Advance l
A Guide for Leaders in Higher Education, Second Edition

"The second edition of this recognized text in higher education leadership development provides a timely update for leaders who must be prepared for a dynamic landscape of issues, accelerating social and cultural changes, and the impact of global and local crises. The aftermath of the COVID-19 pandemic will continue to challenge colleges and universities in new and unforeseen ways and leaders need to maintain and develop their skills to navigate these uncharted waters. This is a text we use in our own leadership development curriculum and highly recommend it to colleagues."
—**Brian Strom,** *Chancellor, Rutgers Biomedical and Health Sciences, Rutgers University*

"After an award-winning first edition, Brent Ruben, Richard De Lisi, and Ralph Gigliotti are back with a second edition of *A Guide for Leaders in Higher Education.* This book could not come at a better time given the leadership challenges facing society like COVID-19 and issues of equity and social justice. The authors not only address higher education's role in meeting these challenges, but they expand their treatment of the book's core concepts and tools. As a result, they bridge theory and practice and underscore the communicative foundation of academic leadership in sophisticated fashion. The continuing importance of their work cannot be underestimated. It is a resource that *all* academic leaders need—and will thoroughly enjoy."—**Gail T. Fairhurst,** *Distinguished University Research Professor, University of Cincinnati*

"This book is unique in providing both frameworks and vital information needed for successful leadership in higher education. I recommend it to all of our department chairs and use it in our leadership development program. Coverage of essential topics such as the changing landscape of higher education, perspectives on leadership, and communication strategies for academic leaders makes this an essential resource for aspiring and current academic leaders."—**Eliza K. Pavalko,** *Vice Provost for Faculty and Academic Affairs, Allen D. and Polly S. Grimshaw Professor of Sociology, Indiana University*

"There is an urgent need for leadership in higher education to confront the complexity of interdependent issues with the relevance and criticality of higher learning. This book offers leadership concepts and competencies for leader development and organizational effectiveness with the greater purpose of impacting higher education for a better society."—**Cynthia Cherrey,** *President and CEO, International Leadership Association*

"Academic leadership is one of the few professions with absolutely no formal training. Leaders in higher education come to their position without leadership training, without prior executive experience; without a clear understanding of their roles; and without understanding the cost to their academic and personal lives. With only 3% of universities and colleges providing professional development for its academic leaders, the time of amateur administration is over. Too much is at stake in this time of change to let leadership be left to chance. *A Guide for Leaders in Higher Education, 2e* is a 'must read and centerpiece' for current and prospective academic leaders—and university professional development programs."—**Walt Gmelch**, *Dean Emeritus and Professor of Leadership Studies, University of San Francisco*

A GUIDE FOR LEADERS IN HIGHER EDUCATION

A GUIDE FOR LEADERS IN HIGHER EDUCATION

Concepts, Competencies, and Tools

Brent D. Ruben, Richard De Lisi, and Ralph A. Gigliotti

Foreword by Jonathan Scott Holloway

1996-2021 25ᵀᴴ ANNIVERSARY

Stylus
PUBLISHING, LLC.

STERLING, VIRGINIA

Library of Congress Cataloging-in-Publication Data
Names: Ruben, Brent D., author. | De Lisi, Richard, author. | Gigliotti,
    Ralph A., author.
Title: A guide for leaders in higher education : concepts, competencies,
    and tools / Brent D. Ruben, Richard De Lisi, and Ralph A. Gigliotti
    ; foreword by Jonathan Scott Holloway.
Description: Second Edition. | Sterling, Virginia : Stylus Publishing,
    LLC, [2021] | First edition: 2017. | Includes bibliographical
    references and index. | Summary: "Taking into account the imperative
    issues of diversity, inclusion, and belonging, and the context of
    institutional mission and culture, this book centers on developing
    capacities for designing and implementing plans, strategies, and
    structures; connecting and engaging with colleagues and students;
    and communicating and collaborating with external constituencies in
    order to shape decisions and policies"-- Provided by publisher.
Identifiers: LCCN 2021036915 (print) | LCCN 2021036916 (ebook) |
    ISBN 9781642672442 (Cloth) | ISBN 9781642672459 (Paperback)
    | ISBN 9781642672466 (Library Networkable e-Edition) | ISBN
    9781642672473 (Consumer e-Edition)
Subjects: LCSH: Education, Higher--Administration. | Educational
    leadership.
Classification: LCC LB2341 .R727 2021 (print) | LCC LB2341
    (ebook) | DDC 378.1/01--dc23
LC record available at https://lccn.loc.gov/2021036915
LC ebook record available at https://lccn.loc.gov/2021036916

13-digit ISBN: 978-1-64267-244-2 (cloth)
13-digit ISBN: 978-1-64267-245-9 (paperback)
13-digit ISBN: 978-1-64267-246-6 (library networkable e-edition)
13-digit ISBN: 978-1-64267-247-3 (consumer e-edition)

Printed in the United States of America

All first editions printed on acid-free paper
that meets the American National Standards Institute
Z39-48 Standard.

Bulk Purchases

Quantity discounts are available for use in workshops and for
staff development.

Call 1-800-232-0223

Second Edition, 2021

We dedicate this book to our families, friends, colleagues, and students who have contributed to and supported our work in higher education leadership.

CONTENTS

PART TWO: LEADERSHIP CONCEPTS AND COMPETENCIES

PART THREE: APPLIED TOOLS FOR LEADERSHIP AND ORGANIZATIONAL EFFECTIVENESS

    SUCCESSION PLANNING
    The Missing Link in Organizational Advancement?   367

20 INTO UNCHARTED WATERS   390

    APPENDIX A
    A Snapshot View of the American Higher Education Sector   405

    REFERENCES   413

    AUTHOR BIOGRAPHIES   437

    CONTRIBUTOR BIOGRAPHIES   439

    INDEX   441

FOREWORD

We live in a challenging age. It is defined by anti-institutional rhetoric, an aggressive populism that has been mesmerized and fueled by assertions of "alternate facts," a racial reckoning on a scale unknown in this nation's history, and a global pandemic that has sickened and killed millions while crippling economies, straining health systems, and exposing the frailties and failings of our social safety network. Serving as a leader during a time of such turmoil is difficult. Doing that work in a college or university setting is that much more challenging given the unique characteristics of higher education.

Consider the cognitive dissonances.

It is uplifting to work with some of the most gifted, ambitious, and interesting individuals on the planet. The faculty are wrestling with everything known and/or imagined in the universe. The students are there to take up as much of that knowledge as possible while also developing the skills that will allow them to thrive beyond college. The staff are dedicated, often in unseen ways, to making sure that this incredibly complex enterprise functions and, ideally, thrives. If one is paying attention to the work of the university it is difficult to suppress a sense of hope for a better tomorrow. And yet we would be remiss if we failed to acknowledge just how complicated this space also is. Protecting the faculty's right to research and teach controversial ideas is critical but doing so also means recognizing that the university could be quickly destabilized because someone's ideas travel into socially or politically uncomfortable spaces. Similarly, creating an environment in which students can feel supported while also challenged lends itself to heated debates about who belongs on a campus and on what terms. Put simply, the very things that make a university so vibrant and exciting also mean that it exists in a perpetual state of contestation.

The people managing that contested state are chairs, deans, provosts, chancellors, and presidents. They work hard to create an environment in which a healthy marketplace of ideas is able to develop. Despite the great attention to detail that these individuals often bring to the task at hand, the work is rarely done perfectly. Further, there is a general acknowledgement that the work can always be done better.

For those who work in higher education these observations will be unsurprising. What is harder to process, though, is that despite this awareness, institutions still devote insufficient time and attention to the kinds of professional and rigorous training opportunities that are necessary to prepare new generations of university leaders. Just looking at the academic side of the ledger is instructive. Chairs become deans who become provosts who become chancellors or presidents. Most of the time, each promotion comes about through others' intuitive assessments that the candidate in question will be able to deliver or perform well. The training associated with any of these posts is most often limited to post-mortem analyses of what went wrong so that it won't be repeated. Given the complexities inherent to any institution of higher education—complexities that are present even in the simplest of times—taking this approach to institutional leadership development is risky.

If universities want to improve and be prepared for the inevitable turbulences in the future, they must commit themselves to developing a new generation of leaders who possess analytic, strategic, and operational skills. The best way to do so is by identifying industry-wide best practices and then inculcating them into one's own institution. This is precisely where *A Guide for Leaders in Higher Education* intervenes. Brent Ruben, Richard De Lisi, and Ralph Gigliotti with a seasoned and insightful roster of contributors who understand the nuances of the higher education landscape, identify the challenges and opportunities that leaders will encounter, and guide the reader through case studies that will move the pursuit of leadership from the abstract toward the concrete.

We are living in an unstable age in which colleges and universities come under withering and relentless attacks for any number of shortcomings, real or imagined. Higher education leaders, if identified and trained properly, can thwart these attacks and change the narrative, ensuring their institutions continue to engage in the essential activities they do best. *A Guide for Leaders in Higher Education* is a major intervention, and it is appearing at precisely the right moment.

—Jonathan Scott Holloway, President
Rutgers, The State University of New Jersey

The purpose of this second edition of *A Guide for Leaders in Higher Education: Concepts, Competencies, and Tools* is to encourage and provide guidance for current and future leaders in colleges and universities. The book was written for faculty and staff leaders alike, and for those who serve in formal leadership roles, such as deans, chairs, or directors of institutes, committees, or task forces, as well as those who perform informal leadership functions within their departments, disciplines, or institutions.

The book can be used as a professional guide, a textbook in graduate courses, or a resource in leadership training and development programs designed for college and university personnel. For this reason, we believe current and aspiring leaders from a variety of disciplines will find it useful. Finally, colleagues coming to leadership positions in higher education from other sectors will find this book a valuable introduction to higher education and a resource that helps flatten what might be an otherwise steep leadership learning curve.

Two core beliefs about contemporary higher education have guided our work on this second edition. The first is that leaders face unprecedented challenges at this point in higher education's evolution. Several of these challenges, discussed in detail in chapter 3, preceded events that transpired in the year 2020. These include economic sustainability, changing composition of the faculty and student bodies, differential retention and graduation rates, declining public confidence in the enterprise, controversies regarding free speech in the classroom and on campus, and making effective use of virtual technologies for instruction, administration, research, and other functions. The health, safety, and broad-ranging institutional challenges ushered in by the COVID-19 pandemic and its aftermath, along with efforts to respond meaningfully to widespread demands for social justice, have only served to heighten challenges already present and to increase the sense of tension and crisis faced by leaders in higher education. Issues related to social justice are of broad and intensifying concern in American society. For higher education, issues related to the marginalization of individuals or groups—and particularly those related to race and gender—are essential considerations. Specifically, these themes are extremely important to the effective recruitment, meaningful engagement, and successful performance of faculty, staff, and students—and leaders of all kinds and at all levels. Although the book is broadly focused on the full array of leadership issues, we endeavor to address these critical issues of diversity, inclusion, and belonging most explicitly in chapter 6 and at other points throughout this book in the context of those chapters' themes.

Our second core belief is that colleges and universities generally have not devoted enough systemic attention to leadership development, evaluation, and recognition. All too often, leaders find themselves unprepared to deal with many of the challenges they confront. This is especially true as it pertains to initial leadership roles such as program director or department chair. Given the diversity of academic disciplines and administrative divisions, it is highly unlikely that newly appointed leaders have the knowledge and background to successfully address the wide array of challenges stemming from today's economic, political, organizational, social, and technological circumstances. The typical approach to filling positions of leadership—such as turn-taking or selecting the most accomplished scholar in a department—often seems unmindful of the complex landscape that confronts higher education leaders. "Learning on the job" may have been acceptable (albeit difficult for leaders and followers) in the past, but this strategy is increasingly inadequate in the current environment. We agree with Bowen and Tobin (2015) and many others who argued that, in light of the challenges confronting modern higher education, there is a need for new forms of governance that are more responsive and effective. Considered collectively, we view increased attention to leadership development in higher education as an essential component to enhanced institutional effectiveness.

Also informing this project are other fundamental principles about leaders and leadership in higher education. These include the following:

- Competencies that are essential for higher education leaders can be identified, developed, improved, and refined over time.
- Ethical behavior and personal integrity are essential for sustained leadership effectiveness.
- Welcoming and respecting the opinions of colleagues and members of other constituency groups and engaging others in the collective work of the institution are essential leadership strategies, ones that create a context within which others may respond in kind.
- An understanding of organizations and organizational dynamics, and a dedication to organizational improvement efforts, are requirements for successful leadership given the ever-increasing complexity of colleges and universities.

- Effective leadership in higher education has as much to do with communication competence and the ability to inspire and influence others as it does with executing formal authority. Even with advantages due to "power" differentials, including control of resources, effective leaders in higher education are as dependent on followers as followers are dependent on leaders.

These principles are foundational to our thinking and to this book, and the many implications that derive from them are explored in the ensuing chapters.

A Collaborative Effort

Working in teams with faculty and staff colleagues at Rutgers University, we have had the opportunity through our Center for Organizational Leadership to develop and conduct leadership training and development programs for senior leaders, midcareer faculty and staff, faculty administrators within our academic health center, doctoral students, and medical students. Our experiences with such programs at Rutgers and other institutions are further detailed in several publications (Connaughton & Ruben, 2005; Gigliotti & Goldthwaite, 2021; Gigliotti & Ruben, 2017; Gigliotti et al., 2017; Gigliotti, Dweyer et al., 2020; Ruben, 2001, 2005; Ruben et al., 2017). Our experiences in designing and leading such programs have convinced us of the value of a developmental, purposeful, rigorous, systematic, and theory-informed approach to leadership in higher education, which will be discussed in detail in the pages ahead, and we express our appreciation to the many participants of these programs who helped us refine many of the ideas, concepts, and models discussed in the pages to follow.

Limitations in Our Coverage

Several excellent resources for leadership development in higher education already exist (e.g., Bolman & Gallos, 2011; Buller, 2014; Eddy & Kirby, 2020; Gmelch & Buller, 2015). Unlike previous efforts, our work does not focus on specific academic leadership positions such as department chair (Buller, 2012), academic dean (Gmelch et al., 2011; Krahenbuhl, 2004), or college and university president (Pierce, 2011). Instead, whenever possible we consider and discuss academic and administrative leadership issues together. We chose this blended approach based on the view that the "cultural divide" between faculty and staff is a source of long-standing, pervasive, and generally unproductive tension within higher education. The lack of a common vision, understanding, and complementary commitment to addressing challenges is quite often a significant source of organizational dysfunction, as discussed in chapters 5 and 6. And, for both types of employees—faculty and staff—the transition to a formal leadership position presents its own set of common issues, many of which are explored in chapter 7.

Chapter 6 is devoted to culture, diversity, and inclusion as they relate to the challenges and opportunities confronting higher education leaders. We recognize and appreciate the important and sometimes unique leadership issues and challenges faced by individuals from underrepresented groups. The lack of representation in academic and administrative leadership positions by race, ethnicity, sex, gender, or sexual orientation is a long-standing issue in higher education (Professionals in Higher Education Annual Report, 2020). Although advances have occurred, White men continue to be overrepresented in leadership positions relative to employee (faculty and staff) and student diversity. Given this history, women and individuals from underrepresented groups face unique challenges when they occupy leadership positions in higher education. These challenges include implicit and explicit biases about their leadership capabilities, difficulty in finding mentors and supportive colleagues, and the expectation that they take on more than their fair share of service obligations to bolster institutional diversity profiles, among other issues. This is a critical topic deserving of continuing discussion and attention. While we share a deep concern about these challenges, the emphasis here is on the broader cultural, diversity, and inclusion goals and approaches that should be of concern to all leaders. We believe the concepts and tools presented in this book will prove useful to those leaders who face special challenges due to their social identity, and we recognize this as an important topic in need of further attention in the leadership and higher education literature.

This work also does not offer detailed coverage of issues in fundraising; the regulatory aspects of governance, including accreditation; city, state, and federal government relationships with universities; and many aspects of student affairs and student development, among other important areas. While we view these topics as critically important for organizational advancement and effective leadership, we also judged that they are relevant for subsets of leaders rather than a broad, cross-cutting swath of faculty and staff leaders in higher education, for whom our book is intended. Again, it is our hope that the tools and concepts presented herein will prove helpful for leaders who find themselves faced with some of the generic challenges in fundraising, government relations and regulation, and student affairs, as well as in efforts to advance the goals of diversity, equity, and inclusion and other higher education priorities.

Last, our experiences and the writings in this book tend to focus most exclusively on higher education in the United States. We have learned over the years of the relevance and utility of the concepts developed by our international colleagues; however, we are also mindful of the unique challenges and needs facing American higher education that deserve special attention.

Those of us who have dedicated our lives to higher education find ourselves at a critical juncture as this second edition is published. The convergence of crises, including a global pandemic and ongoing protests demanding social justice reforms, have unraveled organizations of all kinds, and the impact on higher education has been staggering. There is no doubt that these challenges have important implications for leaders at all levels in higher education. As we collectively navigate the short-term difficulties of the current environment, while also engaging in reinvention efforts to best prepare higher education for its future, we hope this book will be a useful resource.

ACKNOWLEDGMENTS

We are indebted to the colleagues, students, family members, and friends who contributed to the ideas included in this book and in the first edition of *A Guide for Leaders in Higher Education*. Although it is an impossible task to appropriately acknowledge and express our appreciation to each of you individually, we do want to particularly mention the following individuals to whom we are especially grateful.

- Rutgers University president, Jonathan Holloway, for contributing the excellent Foreword to this book at a time when other responsibilities made this a particularly meaningful and appreciated effort.
- Senior administrators and other faculty and staff colleagues whose active support over many years has contributed so significantly to our thinking about leadership and leadership development.
- Faculty, fellows, and alumni from the Rutgers Leadership Academy, Academic Leadership Program at Rutgers Biological and Health Sciences, PreDoctoral Leadership Development Academy, and the Big Ten Academic Alliance leadership programs who influenced in many ways our understanding of the topics addressed in this book.
- Barbara Bender, John Fortunato, Chris Goldthwaite, Sangeeta Lamba, Susan Lawrence, and Sherrie Tromp for their formal contributions to specific chapters within this text.
- Friends and colleagues from other institutions and national associations with whom we have had conversations on leadership and leadership development, and those who adopted and provided feedback on the first edition of the book.
- Colleagues in the Center for Organizational Leadership, Morit Blank, Barbara Corso, Kimberly Davis, Christine Goldthwaite, Kate Immordino, and Sara Spear, for their encouragement and contributions to many aspects of this project.
- Karen Verde, of Green Pelican Editorial Services, and McKenzie Baker and Marianna Vertullo, from Stylus Publishing, for their careful editorial review of all aspects of this book manuscript.
- John von Knorring, president, Stylus Publishing, for his continuing support of our work and the study of leadership in higher education.

PART ONE

LEADERSHIP IN HIGHER EDUCATION

A Critical Need in a Complex and
Challenging Landscape

ACADEMIC LEADERSHIP

Toward an Integrating Framework

In This Chapter

- What are the disciplinary and organizational approaches to leadership in academic settings?
- What are the key sources of influence available to leaders?
- What are the four major dimensions of leadership in academic settings?
- In what ways might considerations of centralized/decentralized strategies and broad/narrow stakeholder engagement be useful for leaders as they address challenges and opportunities?

Leadership has only recently become a topic of great interest within the higher education community. The absence of skilled leadership is often lamented as a root cause of many of the challenges confronting institutions of higher education across the United States. The argument has often been made or implied that more capable and better prepared leaders are needed within colleges and universities.

Those who follow higher education trade publications are accustomed to the seemingly endless coverage addressing the topic of leadership and the corresponding surge in the number of leadership seminars and professional development programs offered by colleges and universities and by national professional and academic associations. The many topics in which more effective leadership is an identified need include strategic planning, access, retention, assessment, diversity, finance, communication, efficiency, innovation, technology, student and faculty/staff relations, crisis management, fundraising and development, university–government relations, and succession planning.

The distinctive nature of higher education as a sector complicates the work of academic leaders and adds a layer of complexity to an already challenging set of circumstances. Academic leaders contend with multiple and sometimes seemingly incompatible organizational missions and aspirations, a broad array of diverse constituencies who often possess differing priorities and perspectives, loosely coupled and relatively autonomous operational systems and units, and traditions of academic freedom and shared governance. These circumstances combine to create significant leadership challenges within academic institutions, which are further complicated by the absence of well-defined markers of excellence and limited incentives or rewards for members of the faculty serving in these roles. The bottom line is that academic leadership is an extremely difficult undertaking, particularly for those dedicated to facilitating meaningful improvement, and successful leadership in higher education tends not to be an inevitable outcome.

In the unusual circumstances that arose during 2020, leaders in higher education were tested in ways few could have imagined. The perilous array of emergent concerns related to campus and societal health and safety, deepening awareness of the need to more forcefully address inequities related to race and ethnicity, along with a widening set of economic and social issues, all interacting in complex ways, exacerbated the already daunting agenda of challenges higher education leaders face. The need for leaders who are sensitive to the broad array of intersecting challenges and who can effectively guide their academic and administrative colleagues and organizations through difficult times has never been greater.

At a time when higher education leadership arguably has never been more critical for the viability and future of these institutions, an understanding of clear and comprehensive concepts and having tools for engaging in the work of academic leadership is essential. Two basic questions take on particular significance if higher education is to successfully navigate this turbulent environment and provide value to an increasingly questioning society: What exactly do we mean when we talk about leadership in academic settings, and what capabilities are required to successfully engage in the work of academic leadership? This chapter previews a leadership framework that begins to address these questions, and in so doing sets the stage for more detailed coverage in subsequent sections of the book.

Beyond Intellect and Disciplinary Expertise

The default view of leadership in academic settings often focuses on mastery of one's discipline and significant accomplishment within core mission areas—education/teaching, knowledge generation/research, outreach/public service/community engagement, and for some professional fields, clinical excellence and translational practices. The formula is generally quite straightforward:

Individuals whose records of professional accomplishment are judged to be outstanding compared with other applicants are selected to lead. Typically, when selecting a leader, a clinical department chooses an accomplished clinician, a teaching institution selects a talented educator, a research-intensive institution seeks accomplished scholars, and so forth.

Reflective of this discipline-based view of leadership, the preparation of faculty and professional staff often begins with a rigorous selection process in undergraduate years—by both the institution and prospective student—and continues with intensive disciplinary socialization throughout the many subsequent years of graduate and professional education. The implicit goal—and one that makes great sense from an academic perspective—is to become distinguished in one's disciplinary and/or technical area and to be recognized as a thought leader, as demonstrated by a superior record of scholarly or professional accomplishments. Disciplinary and/or technical training provide a useful foundation for the assumption of leadership roles in academic settings. In addition to the documentation provided in one's curriculum vitae (CV), another manifestation of disciplinary and/or technical excellence is to have earned distinction among one's peers and colleagues. This might stem from a demonstrated ability to pose questions that cut to the core of the issues being discussed, to engage in a systematic approach to research and/or program development, or to explain and defend one's work in scholarly and professional gatherings in order to advance disciplinary knowledge. Recognized professional advancement in a discipline or technical field is another foundational element for assumption of leadership roles in academic settings.

Viewed from this perspective, leadership in academic settings is related very directly to one's disciplinary and technical knowledge, expertise, and accomplishments within a specific field and the ability to be influential in drawing on one's intellectual knowledge and disciplinary base. No one would dispute the value of these requirements for scholarly or professional excellence and the significance of these capabilities for advancing the boundaries of thought in one's field, as well as for furthering one's own stature and standing in it.

That said, the capabilities that are critical for leadership excellence within a research or technical team or center, or of an academic program, department, or institution, can be quite different than those required for individual scholarly or professional distinction, and this brings us to a second way of thinking about leadership and leadership efficacy. Beyond intellectual mastery of one's field, a broader way of thinking about leadership effectiveness centers on the abilities necessary for designing and implementing plans, strategies, and structures; connecting and engaging with colleagues and students; and communicating and collaborating with external constituencies in order to address the challenges that extend well beyond the parameters of one's area of specialty. This way of conceptualizing leadership in academic settings highlights the need to think broadly about the purposes of higher education and the dynamics of organizational excellence and to apply these insights effectively in goal setting, outcomes assessment, and continuous improvement in one's own leadership development efforts. It also suggests the importance of appropriate diversity among the ranks, not only of faculty and students, but also of leaders at all levels.

One approach to leading in academic settings, then, focuses primarily on disciplinary competencies, documented scholarly accomplishments, and the skills needed in planning one's career to advance intellectual and professional goals. The second approach emphasizes cross-cutting, cross-disciplinary, and generic leadership capabilities that are essential to advancing excellence within any academic or administrative unit. These broader competencies are vital for facilitating the productivity and engagement of colleagues, for creating cultures of inclusion and belonging, for pursuing the larger purposes of the unit, and for building meaningful relationships with the various internal and external constituencies served by the organization and those on which the work of the unit depends. Contrasted with *disciplinary leadership*, this broader set of strategic competencies relate to what can be described as *organizational leadership.*

Each of these views of leading in an academic context—disciplinary leadership and organizational leadership—has value. The first highlights personal accomplishments as a scholar, teacher, clinician, and/or thought leader; the second recognizes the personal, analytic, managerial, and communication competencies necessary for strategic, organizational excellence. Research and experience make it quite evident that excellence and accomplishment in a discipline alone do not ensure excellence and accomplishment as an organizational leader. This fact reveals a weakness in the default, disciplinary view of leadership in higher education.

Further complicating the issue is the fact that, unlike individuals who assume leadership roles in other sectors, most leaders in higher education settings receive little formalized training in competencies that expand beyond the boundaries of their own fields. This helps to explain why leader recruitment, selection, planning, and mentoring and coaching initiatives in higher education generally focus on disciplinary criteria. In addition, it is far easier to document and discern the number of publications and citations, invited keynote presentations, honorary appointments, or other scholarly or professional distinctions one has amassed than it is to define and determine the extent of one's strategic and organizational leadership expertise. But whatever the combination of factors that explains this tradition, the disciplinary approach is limiting when it comes to developing a cadre of leaders and a culture of leadership necessary to convert contemporary challenges into opportunities.

The ideal balance and blend of needed capabilities are not easy to define or achieve. Even after recognizing the critical importance of the broader and more inclusive array of leadership competencies, numerous obstacles remain: How do individuals develop an understanding and skill in each of the competencies recognized as important for leading in an academic environment? In what ways do search committees define and assess candidates' competencies in these areas? How can institutions support the ongoing development of faculty and administrative personnel such that they are able to acquire or refine strategic and organizational competencies, and how might these insights be used for mentoring and succession planning?

Foundational Leadership Concepts

Differentiating and highlighting the value of both disciplinary and organizational approaches to leadership is a central theme throughout this book, and one that elevates the importance of leadership development across all levels of higher education. Toward this end, we next present foundational concepts that are essential building blocks for understanding and demonstrating effective leadership in higher education.

As noted, the most basic issue is defining leadership. The literature on this topic is reviewed throughout the book, most specifically in chapter 8. At this point, however, we preview an integrating view of leadership that guides our approach to the subject. We define leadership as the design and implementation of messages, strategies, processes, and structures in pursuit of social influence (Ruben & Gigliotti, 2019b). Pursuing and affecting social influence pertains to both the disciplinary and organizational approaches to leadership in higher education and is applicable to many other sectors as well. A number of mechanisms are available to leaders as they engage in the formal and informal pursuit of influence. The creation and dissemination of messages through interpersonal, social, organizational, and public media represent one source of potential influence. Less obviously, a leader's tools for influence also include the strategies, processes, and structures designed and implemented to foster, facilitate, or discourage certain outcomes, as depicted in Figure 1.1.

The ways in which leaders can use messages in efforts to influence colleagues and shape organizational trajectories are quite straightforward, and this dimension of communication is a topic of focus throughout the volume,

Figure 1.1. Sources of leadership influence.

A Definition of Leadership

Designing and intiating messages, strategies, processes, and structures to facilitate social influence

Four controllable sources of leadership influences:

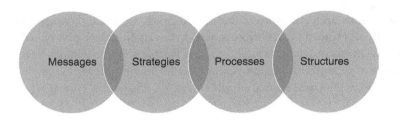

most explicitly in chapter 10. The design and implementation of organizational strategy provide another potential source of influence for leaders. Strategies can be operationalized through the establishment of organizational plans, aspirations, priorities, values, recruitment and hiring goals, leadership targets, or new initiatives. Similarly, through the design and implementation of organizational processes—such as those related to recruitment and hiring, program design and evaluation, personnel review and recognition, the design and facilitation of meetings, embracing diversity and promoting a sense of community, advancing professional development, and the ways in which decisions are made in each of these areas—leaders have opportunities to create and embed their sense of organizational needs, priorities, and values within the operating systems of their units. The design and implementation of organizational structures represents yet another source of potential influence and may include decisions relative to the organizational configuration of a unit, the formation of task forces and committees and the charges each receives, and the launching of new initiatives to focus on areas of a particular need. Each of these sources of leadership influence represents potential opportunities for a leader, and ideally these individual components are linked, integrated, and mutually reinforcing. Our approach highlights the importance of mastering purposeful approaches to leadership and developing a system of engagement in the pursuit of social influence.

Thinking broadly about this full range of approaches available to leaders seems particularly important in higher education, where efforts to influence others may be formal but also informal, planned and unplanned, intentional and unintentional, and mandated and sometimes accidental, as discussed in chapter 10 and more generally throughout the book. We regard leadership as involving both design and development—for instance of visions, plans, goals, programs—as well as implementation and follow-through. In our thinking and experience with leaders across higher education, these two facets of leadership are logically and operationally interdependent for effective leaders and successful leadership outcomes. Brilliant plans for creative new programs do not "automatically" become adopted. Skilled leaders are adept at affecting the design/development and implementation/follow-through phases of organizational change using a combination of the available sources of influence depicted in Figure 1.1.

Mastery of the sources of leadership influence needed to design/develop, implement, and reinforce specific visions, strategic initiatives, or directions requires leaders to be skilled in multiple dimensions. In an academic setting, these key dimensions include competence, communication, engagement, and collaboration, as illustrated in Figure 1.2. As implied earlier, and discussed in chapter 9, those interested in the study and practice of leadership in higher education can benefit from considering the role of various competencies important to leadership in academic settings. In addition to disciplinary and technical competencies, one can consider the ways in which leaders use their knowledge to analyze, manage, and communicate with colleagues, superiors, and subordinates and the reflective processes through

Figure 1.2. Key dimensions of leadership in academic settings.

which one continually reviews and refines personal knowledge and skills in each of these areas.

Despite this deliberate focus on the knowledge and skill demonstrated by individual leaders, we understand and acknowledge the risks of overglamorizing the role and influence that leaders as individuals can have on the dynamics of a group, department, or institution. As detailed further in chapters 8 and 10, we explore the interdependency and inseparability of leaders and followers—working together to create the conditions through which leadership is made possible. Simply stated, without followers, there are no leaders, which has numerous implications for the way one understands their role as leader (Ruben & Gigliotti, 2019b). Moreover, the competencies that are vital as a leader are also vital as a colleague or collaborator as leaders work with followers to define and pursue aspirations to which all are dedicated. Particularly in an academic context where shared governance and collaboration are shared values, the interdependencies between leaders and followers are especially important.

We place significant emphasis on the role of communication as a conceptual and pragmatic tool for leaders. *Communication,* at the most basic level, is a term commonly used to describe the dynamics of creating and sending messages through appropriate media to carefully defined audiences. Far more basically, communication is also the process through which organizational cultures are created, disseminated, perpetuated, and changed (Ruben & Stewart, 2020). It is through communication that we are socialized into the realities of the organizations of which we are a part, and it is through a knowledge of these dynamics that it becomes possible to promote and engage in reflection and change within these cultures.

Additionally, we view engagement and collaboration as particularly important processes, both deserving special attention as important communication goals for higher education leaders. Within colleges and universities, leadership impact is seldom possible without meaningful engagement and buy-in from faculty, staff, students, and many other stakeholders. In this context, insight and skill in designing and implementing messages, strategies, processes, and structures that encourage meaningful engagement and collaboration are indispensable to successful leadership.

Leadership Dimensions in Practice: Charting Your Course

Academic and administrative leaders at colleges and universities confront a broad range of issues, from strategy formulation and goal setting to operational management of personnel and facilities. Some of these arise in response to external challenges; many others relate to internal leadership responsibilities. In either case, fundamental leadership decisions are required to determine how best to address a particular issue. How should a leader most appropriately exercise their authority, while also engaging faculty, staff, and other stakeholders' perspectives in the decision-making process? Prescribed policies and procedures are in place to guide decision-making in many of these areas. However, there are also many contexts in which leaders have considerable degrees of freedom in how they exercise their authority and responsibility.

Two important areas of decision-making relate to the degree to which (a) administrative functions are centrally controlled by the leader and (b) stakeholders are actively engaged in decision-making and problem-solving processes. Decisions regarding these two dimensions are often vital to the success of a leader in addressing challenges and opportunities—both in terms of the quality of decisions and the extent of commitment to and support for the implementation of these decisions.

As noted, in many circumstances, leaders in higher education have a substantial degree of authority in initiating and implementing decisions that affect activities within the institution, department, or division. This authority also comes with important and consequential options. Most faculty and staff have experienced situations where an organization's direction and priorities were very centralized and tightly controlled by one leader or leadership team and, conversely, circumstances where responsibility for control over decisions was decentralized and diffused to a large extent. Leaders can use lessons learned from these experiences as a foundation for defining leadership philosophy and in choosing an approach that is not simply reactive to one's past organizational experiences when options are not prescribed by institutional policies and procedures.

Exercising formal authority with limited or no consultation can be an attractive way to set a new institutional or departmental direction, especially in avoiding the array of different and often conflicting perspectives one might otherwise confront when making decisions. However, comfort and efficiency during the early stages of problem-solving and decision-making may ultimately result in more discomfort—and more time and money spent along the way—than would have been expended had a more collaborative and consultative process been used in the first place. Conversely, adopting an approach that involves iterative consultation with all possible constituencies who might have an opinion or input about a particular decision can paralyze forward momentum. When, who, how, and to what extent to engage in decision-making is no doubt one of the persistent and profoundly important challenges facing leaders in higher education settings.

The following framework is offered as a guide that leaders can consider in thinking through available options. In approaching strategic decisions, consideration of two dimensions can be quite helpful: *locus of control* and *stakeholder engagement*. Each represents a continuum, as Figure 1.3 illustrates.

- *Locus of control* defines a continuum with end points representing two contrasting approaches for exercising control in addressing challenges or opportunities. This dimension defines a range of options, from highly centralized leader control to highly decentralized leader control.
- *Engagement* defines the range of approaches available to leaders with regard to limiting or broadly engaging faculty, staff, and other relevant stakeholders in communication activities relative to thinking through challenges or opportunities.

When combined, these two continuous dimensions define four quadrants —each of which describes actions available for leaders in confronting sector and institutional challenges and opportunities.

The locus of control axis (centralization–decentralization) considers the ways in which a leader chooses to employ or deploy the control and authority vested in them by the institution. For example, leaders typically have a great deal of formal authority in dealing with personnel matters, managing revenues and expenses, setting goals and priorities for future directions, and

Figure 1.3. Addressing challenges and opportunities: Organizational and leadership options.

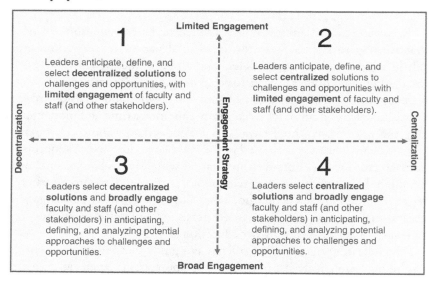

advancing organizational initiatives, among many other issues. In developing and implementing a new initiative, for example, a leader might choose to retain control of the effort, vest control of the process with a centralized executive committee, delegate oversight to one or more committees or task forces across the institution or department, or create a new structure for developing and implementing the initiative.

Closely related and equally important in higher education are leadership decisions about the extent of communication with and engagement of stakeholders. Distinct from centralization/decentralization decisions, leaders must choose how and how much to engage others in developing and implementing initiatives. Efforts to solicit input from stakeholders may be broad or narrow, as these decisions can influence how one chooses to engage the perspectives of others in the design, implementation, review, and evaluation of ongoing activities or new initiatives.

Leadership decisions about the extent and richness of engagement, as with those of related locus of control, have substantive and strategic implications for which leaders need to be extremely thoughtful in their work. For example, when planning to pursue a new initiative within a unit, a leader must decide whether and how to involve faculty or staff who are vocal or well-respected informal leaders. In thinking about this decision, a leader will want to not only consider the substantive value of opinions and advice received in arriving at the best decision, but also the impact of broad representation in helping to reach a final decision. Meaningful engagement with diverse and respected informal leaders often heightens support of and commitment to the success of an idea or project, particularly among stakeholders who learn that respected colleagues were consulted and have endorsed the new direction.

In using this framework, it is helpful to consider one's leadership position and location in the institution's organizational chart. Although leadership control is vested with the individual leader and one's department, in some instances direction might be provided from those to whom you report (e.g., a project leader or administrator in charge; chair, dean, or provost; manager, director, or vice president). When an assignment is received from superiors, it is useful to understand whether they have expectations about how control of the effort is to be vested and whether there is a particular expectation of broad or narrow engagement as you execute the task. The same clarification is important when a leader has decided to delegate responsibility for a project to a direct report. In fact, initiating a discussion about control and engagement is very useful when embarking on any new initiative. In many cases, there may be no external guidance, constraints, or even suggestions about control or engagement, and the decision for how to proceed will ultimately rest with you as the leader.

When you are the person with primary leadership responsibility for initiating or implementing a project, or when you serve as the prime mover behind an initiative, you need to decide whether, how, and when to consult superiors and whether broader or narrower control and engagement of others is optimal. Making these determinations is an important part of leaders' work, an aspect that depends on knowledge of the task at hand, perceptions among members of the unit, inclinations of other stakeholder groups, cultural traditions of the institution or department, urgency of the situation and the time available, one's leadership style and personal preferences as leader, and the importance of shared commitment, all of which are discussed in some detail throughout the book. The framework can be helpful in thinking about and evaluating the costs and benefits of available strategic approaches for addressing challenges and opportunities.

As depicted in Figure 1.4, each quadrant of the organizational framework involves trade-offs and comes with a unique set of assets and liabilities. Some circumstances are particularly well-suited to the approach defined by a particular quadrant. Occasionally, several good options with reasonable alternatives are situated in more than one quadrant; in some cases, an approach that crosses over or blends the approaches of more than one quadrant is most appropriate. Leaders need to weigh the available options and associated trade-offs and select those most appropriate for the circumstances and goals at hand. It is also possible that the best options depicted in the grid will vary

Figure 1.4. Assets and liabilities of organizational and leadership options.

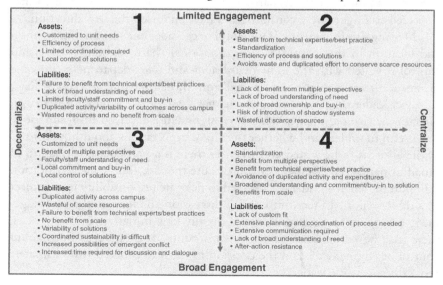

from one phase of an initiative to another depending on the unique circumstances of the initiative, stakeholders, and/or institution.

Figure 1.5 provides examples of various challenges and opportunities and where they fall within each of the four quadrants. Some opportunities, such as strategic planning, might be appropriately initiated within any one of the four quadrants. The same is true for integrating technology solutions for operations or for academics, as in distance coursework and program delivery. For these and other issues, decisions about where to locate initiatives might be based on factors such as the leader's sense of the importance of the activity; how it fits with the broader organizational aspirations, institutional culture, available personnel, the amount of time available, and the manner in which policies and procedures are typically handled; perceived trade-offs in terms of benefits and costs of a particular approach; and a leader's personal competencies and preferences.

Other issues, such as undergraduate core curriculum for an institution, fundraising and development, and assessment of institutional learning objectives, are likely to be addressed with a centralized approach involving many campus stakeholders, although other approaches are possible and the strategy selected may vary from one stage to another in design, coordination, implementation, and follow-through. By way of contrast, the development of a particular major within an academic department or a degree program within

Figure 1.5. Fitting challenges and opportunities to the organization leadership framework.

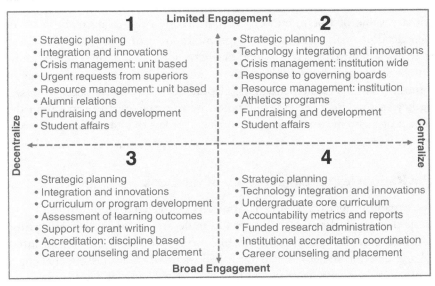

a professional school and assessment of faculty-developed student learning outcomes, or a technical service to be offered within an administrative unit, will typically benefit from a decentralized approach and involve those faculty and staff who will be asked to deliver the program in question.

Some issues—such as a crisis arising within a program, department, or one area of an institution—might become a crisis for the entire campus, college, or university, requiring blended and sequenced approaches involving all quadrants over time. In such instances, leaders have important and often time-sensitive choices to make about how to approach the circumstance and what role they should play relative to control and communication. While a program or department leader might have the formal authority to resolve the issue, communication with and engagement of superiors, colleagues, faculty, and staff are crucial. For example, superiors would not appreciate learning of an issue from the local press or media. It is also the case that the first response to a crisis may need to be centralized and with restricted stakeholder engagement. As the recovery plans progress, and as efforts to consider longer term consequences and strategies become relevant, a shift to more decentralized approaches with more extensive and inclusive engagement become vital. Chapter 17 has much more to say about the factors at play during crisis situations.

In all contexts, leadership decisions have consequences, and process issues often override matters of substance. Adopting approaches that fail to take account of and appropriately engage internal—and, as appropriate, external—stakeholders may not be as immediately consequential for a leader, but resentment can build over time and can undermine confidence in, and the ability of, a leader to be fully effective within the institution or unit. The primary value of this framework is that leaders need to be methodical in their decision-making about the appropriate locus of control for the many activities and initiatives over which they have some discretion—and to know how, when, with whom, to what extent, and in what sequence to engage in communication, engagement, and collaboration with others. These processes are key to the effective implementation of any strategy and can soften the impact of missteps, unanticipated problems, or less than desirable outcomes.

The Rationale and Organization of the Book

The organizational framework is intended as a general guide for leaders to use as they think through the issues and trade-offs discussed. Devoting time to consider the locus of organizational control and the engagement of internal and external stakeholders is time well spent when addressing challenges or pursuing new opportunities within the higher education landscape.

To effectively fulfill their roles, all leaders need a broad understanding of higher education as a sector, including contemporary challenges and opportunities. In addition to having the knowledge of various concepts related to organizations and leadership, there are also a host of competencies, strategies, and tools that are increasingly critical for effective academic and administrative leadership in colleges and universities. Recognizing the importance of concepts, competencies, and tools, this book is organized into three parts that correspond with each of these themes.

- **Part One: Leadership in Higher Education: A Critical Need in a Complex and Challenging Landscape (chapters 1–7)** presents an overview of the specific issues, challenges, and opportunities facing institutions of higher education and those engaged in leadership activities.
- **Part Two: Leadership Concepts and Competencies (chapters 8–12)** explores a series of theoretical topics underlying the study and practice of leadership in higher education and presents a brief review of the relevant literature and perspectives on key concepts that inform leadership practice, such as those related to leadership theories, principles of communication, and behavioral competencies that are foundational for effectiveness in formal and informal leadership.
- **Part Three: Applied Tools for Leadership and Organizational Effectiveness (chapters 13–20)** presents a number of applied models, strategies, and tools for personal, professional, and organizational assessment and improvement, focusing broadly on a wide array of topics, including leadership during times of change, strategic planning, crisis, and leadership succession.

Each chapter concludes with a series of case studies and guiding questions in a section labeled "For Further Consideration." Several of the tools and worksheets referenced throughout the text are included on the website of the Center for Organizational Leadership at Rutgers University (ol.rutgers.edu). We are certain that the "References" section of the book also serves as a useful resource for many readers interested in further pursuing specific topics.

The content and format of this book reflect our view that leadership development works best when it is an intentional, reflective, and systematic experience. The core concepts, competencies, and tools offered herein are intended to contribute to all three areas. We hope your experience with the book is beneficial as you navigate the increasingly tumultuous and complex landscape of higher education—a sector that is surely in need of effective leadership at all levels at this point in its history and evolution.

2

LEADERSHIP AND LEADERSHIP DEVELOPMENT IN HIGHER EDUCATION

A Time of Change

> ### In This Chapter
>
> - What values, assumptions, and practices underlie the disciplinary approach to leadership in higher education?
> - Why has it become important to reconsider the necessary competencies for effective leadership?
> - Why are economic issues becoming an increasingly vital concern for college and university leaders?
> - What are the major approaches to finance and budgeting in higher education, and what are the implications of these approaches for effective leadership at this point in time?

One of the long-standing practices in higher education is the selection of leaders who have distinguished records of scholarly or professional achievement within their own fields. This practice reflects a number of assumptions about the distinctive mission of colleges and universities and the corresponding requirements for effective leadership. While traditional views of institutions of higher learning and their leadership have served well throughout the 20th century, there is value in reexamining the perceived uniqueness of colleges and universities and the nature and needs of higher education leadership in light of the significant challenges and opportunities that confront current leaders.

Issues related to finance and budgeting in colleges and universities exemplify the changes occurring across the higher education landscape that have far-reaching implications and consequences for academic and administrative leaders at all levels. Economic issues have long been a central and essential focus of concern for leaders in complex organizations across sectors, but this knowledge was not always essential for effective leadership in higher education. It is becoming increasingly clear that knowledge and skill in the areas of finance and budgeting are essential for effective leadership in higher education; however, this expertise is not generally acquired on the traditional path to becoming a distinguished thought leader in a particular discipline or technical area. It seems clear that the time has come to reconsider the competencies required for effective leadership in this context and to explore the implications for the training and development of leaders in this sector.

Traditional Values, Assumptions, and Practices

Individual autonomy and creativity have long been considered essential for excellence and innovation in teaching and research. Individual creativity is also critical in technical and professional areas where specialized approaches and methodologies are developed and applied to advance the institution. Placing a premium on personal autonomy and creativity is a core value at the heart of the American higher education system, one that has yielded many benefits. Consistent with this value, reward systems within higher education have traditionally emphasized individual accomplishments and the achievement of excellence within one's academic discipline or administrative domain.

These prized traditions of the academy have both emerged from and reinforced ways of viewing higher education institutions as distinct from other entities. These dimensions and attributes that are often presumed to be unique to higher education include the following:

- a distinctive set of core values
- multiple institutional mission elements serving an array of distinctive constituencies and needs
- traditions of autonomy, self-direction, academic freedom, and collegial decision-making
- loosely coupled administrative and academic units with vastly different structures, cultures, accountability requirements, core values, and leadership traditions and practices
- limited alignment and coordination across units and functions
- decentralized decision-making structures, processes, and criteria
- limited institution-wide approaches to organizational assessment, planning, and strategy development
- lack of systematic approaches to leadership development, leadership succession, and transition planning

Collectively, these characteristics have contributed to the creation of distinctive organizations that present special opportunities and challenges for those charged with the responsibility of leading. One of these is the practice of shared governance (see chapter 5) and the expectation of collegial decision-making within silos that do not necessarily communicate well with each other. Another challenge is an unfortunate status differential between members of the faculty and members of the administrative staff that often elevates the faculty and devalues the staff, either in perception or in practice, as discussed further in chapter 6. Additionally, as noted earlier and discussed in detail in chapter 9, there is the tendency to select leaders based on one's academic and/or technical qualifications, often with less consideration for one's cross-cutting institutional knowledge or organizational leadership expertise.

Another challenge results from the fact that many faculty members avoid positions of leadership—a pattern that says a good deal about the historic status of leadership roles in higher education. Very often faculty perceive— often quite correctly—that the institution does not greatly value leadership performance beyond the provisions of salary increases and/or modifications in workload responsibilities (e.g., reduction in number of courses taught per academic year) while serving in a leadership capacity. Within many institutions, the absence of clear criteria for judging, recognizing, or rewarding leadership presents further impediments to the advancement of leadership practice, as described further in chapter 19.

Particularly relative to academic leadership, limited attention has been given to conceptualizing leadership roles, establishing and communicating clear leadership expectations, defining criteria and markers for assessing effective performance, creating mechanisms to validate the importance of the work of leaders, and more generally deciding where leadership roles fit within the broader scheme of the academy. Service to local, national, or international communities is a foundational aspect of the mission of most institutions of higher education, and service expectations are part of the formal job requirements for most faculty members. Indeed, for faculty on the tenure track, service to one's professional organization(s) is a marker of scholarly recognition that is evaluated in merit and promotion decisions. In contrast, contributions to the institution through service in leadership roles or participation on committees and in faculty governance are often not recognized comparably for tenure and promotion considerations. Unfortunately, an inattention to valuing, assessing, and appropriately rewarding academic leaders has contributed to cynical views of the importance of leadership among many members of the faculty. And, perhaps not surprisingly, colleges and universities have tended to neglect leadership development, recognition, and succession planning, although this pattern is beginning to change, as will be discussed in chapters 18 and 19.

For those engaged in administrative roles, attention and sources of reward and recognition are typically tied more directly to institutional accomplishments. For administrative staff, efforts to identify critical leadership knowledge and skills, provide leadership training and development opportunities, and engage in leadership succession planning are more common, and importantly, transitions into leadership positions typically represent and are regarded as career advancement.

This faculty–staff cultural divide complicates matters considerably for leaders in higher education who must engage both groups in organizational decision-making and governance. Interestingly, as discussed further in chapter 6, the lack of comparability in the way leadership is regarded within the administrative and staff culture compared to the faculty culture is a manifestation of a larger cultural divide between these two critical employee groups.

Are Colleges and Universities Unique as Institutions? (Answer: Yes and No)

Leadership practices within colleges and universities both reflect and reinforce the view of higher education as a distinctive sector. As compelling as this perspective has been historically, one can question whether colleges and universities are as unique as they are often assumed to be—especially in the context of broader institutional and environmental changes. At a very general level of analysis, colleges and universities—and their constituent units—share a number of characteristics in common with business, health care, nonprofit, or government organizations. Some of these features include the following:

- structure—composed of component parts (e.g., programs, departments, schools, divisions)
- stakeholders—internal and external groups and organizations that influence and are influenced by the activities of the organization
- interactions between and among components—necessary to the functioning of the whole
- resources—necessary for continued functioning and for establishing new initiatives, programs, and services
- decision-making—strategic and operational
- traditions and culture—characteristics influenced by past practices

- leadership—informal and formal functions necessary for guidance, cohesion, and planned change
- operating within a larger environment—imposing constraints and creating opportunities
- bureaucratic work structures and processes—necessary for the accomplishment of routine tasks

Other organizations—such as those in health care or business—are extremely complex, are composed of numerous subcultures, and serve multiple stakeholders who often have competing or conflicting needs. Moreover, the "loosely coupled system" (Weick, 1976) label that describes higher education can also be used to describe government or virtual organizations. Like democracies or republics, colleges and universities have traditions of collective governance, and the modern "multiversity" (Kerr, 2001) shares much in common with government. Also, like politics, the power to persuade is often more influential than the power bestowed by any type of formal constitutional authority (Neustadt, 1960). Much like cultural/artistic and civic organizations, among many others, multiple missions, blurry purposes, and competing bottom lines call into question the value of traditional, individually based measures of productivity, value, and performance in higher education. All of this serves as a reminder of the need to exercise caution in treating higher education as wholly unique.

Higher Education as a Business

Thinking in broader terms, modern higher education has features that overlap with the business–corporate sector. Historically, higher education has not been a for-profit enterprise, and the for-profit part of the sector is still small in terms of overall student enrollment, despite rapid expansion in the 1990s and early 2000s. But though the vast majority of colleges and universities are not-for-profit, modern higher education leaders must pay attention to the economic bottom line to a degree that their predecessors did not. While college presidents and other high-level campus leaders have had to attend to the business aspects of the enterprise for some time, a focus on revenues and expenses has now found its way down to leaders at all levels and to individual faculty and staff members. While the assertion that higher education leaders must pay considerable attention to revenues and expenses is troubling for some faculty, students, and other internal stakeholders, these views are changing. The view of higher education as "big business" is widely subscribed to by external stakeholders, such as families whose children matriculate and incur loan debt; government officials who are asked to provide student loans, support research costs, and fund other operating expenses; governing boards who bear responsibilities as fiduciaries for the college or university they serve; and other external stakeholders. Indeed, the escalating costs of higher education have become a major source of criticism and concern among external stakeholders, with a growing chorus of advocates rallying for increased subsidies of various kinds.

The days in which denying the business aspects of higher education might have made sense seem to have come to an end. Derek Bok (2013), former president of Harvard University, acknowledged the following in his book, *Higher Education in America*:

> America's venture in the realm of higher learning gave no hint of future accomplishments. Nor could the handful of young men who arrived in Cambridge, Massachusetts, in 1638 to enter the nation's first college have had the faintest idea of what the future had in store for American universities. . . . From these modest beginnings, higher education in the United States has grown to become a vast enterprise comprising some 4,500 different colleges and universities, more than 20 million students, 1.4 million faculty members, and aggregate annual expenditures exceeding 400 billion dollars. Within this system are schools ranging from tiny colleges numbering a few hundred students to huge universities with enrollments exceeding 50,000. (p. 9)

As Jon McGee (2016) succinctly stated, "Colleges and universities today must be understood for what they are: large-scale business enterprises" (p. 5).

This difference among stakeholders in their perceptions of the business aspects of higher education places additional demands on leaders who must balance perspectives and messages across groups. In addition, the prominent role of faculty in the recruitment, retention, and promotion of colleagues, coupled with the embedded traditions of academic freedom and shared governance, pose challenges for leaders that are not found in other sectors, such as PK–12 education.

Leading Faculty and Staff in the 21st Century

In our view, there is considerable value for leaders in higher education to regard their work from the perspective of two lenses—higher education is a sector that is similar to other service-oriented sectors as well as the business–corporate sector, *and* higher education has unique features that set it apart from business, PK–12 education, health care, military, religious organizations, and nonprofit and charitable organizations, among other sectors. This dual-lens perspective has implications for thinking about what is needed for effective leadership in contemporary higher education. It suggests that effective leaders should possess skill sets that are shared with leaders in other fields, in addition to demonstrating an understanding of the specialized disciplinary and/or technical knowledge and skills that are unique to their positions and to higher education. Put another way, for most individuals, familiarity with and experience in higher education is extremely helpful for effective leadership in higher education. At the same time, the requisite skill set for effective higher education leadership overlaps considerably with the skill sets of effective leaders in other sectors.

The Importance of a Dual Perspective: Issues of Finance and Budgeting

The blend of common and unique features in the higher education sector lies at the core of our thinking about what leaders of colleges and universities need to know and be able to do. For example, economic bottom-line thinking is now essential for effective leadership in higher education. However, a focus on the bottom line alone is countercultural within the academy, and at an extreme, this mindset may lead the organization in directions that compromise its core mission and values.

Regardless of whether one is pleased with this situation, there is little doubt that the economic bottom line now plays an increasingly critical role in higher education decision-making. These realities are a clear influence for those engaged in higher education leadership. Leaders do not have the luxury of being unaware of higher education's cost structures; it is quite clear that the golden age of seemingly unlimited resource investments, especially by federal and state governments, is long gone (Bowen & Tobin, 2015). Especially for those working in public institutions, the political shift in thinking of higher education not as a public good but instead as an individual benefit has transferred the economic burden to pay for advanced degree attainment from state legislatures to students and their families.

Leaders charged with the responsibility of obtaining and managing financial resources are caught between two contextual currents. The public desires reduced higher education costs and believes that institutions could function more efficiently. At the same time, those working inside the academy see a need for increased revenues to keep salaries and benefits competitive, maintain and upgrade classrooms and laboratories, pay for in-demand student life programs and cocurricular services, and fund important yet expensive research, among other needs. This debate is taking place just as colleges receive increased criticism and scrutiny for not fully preparing graduates for their professional roles (Jaschik, 2015). Understanding public perceptions and their factual basis is a necessary first step in positioning leaders to bridge the gap in expectations between external and internal stakeholders. In so doing, leaders have to be realistic and candid with these stakeholders, which requires a general understanding of finance and budgeting issues nationally, within one's own institution, and at the departmental/program level.

The selection of a particular business or financial model does exert a significant influence on leader decision-making at the campus, school, or department level. For example, if the financial model is enrollment based and returns a portion of the revenue earned from student enrollments or majors, there is a significant incentive to increase class size and develop attractive courses and programs to appeal to students. In the case of nonenrollment-based models, issues of course quality, student selectivity, and peer assessments can be influential drivers of change. In general, a key issue is whether the budget model requires return of unused funds to a central pool or permits the unit to retain revenues. Central control systems do less to incentivize cost savings. Note that the influence of budget models and monetary incentives must be placed in the context of the requirements of accreditation agencies and other types of external ranking systems that consider student support, student–faculty ratios, time to degree, student loan debt, and other measures of quality.

An understanding of economic issues and the particulars of finance and budget at a given institution is important for anyone working in higher education. For leaders, an understanding of such issues is not a luxury. Every budgeting model brings with it a number of obvious—and many less obvious—influences that play a critical role in short- and long-term planning and priority setting, as well as in day-to-day operational decision-making.

Popular Budgeting Models and Their Implications

A brief overview of the most popular budget models in use across institutions is presented next.[1] The four most popular types of finance models are as follows:

1. *Incremental.* Traditionally the most common budget model in higher education, an incremental approach, "[was] characterized by central ownership of all unrestricted sources" (Curry et al., 2013, p. 2). Allocations to units and departments are based on the funding levels of the previous

year and are often increased or decreased by a set percentage annually. In institutions that adopt a zero-based budgeting model, where budgets are created from scratch each year, the tendency is still to fall back into an incremental approach.

2. *Formula-based.* Also referred to as *performance-based budget models*, budget allocations in this approach are based on predetermined formulas. According to Curry et al. (2013), when using this model, budget decisions are "made centrally but on the basis of policy formulas or metrics that relate inputs such as enrollment or research volume or outputs such as graduation rates to budget expenditure levels" (p. 4). Resources typically flow to units based on (a) the pooling of funds and the allocations from a predetermined formula (e.g., a division teaching 10% of the credit hours received 10% of the pool) or (b) the application of an agreed-on rate (e.g., $100 per credit hour).

3. *Responsibility center management (RCM).* Also known as *revenue-centered budgeting*, RCM is a model in which each unit is financially responsible for its individual activities and accountable for direct and indirect expenditures. According to Curry et al. (2013), entrepreneurial activities are incentivized by this approach, which "transfers revenue ownership and allocates all indirect costs to units whose programs generate and consume them respectively" (p. 5). Through the use of centralized resource redistribution, also known as *subvention*, senior academic leaders are responsible for the balance of local optimization and strategic investments that are meant to benefit the university as a whole.

4. *Every tub on its own bottom.* A budget model associated with Harvard University and Johns Hopkins University, among others, this model treats each school within the organization as an independent entity responsible for its own management and funding, with minimal linkage to the university as a whole.

More decentralized approaches to financial management, as described by Strauss and Curry (2002), attempt to integrate academic authority and financial responsibility whereby "college and departmental ownership of their revenues is coupled with the responsibility of paying both the direct and indirect costs, maintaining adequate financial reserves for the applicable unit, and funding annual debt service requirements on attributable debt" (as cited in Scarborough, 2009). An exploration into internal economic factors might also consider how money is distributed in a department or unit and to what extent a unit or department relies on students—or in the context of professional education, patients, or clients—for revenue. While there are numerous benefits to decentralized funding approaches, these models can present impediments with regard to support for interdisciplinary or interdepartmental programs and services.

Although these four models can be described as separate budget types, a number of institutions use a combination of these approaches. For example, in a 2011 *Inside Higher Education* survey, over half of the surveyed institutions indicated the use of more than one of the models noted, particularly the more popular incremental (60.2%), zero-based (30%), formula-based (26.1%), performance-based (14.2%), and responsibility-centered (14.2%) models. (Total exceeds 100% due to combination of models at some institutions.)

In a presentation delivered for the National Association of College and University Business Officers, Becker et al. (2012) noted that an institution's character dictates the most appropriate type of budget model. The effective allocation of resources, according to the authors, implements plans, responds to assessment data, combines top-down guidance that is informed by bottom-up knowledge and realities, and uses measures consistently. In thinking about the budget model that your unit, department, or institution uses, consider whether the following ideal characteristics are met throughout the budgeting process:

- driven by strategic, infrastructural, and operational plans
- relies on a broadly participative process
- integrates resource allocation with operational planning and assessment
- emphasizes accountability versus control (Becker et al., 2012)

There was a time when an understanding of budgeting models was only necessary for leaders on governing boards or in the business and finance areas of colleges and universities. Increasingly, knowledge of budgeting assumptions and practices is becoming vital for all leaders, especially given their importance in planning, resource allocation, and organizational assessment activities. According to a 2019 survey of college and university business officers, conducted by *Inside Higher Ed* and Gallup,

> most business officers continue to believe that key campus constituencies are either very (12 percent) or somewhat (61 percent) aware of their institution's current financial health, and that senior administrators and board members are conveying sufficient and accurate information to key campus groups about their institution's financial status (87 percent). (Jaschik & Lederman, 2019 p. 11)

As we have seen, budgeting models vary based on institutional traditions and present circumstances; they also vary as a function of institutional size and type—public versus private and nonprofit versus for-profit, for example. The leadership implications of particular approaches depend on one's position and level and whether one serves in an academic or administrative function. Challenges and opportunities at a presidential or provost level are considerably different from those associated with the role of dean, department chair, or program coordinator. Additionally, because of the shifting landscape, changes are frequent in terms of the way these approaches are conceptualized and implemented by and within institutions. Given this context, leadership challenges associated with these developments often vary from year to year—and sometimes month to month. That said, across a variety of institutions, a number of general strategies are being considered or pursued to control costs and increase available funds (see Box 2.1).

The selection of a financial model and strategy has any number of consequences, for institutions, departments, programs, stakeholders, and leaders at all levels. And, to a greater or lesser extent, each strategy involves planning and change—often at multiple levels within the institution. In such situations, individual leaders may need to initiate these changes, or they may find themselves in more passive and reactive roles where their responsibilities involve thinking through and adapting to changes introduced elsewhere within the institution.

BOX 2.1.
Available Financial Strategies

The following are some typical options for reducing expenses:

- combining programs or services within different levels, organizations, or locations
- implementing shared services models
- introducing new technological alternatives for staffing
- increasing class size or increasing the size of groups for which programs and services are provided
- identifying new instructional delivery models
- reducing the size of programs and services that have decreased in popularity
- increasing responsibilities of particular departments, staff, or faculty
- streamlining and eliminating programs and services

The following are typical options for increasing available resources:

- increasing tuition and fees
- initiating new programs for new constituencies, leading to new revenues
- expanding popular programs and services for which fees are charged
- increasing marketing and recruitment of potential students who pay premium fees (e.g., international students, continuing education students)
- identifying new ways to use existing facilities (e.g., rentals of facilities to outside groups on weekends or summer/winter breaks)
- encouraging entrepreneurial thinking across units, departments, and the institution

Conclusion

The academic culture has a long, proud history in which colleges and universities have been viewed as distinct and distinctive kinds of institutions. Consistent with this perspective, individuals who are highly credentialed and accomplished within their own fields have been viewed as ideally prepared to assume leadership positions. Given recent trends and challenges, however, knowledge and skill sets that extend beyond a particular disciplinary or technical domain—one that includes a knowledge of finance and budgeting, among other broad-based competencies—has become increasingly critical for leadership effectiveness at all levels across institutions of all types.

For Further Consideration

1. Disciplinary leaders
   Consider those individuals who occupy midlevel positions of leadership at your college or university and were chosen from the faculty or staff ranks. How would you characterize their accomplishments in their individual fields of expertise? Did these accomplishments serve them well when they assumed formal positions of leadership? Which aspects of leadership seemed to present challenges for these midlevel leaders?

2. Your institution's approach to budgeting
   Which of the four budget models (or combination of models) described in this chapter is used at your institution? Do you understand the relative contribution of the institution's various sources of revenues? For example, what percentage of students pay the full tuition sticker price? What percentage of operating revenue comes from public monies, such as federal loans to students or state aid? What percentage of operating revenue comes from gifts and endowments? Name one step leaders at your institution have taken to control costs in the last 5 years and one step taken to increase revenues. How were these ideas received when they were introduced? Did you personally support these steps? Why or why not? To what extent did they have the desired impact?

3. Response to COVID-19 disruptions
   In response to the COVID-19 pandemic, how did your college/university pivot to a fully online environment for course instruction? Describe the leadership challenges, successes, and failures of leaders at your institution during the second half of the spring 2020 semester as it pertains to teaching and learning. Carry this discussion forward to consider how the 2020–2021 academic year unfolded. What were the leadership challenges, successes, and failures? What are the primary financial or budgetary challenges posed by the COVID-19 pandemic at your institution? What specific competencies would you identify as most critical for leaders in addressing the short- and long-term challenges triggered by the pandemic?

Note

1. A comprehensive review of higher education budget models is beyond the scope of this book. For additional readings and resources on budgeting and finance in higher education, visit www.nacubo.org/Research.html.

3

THE HIGHER EDUCATION LANDSCAPE

Navigating the Economic, Organizational, Social, and Strategic Terrain

In This Chapter

- What are the critical issues confronting higher education at this point in time?
- What special challenges are presented by COVID-19 and tensions surrounding racial and social justice?
- What other contemporary landscape issues pose challenges and opportunities for higher education leaders?
- How is knowledge of these issues important for leaders, and how can this knowledge be helpful in fulfilling their roles and responsibilities?

L eaders in academic settings are operating in a landscape that has changed fundamentally from what existed some 20 years ago. All colleges and universities today confront an array of economic, organizational, and strategic factors that directly and indirectly shape the work of these institutions. The convergence of crises relating to growing racial unrest and demands for social justice, along with the ongoing impact of the global coronavirus pandemic, are two additional factors that exacerbate the challenges already affecting colleges and universities and their leaders. In this chapter, we discuss three ongoing issues that build on the concepts detailed in the previous chapter. The first relates to the constellation of issues associated with higher education finance. The second concerns the combination of decreasing public support and questioning the value of higher education, and the third pertains to questions related to educational outcomes.

These three challenges provide a backdrop for understanding the challenges and opportunities facing leaders in higher education.

The Higher Education Landscape: Challenges in the 2020s

Attempting to provide a map of the landscape is a risky undertaking, given that the terrain leaders navigate can shift dramatically from year to year, month to month, or even week to week—as has become increasingly apparent to all of us. Indeed, the presumptions that change is rapid and pervasive in higher education and that effectively coping with leading—and, where possible, anticipating—change is critical for effective leadership in higher education are fundamental tenets of this book. At times events require incremental and continuous adjustment; in other instances, as we have learned, an existential threat may require immediate and transformative change within an institution or for higher education more generally. In this chapter, we focus on some of the longer term and ongoing trends in the landscape that do not necessarily rise to the level of a crisis but do require ongoing and systematic attention from leaders at all levels across higher education.

> **Challenge 1**. *Higher education has entered a period of consolidation, increased competition, and (perhaps) contraction due to constraints on revenues and rising expenses.*
>
> a. Higher education is becoming increasingly stratified, such that "elite" private institutions have greater resources than "elite" public research universities, who, in turn, have greater resources than do the vast majority of public colleges and universities that serve the majority of the U.S. population. The concentration of financial resources and the most talented faculty, staff, and students in smaller and smaller numbers of institutions is not a positive trend for the sector or the nation (Bowen & Tobin, 2015).
>
> b. In addition to competing with each other, traditional, nonprofit higher education institutions are also competing with for-profit institutions whose toehold in the sector seems firmly established. Private, for-profit institutions represented 17% of all 4-year institutions and 35% of all 2-year institutions in 2016–2017. Although student enrollment in for-profit colleges/universities is relatively small, nonprofit institutions can ill afford to cede any segment of the market to outside competitors, especially those who have more experience and success with distance-only degree programs.

c. From the period 1980–1981 to 2012–2013, the numbers of institutions of higher education increased by almost 1,500 (46% increase). This period of unprecedented growth has come to an end. In fact, the number of colleges and universities decreased by 366 from 2012–2013 to 2016–2017 (8% decrease). It is unclear as of this writing if this is a new trend or just a temporary shakeout—in either case, colleges and universities face tremendous financial pressures. Institutions that close are typically forced to do so because their business model—balance between revenues and expenses—becomes unsustainable. Leaders and governing boards are advised to err on the side of being hypervigilant about the institution's business model and practices. As detailed in their recent book, *The College Stress Test*, Zemsky et al. (2020) examine four key variables—new student enrollments, net cash price, student retention, and major external funding—to gauge whether an institution is potentially at risk of considering closure or merging with another school.

Implications of Stratification, Increased Competition, and Consolidation for Leaders

In a time of consolidation and increasing competition, it becomes critical to pay close attention to the value and benefits an institution provides to prospective students and other stakeholders, all while sharpening the messaging and strengthening the connections with critical stakeholder groups, especially those that provide sources of funding. One such group is the federal government, which provides considerable funding for student financial aid and research and scientific endeavors.

There are many national, business, and professional organizations that lobby the federal government for continued support of higher education. Leaders can benefit greatly from being knowledgeable about and engaging with the organizations that represent the interests of higher education in Washington, D.C. Leaders at all higher education institutions, particular public colleges and universities, also need to maintain productive relationships with local and state government officials who provide significant sources of funding, despite the aforementioned cuts to 4-year institutions over the past decades that show little sign of being reversed.

Private institutions, and to a growing extent public institutions, also need to engage with alumni and supportive donors to maintain and increase private gifts and grants, making clear the case for doing so. Increasing donor support must become an institutional priority at public colleges and universities given the new realities of decreased state and local funding. (Visit case. org to learn more about institutional fundraising training that is tailored by institutional type.)

In general, except for a small number of elite institutions, leaders at nonprofit colleges/universities should not assume their institutions have a guaranteed future existence, at least in their present forms. (Leaders at for-profit institutions are unlikely to have ever suffered from this assumption.) As we have seen, and as may well be increasingly a sign of the times, academic departments and especially nonacademic departments and services—and in some cases entire institutions—will likely be consolidated or even eliminated in the face of mounting financial pressures. Other features of the contemporary landscape, including questions about the value of higher education, represent an additional source of concern.

Challenge 2. *According to recent surveys and press reports, public confidence in U.S. higher education has declined, and the value proposition of higher education is being questioned.*
   a. This decline in public confidence seems to be driven by concerns about access and affordability of a college education. Despite aid packages and tuition discounting, most undergraduate (and graduate) students must borrow money to cover the costs of tuition, fees, books, and other educational expenses. Escalating costs have led families to focus on employment prospects for college graduates.
   b. Higher education has also been criticized for being overly concerned with political correctness, the promotion of a liberal agenda, and the failure to prepare students for their roles as citizens by being overly accommodating to demands for protection from emotional harm in the classroom and on campus (Lukianoff & Haidt, 2018). Well-publicized instances of colleges and universities placing limitations on (legal) forms of free speech and/or disciplinary personnel decisions due to the exercise of free speech by faculty members have been decried by commentators across the political spectrum. Critics also question the need to institute "trigger warnings" for curriculum content that prior generations of students were routinely exposed to as they completed courses and programs. Note, too, that the connotation of "liberal" in liberal arts has added a political dimension to discussions of the value of higher education, which has contributed further to this challenge. Taken together, these criticisms call into question the

willingness or ability of higher education to fulfill its central purpose—free and open discussion and debate about ideas and social issues, especially those that might cause some student discomfort. If students cannot be exposed to ideas that challenge their thinking while in college, how well is the college experience preparing students for the outside world of work, politics, and community life where diverse and strongly held perspectives and rhetoric are increasingly commonplace? Conservative commentators in particular point to these recent developments in classrooms and on campuses to argue for decreased taxpayer support for higher education (e.g., Milikh, 2020).

c. The "Varsity Blues" scandal of 2019 suggested "elite" schools' competitive admissions systems are rigged in favor of applicants whose families have considerable financial resources. Instances such as this call into question the ethics of college admissions and raise questions regarding the impact of wealth, resources, and privilege in securing admission to some of the country's most prestigious institutions of higher education.

Implications of Decreasing Public Confidence for Leaders

What can leaders do to reverse the decreased public confidence in higher education? Leaders often rely on employment and lifetime income data to defend the investment in higher education from an economic standpoint. Although these data are very favorable for institutions of higher education, this pervasive strategy was recently questioned by the National Association of College and University Business Officers (NACUBO, 2019), whose "Perceptions and Priorities" report opened as follows:

> Higher education faces an uncomfortable reality. While colleges and universities continue to deliver exceptional value, confidence in the sector has dropped precipitously in the past three years—with more than half of Americans now questioning higher education institutions. At NACUBO, we have observed that college administrators frequently dismiss the current doubts, readily pointing to clear evidence of financial value and noting that higher education has long experienced dramatic swings in public perception—particularly as demographics, labor economics, and technology evolve. Far too often, however, this results more in assuaging rather than engaging with people's concerns. . . . The time has come for NACUBO, our members, and indeed all college administrators, presidents, chancellors, trustees, policymakers, and other fiduciaries to step back, take stock of what is working, and highlight trends that institutions can't ignore if

they want to keep delivering great value. The returns to an investment in higher education have never been stronger, but to maintain that value, the sector must continue to evolve. (pp. 1–2)

. . . [Without infusions of monies from federal and state governments, and/or without institutional investments in controlling costs and improving learning outcomes (i.e., retention and graduation rates)], we must honestly ask ourselves to consider at what point borrowing for higher education poses more risk than reward. (p. 6)

The report goes on to assert that for higher education,

equity and affordability must be . . . demonstrated core values. Today, higher education must intensely explore institutional admissions, financial aid, instruction, and academic support practices, and work with vigor to ensure they are working in a way that affords all students a chance to be graduates. (NACUBO, 2019, p. 7)

The report also makes the point that the changing demographics in college enrollments have increased the need for additional student services as more first-time, low-income students enroll.

In reviewing possible solutions, NACUBO (2019) posits that technological advances in teaching might help lower costs, and on a different front indicates the need for improved institutional capacity and successful public relations efforts to influence public perception. Although technology has increased access to instruction, digital forms have not yet lowered the costs of higher education. With respect to public relations, NACUBO recommends that institutional members share in the responsibility of increasing public understanding about the costs of higher education—another instance where expanded leadership capacity is required for coordination and collaboration between and among business, academic, and public affairs departments and other related offices.

With respect to placing limitations on legally protected forms of free speech and scholarship, an understanding of free speech protections and the meaning and scope of academic freedom has become a necessity for those who lead and interact with faculty, staff, and students. Institutions may find it helpful to consider adopting and promulgating policies that govern free speech in the classroom, on campus (including virtual campuses), and in the conduct of everyday operations. For example, the 2015 University of Chicago Report of the Committee on Freedom of Expression developed a statement that many campus leaders might find useful to adopt, promulgate, and discuss at the start of each academic year. Chemerinsky and Gillman (2017) analyzed the topic of free speech and trigger warnings on campus and their "What Campuses Can and Cannot Do" (chapter 5 in their book) is an excellent source for campus leaders to consider. A principled stand on protecting (legal) forms of free speech, scholarly inquiry, and advocacy should guide leaders' decisions when controversies arise. A growing concern is that leaders might compromise core values by the suppression of speech to appease internal stakeholders (e.g., certain students and faculty members). This will almost certainly be met with disfavor by some external stakeholders, including alumni, donors, and legislators. Making reference to and insisting on adherence to principled position statements are important tools for leaders as they seek to maintain core values while appeasing stakeholders with very different senses of what is "right and wrong" with regard to free speech controversies. Over time, principled positions and actions should sustain, not further erode, public confidence in higher education.

The college admissions scandal of 2019 touched a very small number of institutions. In an era of declining public confidence, however, all institutional leaders need to ensure that the highest standards of integrity and morality are maintained, not only in admissions but in every aspect of operations. The increasingly desperate search for continued and new sources of funding has the potential to cause members of any institution, not just a few elite institutions, to take shortcuts with institutional policies and procedures in ways that leave the institution compromised. Leaders need to be articulate about the benefits of a higher education, for individual students and society more generally, and also be vigilant about ethics and integrity in an era of declining support and increased competition for funding.

> **Challenge 3**. *Educational outcomes—especially retention and graduation rates—remain problematic for many groups of students. Across all types of higher education institutions, approximately 40% or more admitted undergraduate students may not obtain degrees in a timely fashion, if at all. In addition, the nature of teaching and learning is being altered by technology at a time when fewer and fewer members of the faculty are tenured or tenure-track.*
>
> a. In 2016, fewer than 55% of all undergraduate and graduate students in the United States were White. Changes in the race-ethnicity composition of college students are ongoing, reflecting changes in the country's demographics. Differential learning outcomes for African American and Latinx students as compared to Asian American and White students is a long-standing issue in PK–20 education in the United States. Despite considerable efforts to address "achievement gaps," definitive, generalizable, and scalable solutions remain elusive.

b. In 2018–2019, 56% of U.S. college students were women; 44% were men. Girls and women have outperformed (as measured by GPA and graduation rates) boys and men in PK–20 education for some time in the United States, and this trend shows no signs of being reversed at present. An important exception to this trend, that is also problematic, is the fact that men are overrepresented in certain STEM fields such as engineering, computer science, physics, and mathematics at either the undergraduate or graduate level and in terms of employment. Again, despite long-standing and ongoing efforts to address differences in STEM fields, differences in educational attainment by sex/gender continue to be a significant challenge for higher education.

c. Due in part to the growing diversity of matriculated students and the costs associated with tuition, fees, books, and other educational expenses, food insecurity is a fact of life for an increasing number of undergraduate and graduate students. Food insecurity has been shown to negatively affect the academic performance of students on college campuses (Brescia & Cuite, 2019; Meza et al., 2019; Payne-Sturges et al., 2017; Regan, 2020).

d. Teaching and learning continue to be transformed because of technological advances, including the availability of course management systems that support face-to-face classroom instruction and make possible the use of distance-only ("virtual") instruction. Traditional, nonprofit institutions have been slow to adopt distance-only courses and programs and have largely ceded this part of the market to private, for-profit institutions. This reality changed dramatically in a remarkably short period of time in response to the outbreak of the coronavirus and the sudden shift to fully remote learning in spring 2020. The longer term impacts of these changes have yet to be realized, and the evaluation of the consequences of this transformative shift on the dynamics and outcomes of teaching and learning will be an issue of ongoing importance to researchers and professionals for some time to come.

e. The composition of higher education faculty continues to indicate decreases in tenure-track positions and increases in nontenure-track positions (Bowen & Tobin, 2015). Critics of 4-year colleges and universities point out that faculty members spend very little time on undergraduate instruction and advisement (Sykes, 2016), another reality that may undergo revision as a consequence of the COVID-19 pandemic and increasing demands for full-time, tenure-track faculty to play an increasingly central role in teaching. This is yet another landscape development that will be important in defining the work of leaders who face larger and larger numbers of nontenure-track and/or part-time faculty members (see chapter 5 for further discussion).

Addressing Learning Outcome Disparities in a Shifting Teaching–Learning Landscape: Implications for Leaders

This third challenge may be the most important for leaders to address. First, improving learning outcomes is at the core of a college or university's mission. Second, progress in this area simultaneously helps to address the other two major landscape challenges we described. An institution that can demonstrate a narrowing of learning outcome disparities—by increasing retention rates, shortening time to degree, and/or equalizing graduation rates by race, ethnicity, and/or sex of student—and postgraduation success in graduate or workplace placement is in an excellent position to address challenges pertaining to institutional survival, support, and public confidence.

Unfortunately, the issue of learning outcome disparities is perhaps the most difficult to resolve, and many institutions have invested considerable resources to do so over the past 2 to 3 decades. We think it is apparent that systematic cross-cutting approaches are needed to address the complex problems of learning and academic achievement. Solutions are unlikely to reside in one academic or administrative unit. Leaders need to be able to work across the institution to address differential learning outcomes. Ensuring that students are not hungry and food insecure, for example, requires a collaborative and cooperative partnership between academic and student service units. With respect to classroom learning, academic departments need to coordinate and share best practices with other academic units and institutions. Academic departments should also work cooperatively with extra-departmental student support services, student life programs, financial aid offices, and so forth. Holistic cross-cutting approaches are needed to support students who are currently underperforming at an institution. This is an area in which institutions would benefit greatly from the identification of "dashboard" progress and achievement markers and their translation into measurable outcomes that can be tracked within individual departments and aggregated at an institutional level (see chapter 16). Leader focus, which includes tracking performance and communicating results over successive years, is a foundational element to building success in this area.

Leaders also need a variety of skills as institutions continue to shift teaching from face-to-face classroom environments to online, virtual environments. Completion of the spring 2020 semester in the face of the global pandemic made this abundantly clear, as many institutions were caught short.

The required expertise for designing and delivering robust online courses typically resides outside academic departments. Therefore, departments may very well need to rely on staff experts to support faculty transitions to online teaching. If an institution wants to create fully online programs, academic departments will also need to work with admissions and enrollment officers, student support services, IT departments, and so forth to recruit, retain, and graduate online students. These cross-cutting points of coordination are best managed by leaders who can successfully navigate the different cultures of the institution (see chapter 6).

The changing composition of the faculty has implications for academic leaders and shared governance, which is discussed further in chapter 5. With respect to learning outcomes, nontenure-track faculty should be carefully vetted and evaluated for teaching effectiveness. Ideally nontenured faculty will be assigned to teach courses in learning environments with which they are most comfortable and experienced, and for the benefit of students, it is best to minimize turnover of nontenure-track and adjunct faculty members. Where possible, teaching contracts with longer renewal cycles (at least 3 years) for those nontenure-track faculty members who are doing an excellent job in teaching and advising students seems appropriate.

Summary of Landscape Issues

The critical elements of higher education described rarely operate in isolation and almost always interact and affect one another, for example, concerns about the ability to sustain financial resources challenge institutions and their leaders in numerous ways. In addition to day-to-day pressures placed on leaders to exercise great care in resource allocation, financial constraints require leaders to be increasingly entrepreneurial and innovative in identifying possible sources for generating new revenues. Limited financial resources and crises such as the COVID-19 pandemic underscore the importance of understanding finance and budgeting models and their implications. They also are likely to require the identification of new and expanded revenue-generating strategies, as well as the utilization of alternative and potentially more efficient options for teaching and learning.

These and other factors also lead many institutions to hire part-time faculty members or contract-based nontenure-track faculty members to deliver instructional programs. Furthermore, financial resource constraints may inhibit the ability of an institution to provide financial support for all students who qualify for admission and to assist students who struggle academically once admitted. While this chain of events, and others, are understandable, they can be problematic. More efficient approaches to teaching and learning—such as the use of technology and more flexible practices in hiring teaching personnel—can be a positive, as well as a necessary, development, but not always. Bok (2013) believes, for instance, that the trend toward having part-time instructors, including graduate students, deliver large segments of the undergraduate curriculum undermines public credibility in colleges and universities and is therefore one that leaders can and must reverse.

We also know that students and large segments of the public think first and foremost about the educational role of colleges and universities, and understandably so. This focus leaves little room for a full appreciation of the research and knowledge-creation aspects of institutional missions that research universities emphasize, particularly when an emphasis on research is perceived to come at the expense of attention to teaching and learning. There are similar issues in other mission areas, such as community outreach and engagement, and patient care for institutions with health and medical units. Because of the richness and diversity of higher education institutions, it is common for stakeholder groups to focus on a particular facet of greatest interest and relevance for them, while failing to recognize the importance and complementarity of other mission areas and the organizational, workforce, and financial interdependencies among all components.

Regardless of specific details, these landscape factors are cross-cutting, and as such, they emphasize the need for academic and administrative leaders who demonstrate competencies and a breadth of understanding that goes beyond narrow training in a specific field, coupled with experience in and familiarity with higher education as a faculty or staff member. In considering the knowledge, skills, and tools required to be an effective leader in higher education, each of the landscape elements highlights the importance of understanding general issues related to leadership and organizational dynamics and a more specific knowledge of finance and budgeting as colleges and universities enter what will likely be an even more competitive and challenging time ahead.

Conclusion

This chapter has presented an overview of the higher education landscape. Students and their families view higher education as critically important (no longer optional) but increasingly unaffordable. This view has led to declining public confidence in the sector and demands for greater transparency and accountability relative to higher education costs. These demands have increased in the aftermath of the COVID-19 pandemic. Several complex issues arise from this dynamic tension, and leaders confront them almost daily. On the other hand, leaders should not lose sight of the fact that there is still a strong perception that the American system of higher education is among the best in the world. Our ideas and approaches to educating students and addressing the problems and deep questions of the world remain a source of envy.

Leaders in American higher education possess a great deal of autonomy to innovate in their approach to addressing challenges and opportunities, which can be both a blessing and a curse. We have used—and will continue to use—the terms *challenges* and *opportunities* extensively to characterize the external environment with which leaders are confronted. In practice, the distinction between the two is very much a matter of how leaders conceptualize and address situations. Engaging in leadership of a unit, department, or institution without an informed perspective on the higher education landscape, a thoughtfully crafted leadership philosophy, an understanding of interpersonal and organizational dynamics, and a clear sense of the mission and aspirations may very well contribute to a prescription for seeing overwhelming challenges and problems.

Periodically, the landscape is transformed by a set of immediate and pervasive concerns, such as the convergence of crises represented by the COVID-19 pandemic and increased racial unrest across the country. In such instances, the challenges of leadership—from both personal and professional perspectives—can be daunting. However, if one prepares carefully, exhibits a clear sense of purpose, employs relevant concepts and tools, and blends the perspectives of faculty and administrative staff appropriately, it is possible to be a proactive leader in transforming challenges into opportunities. While this description is not the classic definition of a transformational leader, about which more will be said later, it is an apt description of the kind of leadership that is certainly needed right now within higher education.

For Further Consideration

1. Higher education and graduate–professional student loan debt
Consider the information presented in Table 3.1 concerning debt incurred by postbaccalaureate students at various types of institutions. Given the large numbers of students who incur debt, and the growing size of the debt, what implications does this have for leaders who are trying to attract students to their graduate programs? What can an institution do to encourage students to apply and complete

these programs in a timely manner? What skills does a leader need to have in order to deal with the issue of graduate student loan debt?

2. Developing distance education courses and programs

Dean Williams is under pressure from the provost to increase revenues for the College of Engineering. The dean is well aware that the faculty have the responsibility and authority to approve courses and programs of study offered by the college. However, the university and college policy manuals do not address whether faculty members need to approve conversion of existing courses and programs from classroom-based to fully online formats. Building on the concepts and ideas presented in this chapter, analyze the benefits and pitfalls for Dean Williams as she considers how to move the college forward to offer existing courses and programs in fully online formats. How might you advise Dean Williams to proceed?

TABLE 3.1

Loan Information for Graduate Student Completers in 2015–2016

		Type of Institution		
Type of degree		*Public*	*Private nonprofit*	*Private for-profit*
Postbaccalaureate certificate	% with loan	49%	58%	78%
	Size of loan	$51,100	$81,500	$97,300
Master's	% with loan	57%	60%	71%
	Size of loan	$59,500	$71,900	$90,300
Doctor's research	% with loan	37%	54%	76%
	Size of Loan	$92,200	$94,100	$160,100
Doctor's professional[1]	% with loan	76%	72%	90%
	Size of loan	$142,600	$221,800	$190,200

Notes. Sizes of loan figures are cumulative from undergraduate and graduate schools. Size of loan averages excludes completers with no loans. Source: U.S. Department of Education, National Center for Educational Statistics, 2018.

[1] Doctor's professional includes chiropractic, dentistry, law, medicine, optometry, pharmacy, podiatry, and veterinary medicine.

4

COLLEGE AND UNIVERSITY MISSIONS AND STAKEHOLDERS

Purposes, Perspectives, Pressures

Barbara Bender and Susan E. Lawrence

In This Chapter

- In what ways does the institutional mission influence an organization's leadership practices?
- Who are the primary internal and external stakeholders of the modern college or university?
- What missions do various stakeholders view as central?
- How can leaders understand and use stakeholder information to strengthen communication about the mission of a unit, department, or institution?
- What sources of information about stakeholder views are available to leaders?

This chapter focuses on the role and importance of institutional missions and stakeholders for leaders in academic settings. When reviewing their offerings and organization, colleges and universities may seem similar, but distinct differences will emerge when studying their practices, cultures, leadership, and reasons for existing. To this end, academic leaders need to possess the vision and communication skills to educate and inform stakeholders about their institution's mission and goals. Especially important, leaders need to understand that stakeholders approach higher education from different vantage points—each bringing unique perspectives, preferences, expectations, and desires. Conveying the institution's goals to a broad range of stakeholders and working with multiple publics to have them embrace the institution's mission is not an easy task, but it is one that academic leaders must address.

The need for leaders to understand, define, embrace, and communicate the mission of their institutions has perhaps never been more critical than in dealing with the extraordinary political and financial pressures posed by the COVID-19 pandemic. The process of closing and later reopening campuses required leaders to set clear priorities as to which mission elements are most important to the institution's identity and fiscal health. Having made these difficult decisions, leaders then needed to clearly communicate their decisions to critical internal (faculty, staff, and students) and external (alumni, donors, public at large) stakeholders. This experience and many others highlight the interdependent relationship between the institutional mission and stakeholders.

The Importance of Mission

How do higher education leaders make decisions on the allocation of resources? What underlying principles and values guide an institution's operational practices? For each of the approximately 4,500 institutions of higher education in the United States, the answers to these questions should be shaped by the institution's mission. A college or university's mission provides a foundation for all the school does and aspires to do.

Table 4.1 provides an example of the diversity of the higher education landscape in the United States. Rather than emerging in a well-planned and systematic manner, the growth of American colleges and universities is the result of a host of extraneous factors, including the need to train clergy in the U.S. colonies, to provide practical training in agriculture for certain regions of the country, and even to allow a wealthy family to create and name a university in memory of a deceased child (Thelin, 2019).

Typically, the mission is embodied in a statement of purpose that serves as a guide for determining the programs and services an institution will offer. The stated mission guides leadership decisions related to institutional operations, including planning, resource allocation, the development of new programs and services, and day-to-day practices and procedures. While mission statements of colleges and universities often have some common characteristics, they are also unique in various ways as a function of the type of institution, primary sources of governance and funding, their history, the populations they serve, and their distinctive aims.

Most often, these distinctive purposes are captured and formalized in a mission statement. Such statements typically include language describing their

TABLE 4.1

Number and Percentage Distribution of Title IV Institutions by Control, Level, and Region: United States and Other U.S. Jurisdictions, Academic Year 2017–2018

Level of institution and region	Number of institutions				Percent of institutions			
			Private				Private	
	Total	Public	Nonprofit	For-profit	Total	Public	Nonprofit	For-Profit
Total institutions	**6,642**	**1,973**	**1,878**	**2,791**	**100.0**	**100.0**	**100.0**	**100.0**
Total U.S. institutions	6,502	1,955	1.626	2,721	97.9	99.1	97.2	97.5
Level of institution								
4-year	2,902	760	1,643	499	43.7	38.5	87.5	17.9
U.S.	2,836	751	1,597	486	42.7	38.1	85.0	17.5
Other U.S. jurisdictions	66	9	46	11	1.0	0.5	2.4	0.4
2-year	1,932	972	159	795	29.1	49.6	8.5	28.5
U.S.	1,905	969	154	782	28.7	49.1	8.2	28.0
Other U.S. jurisdictions	27	9	5	13	0.4	0.5	0.3	0.5
Less-than-2-year	1,808	235	76	1,497	27.2	11.9	4.0	53.6
U.S.	1,761	235	75	1,451	26.5	11.9	4.0	52.0
Other U.S. jurisdictioi	47	0	1	46	0.7	0.0	0.1	1.6

Level of institution and region	Number of institutions				Percent of institutions			
	Total	Public	Private		Total	Public	Private	
			Nonprofit	For-profit			Nonprofit	For-Profit
Region								
New England	373	104	154	115	5.6	5.3	8.2	4.1
Mid East	1,069	274	415	380	16.1	13.9	22.1	13.6
Great Lakes	957	266	292	399	14.4	13.5	15.5	14.3
Plains	566	188	185	183	8.4	9.5	9.9	6.6
Southeast	1,646	541	393	712	24.8	27.4	20.9	25.5
Southwest	708	241	109	358	10.7	12.2	5.8	12.8
Rocky Mountains	258	81	42	135	3.9	4.1	2.2	4.8
Far West	930	255	236	439	14.0	12.9	12.6	15.7
U.S. service academies	5	5	0	0	0.1	0.3	0.0	0.0
Other U.S. jurisdictions	140	18	52	70	2.1	0.9	2.8	2.5

Source: National Center for Education Statistics. (2018). *Postsecondary institutions and cost of attendance in 2017–18; degrees and other awards conferred, 2016–17; and 12-month enrollment, 2016–17.* https://nces.ed.gov/pubs2018/2018060rev.pdf

core values, defined as the philosophical underpinnings or principles that guide the way leaders of particular colleges and universities implement their goals. In some instances, mission statements also make direct or indirect reference to their aspirations—their vision for the future of the institution.[1]

There are many different types of institutions and a wide variety of mission statements. The six statements listed in Table 4.2 illustrate the broad range of institutional missions of U.S. higher education institutions.

For leaders—ranging from members of governing boards to academic and administrative leaders throughout the institution—the mission statement ideally provides a blueprint and a touchstone for organizational decision-making. The statement should serve as a source of guidance when creating strategic plans and goals, designing curriculum, teaching courses, developing programs, and preparing budget models. Leaders' failure to act in ways consistent with the established mission, or drifting from stated organizational principles, may confuse faculty and staff employees; alienate alumni, donors, and other external stakeholders; compromise a leader's credibility; jeopardize the tenure of the leader; or, at an extreme, threaten an institution's survival.

While the importance of consistency of purpose may seem obvious to leaders, the numerous internal and external forces and pressures that influence higher education can complicate planning, decision-making, resource allocation processes, and other leadership actions. Consistency is important, but formalized mission statements also need to be living documents that can guide institutional growth and change as leaders consider new ways of meeting their goals while adapting to the many changes taking place in higher education, including demographic changes of enrolled students, evolving pedagogical approaches, shifting workforce needs, and advances in technology. Although the focus of discussion thus far has been on institutional-level missions and mission statements, the same assets and leadership challenges pertain to statements of purpose developed at the campus, department, or program level.

Although an institution's mission may have evolved or been purposefully modified, the history and original purpose of the institution's founders typically continue to have great influence on the school's mission and practices over the years. In the case of a hypothetical multipurpose university with an exceptionally strong college of education, for example, knowing that the school started as a small teachers' college that grew into a state university can help to explain why, a century later, a particular university has a college of education that is prominent within the institution and serves as a benchmark for other universities across the country. While promoting the strength of its original "teacher training" mission and expanding its college of education

TABLE 4.2
Examples of College and University Mission Statements

Public Research Institution
University of Michigan (n.d.)
The mission of the University of Michigan is to serve the people of Michigan and the world through preeminence in creating, communicating, preserving, and applying knowledge, art, and academic values, and in developing leaders and citizens who will challenge the present and enrich the future.
Private 4-Year Institution
Kalamazoo College (n.d.)
The mission of Kalamazoo College is to prepare its graduates to better understand, live successfully within, and provide enlightened leadership to a richly diverse and increasingly complex world.
Religiously Affiliated 4-Year University
Baylor University (n.d.)
The mission of Baylor University is to educate men and women for worldwide leadership and service by integrating academic excellence and Christian commitment within a caring community.
Historically Black Colleges and Universities
Spelman College (n.d.)
Spelman College, a historically Black college and a global leader in the education of women of African descent, is dedicated to academic excellence in the liberal arts and sciences and the intellectual, creative, ethical, and leadership development of its students. Spelman empowers the whole person to engage the many cultures of the world and inspires a commitment to positive social change.
Public 2-Year Institution
Westchester Community College (n.d.)
Westchester Community College provides accessible, high-quality, and affordable education to meet the needs of our diverse community. Westchester is committed to student success, academic excellence, workforce development, economic development, and lifelong learning.
Medical School
Georgetown University School of Medicine (n.d.)
Guided by the Jesuit tradition of *Cura Personalis*, care of the whole person, Georgetown University School of Medicine will educate a diverse student body, in an integrated way, to become knowledgeable, ethical, skillful, and compassionate physicians and biomedical scientists who are dedicated to the care of others and to the health needs of our society.

into one of the finest education centers in the world, this formerly small college expanded its mission, opened new schools, and created a strong, comprehensive, research-intensive university. In this example, the college of education had a long history of alumni giving, a strong endowment, numerous graduate fellowships, a superb faculty, and the resources it needed to excel. A school's history makes a difference.

Leadership and Mission

The responsibility for interpreting, shaping, promoting, and implementing an institution's mission begins with the governing board and the president. The mission informs daily decisions that need to be made, as well as the short- and long-term strategic planning processes that guide the institution. While a concept such as *embracing the mission* may seem simplistic, fully understanding and supporting a mission is quite often critical to helping determine the success of an academic or administrative leader. Search committees should be especially mindful when listening to candidates for senior leadership roles as they explore mission-related issues.

The overall mission should guide institutional decision-making and, concomitantly, resource allocations. Equally important, every division and unit within the institution should have its own specific mission developed in support of the overall purposes of the college or university. Maintaining a consistency of purpose throughout an institution can be a significant challenge for academic and administrative leaders who may find themselves championing a mission for their particular unit, department, or division that diverges from the institution's broader mission. Ultimately, it is the responsibility of the senior leadership to work with leaders at all levels to create alignment across the institution. Without such a complementary and integrated approach, an institution could easily evolve into a shopping mall of courses, programs, and administrative functions—with no overarching institutional distinctiveness or shared sense of identity among faculty, staff, and students. Worse yet, it can allow unfettered competition between units that are rife with overreaching, divisive, and contradictory messages that are subsequently promoted to internal and external stakeholders.

The financial environment of most colleges and universities is a particular source of conflict for leaders. Pressures to operate with increasing efficiency, reduce costs, and increase available funds may pose specific difficulties for leaders as they strive to adjust to contemporary economic realities while preserving—and, ideally, strengthening—the core mission or missions of their institutions and programs. At the same time, leaders must work to create and foster an academic community that appropriately supports their mission.

Keeping Missions Current

Maintaining one's core mission does not mean that changes can never be made to the curriculum or to the institution's goals. Having a core mission that allows for institutional dynamism can provide colleges and universities with the foundation and flexibility to thrive and adapt to change. For example, as Bender (2002) noted,

> With the ever present demand for accountability and competing pressures from multiple constituencies . . . effective and prudent academic leaders need to be thoughtful visionaries who can develop feasible solutions to institutional problems. The most important factor in effecting change, ultimately, is the courage of the leaders to identify an institution's shortcomings, then convey the findings, with potential solutions, to an audience that will include both proponents and adversaries. (p. 114)

Residential liberal arts colleges, for example, would never have considered including computer game design courses in their curriculum 30 years ago, while today such offerings help provide important educational experiences for their students. Similarly, the inclusion of distance learning courses by institutions with a strong residential component would have been heresy just 15 years ago. But now, in the midst of a global pandemic, almost all institutions provide opportunities for remote learning alongside established online and hybrid offerings, and as public health guidelines allow, in-person traditional seminars, labs, and lectures. In a parallel manner, statements of institutional purpose also provide a rationale for designing and planning new administrative, student life, and campus-related programs and services. They should also provide a basis for reviewing, revising, or eliminating administrative and operational programs and services that are no longer relevant.

As noted earlier and implied in the preceding examples, mission statements should be firmly rooted but also adaptable to the evolving trends that impact institutions of higher education. These may well include broader demographic changes in the local community, state, and region. Despite knowledge of these trends and even with careful strategic planning, an institution might fail to attract enough students to remain viable. An appropriate response to this situation may prompt a shift in mission as a way of addressing changing demographics. Leaders' failure to take note of a dangerous institutional trajectory and adapt the mission to the changing landscape in a timely fashion can, in extreme cases, have dire consequences, as noted in the previous chapter.

The announcement in spring 2015 of the board of trustees' decision to close the 114-year-old Sweet Briar College is, perhaps, an instructive example for at-risk colleges whose missions no longer meet the interest of contemporary students. In cases such as this, one may wonder whether there were possibilities for adapting the mission that would have created options for sustainability. Elizabeth H. S. Wyatt, a member of the board, noted, "The things that made Sweet Briar indispensable in the eyes of many alumnae—its intimate campus, its remote location—did not seem to move prospective students" (Kolowich, 2015). In June 2015, a tentative agreement was reached to keep the school open for at least another year. As part of the plan, the president and many members of the board of directors were replaced (Stolberg, 2015). Under the leadership of a new president, Meredith Jung-En Woo, the college made significant revisions to their traditional academic curriculum with the removal of historic academic departments, replacing them with three centers, Engineering, Science and Technology in Society; Human and Environmental Sustainability; and Creativity, Design and the Arts, and the introduction of a new core curriculum program based around women's leadership (Biemiller, 2017). Their regional accreditor, Southern Association of Colleges and Schools Commission on Colleges, placed Sweet Briar on "warning" status in June 2018, which was later removed in June 2019 (Kelderman, 2018).

As these situations demonstrate, it is possible that one of the most critical capabilities necessary for senior leaders is balancing their attention between continuity and tradition. As noted in previous chapters, maintaining an awareness and responsiveness to critical changes in the higher education landscape is an essential skill for all academic leaders.

Stakeholders

Perhaps no other institution besides government has as many constituencies and beneficiaries—or *stakeholders*, as defined in R. Edward Freeman's (1984) influential work—as the modern college or university. In what follows we identify the wide range of groups that have a stake in higher education today and for whom institutional leaders must be mindful. We also provide a framework for understanding the challenges created for higher education leaders from stakeholders' competing beliefs and divergent expectations about an institution's mission. Identifying what various stakeholder groups understand to be the central mission of a particular college or university, or higher education overall, is critical to effective leadership.

Higher Education on the Public Agenda

Whether higher education ever actually lived in the fabled ivory tower or not, there is no question that it has achieved an unusually high place on the public agenda in recent times. The data presented in Figure 4.1 track this rise by reporting the number of articles referring to higher education institutions that appeared in *The New York Times* over the last 50 years.[2] While the range of topics covered in these articles reflects the breadth of higher education, the pattern of increased media attention is evident. One cause and effect of this increased media attention is an expansion in the scope of who believes they have a stake in higher education and its mission. Individuals and groups across the political spectrum are paying attention to higher education.

The economic downturn of 2008–2009 coupled with the information technology revolution have accelerated the urgency with which attention has turned to colleges and universities over the last 15 years. Government looks to higher education to fix a broken economy of displaced workers and income inequality while largely treating higher education as a private good. Individuals confronting socioeconomic difficulties often view higher education as the potential solution to their circumstances, as demonstrated by countercyclical enrollment patterns. Both see student loan debt as an escalating crisis. A number of states have stepped in with variations on the Tennessee Promise, and the 2016 and 2020 presidential elections saw the introduction of multiple iterations of college affordability plans (Camera, 2019; Smith, 2018).

Tuitions climb while parental worry is fueled by reports that college graduates find it difficult to get jobs that provide adequate return on investment. Online courses and degrees are offered as a way to hold down

Figure 4.1. Increased public attention to higher education.

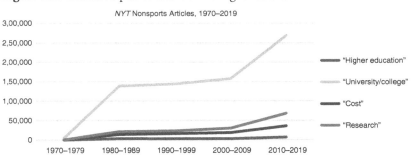

NYT Nonsports Articles, 1970–2019

Legend
"Higher education"
"University/college"
"Cost"
"Research"

tuition, free research faculty from "distracting" teaching loads, and standardize the quality of instruction that students receive; consequently, the online learning environment is touted as a door to economic opportunity for the disadvantaged as well as the elite. In fact, quality online instruction is generally more labor intensive than face-to-face instruction, and the persistent digital divide makes access uneven. Response to the rapid pivot to remote instruction during the COVID-19 stay-at-home orders and the clamor to return to campuses show exactly how much students and faculty truly value the in-person campus experience and the need for the broadband access and computer labs that institutions of higher education provide (Marcus, 2020).

The health care industry, Silicon Valley, and the business community depend on universities' commitment to basic and clinical research but often argue that higher education is not producing the educated workforce that is needed. Meanwhile, political agendas infuse debates over federal funding for research, with a growing chorus from the right accusing colleges of producing "a generation of sanctimonious, sensitive, supercilious snowflakes" (Quintana, 2018). Long before the Black Lives Matter protests in summer 2020, the left had deep concerns that higher education is not doing enough to address economic inequality and systemic racism.

On campus, there has been a rise in the unionization of contingent faculty and graduate students while tenure-track jobs become more and more elusive (see chapter 5). Faculty members face escalating research expectations up and down the hierarchy of colleges and universities. Staff and sometimes faculty feel unseen and undervalued. Administrators struggle to balance academics and athletics, scholarship and student life, dreams and dollars.

But, as discussed in chapter 3, these issues are complex and lack simple solutions. Each of higher education's stakeholder groups appears unhappy. None of these constituencies seems to think they are getting what they want, deserve, or are paying for from higher education. This reality confronts virtually every leader in an academic setting. And then, in 2020, the kryptonite of a global pandemic[3] laid bare long-standing tensions and divisions. Higher education will certainly survive COVID-19, but the recovery will be long and fraught with tough decisions for leaders since the "public agenda" includes multiple and often contradictory perspectives.

Stakeholders and the Higher Education Mission

While a general consensus exists on what higher education institutions and their various programs, services, and activities actually do, as shown in

Figure 4.2, specifics, priorities, and weightings vary across schools to create particular types of institutions of higher education and particular brands.

One may look to a variety of sources to determine how a particular school crafts its identity, including the following:

- mission statement
- strategic plan(s)
- public face (e.g., speeches, major pronouncements, press releases, admissions and recruiting materials, web pages)
- recruitment, promotion, and tenure criteria (staff, administrators, and faculty)
- membership of top leadership bodies and "kitchen cabinets"
- spending/budget priorities

A key task of leadership is to ensure that a consistent vision and purpose of conviction is conveyed and reinforced in and across each of these forums. Institutional priorities should be evident within and across each of these six elements. These institutional documents do not, however, provide information about the mission expectations of various audiences, beneficiaries, constituencies, power brokers, and participants—in short, about stakeholder views of higher education's, or a specific school's, mission (Jaschik, 2015; Labaree, 1997; Rothman et al., 2010).

A significant leadership challenge results from the fact that there is often a fair amount of variance in understandings of a university/college's mission among external constituencies. Figure 4.3 lists and categorizes the multiplicity

Figure 4.2. What universities/colleges do.

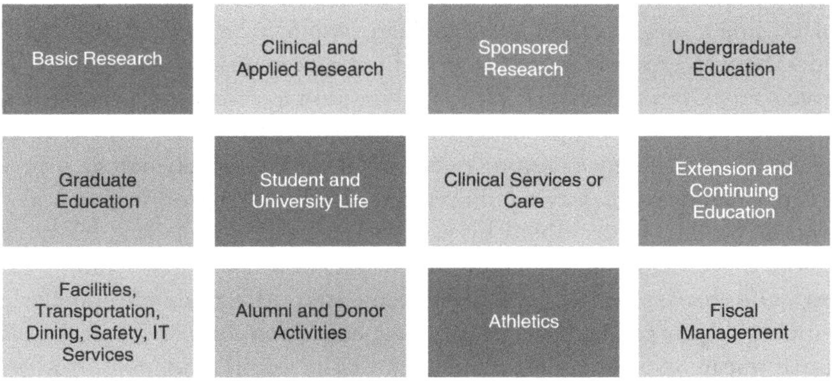

Figure 4.3. Internal and external stakeholders.

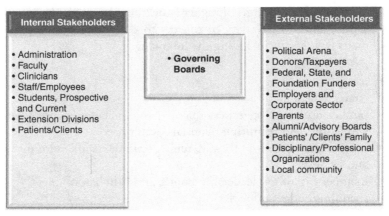

of internal and external stakeholders. As Ruben (2004) pointed out, higher education has been remarkably ineffective at developing the concise descriptions and explanations that would make all aspects of the academy's mission intelligible to laypeople. The expectations of external stakeholders have often reflected the current concerns of society, whether they were the agricultural and mechanical arts added by the Morrill Act, the expansion of federal grants to STEM disciplines due to Cold War concerns, or the civil rights agenda and the expansion of access to higher education through tuition grants, student loans, and affirmative action (Thelin, 2019). Recently, the governors of Florida, North Carolina, Texas, and Minnesota have pitted the need to address workforce concerns against continued investments in traditional liberal arts curricula (Bruni, 2013; Ruiz, 2011) and against the service mission of improving people's lives through teaching, research, outreach, and public service (Associated Press, 2015). A broad range of external stakeholders repeatedly point to the importance of return on investment, prioritizing lower tuition, shorter time to degree, and higher graduate employment rates. Many stakeholders have an expectation that higher education can decrease social and economic inequality and therefore prioritize attention to access and affordability.

Differences in the expectations of external stakeholders may be quite familiar, while differences among internal stakeholders frequently go unnoticed or unaddressed, leaving individuals and groups working at cross-purposes, feeling undervalued by each other, and adding complexity to the role of academic and administrative leaders at all levels. Among the most common areas of internal disagreement are the relative importance of undergraduate teaching versus graduate education, basic research versus applied research versus clinical services, athletics versus academics, student life versus classroom instruction, professional schools versus liberal arts and sciences, STEM versus humanities, and core mission versus revenue generation through auxiliary activities. The job of the leader is further complicated by the fact that while disagreements arise in personnel and budgetary decisions over their relative importance, in most cases, all are important parts of the mission.

Between internal and external stakeholders, governing boards occupy a middle ground; they are "of" the university but not "in" the university, as Figure 4.3 shows. By definition, the board's role is to oversee the institution. The distinguished men and women who serve on boards are often successful leaders in business or government, with experience at institutions with procedures and norms that are very different from those of higher education (Bolman & Gallos, 2011). Generally, their fiduciary responsibilities and their responsiveness to alumni shape their understanding of the institution's mission. See chapter 5 for further discussion of the role of governing boards in institutional governance.

Figure 4.4 depicts these multiple stakeholders under the categories of research, teaching, and service—common elements in the tripartite mission of most 4-year institutions. Not only do different stakeholders emphasize different parts of the triad, their comprehension of what each part is varies and invites misunderstandings. For example, particularly in the budgetary situation since 2008, senior administrators may emphasize funded research and the ability of faculty to secure federal research dollars, leaving many faculty members in the humanities and social sciences—where support funds are often limited—feeling their research is underappreciated. Similarly, students, parents, taxpayers, employers, and increasingly those in the political arena think of the teaching mission as closely tied to career preparation, while some faculty may see the goal of teaching as cultivation of the life of the mind, development of self-actualized young adults, or reproduction of the professoriate. On the other hand, faculty in professional schools may welcome greater attention to their role in improving society by producing well-trained professionals in health services, engineering, education, business, and so on.[4]

Of course, the descriptions presented in Figure 4.4 are stereotypes, and even within the categories of stakeholders identified here, views are not monolithic. Similarly, Figure 4.5 provides a graphic sketch of the constellation of stakeholders and working hypotheses about what appear to be their prominent mission expectations. This graphic brings home the 360-degree vision that higher education leaders need to have. Together, Figures 4.4 and 4.5 illustrate the many opportunities that exist for misunderstanding, miscommunication, and disappointment—all of which challenge leaders.

Figure 4.4. Diverse stakeholders' mission emphases.

Research	Teaching	Service/care
Administration-funded and high-profile research	Students: Undergrad and professional/career	Taxpayers, donors, alumni
Faculty: Pure research	Parents: Undergrad and professional/career	Patients/clients and family
MDs and clinicians: Applied	Taxpayers and donors	Political arena
Extension divisions: Applied	Political arena: Undergrad and professional—access, graduation, employment	Disciplinary and Professional organizations
Corporate sector: Applied Leads to profit-making	Employers and corporate sectors: Both undergrad and professional	Specific constituency Groups for extension Divisions or service missions
Political arena: Applied (especially defense, STEM, and econ Development)	Faculty: Cultivation of life of mind and reproduction of the profession	
Taxpayers, donors, alumni: Applied		

Figure 4.5. Stakeholders' mission priorities.

Communicating Mission and Vision

None of the foregoing analysis is meant to suggest that leaders in higher education must allow stakeholder visions and expectations to define the mission of higher education or of particular universities and colleges. Indeed, the breadth and variation of stakeholder interests makes it impossible to do so. But communicating and realizing an institution's or unit's particular mission and its unique brand requires careful attention to implicit and explicit beliefs of beneficiaries and constituents, attentive listening for these beliefs, and an openness to learning from them. Figure 4.6 provides a simple formula for addressing the challenge presented by discordant visions of the mission of higher education.

These steps are probably obvious to leaders when composing messages that specifically address the unit's or institution's mission, but the emphasis here is for leaders to ask themselves these five questions every time they represent their institution in writing, conversations, committee meetings, and of course speeches and other public presentations. Trying to imagine how others might have addressed these questions can be quite helpful as well.

Taking the time to systematically think through these questions is critical when preparing statements that will be consumed by multiple stakeholders during times of crisis and uncertainty. For example, comparing the various statements leaders made about repopulating campuses in fall 2020, and their timing, reveals much about which external and internal stakeholders are viewed as critical and what leaders perceive their concerns and interests to be (Chronicle of Higher Education, 2020). Responding to the COVID-19

Figure 4.6. Communicating mission and vision.

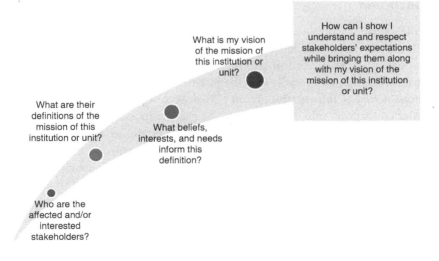

crisis was particularly challenging because so much was unknown and the situation was both fluid and persistent. Unlike getting ready for a blizzard or hurricane, which would be the more common disaster preparedness scenarios for campuses, with the pandemic, the end is distant. Hanging in the balance are not only lives, but the primary revenue streams that allow institutions of higher education to perform their core missions.

The Black Lives Matter protests provide a different challenge. The lack of a statement from leadership is itself heard as a statement (McKenzie, 2020). Because the protests and systemic racism are themselves political and contentious, it is impossible to have an apolitical response. In such situation, leaders must recognize the inescapable intersection between the core values and mission of the institution, the perspectives of stakeholders, and critical issues that must be addressed.

Again, listening matters—as does responsiveness. No institution can be all things to all people all of the time, nor should it try to be. Yet, leaders are wise to take the views of their stakeholders seriously in moving their institutions forward. The 2019 Inside Higher Ed/Gallup survey of American college and university presidents found that only 16% agreed with the statement that "most Americans have an accurate view of the purpose of higher education." While some of this might be rightly attributed to presidents not being very good storytellers, as Noah Drezner suggests, it might also suggest that presidents could be better listeners when it comes to hearing what their stakeholders expect of higher education (Lederman, 2019).

Conclusion

Leaders can learn much through listening carefully and respectfully to each group of stakeholders—learning more of their beliefs relating to the mission of higher education and the expectations that influence their willingness to support the leader and the institution. But leaders can also access other sources of information as they work to bridge the multiple views of higher education's mission. Some will be specific to each institution; others operate at a higher level of generality and pertain to higher education more broadly as a critical societal, economic, and cultural entity. Figure 4.7 reminds us of the multiple sources available to investigate the perspectives of various stakeholders. Leaders at all levels are wise to remain alert to these.

Figure 4.7. Sources of information on stakeholder views of higher education's mission.

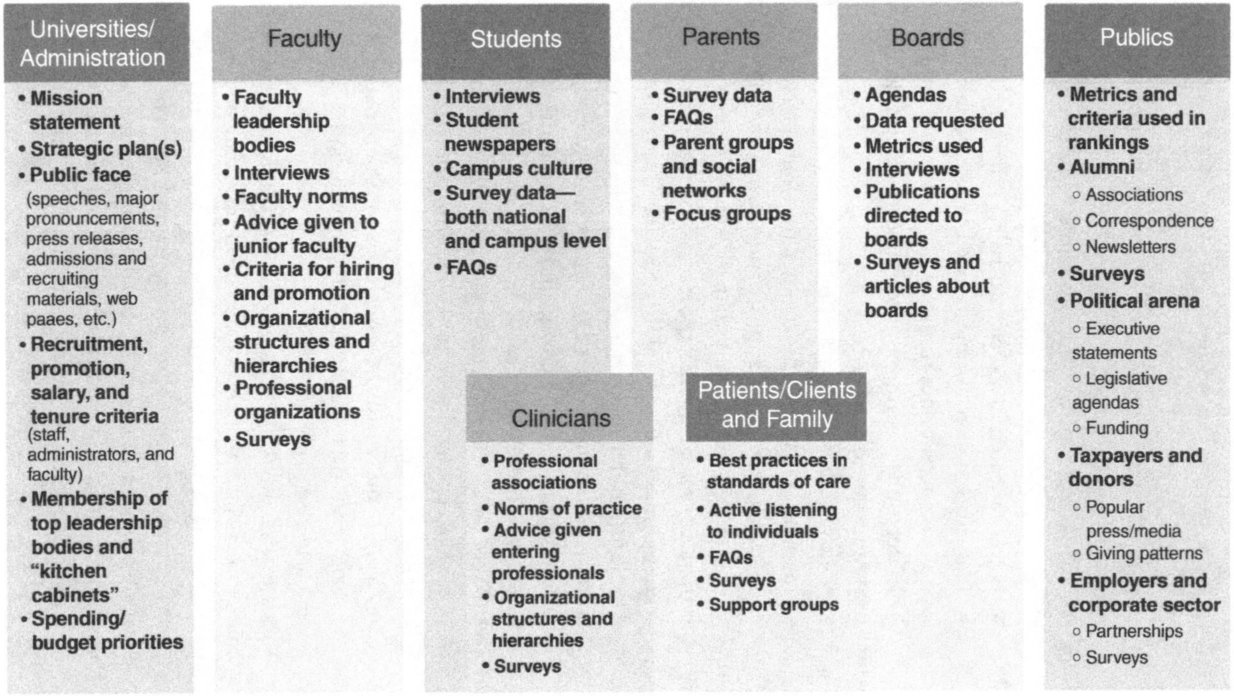

Universities/Administration
- Mission statement
- Strategic plan(s)
- Public face (speeches, major pronouncements, press releases, admissions and recruiting materials, web paaes, etc.)
- Recruitment, promotion, salary, and tenure criteria (staff, administrators, and faculty)
- Membership of top leadership bodies and "kitchen cabinets"
- Spending/budget priorities

Faculty
- Faculty leadership bodies
- Interviews
- Faculty norms
- Advice given to junior faculty
- Criteria for hiring and promotion
- Organizational structures and hierarchies
- Professional organizations
- Surveys

Students
- Interviews
- Student newspapers
- Campus culture
- Survey data—both national and campus level
- FAQs

Clinicians
- Professional associations
- Norms of practice
- Advice given entering professionals
- Organizational structures and hierarchies
- Surveys

Parents
- Survey data
- FAQs
- Parent groups and social networks
- Focus groups

Patients/Clients and Family
- Best practices in standards of care
- Active listening to individuals
- FAQs
- Surveys
- Support groups

Boards
- Agendas
- Data requested
- Metrics used
- Interviews
- Publications directed to boards
- Surveys and articles about boards

Publics
- Metrics and criteria used in rankings
- Alumni
  - ○ Associations
  - ○ Correspondence
  - ○ Newsletters
- Surveys
- Political arena
  - ○ Executive statements
  - ○ Legislative agendas
  - ○ Funding
- Taxpayers and donors
  - ○ Popular press/media
  - ○ Giving patterns
- Employers and corporate sector
  - ○ Partnerships
  - ○ Surveys

For Further Consideration

1. A mission-centered assessment of your unit, department, or institution
   - In your opinion, is the mission of your institution clearly defined and widely understood?
   - Thinking in terms of your academic or administrative unit, is there a clear and agreed-on mission?
     - Is this captured in a specific mission statement?
     - Has this statement been reviewed or revised in recent years?
     - To what extent does this statement serve as a guide for leaders in decision-making, resource allocation, and developing new programs and services?
     - Who are the affected and/or interested stakeholders for this mission? Does the institution's mission correspond to these stakeholders' expectations, and how can the mission be communicated in a way that respects those expectations?
   - Is there any sense in which the traditions embodied by the mission serve to hinder a leader's ability to affect innovation and change?
   - Thinking in terms of your institution or your academic or administrative unit, can you identify specific examples of leader decisions that could be considered mission drift?
     - What was the nature of these decisions?
     - Why were these decisions made? Were they in response to stakeholder interests or did they deviate from invested stakeholder interests?
     - Would you regard these decisions as problematic? If not, why not? If so, what leads you to this conclusion?
2. Liberal arts case study
   You are a faculty/staff member in a small residential liberal arts college. Consistent with its historical mission, the emphasis of programming within the institution has been on arts and humanities. Departments that offer programs and services in these areas have always been priorities in the allocation of resources. Unfortunately, enrollments in particular majors and courses within the college have dwindled in recent years. Foreign language enrollments are down, as are enrollments in history, religion, and art. Programs that began as small units with very limited professional offerings—

among them business, communication, human resources management, and computing—have experienced considerable increases in demand, roughly corresponding to the decreases in the liberal arts fields. Surveys of prospective students, along with preference patterns of incoming students, consistently favor the professionally oriented fields. You have become quite aware that it is impossible to meet this growing demand in these more professionally oriented fields unless faculty and staff resources are taken away from the traditional arts and humanities fields.

- What options are available to cope with this situation, and what are the trade-offs associated with each?
- What stakeholders will be impacted or have their expectations disrupted?
- Are there mission-preserving options that might be considered? Or is a change of mission now necessary and appropriate?
- What role can leadership communication play in responding to this complex situation?
- How will stakeholder expectations influence the communication process?

3. Stakeholder analysis

Consider your current role as you reflect on the following questions:

- Which internal stakeholders have the greatest impact on your unit or department? Do they have the same expectations regarding your mission as your unit or department does?
- Which external stakeholders have the greatest impact on your unit or department? Do they have the same expectations regarding your mission as your unit or department does?
- Using the following power interest grid, prioritize these identified stakeholders by placing them in one of the following four quadrants (see Figure 4.8).
- In what ways does the mission of your unit, department, or institution influence the placement of these stakeholders? Does the relationship between their expectations regarding your mission and your unit's or department's mission influence their placement?
- As a leader, how do you specifically meet the needs and expectations of these diverse stakeholders?

Figure 4.8. Stakeholder power interest grid.

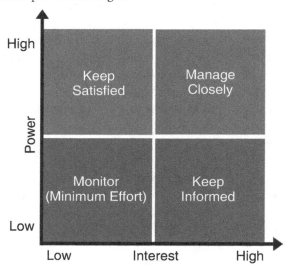

Notes

1. A detailed discussion of the nature and purpose of mission statements, the distinctions between mission, vision and values statements, and the role of each in the planning process are provided in chapter 14.

2. The author's search for *higher education* and then the terms *university* or *universities* or *college* or *colleges* was limited to articles in *The New York Times*, excluding sports and obituaries, and was conducted June 21, 2020. The later searches were also run adding the terms *cost* or *research*. While dwarfed on this chart, the occurrence of the term *higher education* rose dramatically from 94 instances in the 1970s to 6,808 in the most recent decade.

3. Thanks go to Peter March, Rutgers University School of Arts and Sciences, for this turn of phrase.

4. As Ruben (2016b) has noted, depending on the particular higher education institution, the list may include faculty, staff, current and prospective students and parents, law or medical school clients/patients, alumni, advisory boards, academic associations, disciplinary and professional communities, graduate and professional schools and organizations, potential employers, business and industry, state and federal funding agencies, private foundations and donors, local and state government, the citizens of the community or state, disciplinary and administrative opinion leaders at other institutions, and other groups. For administrative departments that serve other departments within the institution—such as facilities, computing services, faculty/administrative councils or assemblies, and other administrative and service units—relevant internal stakeholders are the administrative and academic units for which the organization provides services or that influence or are influenced by the organization.

5

THE ROLE OF FORMAL AND INFORMAL LEADERS IN GOVERNANCE

Locus of Power and Authority

Susan E. Lawrence and Richard De Lisi

In This Chapter

- What is shared governance in higher education?
- What is informal leadership and how does it differ from formal leadership?
- What leadership challenges derive from shared governance and from informal leadership?
- What roles do committees and task forces play in higher education governance?
- How is the nature of the faculty changing in higher education and what are the implications of this change for shared governance and leadership?

Governance is understood to connote the location and exercise of authority (Bowen & Tobin, 2015). As we frequently hear, the collaborative nature of governance, administration, and decision-making in contemporary American higher education differs in many ways from more hierarchical structures, processes, and approaches found in other sectors; however, this was not always the case. In the early history of higher education in the United States, (religious) leaders exercised considerable control and full authority over almost all aspects of operations, including academic matters. Modern-day collegiate governance has evolved and differs in important ways from its religious and secular historical origins. As we look to the future, there are indications that governance in higher education may be undergoing another transformation with significant implications for leadership.

This chapter reviews the unique and changing features of modern higher education governance for leaders in academic settings, focusing specifically on four aspects: formal governance structures, the nature of shared governance, the role of informal leaders, and changes underway in the composition of the faculty. We conclude with brief observations of the ways in which colleges and universities adapted to the global COVID-19 pandemic to learn what these adaptations might reveal about shifts in leadership, governance, and decision-making.

Formal Governance Structures

Colleges and universities are comprised of academic (e.g., schools, departments, programs) and administrative units (e.g., human resources, information technology, facilities) and units that blend these functions (e.g., student affairs and services, libraries, academic support, faculty development) whose leaders report—either directly or indirectly—to the president or chancellor. Depending on the size of a college or university, its organizational chart—depicting the hierarchical relationships between academic and administrative functions—can be quite complex. The numbers and types of academic and administrative units and their lines of authority vary not only with the size of the institution, but also with the type of institution—public versus private, religious versus secular, nonprofit versus for-profit—among a host of other factors. Regardless of the specific institutional context, it is important for leaders to understand the formal relationships among the various divisions of their college or university. This knowledge allows one to enact the steps required to achieve managerial, strategic, and aspirational objectives. A schematic example of a typical college or university organizational chart is provided in Figure 5.1.

Presidents[1] typically have academic backgrounds, almost always have faculty status, and therefore serve as both academic and administrative leaders (Ruben & Gigliotti, 2017). Presidents are expected to maintain and enhance the integrity of the institution, keeping an eye on the present and future of the college or university while honoring the traditions and history on which the institution is built. Being mindful of both internal and external stakeholders, presidents initiate new strategic visions and innovations for the institution. Since the latter part of the 20th century (if not earlier), presidents have served as chief fundraisers for the institutions and as primary spokespeople in representing the institution to the public. In order to lead

Figure 5.1. Schematic organizational chart for a college or university.

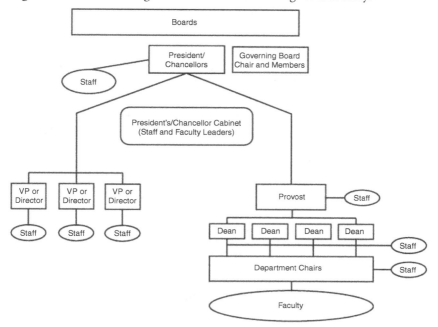

effectively, presidents must build a team of able academic and administrative leaders to whom they delegate authority and responsibility, as depicted in the organizational chart in Figure 5.1.

Virtually all college and university presidents or chancellors report to a governing board that is responsible for maintaining the past, present, and future integrity and success of the institution. Governing boards are typically composed of external stakeholders who may be prominent members of the local/state community and/or distinguished alumni of the institution. At public universities, at least, some members of governing boards are frequently political appointees. While the exact nature and composition vary by type of institution, governing boards typically have ultimate authority on all academic and administrative matters.

Outcomes that result from governing processes and procedures that occur prior to a board's consideration are not "official" until the president brings them before the board for a vote, and the president may well have been engaged in prior consultation with university leaders on these topics before they are brought forth for formal approval. In practice, because of ongoing interactions between university leaders, boards, and board committees, the vast majority of final votes for board approval are pro forma. In the case of public colleges and universities, certain board decisions might also have to garner approval by a state-level commission or department of higher education.

Another aspect of governance within the purview of boards is working with the president to create new strategic directions or initiatives for the institution. A board might urge a president to alter the profile of the student body, such as decreasing the size of the undergraduate student body, increasing the ratio of in-state and out-of-state students, or increasing the diversity of the incoming student cohort. Or a board might recommend mission-related changes such as an increased or decreased emphasis on athletics or the new pursuit of new strategic ventures. Perhaps most important, boards have oversight over an institution's resources and expenditures. As part of this fiduciary responsibility, governing boards are often expected to assist the president in obtaining the necessary funds for operations and infrastructure. For example, governing boards at public colleges and universities must approve proposed increases in tuition, fees, and room and board. Governing boards might also help identify donors capable of making substantial private gifts to support the institution. In addition, governing boards approve, maintain, and promulgate institutional policies and procedures that guide governance and administration throughout the institution.

Internal stakeholders often overlook or fail to recognize the influential role of the governing boards in policy- and resource-related issues. Many faculty, staff, and students view upper level administrators, especially the president, as the final authority for all aspects of the operations of the college or university. It is important to recognize, however, that presidents serve at the pleasure of the governing board and seek to maintain a healthy working relationship with members of the board, especially its president. That said, a college or university's president is *the* institutional leader and often the public face of the college or university.

For colleges and universities of a certain size, the chief academic officer reporting directly to the president is a *provost* who serves at the pleasure of the president. The provost oversees and allocates resources to support academic and research initiatives and priorities for the entire college/university. The provost might serve as acting president if a vacancy were to occur. Academic *deans,* who are the chief academic and administrative officers for separate colleges or schools (e.g., arts and sciences, business, education, engineering, law, and medicine, among others), are appointed by the provost to whom they report and at whose pleasure they serve. Working in concert with the provost, academic deans set strategic priorities for their schools and allocate resources in accordance with these priorities. Deans are responsible for performance evaluations of faculty and staff members who reside within their respective colleges or schools and typically are assisted by a number of associate or assistant deans—for instance of research, student life, administration, IT, and others that vary with the size and complexity of the unit—who are appointed by the dean.

Colleges and schools typically have two or more academic departments that are run by department *chairs* or *heads* who are appointed by the dean to whom they report and at whose pleasure they serve, often after a nomination process involving department faculty. Working with the dean, chairs set strategic priorities for their departments and manage resources allocated by the dean in support of these priorities.

Chairs are responsible for the evaluations of faculty and staff members who reside within their department. Within schools, and more often within departments, program directors for graduate and undergraduate studies and other specific functions may be appointed or elected and serve in these positions at the pleasure of the administrator to whom they report.

Each of these key positions of academic leadership (i.e., provost, dean, chair) is almost always occupied by a tenured member of the faculty who returns to faculty status when the term of appointment is completed or not continued. The conditions of employment and compensation for service as provost, dean, or chair differ from those received as a member of the faculty. For example, teaching responsibilities might be reduced, resources might be provided to support continuation of research and scholarship, and salary might be enhanced or increased during the term of service.

Complicating the role and responsibilities of chairs and program directors is the fact that at many larger institutions these individuals are also expected to engage in research, instruction, institutional service, and community engagement—areas that are typically required of all tenure-track faculty. Moreover, as distinct from appointments or reappointments to higher level leadership positions, chairs' and directors' progressions through academic ranks (to associate, full, and, where available, distinguished professorship) depend largely on their contributions and impact as faculty scholars and teachers. Their institutional leadership contributions are generally of far less significance in considerations for academic promotions. These two rather distinct tracks of employment responsibility, each with their own promotion criteria, coupled with the fact that deans and their departmental faculty colleagues each presume that chairs and directors are primarily accountable to them—combine to make the role of the academic chair or program director one of the most complicated in the university, both theoretically and operationally (Gmelch & Parkay, 1999; Hecht, 1999).

On the administrative side of the college or university are various high-level officers who lead different divisions such as athletics, budget and finance, communication and marketing, facilities, human resources, information technology, and student affairs, among other possible administrative units. Depending on the size of the institution, these high-level administrative officers might hold a title of executive vice president, senior vice president, vice president, or director. At large colleges and universities, separate schools have personnel who address several of these key administrative functions. For example, a school or college typically has local units dedicated to communication, information technology, student affairs, budget and finance, and so forth. Working with their respective deans, such personnel serve to connect or link the academic and administrative arms of the university.

The preceding description of academic and administrative positions that comprise college and university formal governance structures is referenced next as we consider shared governance and informal leadership. The leadership team—governing board, president, provost, senior vice presidents, and so forth—is responsible for the recruitment, selection, and retention of outstanding individuals to serve as members of the team. In so doing, those in positions of authority consider many factors, including academic accomplishments, prior administrative experiences and achievements, stature within one's discipline, organizational and communication skills, contributions to the advancement of diversity goals, and broadening the representation among sex, gender, race–ethnicity, sexual orientation, and other cultural attributes. Increasingly, governing boards seek to have the leadership team reflect the growing diversity of the students, faculty, and staff who comprise the institution.

Shared Governance

The formal lines of authority depicted on an organizational chart do not paint a complete picture of governance in higher education as far as the pragmatics of leadership are concerned. Indeed, a main theme of this chapter is that leadership in higher education is complex, even unique, because leaders in academic settings share authority with other key stakeholder groups. Of special importance is the 100-year-old tradition of shared governance that vests responsibility and authority to full-time members of the faculty and the departments or divisions in which they reside. In general, shared governance is understood to be the province of members of the faculty. It is important to recognize, however, that shared governance arose in an era in which the vast majority of faculty received tenure after a probationary period. This tradition and its implications, along with the very definition of "the faculty," are evolving—a topic to be discussed in a later section. At some institutions, undergraduate and graduate students might also have a formal role in governance—for example, members of the staff or student representatives might serve on a collegiate senate or even as members of large governing or advisory boards. In this section, our discussion of faculty roles refers to tenure-track and tenured faculty members, not "contingent," "contractual," or similarly titled faculty appointees who have no opportunity to achieve continuous tenure at an institution.

The system of shared governance has produced another unique feature that is not accounted for in an organizational chart—informal leadership, which is the topic of the next section of the chapter. The culture of shared governance and the role of informal leaders affect all levels of leadership in a college or university. Successful leaders are ever mindful of these realities, even though many rank-and-file members of the faculty, staff, and student bodies view their leadership powers as unconstrained, even limitless. Those new to positions of leadership in higher education are often surprised by the gap that exists between outside perspectives on a leader's possibilities for exercising authority and the real-world constraints felt from the inside.

Organizational charts of colleges and universities seem to indicate that members of the faculty who do not hold formal positions of academic leadership (e.g., president, provost, deans, or chairs) have no role in leadership decisions but instead are subject to the decisions of others. It is the case that in terms of the formal organizational charts of colleges and universities, faculty members are far removed from presidential and senior leadership officers, as well as from the governing board, but in fact a great deal of responsibility and even authority is delegated to members of the faculty working within their respective departments or schools. At most institutions of higher education, faculty members have formal responsibility and authority for curriculum (e.g., approval of course development, modes of instruction), for degrees and degree requirements, and for judging whether students have completed all the necessary degree requirements, which authorizes the president and governing board to bestow degrees upon graduates. Although a president and board have the formal authority to confer degrees upon student candidates, they do not do so without prior faculty approval. Faculty also play a role in student disciplinary matters that involve academic misconduct.

Faculty members are directly involved in masters' and doctoral student admission decisions. At the undergraduate level, operational aspects of this process are typically overseen by admissions officers—generally serving in various enrollment management functions. Faculty members serve critical functions in faculty recruitment, mentoring, recognition, and promotion review processes. Faculty judge and evaluate each other for initial hiring decisions, for membership on certain committees or faculties (e.g., status on a graduate faculty), for promotion and tenure decisions, for faculty honors, and for merit-raise decisions (e.g., salary increases for faculty colleagues). In many of these instances, the faculty voice is necessary, but advisory, to a dean or provost. For example, a committee or departmental faculty might vote to hire a given finalist for a faculty position, but a dean or provost could select a different candidate. (See chapter 10 for an example and an analysis of a communication breakdown that might occur in the hiring process.) Many deans require a short list of two to four faculty-approved candidates and pledge to make a selection from the faculty-approved list without being bound to faculty ranking of these finalists. Faculty at some, but not all, institutions are given a role in the nomination and/or hiring of academic administrators, such as department chair/head, dean, provost, and even the president. This is often done by faculty representatives, not the entire faculty body. However, in recent years, governing boards and top-level administrators on many campuses have instituted hiring procedures that omit faculty participation for some of these officers. Faculty members often play a role in certain aspects of student affairs such as residence life, fraternity and sorority life, or athletics. Additionally, faculty members play a role in other governance decisions via participation in local and schoolwide faculty meetings and collegiate senates or councils, and via committee participation (discussed in detail later in this chapter).

It is important to appreciate the considerable power delegated to the faculty at a college or university as part of shared governance. A provost or dean might wish to have a new degree program developed, for example, based on input from key external stakeholders. The dean might make a good case for this new degree with the relevant department chair and ask that chair to obtain the necessary faculty approval. If the departmental faculty votes not to approve this program, it is unlikely to move forward despite the wishes of the chair and/or the dean. Many other examples could be listed. Perhaps the most important responsibility of faculty is their role in tenure and promotion decisions of their colleagues as they become candidates for advancement. While a positive vote may not result in a positive promotion decision, a negative vote from faculty colleagues almost always results in the candidate being denied the promotion.

The faculty role in initial hiring, in renewal of contracts, and in advancement of their colleagues is considerable, and different from almost any other sector. A junior faculty member (e.g., an assistant professor on the tenure track) does not "report" to other faculty members except for the department chair—or in some instances a program director—who has a formal position of leadership. Despite this lack of employee–supervisor relationship, a junior faculty member's advancement hinges on performance evaluations offered by senior faculty members who do not occupy formal leadership positions. The role of tenured faculty in hiring and firing decisions is considerable and differs from most other sectors, including PK–12 education. In short, despite their apparent insignificance as reflected in an institutional organizational chart, faculty members play a considerable and substantial critical role in higher education governance. Clearly, the nature of shared governance requires that leaders in academic settings take account of the faculty perspective related to issues of personnel and curriculum, broadly defined.

Two other aspects of shared governance involving members of the faculty include the advice (and sometimes consent) they offer to their academic administrator colleagues about resource and expenditure allocations and about the strategic vision for their department, school, college, or university. There is considerable variability across the sector on each of these matters, and in general the faculty voice on budgetary matters and matters of strategic direction has been diminished in recent decades. Faculty perspectives and input are typically garnered via representative bodies such as a budget and planning committee, but these perspectives do not necessarily include formal governance authority. However, for reasons discussed in the next section, ignoring faculty perspectives on matters of institutional priorities and future directions, especially when such perspectives are obtained through deliberative processes or where faculty endorsement and support are important, can be perilous for leaders in academic settings.

Informal and Formal Leadership

The role and importance of the many informal leaders who play a part in shaping the direction and outcomes of governance decisions—to the delight or frustration of leaders vested with formal authority—is not represented in formal organizational charts. Uniquely, in higher education, a leader's formal authority is limited not only by the superiors to whom they report but also by informal leaders who might report to and engage with them.

We define *informal leadership* as forms of social-organizational influence exercised by individuals who do not occupy a position of formal authority within a particular context. The impact of informal leadership is especially profound in college and university settings. The academy encourages discussion and debate both in the classroom and beyond. As part of this culture, certain members of the faculty and staff feel free to question or challenge leaders as they engage in governance activities. In addition, as discussed in the previous section of this chapter, the tradition of shared governance delegates authority to members of the faculty and staff working within committees, departments, task forces, senates, and other faculty and staff bodies. Individuals whose work on important committees and other deliberative bodies recognized as significant and exemplary often find that their opinions are sought on matters unrelated to their designated committee work. The involvement of these individuals is also likely to be sought out for additional committee appointments. Informal leaders can support or work against the stated goals of formal leaders.

Examples of Informal Leaders

Informal leadership includes a broad range of behaviors, from being an exemplary role model to being a purposeful and strategic opinion leader or change agent. For example, highly capable individuals whose work products are excellent (Collins, 2001) and who model helpful behaviors that advance organizational efficacy may be considered one class of informal leaders. These good citizens of the academy lead by example. Another class of informal leader includes those who wield influence behind the scenes or in assigned committee work. These informal leaders demonstrate particular skill in working with others (Collins, 2001). Their opinions are valued and sought out by colleagues. Those who serve on, and especially those who chair, standing committees, college senates, ad hoc task forces, and other deliberative bodies may be considered both informal and formal leaders. Their leadership status depends on the individuals' sphere of influence and on the roles and responsibilities conferred by the committee members and the chair position at a particular institution (e.g., the chair of the faculty tenure and promotion committee).

Particularly respected senior members of a department, program, or unit often function as what we might term *underground leaders*. Such leaders may have acquired their influential status through professional accomplishments, seniority or tenure, former formal leadership positions they have occupied, personal relationships, or personal style. The presence of a very powerful leadership underground is one of the particularly interesting and unique features of higher education. These informal leaders can facilitate or disrupt, focus or shift the focus, support or stall the efforts of those in formal leadership roles.[2] Finally, those with formal leadership roles, such as directors, department chairs/heads, or deans, serve as informal leaders when they exercise influence among their peers within the institution in activities not directly related to their formal positions of authority.

As these examples show, there are many opportunities for leadership available to members of a campus community. In higher education, leadership extends beyond institutional appointment and is often the result of personal choices. Stincelli and Baghurst (2014) note that, even in the business sector, "leadership, the process of influencing individuals to work jointly toward common goals, is carried out by both formal and informal leaders within an organization" (p. 1). The structure of a college or university, with its norms of faculty governance and individual autonomy, and multiple discrete administrative units, makes higher education particularly open to, and in need of, informal leadership.

Formal Leaders and Informal Leaders

As implied, in practice, the distinction between formal and informal leadership is typically more a matter of degree than a rigid dichotomy. At the extremes of the continuum, we find that formal leadership positions are organizationally defined, whereas informal leaders are behaviorally identified. Formal leaders hold officially designated and titled positions of power and authority at a specific location in the institutional hierarchy. Informal leaders gain their influence from credibility, respect, and interpersonal relationships (Peters & O'Connor, 2001; Stincelli & Baghurst, 2014). Informal leadership is often exercised among lateral peers or within interpersonal networks that may cut across formal unit divisions and status hierarchies in the university. While formal leaders are formally accountable for their actions and are required to discharge administrative and managerial tasks, informal leadership roles are not generally associated with specific responsibilities or administrative duties.

The informal leader has no portfolio for which they are accountable and no formalized metrics in terms of which to assess effectiveness. This does not mean that informal leaders may not be held accountable when disruptive, or credited when constructive, but rather that they typically lead at their own pleasure and set their own standards for success. This freedom, though, comes with a price. Unlike the formal leader, who controls tangible and intangible resources that can be used as carrots and sticks, the informal leader has nothing to dispense beyond the intangible social rewards and sanctions deployed within social networks. Table 5.1 summarizes these distinctions between formal and informal leadership.

Exercising Informal Leadership: Processes of Social Influence

There are different ways to exercise informal leadership in a college or university setting. Context, objectives, and personalities in one's unit, department, or institution determine which informal leadership approach is most appropriate at a given moment. One of the simplest leadership behaviors is to become a supportive follower. Leadership is always an interactive process;

TABLE 5.1

Organizational Characteristics of Formal and Informal Leadership

Formal Leadership	Informal Leadership
Organizationally defined; carries a title Officially designated position with specified responsibilities and authority	Behaviorally defined; no official title
Part of hierarchy within the organization	Credibility and respect in the context of interpersonal relationships; typically exercised among peers within committees or interpersonal networks
Accountable to higher levels of authority; must ensure that routine administrative tasks are completed	Does not carry specific responsibilities or administrative duties; no specific accountability*
Controls tangible and intangible resources; can use carrots and sticks as means of influence	Does not control tangible or intangible resources; influence is embedded within peer networks, interpersonal rewards, and sanctions

* Informal leaders might serve as chairs of committees or task forces and therefore have a committee chair title and the responsibility to work with others to complete a specific charge. Committee chair roles include elements of both informal and formal leadership.

consequently, in practice the follower may exercise as much power as the leader (see chapter 10). Supporting and mobilizing others to adopt the vision or a decision of a formal leader can be a challenging exercise of social influence. Similarly, modeling the kind of behavior and speech you would like to see your colleagues engage in can also be a powerful leadership strategy. Taking care to align behaviors with professed values demonstrates integrity and understanding, two attributes critical for leaders to possess, especially in the eyes of their colleagues. Informal leaders see opportunities in their multiple roles as colleague, ambassador, teacher, researcher, steward, opinion leader, and change agent to further the university's mission and particular policy objectives.

Building dense social networks within the university can be an extremely valuable strategy for formal and informal leaders. Being an active mentor and supportive colleague across rank, role, status, and culture builds social capital, trust, and influence. Institutions of higher education are well known for silos—multiple distinct cultures and complex reporting lines—as well as the faculty–staff divide (see chapter 6), yet all units have important interconnecting roles to play in furthering the college's or university's missions. Developing cohesive networks that build bridges of mutual understanding and reciprocal respect across faculty–staff lines and between disconnected groups creates a space for compromise, cooperation, and compliance. Informal leaders often have more freedom than their superiors to work across silos, and potentially help to foster connections among them, since it may be easier for informal leaders to appear to move beyond or rise above their formal affiliation with a particular group or unit.

Formal leaders brought in from outside the university are often at a disadvantage precisely because they are new and therefore do not have cross-silo informal leadership networks throughout the institution on which to draw. This is particularly the case when new leaders come to higher education from other sectors (Ruben & Gigliotti, 2017). Leaders who are new to an institution can benefit greatly from working to develop networks that allow them to leverage the knowledge and relationships of local informal leaders who are well-known and respected. For informal leaders within an institution, offering such assistance to new leaders and colleagues represents an important strategy to advance the institution and at the same time create further opportunities for informal influence.

The open nature of higher education allows change to percolate up from the grassroots as well as to be mandated from the top, and because of this, informal leaders are often able to adopt visibly proactive approaches and develop new initiatives through their own initiative. For example, new programs designed to train graduate students in effective pedagogy may be initiated by faculty in departments, and initiatives to support transfer students may be launched in advising offices. Also, new strategies for using information technology and social networks for student support may start as an individual faculty or staff member initiative, and activities promoting nutritional health on campus may grow out of the efforts of line employees in dining services.

Mobilizing support for a policy change and lobbying those with the formal power to implement such a change is another strategy open to those aspiring to informal leadership. While the endorsement of new initiatives by formal leaders should be cultivated, success usually requires informal leaders to follow through with close attention to implementation, perhaps doing the implementation work themselves. These and other types of informal leadership activities generally require dedication to the institution and call for one to take ownership of one or more of its mission elements—actions that can simultaneously advance the institution and the influence of the individual.

Exercising Informal Leadership in Small Groups: Committee Work

In sectors other than higher education, informal leadership has most often been studied in groups, teams, and committees as individuals take on roles as task leaders, social leaders, and opinion leaders (Benne & Sheats, 1948; Luria & Berson, 2013; Neubert & Taggar, 2004; Zhang et al., 2012). These roles are also exercised in multiple sites within the loosely coupled structure of the university (Birnbaum, 1988), including academic departments, intraschool administrative initiatives, forums of faculty governance, and broad committees that include academic and administrative personnel (Farris, 2020). Academic and administrative leaders need to consider the strategies for effective social influence at an informal level. Some of these seek to enhance and some to derail group functioning.

In 1965, Bruce Tuckman published a classic article defining four stages of group development, as depicted in Figure 5.2. Informal leadership behaviors play a role in each stage. Tuckman labels the first stage *forming*, during which group members establish relationships and identify the boundaries of the task before them. This stage is characterized by processes of "orientation, testing, and dependence" on authority figures. The second stage is *storming*, during which conflict arises around relationships within the group and the requirements of the task with which the group is charged. It is a heavily emotional stage in the group process. The *norming* stage occurs as the group begins to coalesce and members begin to identify as part of the group. Standards and roles emerge as individual opinions are expressed. Finally, having developed a functional interpersonal structure, the group's attention and energy are more clearly focused on *performing* the task at hand. Roles are now viewed as more flexible, and shifting occurs as necessary for functional effectiveness (Tuckman, 1965). In 1977, based on several additional studies, Tuckman and Jensen added an *adjournment* stage characterized by

Figure 5.2. Tuckman's four stages of group development.

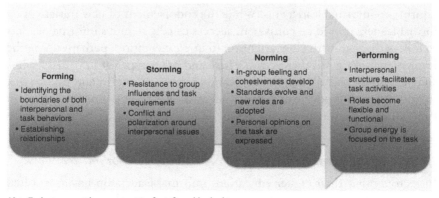

Note: Each stage provides opportunities for informal leadership.

dissolution of the group, often with members experiencing some sadness and self-reflection.

Each of these stages of group development provides opportunities for informal leadership as members adopt different roles within the group. Writing in 1948, Benne and Sheats argued that improving group functioning could not rely solely on improving the skills of the formal leader of the group, but must attend to membership roles as well. They identified almost 30 functional roles open to people in groups, providing many opportunities for informal leadership of several types. These roles can be classified according to their likely contributions to the stages of group development, as depicted in Figure 5.3.

All of these roles are avenues for social influence and can be adopted as strategies of informal leadership by individuals with and without formal leadership titles. Within any group, these roles may be centralized with a single leader or small group of leaders or disbursed widely throughout the membership. Social leadership roles include acting as an energizer, encourager, gatekeeper and expediter, harmonizer, follower, or coordinator. As shown in Figure 5.3, they are especially important during the forming stage and again during the norming stage. Disrupter roles, such as aggressor, dominator, blocker, recognition-seeker, loafer (or playboy, as labeled in the 1948 typology), special-interest pleader, help-seeker, or self-confessor, are manifested

Figure 5.3 Exercising informal leadership in groups.

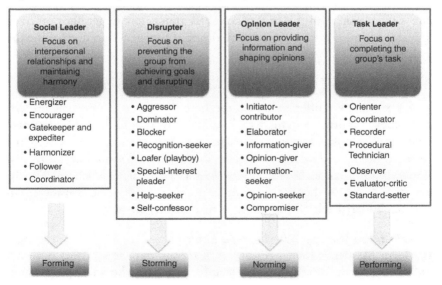

prominently during the storming stage and can derail the group if not balanced by other members. Even though elements of these roles can be frustrating, as noted earlier, dissent, debate, challenge, and so on can contribute to better solutions and processes—sometimes in spite of the motives of those who enact those roles. Opinion leader roles include initiator-contributor, elaborator, information giver, opinion giver, information seeker, opinion seeker, and compromiser. These roles are crucial during the norming stage. Task leader roles—including orienter, coordinator, recorder, procedural technician, observer, evaluator-critic, and standard setter—are essential during the performing stage. Social leadership roles are likely to come to the fore again during the adjournment phase. Individuals can move in and out of each of these roles at different stages of the group's work and can engage in several simultaneously. Disaggregating and labeling common postures and roles that members take on in a group and identifying them throughout particular stages provides a language and framework for understanding and influencing group processes. A great deal of frustration can be avoided and strategic advantage gained by recognizing certain behaviors as typical parts of the process of group work. For example, a committee member might express frustration to a leader about a colleague on the committee who is engaging in what they view as disruptive behaviors during committee meetings. If the leader understands that the committee is early in its work—still within the storming stage—the leader might not see a need to intervene since such behavior can be common in early stages of group work. The same behavior would be viewed as more problematic, however, if it occurred later in the committee's work, within the norming or performing stage. The leader could have a discussion with the committee chair about how to get back on track or decide to intervene personally if disruptions threatened to undermine the goals of the group.

Practical Tips and Considerations Concerning Informal Leadership

In this section we offer guidance for both formal and informal leaders. Given their importance in higher education, how should formal leaders take account of informal leaders and encourage their participation? Given the nature of the reward system in higher education, why should an individual choose an informal leadership role within a department or school? Finally, how does one gain the respect of one's peers in order to be considered an informal leader? Each of these issues is taken up in this section.

Formal Leaders Working With Informal Leaders
As a formal leader in higher education, it is important to cultivate informal leaders among the administrators, faculty, and staff who share your vision and commitment to the institution. Those who function as good citizens of

the academy are prime candidates for nurturing as informal leaders. As a rule, cultivation efforts are more successful when leaders create a governance culture in which debate and discussion are encouraged. As decisions are made and implemented, those who voiced opposition should not feel permanently disenfranchised. It also helps to have key members of the faculty and staff work together where possible. The staff may not appreciate the role of informal faculty leaders, and faculty members also should understand the role of key staffers who exercise considerable leadership influence. As a formal leader, the example you set will help with these cultural considerations. For instance, maintaining one's equilibrium and professionalism when votes do not go your way is an important behavior to model.

Titled leaders should also fully understand the governance limitations on their formal authority. Campus policies and procedures must be adhered to with fidelity. On issues that require faculty approval, faculty governance policies and procedures should be faithfully followed in letter and spirit. As a formal leader, the more radical your proposals, the more important it is to solicit the views of informal faculty and staff leaders prior to formal processes (e.g., committee fact-finding) and discussions. Sharing the rationale for your ideas about new paths and directions early on with informal leaders is often a critical step in the governance process. Often, the ideas of informal leaders—whether in support of or opposition to these new paths and directions—can be accommodated to the benefit of the institution. Whenever possible, avoid the invocation of unrealistic deadlines or perpetual states of crises as an excuse to trample on faculty governance procedures or institutional policy. Without also winning the hearts and minds of informal leaders, successes may be short-lived, reflecting compliance without commitment and leading to an abandonment of the idea or initiative once you no longer hold the formal position of authority. Disregard for established procedures and cultural norms is likely to create an oppositional culture in which even routine completion of everyday operations is met with resistance and foot dragging.

Many informal leaders are dedicated individuals who behave in ways that are supportive, constructive, and supplemental in pursuing institutional missions and goals. These individuals are great assets to an institution's formal leaders. It is also the case that higher education is full of smart and independent thinkers, and not surprisingly, conflicts sometimes arise about how to best achieve the department, school, college, or university missions or how those missions should be prioritized. At times, informal leaders are those who generate, mobilize, and organize dissent. Such dissent is often not intended to be obstructionist, and the most influential leaders promote constructive conversations and listen closely to the explicit and implicit messages conveyed. Often the final outcome is better because of the contributions of dissenters. Even dissent that seems less than constructive provides formal leaders with important information about the concerns of stakeholders within the university, and these should not be dismissed too quickly.

It is essential to understand that, at times, formal leaders may be suspicious of the influence of informal leaders, recognizing that their informal leader influence may well be outside of their control and may become a potential threat to their own leadership. But as discussed, informal leadership can be exercised in support of formal leaders, not just in opposition, and in such cases establishing a mutually supportive relationship between formal and informal leaders can work well.

But at times, informal leaders are indeed oppositional, and in such cases may simply be bent on obstruction, perennially suspicious of administrators and formal leaders, or unwilling to give up battles that were lost long ago. Formal leaders must develop strategies to address the challenges—and the opportunities—that arise with the informal leaders with whom they interact. Finally, because of the autonomy that the academy allows and encourages, opposition based on individual self-interest sometimes emerges. In some instances, when policies seem to similarly threaten the autonomy or self-interest of a category of individuals, an oppositional informal leader may emerge. Despite the encouragement of the free exchange of ideas on college campuses, faculties and career staff and administrators are often conservative when confronted with pressure to change long-standing policies and practices (Tagg, 2012). Formal leaders are well advised not to be surprised by these dynamics, and in fact may be encouraged to learn to predict when they might occur, take advantage of insights they might provide, and develop strategies to mitigate any damaging impact they may have on the overall well-being of the institution.

Given that colleges and universities contain fertile conditions for the growth of informal leaders, it is important for those with formal leadership positions to be aware of the powerful role informal leaders can play, especially if one is an outsider new to the campus. By being an astute listener and observer, leaders can learn rather quickly who the informal leaders are within their unit. In this process, it is also necessary to minimize the tendency to permanently classify informal leaders as either supportive or oppositional as they offer advice, sometimes seeking to advance their own goals. Evaluating ideas and opinions of informal leaders on the ideas' merits, and not based on personal relationships, is generally the best strategy—keeping in mind the impact of those evaluations not only on the informal leader, but also on others who are learning about a formal leader's style from the choices made in these situations. Leaders also need to examine their own contributions to dysfunctional patterns that may have emerged before blaming others

(Feiner, 2004). Informal leaders can be a vital source of information for these reflections—even when this may not be their conscious goal.

Choosing to Become an Informal Leader
What considerations should guide an individual's decision to adopt—or attempt to avoid—seeking informal leadership opportunities? If a person aspires to contribute as an informal leader, how can one gain effectiveness and influence? We consider these issues next. As we have seen in this chapter, there are numerous opportunities in higher education for those who do not exercise a position of formal authority within a particular context to exercise social-organizational influence on issues about which they feel passionate. Some informal leadership behaviors, such as being an exemplary role model or effective committee member, present themselves naturally. Others, such as change agent or strategic opinion leader, may require a conscious choice, and may also require considerable time and commitment.

Decisions about how active to become as an informal leader are contextual and personal. Such decisions may reflect the level of passion one has for a particular issue. They may also reflect an individual's career stage and the professional and personal resources one has to devote to engaging in proactive informal leadership. At times, informal leadership may require putting the needs of the institution above one's own individual advancement. Faculty members often see informal (and formal) leadership opportunities in this light since advancement in faculty rank generally depends on *individual* accomplishment in the classroom, in scholarship, and in the profession, and there may be little institutional reward for service in informal leadership roles.

For others, especially staff and faculty who aspire to occupy formal leadership positions, informal leadership may be an important way to advance one's career. Both groups should consider their own need for formal approval or recognition and recognize that these may or may not be forthcoming—particularly in the short term—in spite of their contributions. Indeed, the most frequent reward for being an effective informal leader and getting things done might be more assignments of a similar nature in the future. That said, nearly everyone, whether content to exercise social influence through being a model citizen or aspiring to be a widely recognized opinion leader, can benefit personally and contribute to the well-being of the organization by dedicating some level of energy and commitment to informal leadership activities.

Gaining Respect and Influence
Much of what has been discussed here as strategies for informal leadership applies equally to those holding formal leadership roles, particularly because the decision-making structures in higher education are often fluid

among groups of people of various ranks and positions. As a process of social influence, everyone can develop the potential for leadership through some practical everyday activities that also, along the way, make the college or university a more effective and pleasant place to work for all involved (Edmunds & Boyer, 2015). The hope is that these behaviors are not adopted simply as instrumental strategies, but rather emerge as a genuine outgrowth of individual personal values and commitment. Not all of these will fit every personality, and pursuing such behaviors can seem inauthentic, leading to results that may well be counterproductive. Small behaviors, such as the following, make a difference in advancing one's potential as a formal and informal leader:

- Earn a reputation for integrity, discretion, genuine interest, helpfulness, and reliability.
- Follow through on promises, big and small.
- Model hard work and dedication to the common good.
- Become an asset to those above and an assistant to those below. Cultivate the support of the people doing the day-to-day, on-the-ground implementation and get the support of the various implementers and stakeholders to whom they report.
- Develop a broad network across rank, role, status, and culture.
- Express gratitude by thanking people for their contributions and being genuinely appreciative. It can be especially powerful to recognize those contributions that many others overlook. Praising those who contribute to others, particularly to their formal leaders, earns loyal friends.
- Know your peers and cultivate goodwill among them.
- Know the relevant formal and informal leaders and their views; cultivate their support.
- Make the lives of formal leaders easier by securing buy-in from those who report to them so that your project is not their problem.
- Always show up prepared and provide appropriate information.
- Ask strategic but constructive questions that can help reframe the issue.
- Volunteer for tasks and follow through on completing them.
- Frame discussions or debate by introducing drafts or other materials to use as starting points for discussion in a way that makes following your lead easy.
- View the situation from other participants' points of view and in light of their various interests—this includes the perspective of more senior leaders who also have a stake in the process and outcomes.

- Be open to other views; accept suggestions that improve the outcome; compromise when it will get to "the good," even if not to "the perfect."
- Share the credit. Be more concerned with getting good ideas adopted or the task completed than getting credit for it. Patience may be required. You are often planting seeds that may take a while to germinate.
- Mentor and be mentored.
- Be humble and have a sense of humor.

Implications of Changes in Faculty Workforce for Governance and Leadership

Up to this point we have seen that, despite their apparent lack of status in formal structures of governance, tenured members of the faculty have significant roles to play in higher education governance. The century-old tradition of shared governance delegates many important responsibilities to faculty members. Aside from the parts they play in the exercise of shared governance responsibilities, certain members of the faculty are informal leaders who exert considerable influence in shaping institutional culture and possible future directions. While these characterizations still hold, it is the case that the landscape is changing due to the steady increase in the proportion of contract, term, and adjunct faculty and the corresponding decrease in full-time tenured members of the faculty. In this section, we briefly describe this trend and discuss its implications for leaders and governance.

A decrease in the percentage of faculty who are tenured and tenure-track has continued unabated for several decades—from almost 80% of the faculty in 1969 to approximately 33% of the faculty in 2009 (Bowen & Tobin, 2015) and about 25% in 2016 (Flaherty, 2018; Selingo, 2016). Course instruction has been assumed by *nontenure-track faculty* who may be full-time employees but are most likely part-time employees. Part-time instructors or adjunct faculty members represent the vast majority of nontenure-track instructors (Selingo, 2016). According to a 2011 study from the American Association of University Professors (AAUP), an estimated 56% of college professors are part-time or full-time, non-tenure-track faculty members. More recent reports reveal that roughly 75% of instructors teaching in classrooms today are off the tenure track (Flaherty, 2018). Part-time, nontenure-track faculty members work with little job security, often on a semester-by-semester basis.

In contrast, full-time nontenure-track faculty members typically receive multiyear renewable contracts that require an emphasis on *teaching*, including curriculum development and supervising and advising students. Some universities have additional types of full-time nontenure-track faculty who focus on aspects of the university's mission beyond teaching. For example, a *clinical* professor might work in a department of applied psychology, law, journalism, or a dental, medical, or nursing school and will be required to provide clinical services. A fully grant-funded *research* professor might be hired to help the principal investigator conduct research outlined in the grant. A research professor's term of employment is contingent on the continuation of grant funding. Some universities have codified titles for nontenure-track faculty members that signal stature in the field at the time of hiring or advancement at the institution with successive contract renewals—assistant teaching professor, associate teaching professor, and teaching professor, for example.

In discussing these trends in faculty composition, Selingo (2016) spoke of the emergence of a "bifurcated faculty" in higher education. The bifurcated nature of the faculty consists of senior members, many of whom obtained tenure in a different era and those more junior members who increasingly are not hired on the tenure track and are asked to address only certain aspects of the overall mission, such as teaching or clinical activities. Both Bowen and Tobin (2015) and Selingo (2016) think it is a positive development that faculty who specialize in teaching (only) are being hired in significant numbers.

As we consider these trends in faculty composition, it is important to remember that the tenured members of the faculty are, on average, older and either close to or beyond traditional retirement age (Selingo, 2016). Thus, the bifurcation of the faculty not only reflects tenure status but also pertains to career stage. This means that the tenured members of the faculty were socialized into the profession during a time when the traditions of shared governance were preeminent values, and many are invested in keeping this value alive. The same commitment is unlikely to be present for their younger, newly hired, nontenure-track colleagues who remain focused on continuing employment and contract renewal procedures.

In what follows, we discuss the impact of this duality on shared governance, informal leadership, and formal leadership in higher education. The trends and impact we note are only exacerbated by the larger numbers of part-time adjunct faculty members whose status is not specifically discussed here.

The decrease in tenure-track faculty has implications for formal leaders as they fulfill their governance and administration roles. For example, some responsibilities that are delegated to faculty in official policy and procedures manuals of the institution (e.g., serving on a committee to evaluate faculty for promotion) require that the members have obtained tenure and the rank of associate professor or higher. This same requirement might be in force for a member of the faculty to be eligible to assume a departmental chair position, a graduate program director position, and other positions of academic leadership. As the tenured ranks have decreased over time due to replacement with nontenure-track faculty, these formal and shared governance roles have fewer faculty members available to serve in these capacities. This reduction in the pool of available tenured faculty increases the service burden on the remaining tenured faculty members due to limited available options.

In some cases, the available tenured members may not be well-suited to assume certain shared governance roles and responsibilities, or have already served in these roles one or more times in the past and, as noted earlier, may do little to advance their professional standing or career trajectories to the extent that these are based primarily on research, publication, grants, and instruction. Small departments, for example, may find they have no viable candidates to assume the role of department chair due to the lack of capable or willing tenured professors. In short, increases in full-time nontenure-track faculty might reduce budgetary pressure to meet course offering demands, but at the same time might weaken aspects of shared governance and administration. Provosts and deans need to be mindful of these possibilities and pay attention to time limitations for key shared governance positions with an eye toward "grooming" replacements for department chair and program positions, membership key committees, and so forth. This situation has significant implications for leadership development and succession planning, which are discussed in extensive detail in chapters 18 and 19.

Trends in faculty hiring and role responsibilities introduce other complexities. Nontenure-track faculty who specialize in teaching or clinical service are typically not required—and may not be encouraged—to conduct research or scholarship as a condition of employment. However, if the institution is research intensive, hiring teaching or clinical specialists may detract from the research mission and even from the teaching mission. For example, a teaching or clinical faculty member would not be expected to secure external grant funding and may not be available to mentor and direct either undergraduate or graduate student research projects. To the extent that a department or division is evaluated in terms of research and scholarship, including grant awards, a leader must take account of these realities and not lose sight of the overall balance in mission fulfillment by the entire faculty. As already mentioned, solving a problem in course coverage might create an unanticipated problem in the areas of research and scholarly productivity. And addressing needs in these areas may well come at the expense of having sufficient coverage of various committee functions. While most individuals who have obtained a doctoral degree have a range of scholarly capabilities, it may be inappropriate—even contractually precluded—to ask nontenure-track faculty members to perform duties outside of their contractual obligations, even if the faculty member is willing to do so. Stated differently, nontenure-track faculty contracts need to be carefully and thoughtfully constructed to protect the institution and the individual. Leaders also need to ensure that the contractual terms are upheld by all members of the department or unit.

Another complexity of the present circumstance is that the restricted availability of tenure-track openings may mean that new graduates of doctoral programs end up accepting a nontenure-track teaching position in what they hope will be an interim measure. While a supportive department chair might empathize with the dilemma such an individual faces, caution is advised when it comes to providing support or encouragement to conduct research or apply for grants if the individual's contractual renewal does not specify research/grantsmanship as a basis for reappointment. Both the administration and the faculty member must understand and adhere to the contractual terms of the appointment.

Further issues arise with regard to the role and responsibility of nontenure-track faculty in the day-to-day operations of a department. For example, such faculty colleagues could participate fully in discussions and deliberations pertaining to matters of curriculum and instruction, supervision of students, and advisement of students. To the extent that discussions of budgetary matters and the allocation of resources touch on the impact on teaching, nontenure-track faculty could also be included in discussions and decision-making processes. But there are obvious sensitivities and tensions here. Leaders need to strike a careful balance between proper inclusion of nontenure-track faculty in shared governance while not taking advantage of these colleagues by asking them to perform duties that exceed their contractual obligations. And, in this regard as in others, the issue of consistency in the treatment across all members of each employment category is an important consideration.

Increases in nontenure-track faculty also decrease the pool of informal leaders. Given their contractual status, nontenure-track faculty members are similar to members of the administrative staff in that they serve at the pleasure of their faculty colleagues (who play a role in their evaluations and renewals), and also at the pleasure of formal leaders (e.g., department chair). Such individuals have little to gain and much to lose by taking controversial stands, siding with either party in a debate and thereby risking the endorsement of either the faculty or the formal leadership team when their contracts are up for renewal. In some respects, nontenure-track faculty members have one foot in the faculty culture and one foot in the administrative staff culture, as detailed further in the next chapter. These faculty colleagues might take a lead in areas related to teaching, but to the extent that issues are controversial, nontenure track faculty might feel compelled to defer to faculty members with tenure. The reduction in the tenured ranks also increases the influence and power of tenured faculty members who are recognized as informal leaders. In essence, there are fewer voices that might offer an alternative perspective.

In their discussion of the increase of nontenure-track faculty members, Bowen and Tobin (2015) make a number of useful suggestions for leaders. If some of these suggestions are carefully implemented on a given campus, it will help avoid some of the pitfalls mentioned. Bowen and Tobin (2015) recommend the following with respect to full-time nontenure-track faculty:

- Have a well-formulated set of titles along with compensation and benefits that are commensurate with contributions; titles should indicate roles/duties and convey respect.
- Be clear about appointments and opportunities for reappointment (e.g., renewable contracts).
- Have a well-defined evaluation process for making decisions about advancement, promotions, and nonappointments.
- Provide basic organizational protections for the core elements of academic freedom—protect nontenure-track faculty from unprofessional obstacles to promotion and advancement.
- Encourage suitably qualified nontenure-track faculty members to participate generally in the life of the institution; treat them as members of the faculty and make them eligible to serve on appropriate faculty committees (e.g., a curriculum committee).
- Include nontenure-track faculty members in the same academic chain of command used for tenured and tenure-track faculty members (i.e., they report to a department chair and a dean).

In summary, the changes in faculty composition that have evolved over the past 50 years are changing the nature of shared governance and shifting the locus of power and authority away from the faculty as it has been traditionally conceived. Some of these changes have already occurred at institutions in which the influence of the faculty role has been diminished on matters of budget and priority setting. For other areas in which shared governance continues to be a core value operationally as well as rhetorically, nontenure-track faculty will not be available or willing to perform certain duties required for broad faculty engagement in institutional leadership. In areas such as the hiring and evaluation of members of the faculty, for example, it would be awkward—and likely not permitted by regulations—for contractually appointed faculty members to vote on the appointment, reappointment, or promotion of another contractually appointed faculty member, especially in a year when each of their contracts is up for renewal.

In many respects, a bifurcated faculty—some only teach, some only conduct research, some only conduct clinical services—does not match the assumptions that underlie the shared governance traditions, and as a result leaders confront numerous complexities as they try to develop appropriate strategies to define responsibilities, preserve the continuity of core department values, and adhere to contract terms, all while promoting meaningful innovation and satisfying engagement for colleagues in all positions.

2020 World-Wide Pandemic

In March 2020, colleges and universities were confronted with a crisis of epic proportions—the outbreak of the COVID-19 pandemic. Institutions were forced to abandon campuses and to deliver emergency remote instruction through fully online modalities. The "shuttering in place requirement" except for "essential workers" was mandated by state and local governments and applied to government agencies, businesses, restaurants, sports and entertainment venues, and virtually all aspects of U.S. society, including PK–12 and higher education. In response to this crisis, leaders decided to require the completion of courses for the spring 2020 semester via distance education. In general, this decision was made using the formal mechanisms of governance and not via collaboration with members of the faculty under a shared governance model that delegates authority on curriculum matters (broadly defined) to members of the faculty. In our view, changes that were afoot prior to the pandemic set the stage for the manner in which most institutions relied on formal governance structures and authority to make decisions about operations.

Despite the hardships for faculty, few questioned the necessity for swift decision-making and action so that the spring 2020 semester could be salvaged with regard to teaching and course completion (Gigliotti, 2020a). The longer term impact of the pandemic and the decisions made in response to the pandemic and other converging crises during this period, as well as the way in which they were made, will be interesting and important to track.

What might these experiences during the COVID-19 pandemic augur for shared governance going forward? The AAUP published a position statement in March 2020, entitled "The AAUP Position and Standards for the COVID-19 Crisis." This document emphasized the centrality of the faculty in higher education decision-making and stated that consultation was perhaps even more important in a time of crisis. In essence, the AAUP questioned the lack of faculty participation in the response to the pandemic and emphasized that shared governance should continue to be exercised in both virtual and on-campus environments. The AAUP position seems to evidence a concern about further devolution in the faculty's participation in college and university governance postpandemic. It is worth acknowledging that the AAUP statement dealt with other concerns, such as faculty intellectual property being placed online and the use of teaching evaluations obtained during the spring 2020 semester, among other matters.

Conclusions

In our view, the effects and implications of the COVID-19 pandemic on governance, formal leadership, and informal leadership will likely extend well beyond the spring 2020 semester and 2020–2021 academic year. As detailed in chapters 2 and 3, higher education was in a difficult period prior to the spring 2020 semester. These difficulties necessitated a rethinking of shared governance as it had been exercised for a century or more (see Bowen & Tobin, 2015), which requires capable and effective leaders at all levels of the institution. We believe the extraordinary stresses and strains on colleges and universities due to the pandemic only serve to deepen and exacerbate trends that were already in motion. To the extent that the higher education landscape was rocky, it is even more rocky now. To the extent that leaders were starting to reshape shared governance in favor of formal governance structures, we expect this trend to continue and perhaps accelerate, especially if campuses remain less than fully occupied and interactions occur virtually. To the extent that leaders are shifting away from hiring tenured and tenure-track faculty members, this pattern will continue as a means to provide budgetary cushions. All of this increases the importance of leaders and leadership excellence in higher education. This includes the ability to recruit and retain others for both formal and informal positions of leadership as the full-time faculty ranks diminish. Perhaps now, more than ever, higher education needs capable and responsive leadership to deal with the challenges of a postpandemic world.

For Further Consideration

1. Governing board
   What type of governing board does your institution have? Who are the members of the governing board at the present time and how were they selected? What issues is the governing board working on right now? How would you characterize the relationship between the governing board and the college president, deans, and the faculty and staff?
2. Your experiences as an informal leader
   As you reflect on your own leadership experiences, select an instance in which you exercised an informal leadership role. Were you successful as an informal leader? How would you define success in this instance? Which of the informal leadership strategies presented in this chapter did you use? How would you characterize the outcomes of the experience—for the institution and for you personally? What might you do differently next time?
3. The influence of informal leaders
   Identify two informal leaders in your department, unit, or institution. In what ways do these individuals demonstrate informal leadership? How would you characterize their behaviors and attitudes? What factors have led them to be able to function as informal leaders in your unit? In what ways do these leaders—who do not occupy a formal position of authority—influence others in your organization?
4. Nontenure-track faculty members
   How many nontenure-track faculty members teach courses in your department or unit? How many are full-time and how many are part-time? Are nontenure-track faculty members welcomed to participate in formal and informal gatherings by other members of the faculty, and do they choose to participate? What roles do nontenure-track faculty play in shared governance activities in your department or unit?
5. COVID-19 response
   How did the leadership at your institution handle the pandemic in March 2020? Would you characterize the communication from leaders as informative and effective? What strengths would you identify, and what relative weaknesses? Who was involved in decisions about how to complete the spring 2020 semester? Were members of

the faculty consulted? In terms of timing, debate, and involvement, how unusual was it to have so many critical decisions reached in such a short period? What does this indicate about higher education governance?

Notes

1. *President* is the most common title for the senior leader of an institution. In some instances, the term *chancellor* is used. When a college or university is part of a larger configuration or system, both these titles are typically used. One denotes the leader of the whole system; the other denotes the leader of a particular institution.

2. Our use of the term *underground leaders* draws on the concepts of the opinion leader developed and widely applied in political science and mass communication studies (Katz & Lazarsfeld, 1955) and of the public character used in sociology and ethnographic studies to describe informal leadership roles within urban communities (Duneier, 2000; Jacobs, 1961).

6

CAMPUS CULTURES AND THE LEADER'S ROLE

Building Capacity to Enhance Diversity and Create Inclusive Campus Communities

Sangeeta Lamba and Brent D. Ruben

In This Chapter

- In what ways is an understanding of culture essential for effective leadership?
- In what ways do diversity, equity, inclusion, and belonging contribute to organizational and leadership excellence?
- How can leaders in higher education integrate the skills of ethnography into their leadership practices?
- What differences between academic and administrative cultures lead to tensions, and in what ways can higher education leaders navigate these important cultural differences?
- Why are skills in cross-cultural communication important for the success of higher education leaders?
- What can a leader do to ensure diversity and inclusion are integrated as core values within their organizations?

B y their very nature and by virtue of their core values, colleges and universities are incredibly complex and diverse organizations. The vast array of multiple, blended, and dynamic identities and affiliations represented within colleges and universities contributes to a cultural richness that enhances the living and learning experience for everyone involved in the community. This cultural richness presents communication opportunities and challenges. An understanding of cultural concepts and a sensitivity and responsiveness to cultural differences are increasingly vital given the recognized importance of diversity, equity, and inclusion.

Whether in instruction, research, or clinical and community outreach, achieving and sustaining excellence requires a blending of the experiences, cultural traditions, and expertise of a broad array of individuals. Each member of the faculty, staff, and student body enters the campus community with an identity shaped by and in some ways reflective of their discipline, occupational role, nationality, sex, gender, race, ethnicity, age, religion, political orientation, and many other social identities and characteristics. Identities are further developed through affiliations with and active participation in campus, community, or national groups.

The dynamic nature of the college or university experience presents many opportunities for learning, engagement, and collaboration, but these factors also pose important challenges for members of the campus community, especially those engaged in formal leadership. The extent to which these challenges become opportunities depends to a large degree on the community's ability to foster an appreciation and respect for diversity as a core value and to promote inclusive practices that result in individual fulfillment and organizational engagement. In each of these respects, the approaches, behaviors, and decisions made by leaders are central.

Becoming adept at observing, understanding, appreciating, valuing, and enhancing the many cultural identities in higher education is clearly one of the requirements for leadership effectiveness at any level. Through messages, processes, strategies, and structures—along with a strong commitment to role modeling desired behaviors—leaders can advance appreciation and inclusion of varying cultural identities and perspectives. Such efforts can lead to meaningful collaboration with individuals representing varied cultural influences, experiences, and affiliations, each of whom comes together to advance excellence.

Culture

There are a number of definitions of *culture*, including one by noted anthropologist Clifford Geertz (1973): "[Culture] denotes an historically transmitted pattern of meanings embodied in symbols, a system of inherited conceptions expressed in symbolic forms by means of which [members of a community] communicate, perpetuate, and develop their knowledge about and attitudes toward life" (p. 89). Another definition, posited by Edgar Schein (2015), also reflects an emphasis on shared patterns of meaning "taught to new members as the correct way to perceive, think, and feel in relation to . . . problems" (p. 287). Ruben and Stewart's (2020) description of culture focuses attention on the role of an organization's history, language, stories, rules, traditions, customs, and preferred practices.

Organizational Culture

The particular focus within this chapter will be on organizational culture and the meanings, preferences, and practices that combine to give a program, department, discipline, school, or institution overall its distinctive character. The concepts to be discussed are also broadly applicable to thinking about the vast array of individual and group identities and affiliations that are so significant to virtually every aspect of campus life.

Approaching the topic of organizational culture from the perspective of communication, Joann Keyton (2011) describes the phenomenon as "the set(s) of artifacts, values, and assumptions that emerges from the interactions of organizational members" (p. 28). Each of these cultural elements—along with the blending of cultural identities of faculty, staff, and students—comes into play in quite significant ways as leaders endeavor to support and guide an organization.

Like other cultures, those represented in higher education organizations develop and evolve over time, are taken for granted, and often go unnoticed and unanalyzed. As Ruud (2000) suggests, "The concept of culture . . . [is] a resource for describing and analyzing organizational life. . . . [It] provides a way of understanding how members within the organization make sense out of their everyday interactions" (pp. 118–119). Cultures are not right or wrong, but there exists a logic for why they developed in the way they did and why particular groups value the things they do. Cultural traditions tend to be fairly stable over time and naturally resist change, much as our human immune systems resist irritants.

Leader as Catalyst for Organizational Inclusive Excellence

What makes people feel like they belong in an organization? How does a leader foster this feeling of belonging, where individuals feel that they are valued, respected, and heard? These so-called inclusive leadership skills are competencies that organizations increasingly value. These qualities are important not only attracting and retaining diverse talent but also for ensuring a collaborative culture that will enhance organizational performance, recognizing that diversity and inclusiveness are not just "nice to have" but are, in fact, fundamental to achieving excellence. When diverse employees feel a sense of belonging in the organization, there is potential to accelerate innovation and productivity, while a feeling of citizenship and a sense of community may lead to more employee satisfaction and less turnover (Cottrill et al., 2014).

Inclusive leadership skills begin with a clear understanding of the terminology used in this space. The words *diversity*, *equity*, and *inclusion* themselves are often misunderstood, interchangeably used, and frequently left to an individual to ascribe their own meanings to the terms. Therefore, leaders may benefit from creating a common language and shared understanding so that the organization is aligned in their understanding of these concepts. A simple and helpful analogy that is often used to define and differentiate these concepts is the example of diversity being invited to the dance party, inclusion being asked to dance, and belonging as dancing as if no one is watching. As discussed next, there are a number of useful considerations regarding each of these terms.

Diversity

Often *diversity* is used for individuals (e.g., a diverse candidate) when it implies "different," most likely referring to someone from an underrepresented group. However, diversity should be understood to be a relational term. A person is not diverse in themselves; rather, a team may exhibit diversity when individuals bring different lived experiences or different perspectives. Many consider diversity only as compositional (what we look like) or proportional (quantity), but cognitive diversity (how we think differently) is also important to consider, and the impact of each kind of diversity is enhanced by the other.

Inclusion

Addressing compositional diversity will not guarantee inclusion. Inclusion reflects the *quality* of the experience and the sense of being valued as a core part of the organization such that one feels engaged and eager to contribute. Designing inclusive organizations will therefore require engaging members of the institution, school, or unit in order to understand what they need for a quality experience.

For leaders of transformative organizations, addressing both diversity (who) and inclusion (how) is critical. Diversity of representation and a culture of inclusion must be intertwined and inextricably linked since diverse representation without a culture of inclusion is likely to fail to achieve either short- or longer term goals, while an inclusive culture without diverse representation lacks credibility.

Equity and Equality

Equity and *equality* are two other terms that have different meanings and yet are often used interchangeably. Equality assumes everyone will benefit when given the same resources. Equity acknowledges that differences exist and seeks to identify resources to fit the different needs of a person/community in order to achieve similar outcomes (Race Forward, n.d.) or as a way to "level the field." For example, if an educational webinar is offered to all, we ensure equality in access to all; but if 30% of the community is Spanish speaking, then offering the webinar in both English and Spanish would also ensure equity.

Once we reach a shared understanding of key terms and concepts, we can then attempt to integrate strategies that weave diversity, equity, and inclusion into the fabric of the organization. This requires promoting a shared commitment to these ideals and demonstrating that commitment in practice by assuring that these principles are consistently reflected in leadership actions and decisions. For example, we might consider diversity when search committees are being formed or when selecting applicant pools, along with being mindful of what (or who) we honor or celebrate on the walls and websites of the organization and who we choose to invite to speak at major college or university events.

Leadership Ownership

Inclusive leaders take ownership for diversity and inclusion in the organization instead of relegating it to a select few representatives. They exhibit a commitment to these aims in their messages and in their behaviors such that they exhibit a genuine and nonjudgmental curiosity about others, and have the ability to listen deeply and practice cultural humility (Center for Talent Innovation, 2013), which together promote a "speak up" culture.

Effective inclusive leaders also demonstrate cultural fluency and recognize that there is a learning continuum that begins with an awareness of their own biases (both conscious and unconscious) and extends to actively seeking ways to mitigate these biases. Unconscious bias includes those attitudes or stereotypes that are outside our awareness but affect our understanding, our interactions, and our decisions. We all harbor unconscious associations—both positive and negative—about other people based on characteristics such as race, gender, age, and appearance. These associations may influence our feelings and attitudes and result in involuntary discriminatory practices, especially under demanding circumstances (Association of American Medical Colleges [AAMC] & Kirwan Institute, 2017).

Unconscious bias often emerges in the form of microaggressions that negatively impact organizational culture. Microaggressions are the daily, commonplace interactions (verbal, nonverbal, behavioral, environmental), whether intentional or unintentional, that communicate hostile, derogatory, or negative slights and insults toward members of marginalized groups (e.g., people of color, women, LGBT persons, persons with disabilities, religious minorities, etc.) (Sue, 2010). They may well be outside the conscious awareness and intentions of the individual displaying these behaviors, but they nonetheless may be a very negative influence because of the impact they have on others. Microaggressions are often constant and cumulative, and they send messages that are often devaluing and convey disrespect, resulting in a negative impact on an individual's mental and physical health (Sue et al., 2008), creating a suboptimal learning or work environment and undermining efforts to establish a positive, satisfying, and inclusive campus climate. It is important that leaders create opportunities that increase awareness of bias and empower their colleagues and others in the community to mitigate microaggressions.

Inclusive leaders recognize that a diverse culture may not necessarily be an inclusive one and that inclusion is both an individual and collective task for the organization. What leaders say and do has an incredible impact on others, and being intentional in using the diversity, equity, and inclusion lens for every decision is important. Building trust and engaging in lifelong learning will nourish an organizational culture of inclusion and belonging—one that contributes to the overall quality of organization and the community.

Leader as Organizational Ethnographer

Developing an understanding of culture and organizational culture and employing some of the insights and skills of an ethnographer can be extremely important to successful leadership. According to Spradley (1979), "Ethnography is the work of describing a culture. The essential core of this activity aims to understand another way of life from the native point of view" (p. 2). The practice of ethnography involves a deep and meaningful immersion into the lived experiences of a group, organization, or community.

The benefits of ethnographic techniques extend beyond anthropological and social science research and into the domain of applied leadership practice. Academic leaders, as organizational ethnographers, can develop a nuanced understanding of the varying disciplinary, professional, national, ethnic, gender, religious, and other groups represented within the college or university, and this knowledge can be invaluable to the ways in which a leader conducts their work. To cultivate this level of understanding, leaders need to essentially become students of the various cultures they encounter within the institution, focusing thoughtful attention on observation, listening, and performing the careful and systematic analysis of traditions, sensitivities, expectations, and preferences.

How and where can an individual who is new to an organization or a leadership role undertake their work as an ethnographer? Observations might take place during formal meetings, lunchroom conversations, or chance encounters within the classroom or in offices, student unions, coffee shops, or hallways. Focusing on meetings, for example, one might observe the patterns of arrival, attendance, and departure. What time do individuals tend to arrive for a meeting? How are meetings begun? Are there formalized agendas? If so, how are the agendas constructed, and when and by whom are they distributed? Do members contribute items to the agenda? How is meeting time allocated among activities such as leader announcements, group discussion and analysis, group decision-making, and the development of action plans? How fully are members engaged? Is attendance expected of all? Are explanations expected from those who miss a meeting? How are meetings ended? What materials, if any, are prepared and shared after the meeting?

Communication patterns—in both face-to-face and digital contexts—should also be observed. What are the typical patterns of interaction? Do some, most, or all members speak? Are some colleagues predictably involved in these discussions and others not? How do patterns of participation relate to gender, race, area of expertise, rank, or seniority? What themes, analogies, and metaphors are commonly used? Do the content and tone of discussion tend to emphasize collaboration and cooperation within the unit and with other units, or are competition and individual pursuits more common themes? Do some other terms have predictably positive or negative connotations? Is "the administration," "the faculty," "staff," or "students" talked about in predictably positive or negative ways? Is business language commonly and comfortably used, or are these associations avoided or negatively regarded? How candid are colleagues with one another about their views and opinions? Do members openly question or challenge their leaders or one another? When challenges occur, how do leaders and colleagues respond? Are post-meeting and back-channel conversations among colleagues a common practice? What function do such discussions seem to serve? How are decisions made and implemented? How would you characterize the pace of decision-making?

Other topics of focus might be as follows: Who are the formal and informal opinion leaders? What approaches to problem-solving and decision-making are common to the organization? What role do informal leaders play? To what extent is control for various functions distributed within the organization? How broadly engaged are members of the unit or institution? Are the views of external stakeholders typically sought and when and how is information used in problem-solving? Are comparisons to other organizations a common strategy in decision-making? Are there patterns in the organizations used for comparative purposes?

One can also devote attention to cultural conventions regarding email behaviors within the unit. For what purposes are emails used? Is it customary for all department members to respond to each email that solicits information or poses a question? Are "CCs" and "BCCs" typically used? In what instances, and for what purposes? Are there topics that are less often or never discussed through email?

In a general sense, an ethnographic approach is a systematic method for gaining a deeper understanding of the cultural practices of particular groups, organizations, and subcultures. For the purposes of organizational leadership, one might focus particular attention on the dimensions included in the organizational culture framework developed by Ruben et al. (2020) and displayed in Figure 6.1. Applying skills of careful observation,

Figure 6.1. Dimensions of organizational culture.

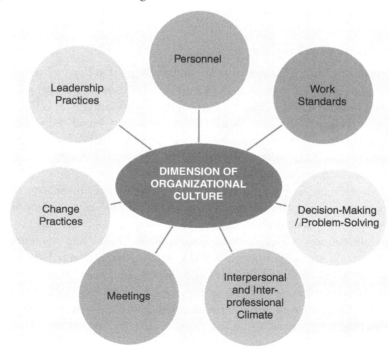

listening, and analysis allows a leader to gain insights that will help them predict approaches that are quite likely to resonate well with the culture and those that will not. These insights can also help to differentiate leadership and communication styles that will be familiar and well-received from those who will likely create turbulence.

The foregoing comments are not intended to suggest that it should always be a leader's intention to enact leadership approaches that will be consistent with or reinforce cultural traditions or the common practices of particular groups or subgroups. Indeed, in some instances, an important goal of a leader may be to confront or transform some elements of the culture. Those strategic choices need to be made on a case-by-case basis. But in all instances, one hopes to make *informed* choices reflective of a nuanced understanding of the cultures in play and with a sense of likely responses rather than random or arbitrary choices made without forethought and planning. We might borrow and adapt Alice Goffman's (2014) observations in her ethnographic study of life in an urban neighborhood in Philadelphia, in thinking through the intersection of leadership, organizational ethnography, and culture: "To survive . . . [and succeed as a leader] . . . [one] learns to hesitate when others walk casually forward, to see what others fail to notice, to . . . [carefully analyze] what others trust or take for granted" (p. 25).

Organizational Climate

One additional idea related to organizational culture that deserves mention is organizational climate, which is an expression of culture. A wide range of factors may be considered elements of an organization's climate, as is illustrated within the "Great Colleges to Work For" framework summarized in Box 6.1. How do faculty and staff treat one another? How are students treated? Is the tone one of genuine interest, supportiveness, and respectfulness, or is a sense of disinterest, disregard, and disrespect apparent?

A visitor may get a feel for the climate of a college or university, or of the programs or departments within it, by walking around campus, stopping in an office to meet with staff or faculty, or reading campus-wide emails from the administration. Conversations among faculty, staff, and students may also convey a sense of how people working in an organization feel about their work, their workplace, and the services they provide. Even the tone and style of conversations among colleagues, the layout of the facility, and whether and how colleagues respond to routine emails can contribute to the sense of the organization to those inside and outside the organization (Schein, 2015;

Schneider, 1990; Tagiuri & Litwin, 1968). Through these micro behaviors, actions, and elements, an organization's climate takes on a life of its own, one that is often self-perpetuating.

BOX 6.1
(Edmunds & Boyer, 2015)

In 2008 the *Chronicle of Higher Education* and ModernThink LLC created the Great Colleges to Work For program. Annually they report the results of employee surveys at participating colleges and universities. The 2015 results are again instructive for formal and informal leaders in higher education.

Employee satisfaction is highest when

- Leaders are
  o Credible
    ▪ Leaders engage in interactions that build trust and behaviors that are consistent, reliable, and reflect integrity.
  o Capable
    ▪ Leaders demonstrate that they have the knowledge, skills, and experience to effectively lead the institution.
- Communication is
  o Transparent
    ▪ Leaders are open concerning both good and bad news, provide the context and rationale for decisions, and ensure that the campus community receives regular and timely updates.
  o Interactive
    ▪ Leaders foster interactive communication that creates opportunities for two-way exchanges.
- Alignment between goals and people emphasizes
  o Collaboration
    ▪ Leaders support faculty and staff members and require faculty and staff to support each other, solicit input from one another, and pay little attention to who gets credit for what.
  o Contribution
    ▪ Leaders position people to contribute at their highest level by putting the right people in the right jobs and providing them with the training, tools, and resources to succeed.

- Respect is demonstrated through
  - Fairness
    - Leaders treat employees fairly, regardless of personal attributes or position.
  - Acknowledgment
    - Leaders provide specific and regular rewards, recognition, and feedback designed to motivate faculty and staff members to treat one another well and do their best work.

Synthesis by Susan E. Lawrence.

Clearly, organizational climate is an important topic for leadership attention. Climate is significant to the fulfillment of its mission, the efficiency of day-to-day operations, the experiences of students, and the satisfaction of faculty and staff. Because climate issues are generally manifestations of deeper issues of organizational culture, efforts by a leader to address them directly is often analogous to focusing on symptoms rather than underlying root causes.

The Organizational Climate Inventory and the Dimensions of Organizational Cultures Inventory provide useful tools to assess the culture of one's department or institution. These inventories allow leaders to focus on a deeper understanding of the workplace experience, promote employee well-being and workplace satisfaction, and identify areas for climate and cultural improvement.

Higher Education: A World-Class Leader in Cultural Complexity

In a classic ethnographic study of a community symphony, Ruud (2000) discovered two distinctive and competing cultural perspectives within the organization: Musicians tended to embrace an artistic code while managers embraced a business code, and each code competed with another for organizational prominence. He illustrated how a person's responsibility in the organization had a significant influence on that person's organizational identity—with administrators taking on a business orientation and musicians attending to the more performance-oriented components of the symphony. Ruud (2000) explains,

The artistic and business codes, analyzed individually or in opposition, are meaningful in that they express, in a culturally specific manner, the way in which performers and business personnel experience and evaluate organizational life. Each code . . . suggests a particular set of . . . premises that guide organizational members as they assess past, present, and future organizational actions. (p. 124)

These communication codes shape the reality for members of the organization. Moreover, members of the business, artistic, and other groups embody elements of other cultural traditions associated with their gender, ethnicity, political orientation, race, religion, and so on. Ruud (2000) also found that "certain groups [those with a business orientation] wield more power [than the performers] and . . . have more opportunity to ensure that their interests are maintained" (p. 138). By way of analogy, the findings from this study provide a glimpse into the cultural complexity of higher education and the value an ethnographic approach may have for leaders as well as researchers.

When it comes to the number, complexity, and variety of cultures within a single organization, higher education institutions may well lead all others. Even focusing specifically on professional roles within a college or university, there are a very large number of groups with distinctive cultures. In the most general terms, the administrative–academic divide—which may be seen as paralleling the cultural divide identified by Ruud (2000)—is particularly important for leaders to understand. Generally, this divide cuts across the institution as a whole. Additionally, the arts and sciences, humanities, performing arts, professional schools (e.g., medical schools and law schools) also have their own cultures and subcultures. Within an academic health context, one might consider the critical differences among the cultures of physicians, patients, researchers, residents, and postdoctorates, not to mention the various cultures within schools of nursing, pharmacy, public health, and dentistry; the teaching hospital; and the many other health and medical units represented within many colleges and universities. In addition, the distinctive cultures of student affairs, facilities, residence life, business services, and so on collectively comprise an amazingly complex, intersecting, and overlapping array of cultural groups within any institution.

Although subgroups are loosely united around the shared goals of higher education, it is also the case that among the various cultural groups distinctive and sometimes competing goals, values, expectations, and language codes exist. Distinctions between the cultures of musicians and managers in the case of a symphony orchestra parallel some dimensions of the contrast between members of the academic and administrative cultures, and noteworthy cultural differences exist and are characteristic of the broad landscape of schools, divisions, and departments within any college or university. Additionally, each of these numerous subgroups has its own nuanced cultural identity, reflecting differences in discipline, rank, gender, age, race/ethnicity, technical area, source of funding, tenure status, union status, and a variety of other factors that may be important either in the background or foreground in particular situations (Snow, 2012; Tierney, 1988).

A Focus on Academic and Administrative Cultures

The two largest and most important employee groups within higher education institutions are the staff/administrators and the faculty, each of which plays a vital and significant role in any department, school, or institution. A large percentage of the plans, decisions, and initiatives undertaken by higher education leaders involve both of these cultures in some way. Differences between the administrative (administrator/staff) and academic cultures are critical to the functioning of any college or university, but they also create significant challenges. Each culture tends to be somewhat distinctive because of the unique makeup of the group's members, including differentiating roles and responsibilities, education and training, incentive and reward structures, and professional backgrounds. From the perspective of leadership, it is critically important to understand these cultures and the nuances that define and differentiate one from the other. For example, one might identify the following traditional core values of the academic culture:

- freedom of expression
- collegial decision-making
- creating, advancing, and imparting knowledge
- primary loyalty to discipline rather than institution
- higher education as unique and special—not a business
- a view of faculty as the most important group in the institution
- students as learners—not customers
- self-determination (individual and institutional)
- customization of processes and procedures
- aversion to board, state, national, accrediting, and U.S. Department of Education perspectives as important in decision-making

These core values often clash to a lesser or greater extent with the primary values of the administrative culture, which might include the following:

- operational effectiveness
- hierarchical decision-making
- efficiency
- cost effectiveness/cost savings

- service orientation and loyalty to institution
- the university as a business
- return on investment
- compliance with regulations as a critical concern
- valuing standardization of processes and procedures
- attuned to board, state, national, accrediting, and U.S. Department of Education, and other regulatory agency perspectives as important in decision-making

We believe these lists capture some important and generally predictable differences between the cultural values of academics and administrators that leaders need to understand and take into account in their work. Often, these differences in core values can play out in the ways that work is structured and accomplished and in the ways that members view one another. That said, it is important to note that these lists are cultural generalizations, and as with all cultural generalizations, their validity and value differ from individual to individual, situation to situation, and institution to institution.

Where these cultural differences are present, contrasts become evident in any number of areas, including the way in which these groups think about and approach meetings, how they think and talk about their organizations and work activities, and in their language preferences and usage. In general, within the administrative culture, attendance at scheduled meetings is assumed to be mandatory unless a major problem arises. In that case, notification is expected, and, if possible, the individual who must miss a session will send a substitute. Within the academic culture, attendance at most meetings is considered desirable but not mandatory. If a faculty member has a research, teaching, professional, or service activity that they regard as a priority, that may take precedence over attendance at a meeting.

In general, timely arrival to the meeting is more valued in the administrative than the academic culture. Academic meetings often begin when it seems that a critical mass of participants has arrived, even if that is later than the scheduled time. Members of the administrative/staff culture are also generally more likely to regard preparation for a meeting as essential; faculty, on the other hand, tend to place greater importance on the discussion that occurs at the meeting. The same relative rules of formality and informality that relate to meeting start times apply to the ending of meetings and to whether and how attendees follow up afterward. Not surprisingly, each group is somewhat puzzled, and sometimes frustrated, by these different patterns of behavior when meetings include a mix of faculty and staff members.

For a leader who must organize, conduct, and follow up on meetings that involve individuals from both cultures, the task can be daunting. At least during initial meetings, it may be prudent to prepare for, accept, and work around the deep-seated cultural differences that may present themselves— and to display understanding and patience as you work to establish shared expectations within the group.

Cultural differences between administrators and academics may also be significant in work patterns and styles. While faculty work on projects at varying locales and at all hours of the day (or night), under normal circumstances, staff responsibilities are more traditionally performed in their offices in the 9-to-5 window. For staff—and sometimes students and visitors—it can be frustrating that faculty are not necessarily available and/or in their offices during "regular" working hours; they may fail to realize that for many faculty members there really are no regular working hours. Conversely, it is sometimes a bit troubling to faculty that staff members may not be inclined to respond to emails in the evenings or on weekends—although, increasingly, this distinction does not necessarily hold. While the faculty work style is often characterized by greater autonomy, in fact, regular, 3-year, tenure, and post-tenure reviews provide many accountability points. These may be less apparent to staff who are likely to have more frequent and sometimes more formalized performance reviews. Accountability exists for both groups, though the form and timing differ. Consequently, differences between these accountability models can be a source of misunderstanding and resentment.

As noted, differences between the two cultures are also apparent in the way they each think and talk about organizations. Faculty members are likely to describe their department, school, or university as unique and often talk about issues as if they are particular to their organization. Administrators, on the other hand, are more likely to use generic language, such as "organizational issues," "process issues," or "leadership issues"—reflecting a perspective that focuses more on commonalities across units than on differences.

Another difference in language surfaces in the way administrators and faculty communicate about the business operations of colleges and universities. In an article in *Inside Higher Education*, for example, Kellie Woodhouse (2015) explores the different sets of vocabulary faculty and staff use. She quotes Margarita Rose, chair of the faculty leadership at King's College, who presents the difference as follows: "There's an expectation . . . that the financial officer will have the same language and understanding as the academic administration and faculty. Perhaps that's an unfair expectation since we don't always use language the same way." However, as Richard Kneedler, president emeritus of Franklin & Marshall College, suggests,

> It's important that faculty have a willingness to learn some terminology with which they might not be familiar, because the institution where they

find themselves very likely needs to have skills in a variety of areas where they might not have been necessary 15 or 20 years ago, but they are absolutely vital today. (Woodhouse, 2015)

The university-as-business issue is but one example of the underlying tension between these two dominant subcultures.

Other variations in language use and interpretations can also be a challenge. Sometimes unique academic words and phrases are subject to criticism—and may evoke sarcastic responses—from administrators. For example, when academics say *collegial decision-making*, administrators may interpret the phrase to mean "a time-consuming process that results in no clear outcomes, and by the time this outcome becomes evident, the time to act has probably passed." The term *tenure* may be interpreted by some staff as "immunity to accountability and organizational responsibility." The phrase *faculty participation* may well be understood by some to mean "lots of talking, not many tangibles/deliverables." Conversely, when faculty hear that "consultants have been hired to assist with strategic planning, branding, marketing, or process reengineering," their translations traditionally have been equally unflattering. Faculty may interpret this reference as "Here we go again—an investment of time developing a list of priorities that are obvious or predetermined by administrators to be published in a brochure that will likely accumulate dust on the bookshelves when that time and money should be spent on teaching and research." Furthermore, the language of *efficiency, higher education as a business,* and *standardized processes and procedures* is sometimes viewed by faculty as an implicit attack on academic freedom, autonomy, and the core academic values of higher education.

One quite predictable language pattern is particularly troubling to staff and is, therefore, worth singling out for special mention. Often in discussions of the mission of a unit or institution, emphasis is placed on the role of the faculty, research, and classroom or laboratory instruction. Inadvertently, this representation marginalizes the essential contributions of administrators and staff—stakeholders who play mission-critical roles throughout the institution. In a sense, it represents an instance of what is often termed unconscious or unintentional bias and is another reminder of the need for sensitivity to cultural issues of all kinds.

Though not employees, students represent a third critical stakeholder group—better thought of as multiple groups, each with their own cultural priorities. These groups consist of undergraduates and graduate students, full-time and part-time students, residential and commuting students, and the growing number of distance learners. Each of these subcultural groups may also feel strongly about their affiliation with their department, campus, or discipline.

Beyond Role-Based Cultures: Identities and Differences

Many of the issues related to cultural difference and sensitivities with regard to academic and administrative cultures are also applicable to various other campus cultural identities and affiliations. Beyond role-, discipline-, and specialty-based cultural affinities and identities are those related to sex, gender, race and ethnicity, religion, political orientation, age, lifestyle, and nationality, among others. Each individual's identity reflects a unique blend of cultural influences. As Harold Silver (2008) suggests, "In terms of . . . shared norms, values and assumptions, as well as symbols, myths or rituals, universities do not have a [single] culture. [Universities are] . . . a system of subcultures in perpetual, erratic, and damaging tensions" (p. 167). There is no such thing as a unified culture, and there exist a number of competing ideas within the academic and administrative subcultures (Martin, 1992; Silver, 2008).

The lack of individual or institutional awareness of these cultural complexities and differences can lead to unintentional and damaging missteps, including the potential for behaviors that are viewed as culturally insensitive. Furthermore, a lack of awareness and understanding can lead one to engage in stereotyping, acts of individual and institutional bias, and macro- and microaggressions that can have a wide range of negative implications on colleagues from across the institution and may also result in major problems for institutional leaders. Unfortunately, individuals often become targets of discriminatory practices based on their geographic region or country of origin, gender, race, religion, political orientation, or other cultural factors. Sometimes these practices are overt and intentional; in other instances, they may be accidental. Such behaviors may be deemed simply annoying or inconsiderate—as with a thoughtless comment by a staff member about the preferences afforded to faculty when it comes to freedom of speech or scheduling flexibility. In other cases, comments or actions can be highly offensive, marginalizing, emotionally charged, and even illegal. In any case, when they occur, their consequences can be extremely problematic and may very well undermine the mission, values, and efficacy of a group, organization, and institution as a whole.

Leaders as Agents of Inclusion and Community-Building

For values-based and pragmatic reasons, promoting diversity, equity, and inclusion is a critical area of responsibility for leaders. The goals of inclusivity apply equally to considerations relative to faculty, staff, students, and other stakeholder groups with whom leaders engage. It is clear that any and all identity and affiliative groups have a potentially significant impact on organizational functioning, and maintaining vigilance and sensitivity to cultural issues can be a key factor in both organizational and individual effectiveness and in creating a sense of community.

In thinking through the various means by which a leader can promote inclusive practices, the definition of leadership provided earlier can be helpful. Recall that the influence of leaders can take place through the design and implementation of messages, strategies, processes, and structures.

Messages

Perhaps most obviously, a leader can be influential as a voice for inclusive practices through formal and informal communication—in speeches, on websites, in casual conversations, repeatedly and regularly. Messaging can make clear that inclusivity is important—to represent the diverse groups served by the institution; to promote appropriate and respectful practices among faculty, staff, and students; to broadly engage diverse voices in the collaborative work of the institution; and to provide role models for appropriate practices in an environment where teaching and learning are central to the mission. While grand pronouncements and widely distributed policy statements are important, subtle but consistent messaging and actions repeated over time and across contexts promote inclusion as an aspirational and realized goal.

Strategies

Falling within this category are leadership initiatives designed to reinforce diversity and inclusivity goals. These could include the review of courses and cocurricular activities to ensure that they broadly support these goals. Another approach would be the development of a plan for assuring appropriate diversity on committees and task forces. Leaders might also initiate a regular series of informal and/or social activities such as colloquia or receptions for faculty, staff, or students at which efforts are made to foster conversations across differences to promote inclusiveness. Regular efforts to recognize accomplishments by members of the unit in publications at meetings, on websites, and in announcements to external stakeholders are additional strategies that can be utilized.

Taking a longer term perspective, a useful strategy might be the creation of in-person or online pathways and partnership programs to recruit a broadened base of individuals from underrepresented groups and a similar pathway that allows for their growth once they are part of the organization. Programs along these lines can identify specific groups to foster based on gender, racial/ethnic, or disciplinary background and expertise, depending on the needs and aspirations of a department or institution. For example, first-generation college students, international students, and staff recruits from other sectors may all be groups for which some specialized programming may be helpful in both recruitment and retention.

Processes

Designing organizational practices that promote attention to broad and inclusive participation may enhance the quality and richness of programs and activities, while facilitating the meaningful engagement of individuals representing varying demographics and perspectives. Examples of processes where leadership efforts can be quite influential include search, onboarding, planning, personnel review, program assessment, and curriculum review. As an example, instituting peer mentoring processes as a component of orientation and personnel review processes affords an opportunity to enhance the richness of personnel processes and inclusivity simultaneously. More generally, instituting processes to encourage leadership development and distributed leadership is another mechanism to support these goals. Finally, introducing performance goals that take account of diversity and inclusion as a part of annual reviews for leaders of programs, units, centers, and departments is another example of a process that can be quite influential. In addition to having a direct influence on actions and behaviors in the workplace, these processes help to advance and normalize expectations relative to diversity and inclusion across an organization.

Structures

Leaders can influence goals by forming task forces or committees, creating titled leadership positions, or forming dedicated offices to foster and/or coordinate diversity and inclusion programs and services for faculty, staff, and students. The creation of offices, centers, or programs designed to meet the specialized needs of individuals or groups within the organization is another possibility. Forming department, school, or campus programs or committees to focus on topics such as inclusive teaching, attention to diversity and inclusion in course materials for faculty and staff, and inclusivity in student clubs, activities, and organizations are additional examples of structures that can help advance goals of diversity and inclusion (Nevin, 2020).

In pursuing any of these messaging approaches, strategies, processes, or structures, it is obviously important to take account of the perceptions of all members of the organization—recognizing the importance of all individuals and groups within the unit.

Leaders as Cross-Cultural Communicators

Leaders and leadership behaviors are essential to creating a community that values and benefits from diverse individuals, groups, and cultures. Indeed, it is increasingly unlikely that leaders will be effective if they are unable to bridge the broad individual and cultural differences that are present in their leadership context. To a significant extent, success as an academic or administrative leader is dependent on one's ability to apply the basic skills of ethnography to heighten one's sensitivities to the perspectives of various cultures within institutions of higher education. Skills in intercultural communication are also extremely valuable, and competencies in this area help to translate and leverage ethnographic insights in pursuing leadership and organizational goals (Ruben, 1977; Ruben & Kealey, 1979).

As leaders navigate the array of subcultures within the academy, it is helpful to realize that they are essentially operating in an intercultural environment. The implication is that a leader must be an organizational ethnographer, as well as an adept cross-cultural communicator. Typically, the issue is not whether particular perspectives are right or wrong. Elements of every culture take on a reality of their own—one that reflects the norms of a culture that are understood to be "correct," whereas others might seem incorrect or inappropriate. All perspectives have a historical explanation and logic (Ruben & Stewart, 2020). Effective leadership requires cultural sensitivity, avoiding overgeneralization, and finding creative ways to utilize and leverage the strengths of all perspectives.

While they may not be the most socially consequential challenges, some of the most common cross-cultural communication situations in higher education involve bridging the academic–administrator/staff cultural divide. Janet Mason Ellerby (2009), professor of English at the University of North Carolina at Wilmington and former interim director of the Women's Studies and Resource Center, describes this challenge:

> Having had the opportunity to look at academe from both sides now—as professor and administrator—I'm disillusioned. The divide I had always suspected between faculty and administration seems quite real, and any ideals I might have entertained of mutual respect have been tarnished. . . . What I can see from both sides now is what could have happened, what still could happen. Administrators need to work harder to raze the divide between administration and faculty, to construct sturdy bridges of mutual respect that encourage communication, consultation, and collaboration. It is too facile to say, "We're all in this together."

Strategies to Increase Culturally Responsive Communication

Functioning effectively in such cross-cultural situations requires leaders to value outcomes and process equally and to emphasize shared goals. There are a number of specific strategies that can be helpful in anticipating and responding to cultural differences, including the following:

- Leaders are quite likely to have their own opinion of the merits of a particular initiative, project, program, change, or activity based on their experience. Predictably, these views will be reflective of their role, gender identity, discipline, or specialty. When serving in a leadership position, one's personal perspective may have to be sublimated or sidelined. Bluntly stated, as a leader, the task is often less about advocating one's own point of view and more about creating constructive dialogue, developing high-quality decisions that are informed by multiple perspectives, and cultivating buy-in and support for the directions to be pursued. It is also the case that multiple perspectives generally heighten the probability of sound decisions, and the act of engaging others greatly increases the likelihood that the chosen directions will have traction and sustainability.
- Clarify the perspectives that varying groups have—and the array of assets, liabilities, risks, and opportunities each is likely to identify—and develop plans and processes that take account of varying cultures and relevant cultural differences.
- Work to develop solutions that take account of goals and cultural realities of others whose support will be critical to one's success as a leader in this instance and over time.
- Identify and engage individuals who represent the interests of groups that have a stake in an initiative, project, change, program, or activity being contemplated, planned, or implemented.
- Commit to increasing one's competence as an intercultural communicator by enmeshing oneself in a network of friends and acquaintances from a variety of cultural groups across the institution and invest in understanding their unique cultures, perspectives, and experiences.

Thinking specifically in terms of role-based cultures, if you are a faculty leader, some of your best friends really do need to be administrators; and conversely, if you are a staff administrator, you need to be able to count faculty members among the friends who you know and appreciate. The same need for multicultural competence extends to students and external stakeholders. Simply put,

> There is the need to be alert and sensitive to the needs, orientations, values, aspirations, and . . . communication styles of other persons with whom one interacts. One needs to know how respect, empathy, non-judgmentalness, turn-taking, orientation to knowledge, and group and organizational roles are *regarded* and *expressed* in a given culture. Of equal or greater importance to effectiveness at transfer of skills is the willingness to be introspective, and committed to see, to examine, and to learn from one's failures and weaknesses as well as one's successes and strengths. Only in this way can one's behavior be brought into congruence with what one believes and intends. (Ruben, 1977, p. 102)

Organizational Culture Change

Perhaps the greatest test of a higher education leader's ethnographic and cross-cultural communication skills is provided by situations where the goal is to alter an existing organizational culture or shape the culture of a new organization. One very effective approach is to engage colleagues in reflective assessment. Ideally, this process can provide the basis for constructive dialogue and critique and also form the foundation for envisioning improvements or alternatives. The excellence in higher education model (Ruben, 2016) discussed in chapter 13, is one possible framework for guiding this kind of process. Another useful tool is *Diagnosing Your Organization's Culture* (Ruben et al., 2020). While there is no simple set of strategies that assure success in such instances, the following suggestions can be helpful:

- Create and articulate a vision of a desired organizational culture, being specific about how and why it would differ from the present culture.
- As a new leader, identify, recognize, and validate the good work done by predecessors (leaders and units), emphasizing accomplishments that exemplify dimensions of the desired new culture.
- Recruit diverse employees who embody the desired aspirations and values of the new or modified culture.
- Be visible and associate yourself personally and behaviorally with the values and principles embodied in the new or modified culture (e.g., role modeling and finding ways to visibly walk the talk).

- Identify previous and present leaders, including thought leaders, who are talented, and make an effort to engage them fully in the new directions.
- Disseminate and engage diverse colleagues in discussions of an alternative organizational vision to internal and external constituencies.
- Commit to making decisions that are transparent and consistent with the alternative organizational vision.
- Establish goals and strategies for both the short and long term that are consistent with the desired culture.
- Hire and promote in ways consistent with the desired vision and values. For example, take professorial criteria and peer review processes seriously for external hires and internal promotions and do not use promotions as a strategy to move weak leaders out of their present positions. Doing so sends precisely the wrong message to colleagues.
- Give visibility to exemplary projects and outcomes.
- Create reward and recognition systems that encourage movement toward the new cultural vision, including public forums and communication mechanisms to publicize changes that exemplify the desired new directions.
- Work with and through diverse leaders at all levels.
- Align organizational rhetoric with organizational practices (e.g., selection, promotions). Maintain alignment between what is said and what is done and assure that this consistency is apparent to diverse internal and external stakeholders.

Conclusion

Inclusive leadership skills that promote meaningful engagement and collaboration are imperative for leaders today. Regardless of whether one is an academic or administrative leader, success in this respect requires one to have cultural humility and endorse broadly inclusive perspectives, practices, and personal behaviors along with efforts to promote engagement, respect, and understanding among the many subcultures of the institution. These goals can be pursued through the design and implementation of messages, strategies, processes, and structures that promote inclusive excellence, and through the application of ethnographic and cross-cultural communication skills.

7

THE TRANSITION
TO LEADERSHIP

From Pilot to Air Traffic Controller

In This Chapter

- What are the fundamental differences between the role of a faculty or staff member and that of an academic or administrative leader?
- What challenges and opportunities are typically associated with the transition to a leadership position?
- What are the cross pressures that leaders must understand and address?

As highlighted throughout this book, leadership in higher education is distributed across the institution, and there are abundant opportunities for influence through informal as well as formal roles. We recognize, however, that for many scholars and practitioners references to "leadership in higher education" brings to mind thoughts of formalized academic and administrative positions of authority. Thus, this chapter will focus more specifically on the transition that one might experience from the role of a faculty or staff member to a position of academic or administrative leadership—a transition that is often far more turbulent and paradigm shifting than might be expected.

In our positions as faculty or staff members we have a familiarity and comfort with our colleagues, our work, and the organization. Over the months or years of employment, we have likely achieved a level of personal efficacy, technical expertise and confidence, and an operating style that fits with the culture of the organization. The existence of performance goals and measures of accomplishment help to guide us in our roles as individual faculty and staff, and we are generally mindful of these as we develop and pursue personal plans and goals for our envisioned futures. Over time, we develop our own personal and professional networks and likely establish a number of peer relationships with colleagues in the unit—relationships we particularly enjoy and that contribute to our overall satisfaction in the workplace. In these relationships, we tend to be casual and candid in our conversations, and there is a sense that we can share our perspectives about work and the organization without concern about any broader institutional significance or impact those conversations might have. As an individual faculty or staff member, we speak for ourselves, with "I" being the pronoun of choice.

Along with pronouns, many other aspects of our work situations change—and sometimes quite dramatically—when we step into a leadership position and begin to speak not only for ourselves but also for the program, department, school, or institution for which we serve as a leader. Suddenly, "we," "us," and "our" become far more relevant—and appropriate—than "I," "me," and "my." Key issues are now what *others* think and believe, what *others'* motivations and concerns are, what *others* expect and need. Even more critical are questions about the collective organization, including how senior institutional leaders view the unit, what the unit aspires to become, what resources the unit needs to function effectively now and in the future, and what role the leader must play to achieve these outcomes.

Shifting from a focus on one's own faculty or staff career trajectory to a more encompassing view that includes understanding and nurturing the work of others and the accomplishments of a team requires a significant change in outlook and behavior. Gone is the freedom to make person-ally oriented choices about who in the department to be most attentive to and with whom to spend the most time. Gone also are the days when one could share an opinion informally with colleagues without thinking of its precedent-setting or broader policy implications. Early in the transition to a formalized leadership position, one realizes that effective leadership—whether in academic or administrative positions—requires sublimating some of one's own interests in favor of priorities that are critical to the suc-cess of one's colleagues and the unit.

New leaders also discover that measures of success are more numerous—and often quite different—than those they were socialized to value in their faculty or staff roles. As an academic leader, for example, it becomes impor-tant to focus on familiar metrics associated with scholarship, teaching, or outreach for the unit as a whole rather than solely for one's own perfor-mance. Beyond those measures, newly relevant markers for leaders relate to one's contributions to performance and advancement, and to organiza-tional aspirations and plans, such as creating a more diverse and inclusive culture and work environment for faculty, staff, and students, or enhancing the commitment to collegial mentoring.

The role of leader also requires one to understand a much broader landscape and to appreciate the perspectives of multiple and diverse stakeholders within and outside the institution. The education and socialization that prepares us for individual success typically provide little guidance when it comes to leadership and organizational effectiveness. Unfortunately, many of the capabilities and skills that are essential for individual success are unrelated— even antithetical—to those necessary for effective organizational leadership. Individual staff and faculty members become adept at guiding their own professional advancement. As noted previously, however, criteria for judging effectiveness in the new leadership role will broaden from a sole focus on individual disciplinary and professional efficacy to give prominence to the collective accomplishments of the group internally and in relationship to its multiple stakeholders.

For most incoming leaders, the sense of competence and mastery achieved in prior roles is challenged by the demands of the new position. For these reasons, the move to a leadership role is a significant change personally and professionally, providing new and exciting opportunities on the one hand, but also bringing what can be an unsettling shift in one's identity, on the other.

Leadership transitions are predictably complex events and come with some turbulence for all involved. When new leaders represent a change for the organization—whether it be a change of disciplinary and methodological orientation, or perhaps even a change in the demographics of the leader, including race, nationality, age, or gender—additional challenges and opportunities are likely to accompany the transition. Clearly there is no prescription for fully realizing the potential opportunities provided by these circumstances; however; by embracing the virtues of intentionality, reflection, patience, persistence, and flexibility—new leaders and their colleagues may come to a shared understanding and appreciation upon which to engage in the work of the unit, department, or institution in satisfying and productive ways.

Higher Education Leader as Air Traffic Controller

As a staff member, and to a greater extent as a member of the faculty, you are the pilot of your own plane. Faculty in higher education are largely responsible for planning their own trips, establishing flight plans, and taking off and landing when and where desired within the agreed-on rules and boundaries of an institution. This characterization is somewhat less accurate for technical and professional staff, who are generally provided with a more structured flight plan and expected to follow the provided guidance to arrive at the intended destination employing their own knowledge and skills.

When a faculty or staff member assumes a formal leadership role, the individual pilot is suddenly transformed into an air traffic controller, concerned not only—or even primarily—with their own plane, but rather with all the planes and pilots for whom one has responsibility. The efficacy of the flight industry hinges on the role of the air traffic controller, leading many to classify it as one of the most stressful occupations (Brown, 2011; Costa, 1993; Zeier, 1994). Indeed, many of the responsibilities of the air traffic controller have their parallels in the work of higher education leaders:

- helping to establish flight plans
- tracking weather conditions
- overseeing runway movement and gate departures/arrivals
- establishing takeoff/landing sequences
- coordinating departures and arrivals
- monitoring flight trajectories
- assuring the safety and well-being of all

The coordination of academics or professionals within colleges and universities depends on the capabilities of formal leaders in much the same ways that the efficacy of the flight industry hinges on the role of the air traffic controller (Brown, 2011; Costa, 1993; Zeier, 1994). The air traffic controller role—or the role of a leader in higher education—challenges one to think and act strategically and to consider the totality of the "friendly skies" rather than just one's own flight trajectory. The transition requires faculty or staff members to become more reflective and set aside familiar habits and routines. Traditional sources of personal satisfaction may also undergo a shift to take account of one's contributions as a leader. That change is likely to be important not only in formally evaluating your performance, as noted previously, but also in recognizing and valuing your personal and professional efficacy in a very different role (Gracias, 2018). As Box 7.1 points out, the shift in focus and behavior is not easy, seldom comes naturally, and for most leaders requires the acquisition of a new compass, new navigation settings, and perhaps even a new way of thinking about one's career.

BOX 7.1
A Message From the Chair

A recently appointed department chair sent the following email to all faculty and staff in her unit:

Hey Everyone, I usually just delete the University Faculty and Staff News-letter that comes each week, but today I happened to notice—and wanted to let you know—that the news about William's new appointment was noted in today's edition.

—Jamie

The opening of this email might be fairly routine and unremarkable for an individual faculty member to send to colleagues. This same message, however, coming from a formally appointed institutional leader may take on quite a different significance. One can imagine potentially unanticipated and undesirable consequences when such a message is sent to new full- and part-time faculty or staff, or is inadvertently forwarded by colleagues around the university. This simple example highlights the potentially different responsibilities of an individual faculty or staff member acting as a free agent—a solo pilot—in comparison to that same individual's responsibilities upon assuming the role of unit leader.

Navigating at the Crossroads

Earlier chapters of this book described the following complexities confronting college and university leaders:

- shifting and increasingly tumultuous landscape of higher education
- differing types of institutions
- varied missions and perspectives
- diversity of institutional stakeholders
- evolving organizational structures and roles
- complexities of cultures within colleges and universities

Leaders in higher education are positioned at the crossroads of these influences and pathways. The route that each of us chooses for ourselves—and the priorities we define and the balance we achieve—are all critical. This section presents a set of practical considerations for developing a road map for decision-making given the many competing influences. We believe that effective leadership involves working at the intersection of what matters to others and what matters to you, as depicted in Figure 7.1. Working at this crossroads involves everything from making strategic choices that will have a lasting impact on a department or academic unit to the seemingly minor choices made about which email to respond to first as messages flow in rapid succession into one's inbox.

In confronting both macro and micro events, a leader is positioned at the nexus of many influences, and the choices one makes can be extremely important in both professional and personal terms. Each decision provides a statement of values and priorities, sets precedent, shapes the organization's culture, and contributes to one's legacy as a leader. The daunting challenge is to attend to, prioritize, and balance the distinct needs and expectations of others, while remaining true to one's own leadership values and aspirations.

What follows is a set of practical suggestions for planning and evaluating the choices you make in balancing priorities at the crossroads:

- Develop an understanding of the implications of the professional role you will play as the leader and determine what changes it implies.
- Assess your personal skills and behavioral strengths and limitations and strive to leverage your strengths while enhancing or overcoming deficiencies.
- Invest time to study and gain a deeper understanding of the perspectives, values, needs, and leadership expectations of colleagues,

Figure 7.1. Leadership: Working at the intersection of what matters to others.

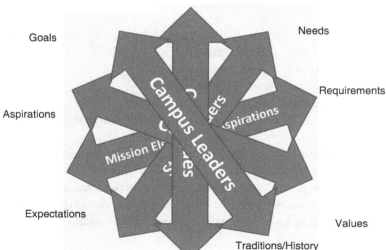

campus leaders, and other stakeholders who will be critical to your work and to success in your role. Identify key issues to keep in mind relative to each group.

- Give careful consideration to what matters to you as a person assuming a leadership role, reminding yourself why you decided to pursue this role. Determine where you hope the organization will be in 5 years and what you hope your legacy and lasting contribution will be.

- Prioritize your leadership responsibilities and develop a preliminary plan for prioritizing and balancing various facets of your work and personal life.

- Recognize the importance of having a collaborative and supportive leadership team, determining what strengths need to be represented on the team, where those exist, and how to engage individuals who possess them.

- Remember that every decision or action is precedent setting when you are in a leadership role and strive to reinforce the values of consistency, reliability, and transparency in your work.

- Develop criteria for leadership success, using new indicators and unlearning some past behaviors. This may require some new language or new metaphors—for example, the air traffic controller rather than pilot of a small plane, as suggested previously. Develop unit- or system-level ways of thinking about important functions like communication and leadership and make use of concepts such as leadership architecture (i.e., the design of leadership structures and teams) and communication analytics (i.e., clarifying strategy, goals, audience, and communication implications).

- Develop methods for reflecting on your performance and success in achieving the purposes and aims of all relevant stakeholders and develop way to review and record your personal assessments.

- Solicit and carefully consider feedback from members of your team and from those to whom you report. Determine how you will solicit input and advice from colleagues, supervisors, and friends and how you will engage in more formalized consultations or mentoring with peers or experienced leaders at one's own or other institutions.

- Be aware of your level of emotional stress stemming from professional responsibilities. Strive to attain a healthy work-life integration. Develop a plan to manage stress in ways that work for you, such as a regular, scheduled time for exercise, spending time with family/friends, pleasure reading and other hobbies, and so forth. Some leaders find it useful to maintain electronic silence at certain hours or days of the week as a way to manage the stress caused by the tremendous volume of incoming messages and emails.

Conclusion

Within the context of higher education, it is appropriate that we privilege a commitment to learning and personal and professional development. Do not assume that you know everything you need to know coming into a leadership role. Unquestionably, you should remain open to new concepts, new language, new metaphors, and new ways of accomplishing the work that needs to be done; these ways of thinking can shape the insights and behaviors of leaders in very powerful ways.

Recognize that years as a faculty or staff member with technical or disciplinary expertise may impede one's ability to learn across disciplines, units, or systems. As Epstein (2019) advises, "The challenge we all face is how to maintain the benefits of breadth, diverse experience, [and] interdisciplinary thinking . . . in a world that increasingly incentivizes, even demands, hyperspecialization" (p. 13). He advocates for the development of "habits of mind that allow [people] to dance across disciplines" (p. 49), and there is no doubt that such habits can guide leaders in navigating the many cross pressures that exist within higher education institutions. Furthermore, as a leader, it is useful to commit oneself to reflective practice and working to understand and derive satisfaction from responding to the multiple and challenges and opportunities that inevitably arise.

In the pages ahead, we will further examine the idea of leadership, exploring the connections between leadership and communication, and proposing a variety of models, lenses, and ways of thinking about social influence—all of which are useful tools when pursuing careers and experiences that require careful coordination, collaboration, and engagement.

For Further Consideration

1. Shift in focus
   Identify an issue that might arise within your unit, department, or institution that demonstrates the conflicting expectations, needs, or perspectives of internal or external stakeholder groups. In what ways would this issue challenge you as you shift your perspective from that of a faculty/staff member to that of a leader? Identify the strategies you might pursue in balancing the needs of internal and external stakeholders in responding to this issue. Which concepts from this chapter are most useful as you think through your response?

2. Faculty member salary request

   As a new leader, you are approached by a faculty member who asks for a salary increase to offset an offer from another institution. You learn that this same faculty member received an offer from another institution the previous year, and your predecessor made a counteroffer to retain the individual. You check with the administration and learn that it is within your prerogative to make a counteroffer again this year, if desired, in order to retain the person. What do you do? What issues are at stake? How might you go about seeking information and advice that will be helpful in your decision-making?

3. Blogging dean case study

   As a faculty member in your institution's School of Health and Medical Sciences, you have developed a number of personal concerns about the growth of online education within the School of Public Health, a school that offers an array of online and hybrid courses, along with two fully online degrees. Your personal philosophy of education leads you to place great value on the interpersonal interactions with your undergraduate and graduate students—and you believe that online education mechanisms compromise the mutual learning that takes place inside of the physical classroom. After years of notable accomplishments as a public health teacher-scholar, you apply for and receive the position of dean of the School of Public Health. One of your goals in the new role is to openly communicate with your internal and external stakeholders through a monthly blog. You decide to launch your blog with a candid post on your concerns about virtual education in undergraduate and graduate health and medical programs.

   • What are the benefits of writing a blog on this topic—for you or your institution?
   • What are the likely upsides and downsides of your decision?
   • What type of reaction might a blog on this topic solicit from the faculty, students, and alumni of your school?
   • Might there be a better format for sharing your concerns on this subject with your internal and external stakeholders?
   • How does this example capture the different responsibilities and expectations in play as one makes the transition from the role of faculty member to dean—from an individual pilot to an air traffic controller?

PART TWO

LEADERSHIP CONCEPTS AND COMPETENCIES

8

WHAT IS LEADERSHIP?

Making Sense of Complexity and Contradiction

In This Chapter

- Why is it important to think about the nature of leadership?
- Why is there such a diverse array of views about leadership theory and practice?
- What makes leadership effective or successful?
- What are the major concepts, approaches, and theories of leadership?
- How does leadership theory provide a useful foundation for leadership practice?

Leadership is widely discussed and studied, and the term is used with increasing frequency in settings ranging from business and politics to sports, education, and religion. For all of the interest that exists in the topic, there is considerable ambiguity over how to conceptualize and define leadership and substantial difference of opinion as to what constitutes effective leadership practice. Texts, news articles, professional papers, and podcasts abound that address the subject, presenting a myriad of strategies presumed to be relevant for effective leadership, many of which capture the accomplishments—and, more often, the perceived failures—of contemporary leaders. Clearly, the diverse theories, approaches, models, and guides that offer practical advice are expansive—and expanding. This chapter provides an overview of core leadership concepts that are central to the study and practice of leadership, particularly in higher education settings.

Competing Perspectives on Leadership

Given the popularity of the term *leadership*, it is not surprising that there are many folk theories related to the topic. On the one hand, these signal the importance attached to understanding leadership, yet they also reveal and contribute to what are often overly simplistic theories of leadership dynamics and practices. One such notion is the belief that some individuals are natural leaders while others are not. This view is sometimes accompanied by the presumption that leadership traits are an inherent part of an individual's personality and less the product of experiences; therefore, efforts to become more adept as a leader are not likely to be of much value. While this idea was quite common in early theoretical conceptions, the prevailing view is that a person's natural leadership capacities are honed through experience and that any of us can acquire enhanced leadership capability if we dedicate ourselves to that goal (Northouse, 2019; Parks, 2005; Velsor et al., 2010).

Another common notion is that to be influential, one must be outgoing and highly verbal. There are certainly instances where this style is associated with those in successful leadership positions, and it is not difficult to see how these skills can be helpful in many settings. Being skilled at selective communicative engagement, especially careful decision-making about with whom and when to assert one's views, can be a critical leadership quality in a range of circumstances. However, there are also situations where these behaviors are associated with a tendency to be overpowering and domineering, thereby causing a backlash and increasing resistance to intended outcomes and, over time, diminishing the respect and influence the leader may enjoy.

It is also commonly believed that those with advanced degrees are inevitably more effective leaders than those with less formal education. While intellectual capability associated with educational attainment certainly can contribute to a person's knowledge and analytical skills, possessing these capabilities provides little assurance of one's ability to apply them effectively in a manner that leads to effective leadership. Also, in many situations, technical expertise and advanced education may actually impede the ability to engage successfully with others—particularly with those who lack a similar background or set of capabilities.

The term *leadership* is often associated with formal positions or titles, and we often assume that those who occupy these roles represent the essence of what leadership means. While this way of thinking is certainly familiar and understandable, informal roles also afford excellent opportunities for leadership influence, as discussed in chapter 5.

Another concept that provokes opinions and debate is the question of whether there is one single constellation of leadership knowledge and skills that, if possessed and applied, will lead to consistently positive outcomes across a broad range of situations, sectors, and cultures. We examine this topic at greater length in chapter 9, but suffice it to say here that some universal leadership capabilities are important across multiple settings. There also exist situation- and context-specific knowledge and skill sets that can be vital to producing desired outcomes, such that there is no simple or single profile of *the* successful leadership approach. Perhaps the greatest challenge is to know which cross-cutting capabilities are most essential and which setting- and position-specific knowledge and skills are critical—and how to determine and apply the appropriate blend when engaged in formal and informal leadership endeavors.

Defining Effective Leadership

One additional issue deserves mention. Frequently there occurs a blurring of the distinction between good or effective leadership practices, on the one hand, and good outcomes on the other. Clearly, an individual can exercise what can be considered effective and successful leadership, even when the outcomes of those efforts may be negative or undesirable, either by intention or default. There is no shortage of historical or contemporary examples of situations where a leader's purposes seemed questionable to many, but their effectiveness in pursuing these purposes was quite evident.

Aside from the ethical issues that these situations raise, when the goal is to learn about leadership, it is important to distinguish between how we value a leader's intentions, strategies, and practices and how we assess one's effectiveness in achieving particular outcomes. It seems clear that we can often learn a great deal about leadership from those who are successful in achieving particular purposes—regardless of how we might feel about the value or appropriateness of particular outcomes or their motives. By the same token, much can be learned from those whose aims we view as worthy and desirable but whose efforts to achieve these ends are not successful.

What Makes a Great Leader?

Traditional approaches to leadership tend to focus on personal traits or attributes that are presumed to be characteristic of successful leaders, often including confidence and extroversion. Libraries and bookstores, however, are filled with the biographies and narratives of individuals—born into poverty, exhibiting an introverted personality and, by most formal measures, powerless—who have gone on to excel as leaders. Conversely, many individuals who seem to excel as leaders based on their credentials, personal style, attitude, and position in the organization may ultimately fail as leaders. In some instances, a particular critical incident and highly visible leadership moment may create a leadership impression that becomes emblematic of an individual leader's legacy. What then are the necessary qualities for a great leader? Various scholars have addressed the question. One prominent author, Warren Bennis (2007), for example, offers the perspective that great leaders

- create a sense of mission,
- motivate others to join them on that mission,
- create an adaptive social architecture for their followers,
- generate trust and optimism,
- develop other leaders, and
- get results.

This focus on social influence and effective engagement with others is reflected in other definitions of leadership, such as Northouse's (2019) view of leadership as "a process whereby an individual influences a group of individuals to achieve a common goal" (p. 5). For Northouse, leadership involves influence, centers on leader-follower interactions, occurs within the context of groups, and addresses a common or mutual purpose. Many others, including Arnett et al. (2018), Fairhurst and Sarr (1996), Johnson and Hackman (2018), Middlebrooks et al. (2020), Ruben and Gigliotti (2019b), and Witherspoon (1997), present perspectives on leadership that depend on social influence and effective communication. The many writings on effective leadership tend to posit nuanced and slightly different angles on the topic, such as the following. Leadership is said to consist of the following:

- attracting people (Maxwell, 1999)
- building community (DePree, 1999)
- creating and sustaining culture (Schein, 1999)
- change management (Kanter, 1983)
- pursuing mutually beneficial purposes (Johnson & Hackman, 2018)
- influencing individual or group behavior (DuBrin, 2004; Hersey, 1984)
- problem-solving (Luke, 1998)
- vision plus action (Useem, 1998)
- vision plus strategy (Ruben, 2006)

Thus, the definition of effective leadership varies in some ways based on the perspectives of the authors addressing such matters and also the perspectives of those who are impacted directly and indirectly by the efforts of leaders in one's organization.

Dichotomies: The Yin and Yang of Leadership

As the title of this chapter suggests, the literature on leadership is voluminous and diverse and includes many often complementary but sometimes
contradictory views. The complexity and contradiction are particularly
apparent when one considers various dichotomies represented in discussions
of leadership, such as the following:

- management versus leadership
- leadership versus followership
- science versus art
- theory versus practice
- transparent versus opaque
- authentic versus calculating
- planning versus execution
- servant versus master
- incremental versus strategic
- great influence versus influence often overstated
- formal versus informal leadership
- directing versus role modeling
- transactional versus transformational
- leadership as decision-making versus leadership as process facilitation
- context specific versus context general

Three of these dichotomies, to be explored further, are particularly common
and inform the ways in which leadership is both studied and practiced: lead-
ership/management, leadership/followership, and leadership as science/lead-
ership as art.

The Leadership/Management Dichotomy

Perhaps the most familiar of these distinctions is between *management* and
leadership. Leadership is generally described in terms of creating a vision
that mobilizes followers and produces change, whereas management is
typically characterized as maintaining order and consistency through the
enactment of systematic procedures and routines (Bennis & Nanus, 1985;
Kotter, 2012; Rost, 1993; Zaleznik, 1992). Consistent with this distinction, one often hears management described as "keeping the trains running
on time," while leadership is about "deciding where the trains should go."
This dichotomy highlights significant differences in roles and responsibilities; however, such distinctions between leadership and management tend
to set off and privilege leadership as the more glamorous and enviable role

in a way that positions attention to detail and routine work as less significant for effective leadership.

In practice, this is often a dysfunctional dichotomy, and a closer look at the work of managers or leaders often reveals a blurring and overlap of responsibility. Whether one thinks in terms of successful efforts in planning, change, team-building, or contending with an organizational crisis, for example, leaders engage in a variety of management responsibilities of a more routine and granular nature. Conversely, effective management of such endeavors also requires individuals to energize, mobilize, and engage followers to pursue shared purposes. The critical point here is that drawing this distinction generally provides little guidance as to the nature of leadership or management, or the practices necessary for either one, given that ideally an individual described with either label is called on to apply a blend of the capabilities associated with both terms in order to be successful.

The Leadership/Followership Dichotomy

A second dichotomy, leader versus follower, is also common in the leadership literature and in professional practice. Much of the literature presents a clear distinction between *leaders*—those who exercise power (e.g., make critical decisions, supervise, influence, create vision, direct activities, manage resources, etc.) and *followers*—those who are led (e.g., subordinates who carry out the directions of leaders, receive guidance and supervision, report to leaders, etc.). This delineation has value in some respects. For example, individuals in designated leadership roles are more often responsible for initiating direction and creating communication linkages and are likely to be held accountable and recognized for the collective accomplishments of a group, team, or organization. However, the dichotomy oversimplifies the boundaries between these roles, and in practice, the activities of leaders and followers are fluid and overlapping.

Paralleling the oversimplified distinctions between leaders and managers discussed previously, in practice, leaders often follow, and followers often lead. In fact, in the ongoing dynamics of group and organizational life, it may be quite difficult to discern who is leading and who is following at any moment in time, and the roles are dynamic, fluid, and interdependent. Recent scholarship goes so far as to suggest that leadership itself is coconstructed through interactions between leaders and followers via communication (Barge & Fairhurst, 2008; Ruben & Gigliotti, 2019b; Smircich & Morgan, 1982; Witherspoon, 1997). The simple test of the concept of the interdependency of leaders and followers becomes evident when one recognizes that unless there are people who follow, the concept of leader has little or no value (Platow et al., 2015; Ruben & Gigliotti, 2019b).

The Science/Leadership as Art Dichotomy

A third common but oversimplified dichotomy is apparent in discussions of whether leadership is a science or a form of art. Viewed from a scientific perspective, one can identify any number of generalizable theories and concepts that are useful in informing our understanding of leadership, as the forthcoming review provided in this chapter illustrates. However, it can also be argued that the practice of leadership is ultimately an art (Grint, 2001). This way of thinking points to the personalized, subjective, and creative actions of leaders, all of which are reflective of individual strengths, weaknesses, and idiosyncrasies.

As with the dichotomies discussed previously, a richer understanding of leadership becomes possible by recognizing the limitations of dichotomous thinking and embracing instead the notion that leadership lies at the intersection of science and art—and benefits from the perspectives of both. Scientific and scholarly theories can be very helpful in informing our understanding of the nature and dynamics of leadership, and in familiarizing us with successful leadership outcomes in various settings, but in practice, every would-be leader must ultimately personalize, enact, and apply these theories in their own way—and that translational process often unfolds as more of a subjective art than a prescriptive science.

Multiple Approaches to Leadership

As is apparent from the foregoing discussion, there are many ways of thinking about leadership. One explanation for this diversity relates to the fact that there are personal, professional, and scholarly perspectives on leadership. Definitions and concepts emerge from all three, including personal/native theory (e.g., autobiographies and biographies of famous leaders), professional theory (e.g., current practices/policies and case reports of leadership in an applied context), and scholarly theory (e.g., qualitative and quantitative research studies that are descriptive, explanatory, and predictive).

The scholarly leadership literature is both expansive and fluid, and there is no shortage of theoretical perspectives available for individuals seeking to make sense of, explain, and better understand the complexity of leadership behavior. Some of the more classical theories focus on traits, skills, styles, and the particular leadership situation. Building on these theories, scholars have also broadened their lenses to explore the deeply connected relationship between leaders and followers, such as contingency, path–goal, and leader–member exchange theories. Additional perspectives on leadership include contemporary views of transformational leadership, authentic leadership, servant leadership, and team leadership. Finally, as mentioned briefly later and noted in chapters 9 and 10, competency and communication approaches to leadership have had an influence on the view of leadership that is presented in this book. Specifically, competency approaches to leadership tend to emphasize the importance of both leadership knowledge and skill, and the ability to apply these with strategy, flexibility, and selectivity to pursue specific goals and to address personal and situational challenges and opportunities. Communication approaches to leadership explore the inseparability of communication and leadership theory and how this connection enhances both domains through a focus on the negotiation of meaning and the role of framing in social influence.

The following section provides a cursory overview of major classical and contemporary leadership theories based primarily on the extensive work by Peter Northouse (2019) and a number of the original scholars of these theories. For each section, we offer a summary that includes an overview of key concepts advanced by the theory and a brief discussion of key strengths and criticisms associated with each perspective.[1] Each section concludes with a brief explanation of the linkage to the work of higher education leadership—applications that showcase ways of using the theories to inform leadership practice in academic contexts.

Trait Approach

The trait approach to leadership captures the thinking of many of the early classical theories, including the great man and so-called trait theories. From this perspective, leaders are viewed as possessing innate leadership qualities that differentiate them from nonleaders, including qualities such as intelligence, self-confidence, determination, integrity, and sociability (Northouse, 2019). Historically, this approach has been appealing because of its simplicity and the substantial body of research that it has generated. The perspective implies that specific traits can be measured and matched to specific jobs. A major weakness of this approach is its assumption that only individuals with particular fixed traits can be effective leaders, and despite extensive research, an exclusive list of traits that would distinguish leaders from nonleaders has not been identified.

The literature has tended to move away from the idea that certain individuals possess personality traits that make them effective leaders, while others lack this potential. That said, various authors continue to point to research that suggests certain traits are associated with leadership effectiveness. In a study on leadership in corporations compared to higher education, for example, the executive search firm Witt/Kieffer (2013) found that some traits were common to leaders in both groups, while others were more likely to be present in one than the other. The traits that were more prevalent among higher education leaders were initiative, tact, creativity, and self-expression.

Skills Approach

The skills approach to understanding leadership reflects a shift in focus from innate and generally fixed traits to individual capabilities that are cultivated and developed over time (Northouse, 2019). Various taxonomies have been advanced, including the three-skill approach, which highlights technical, human, and conceptual skills required for effective leadership (Katz, 1955). Within the context of higher education, leaders must develop the technical, human, and conceptual skills needed to lead these complex organizations effectively. To illustrate, this approach to leadership would focus on the cultivation of particular capabilities—in public speaking, strategic planning, or critical thinking, for example—that would be important to successful leadership within a program, department, or institution.

This leader-centered model portrays leadership skills as being accessible to all and suggests that anyone can learn them. A key limitation of this approach, however, is its lack of predictive value. In particular, this approach fails to explain how variations in skills affect overall leadership performance or effectiveness.

Style Approach

A style approach to leadership focuses on common leadership behaviors in a variety of contexts. Unlike the previous two approaches to leadership, a style approach considers the needs of subordinates in determining one's leadership effectiveness (Northouse, 2019). Seminal studies conducted at The Ohio State University and the University of Michigan point to various styles that leaders may typically exemplify, distinguishing task-oriented behaviors from more relationship-oriented behaviors. Blake and McCanse's (1991) leadership grid (formerly Blake and Mouton's managerial grid) is one of many tools available for leaders to use to self-assess, change, and improve one's dominant leadership style.

A benefit of this approach is its emphasis on leadership behavior in a broad range of situations and contexts. As with the skills approach, however, no consistent link exists between task and relationship behaviors and outcomes, and thus the approach is not particularly helpful in identifying an ideal leadership style. Within the context of higher education, the traditions of shared governance seem to privilege democratic approaches to leadership in these contexts. As Lewin et al. (1939) found in their seminal research, followers exhibit more commitment and cohesiveness under democratic leaders, but one might also think of situations in higher education that demand a more authoritarian leadership style, such as times of crisis when immediate action becomes necessary.

Situational Approach

One explanation for why other approaches have not been successful in identifying a single "best" leadership style relates to the dynamic and evolving setting in which leadership occurs. Taking account of this fluid context, the situational approach, based on research by Hersey and Blanchard (1969), suggests that the traits needed for effective leadership vary depending on the circumstances. Different situations call for different approaches to leadership, including, for example, directing, coaching, supporting, and delegating. According to this perspective, to be successful, leaders must adapt their style to adequately meet the demands of the situation (Northouse, 2019). This approach is intuitive and prescriptive, yet it lacks a strong body of supportive empirical research.

The situational approach calls attention to the need for leaders to be able to demonstrate an awareness of the nature of the context in which they are leading. As suggested previously, colleges and universities experiencing a crisis require a different approach to leadership from that needed during times of stability and tranquility. More generally, quite different leadership capabilities may be required when dramatic change is deemed necessary within a program, department, or institution compared to a time in that same organization once major changes have been instituted when a calm and reinforcing approach to leadership is needed.

Contingency Theory

Building from the situational approach, contingency theory focuses on the match between a leader's style and the context in which that person is leading (Northouse, 2019). Contingency theory identifies specific styles of leadership that may be best or worst for a particular organizational context. For example, Fiedler's (1967) model offers a series of preferred leadership styles based on the leader–member relations, task structure, and position of power in a particular situation. This theory is supported by empirical research and allows for predictions to be made whereby it is possible to determine the probability of success.

Through environmental scanning strategies, leaders in higher education can use this framework to develop a more sophisticated understanding of the situation and to adapt one's behaviors accordingly. This theory suggests—as noted in previous discussion—that behaviors and competencies required for effective performance as a faculty or staff member are often not the same as those necessary for effective leadership. Contingency theory focuses attention on the match (or mismatch) between style and context and points to potential misalignments that might be expected when a faculty or staff member is promoted to a position with leadership responsibilities. A key criticism of this theory, however, is that it is cumbersome to apply in real-world settings. Moreover, it does not explain why certain styles are more effective in some situations than others.

Path-Goal Theory

Path-goal theory seeks to explain the ways in which a leader motivates followers to accomplish desired goals. Based on this approach, subordinates will be motivated if they think they are capable of performing the work, if they believe efforts will result in a specific outcome, and if they trust that the payoffs for doing the work are worthwhile. Leaders can motivate followers by clearing the path to the goal (Northouse, 2019). This theory deals directly with motivation in a way that other theories do not. Furthermore, by exploring the relationship between style and goal, this perspective instructs leaders regarding ways of choosing a particular style based on both the demands of the task and the goals of the subordinate.

Path-goal theory is often criticized for being overly complex and for lacking conclusive supportive research. Additionally, this approach treats leadership as a one-way event and fails to fully recognize the significance of the abilities of followers. That said, a benefit of this approach is that it allows for consideration of the ways in which academic and administrative leaders motivate others to accomplish specific tasks for the overall benefit of the institution by clearing the path for others to succeed. For example, how might a college or university leader remove obstacles that obstruct innovative thinking? As the competition for resources continues to increase, in what ways can leaders in higher education encourage others to think creatively about the work they do in order to maximize institutional resources, collaborate across units, or seek new avenues for external funding sources? The path-goal perspective focuses attention on these dimensions of leadership.

Leader–Member Exchange Theory

Leader–member exchange theory regards leadership as a process, paying particular attention to the interaction between leaders and followers.

According to Graen and Uhl-Bien (1995), the quality of leader–member exchange is related to positive outcomes for leaders, followers, groups, and the organization in general. One classification to emerge from this theory is the distinction between in-group and out-group leader–member relationships, whereby managers sort team members (often unintentionally) into one of these two groups (Northouse, 2019). In-group members maintain the trust of the leader and often receive challenging and meaningful work assignments, unlike the out-group members who have limited access to the leader and are often restricted to less challenging work responsibilities. Leader–member exchange theory focuses on the ways in which leaders use some subordinates more effectively than others to accomplish goals. The leader–member relationship is the focal point of this approach, yet some suggest that this model gives insufficient attention to the role of subordinates. Furthermore, the theory does not adequately explain how leaders might create high-quality exchanges with followers.

This theory does lend itself to an exploration of higher education leadership. Much of the work undertaken in colleges and universities is accomplished through a committee structure. The leader–member exchange theory allows us to consider the ways that leaders select, organize, motivate, recognize, and reward the members of the committees. Committee members too often receive little direction, support, or recognition for the important work they do, and the quality of leader–member interactions has the potential to influence the work of current and future committees. Furthermore, this theory may allow for a deeper understanding of the in-group and out-group relationships developed within the committee structure and more generally within programs, departments, and schools.

Transformational Leadership

A more contemporary approach, transformational leadership focuses on the ability of leaders to create change in the individuals and organizations they lead. A concern with the collective good is central to this leadership approach (Northouse, 2019). As described in the framework, transformational leaders demonstrate an exceptional influence that moves followers to accomplish more than would normally be expected. Four factors of transformational leadership include idealized influence, inspirational motivation, intellectual stimulation, and individualized consideration (Bass & Avolio, 1994).

This theory is intuitively appealing because it is possible to identify a number of noted leaders who embody this approach. It also provides an expansive view of leadership that has utility across a variety of situations. Despite the wealth of research on this approach, it has been criticized for its breadth and a lack conceptual clarity. Furthermore, by focusing so heavily on individual leaders and their impact, some see the approach as elitist and unduly marginalizing of the role of followers. With the emphasis on the leader's vision that is fundamental to this approach, questions often arise about who determines the ultimate value of this vision—in particular, which followers? There is often a widely shared admiration for individuals who exhibit the qualities of transformational leadership, particularly those who have the unique ability to envision and inspire individuals and groups to move in new, bold directions. But these capacities may not be accompanied by the interest and skills needed to manage the more routine and less glamorous aspects of academic life. Frequently, aspects of these "management" skills are critical to following through on a vision, and to successful implementation, as discussed earlier in the discussion of the leadership/management dichotomy. This is a potentially important concern whether the initiative under consideration is a new degree program, a new school, or a new service for users.

Servant Leadership

According to Robert Greenleaf (1977), who coined the term, *servant leadership* "begins with the natural feeling that one wants to serve, to serve first. Then conscious choice brings one to aspire to lead" (p. 13). This approach to leadership suggests that servant leaders are those who place the good of followers ahead of their own self-interest. Servant leadership extends beyond the act of doing and reflects a specific way of being (Gigliotti & Dwyer, 2016; Sendjaya & Sarros, 2002). One model of servant leadership outlines a series of antecedent conditions, behaviors, and outcomes associated with this other-oriented approach to leadership (Liden et al., 2008).

Servant leadership is unique in making altruism the central component of the leadership process, and it presents a provocative, and perhaps even counterintuitive, view of power and influence (Northouse, 2019). Some criticisms of this approach include the lack of a consistent theoretical framework, the contradictions between principles of servant leadership and other traditional concepts of leadership, and the perceived moralistic tone of the approach.

One of the tensions related to the implementation of servant leadership lies in the ways that leaders in academic settings balance individual, interpersonal, group, and organizational commitments. Specifically, a leader who privileges service to the university above all other values appears to ideally exemplify the values of servant leadership. However, in any number of instances, the goals of service to the institution may conflict with commitments to one's colleagues, administrators, other stakeholders, and to one's own interests. One example might be the challenges that department chairs face when preparing the academic course schedule. How should they balance and prioritize the needs and expectations of the students, other faculty members, the dean, the institution, and oneself, and how should they respond when conflict arises from these competing sources?

Authentic Leadership

Authentic leadership calls for an approach to leadership "that is consistent with our personality and character" (George, 2003, p. 13). Authentic leadership consists of four components: self-awareness, internalized moral perspective, balanced processing, and transparency in relationships. Another approach to authentic leadership focuses on purpose, values, relationships, self-discipline, and heart (George, 2003). Similar to servant leadership, authentic leadership calls for leaders to do what is "right" and "good" for both followers and society. Being true to one's self and forthright with others is fundamental to this approach. Trustworthiness is also understood to be critical for effective leadership. Some of the other concepts of authentic leadership, including the moral component, are not fully substantiated. Moreover, these determinations necessarily rely on personal and subjective judgments, and the specific connections between authentic leadership and positive organizational outcomes remain unclear (Northouse, 2019).

This perspective emphasizes the idea that "knowing thyself" and behaving in a way that is consistent with one's true self is a positive aspect of social influence. Those who aspire to be authentic leaders need to have a clear sense of who they are, and their behaviors need to reflect this self-perception. Yet in her book on the authenticity paradox, Herminia Ibarra (2015) casts authenticity in a different light. She notes that all of us have multiple identities and approaches, potentially calling into question the existence of one, true authentic self. Being preoccupied with a single authentic identity as a leader can create an inflexibility and "can be a recipe for staying stuck in the past" (p. 59). Fear of acting in an inauthentic manner can also serve as an "excuse for sticking with what's comfortable" (p. 54). Ibarra points to the value of leaders recognizing and experimenting with their multiple identities and different leadership styles and behaviors. Although some may label these actions inauthentic, Ibarra considers this an adaptive approach to creating opportunities for learning and leadership development. In the course of a leader's daily responsibilities, a number of situations present themselves where candor, disclosure, and transparency are appropriate and highly valued; but there may be circumstances involving human resource or financial matters, for example, where one is obligated to maintain confidentiality and where the commitment to transparency and authenticity can present challenges for all involved.

Team Leadership

A team leadership model explores the ways in which interdependent members of groups coordinate activities and accomplish common goals (Northouse, 2019). The leader of the team is considered responsible for the effectiveness of the group, which demands behavioral flexibility whereby a leader matches their behavior to the complexity of a particular situation. According to McGrath (1962), team leaders play a critical role in diagnosing group deficiencies, taking remedial action, forecasting environmental changes, and preventing deleterious outcomes. As an increasing amount of work is accomplished in teams, this approach strikes a relevant chord for leadership scholars and practitioners. Furthermore, it addresses the dynamic and evolving roles of leader and follower in a team setting. A criticism of this model is that the list of skills needed for effective team leadership is somewhat limited and fails to fully address the specific problems associated with team dynamics.

Teams can be a very important mechanism for sharing expertise, and the reliance on teams and committees to engage in unit-based and interdepartmental activities is an important dimension of the work of higher education. Team leadership supports concepts of engagement and collective problem-solving. Taking full advantage of these attributes, however, often requires considerable time and effort on the part of leaders in order for teams to develop to a point where they function effectively.

Communication and Social Influence Theory

Communication has long been recognized as an important component of leadership theory and practice. Traditionally, it has been viewed as a useful tool available to leaders to promote ideas, attract support, motivate action, and advance informative and persuasive efforts of all kinds. In the context of leadership, interest in the communication process is focused on message sources, messages, dissemination channels, and the ways these work together to achieve intended outcomes (Ruben & Gigliotti, 2019b; Ruben & Stewart, 2020). As useful as this perspective is, contemporary communication theory views the process as more than simply a strategic message-sending tool for leaders. In this broader view, communication provides a lens through which to understand the dynamics of leadership and social influence. This more generic view of the process, which will be discussed in detail in chapter 10, describes communication as the process through which relationships, groups, and organizations are created, maintained, and changed (Fairhurst & Putnam, 2004; Ruben & Stewart, 2020; Weick, 1995). Leadership, in turn, is recognized as playing an important role in each of these endeavors.

Conceiving of leadership in terms of social influence leads to the identification of four mechanisms through which leaders can achieve impact: (a) messaging, (b) strategy, (c) processes, and (d) structures (Ruben & Gigliotti, 2019b). First, and most obvious, *messaging* includes verbal and nonverbal messages created and disseminated through interpersonal, social, organizational, and public media. The formulation and implementation of *strategy* is a second potential source of influence for leaders. A third involves the design or modification of *processes* within their organizations, and the fourth consists of the design or redesign of *structures* to support social influence efforts.

In addition to message creation and dissemination, specific leadership processes, strategies, and structures may be used to create or advance new or redefined visions, plans, goals, or policies. Each can be a mechanism for influence within a team, group, or organization and may ultimately contribute to a leadership agenda. For example, a leader's decisions and actions relative to processes and structures may be used to reinforce or reshape work roles and responsibilities, the nature of reporting relationships, or the locus of control for decision-making, among other possible influences. All four actions have the potential to foster, facilitate, encourage, or discourage particular outcomes.

While each of these mechanisms offers various possibilities for leadership impact, a broadened understanding of communication and social influence also comes with a caution about ascribing too much power to the actions of leaders. The impact of what an individual leader says or does, along with the strategies, processes, and structures they put in place, always depend on the communicative interplay among leaders, followers, and context and are a consequence of the way actions are initiated, interpreted, and acted on. As we noted earlier, leadership outcomes are defined as much by followers as they are by leaders, and context and history also matter (Ruben & Gigliotti, 2016, 2017, 2019b). While offering a range of ideas about how leaders can shape a situation, communication theory also provides a reminder that, ultimately, it is the attention and buy-in from followers that empowers an individual to serve as an agent of social influence.

Strengths of this perspective include highlighting theoretical connections between communication and leadership and placing both concepts in the broader context of social influence. This approach also promotes creative thinking about actions and behaviors that may be undertaken by leaders to support particular priorities. While advancing understanding of leadership and organizational dynamics, a limitation of this approach is that it is somewhat abstract and does not translate into simple prescriptions regarding how leaders should act or what they should do or say to be effective in particular settings or circumstances.

Macro and Integrative Theories

As is apparent from the foregoing review, approaches to leadership have evolved considerably over the years, from those focused solely on the individual's inherent capabilities to theories that acknowledge the importance of developmental influences in the acquisition of leadership capabilities. In the evolution of leadership theories, an increasing emphasis has been placed on the choices leaders make and the importance of situation, timing, goals, followers, and the interactions between and among these factors in explaining leadership successes or failures.

While the boundaries between the various theories presented are overlapping, each tends to emphasize particular facets of leadership. As discussed, the classic literature focuses specifically on traits, skills, or styles. Contemporary theories seek to explore leadership more broadly, considering the individual leader's approach and the influence of followers and the context in which leadership occurs, such as highlighted in transformational, authentic, and servant leadership theories. As will be discussed further in the next chapters, the communication-oriented approach suggests that leadership and communication are inseparable phenomena, with a relationship that, when understood, provides useful messaging strategies, and also very useful insight into the nature of social influence and the role of leadership in that process. The competency approach, which builds on these approaches and focuses on the combined knowledge and skills that successful leaders may apply strategically in a variety of settings, will be discussed further in chapter 9,

The ongoing research on these theoretical perspectives is expansive, and the brief summaries offered are inherently limited and cursory. Each theoretical approach has strengths and weaknesses; each is a way of seeing and *not* seeing. By understanding and using a number of theoretical lenses, one may gain a more thorough understanding of leadership and the factors that are important to leadership outcomes in practice. As Johnson and Hackman (2018) suggest, "Sometimes the approaches overlap; other times they contradict one another. No single approach provides a universal explanation of leadership behavior, but each provides useful insights" (p. 75). For a more thorough summary of each theoretical perspective, see Northouse (2019) and Johnson and Hackman (2018).[2]

A Comprehensive Leadership Megamodel

As a way of making sense of the voluminous leadership literature, Hernandez et al. (2011) offer a comprehensive "megamodel" of the leadership system that integrates diverse theoretical perspectives. In their model, the authors locate a number of dominant leadership theories within the two-dimensional framework based on the mechanism and locus of leadership. This framework presents a useful structure for understanding the theoretical constructs and connections between the aforementioned leadership theories.

Their review of the literature leads to the development of a common language across theories—the loci of leadership (where leadership "comes from") and the mechanisms of leadership (how leadership is transmitted). Based on their findings, the authors identify five dominant loci, or sources, from which leadership is thought to arise according to various theories—including the leader, context, followers, collectives, and leader–follower dyads. These points of origin for leadership are not seen as positions on a fluid continuum; rather, they represent distinct and independent sources for leadership. The authors identify four common mechanisms of leadership—what they describe as the *means by which leadership is transmitted*—traits (personality characteristics), behaviors (actions), cognition (thoughts and sensemaking processes), and affect (emotions and moods). Similar to the loci, the mechanisms are not ordered in a continuum but rather stand alone as independent categories.

This comprehensive model provides an expansive and inclusive way to think about leadership, and it offers a common language for understanding and describing the complexities of leadership dynamics. As noted in the article,

> By way of analogy and for ease of use, the two dimensions can be compared to grammar: the locus of leadership is the subject of the sentence (that which acts) and the mechanism is the verb (the action). It follows that combining the two will result in a complete sentence such as "The leader behaves" or "The follower feels." To push the analogy further, a substantive analysis of leadership is not possible unless both dimensions are considered, and we posit that the loci and mechanisms of leadership can be used as fundamental building blocks to understand what constitutes leadership. A list of nouns and verbs, however, is of little use unless one combines them into a coherent story. Hence, while we started with a simple sentence employing only a noun and verb, we tell the story of leadership theory through a combination of multiple loci and mechanisms that we suggest form a more comprehensive leadership system. (Hernandez et al., 2011, pp. 1168–1169)

The locus-mechanism imagery captures the evolution and expansion of leadership theory from the "great man" perspective to a view of leadership that is interactional. This perspective also makes the point that context—for our purpose, a higher education context—can be an important factor in understanding leadership dynamics.

Despite the many contributions of this megamodel, a few limitations can be noted. Their comprehensive model focuses on purposeful or intentional leadership efforts, or both, and in so doing it overlooks or diminishes the relevance of informal, unintentional, or unplanned leadership processes. If leadership is understood to be about social influence, as we and a number of authors suggest, then it seems important to recognize that social influence is often an intended goal of leaders, but not always. For instance, an administrator's choice to respond to an email in a particular way clearly fits the traditional definition of an intentional leadership act. But a decision not to respond, whether an active choice or not, would also constitute a potential leadership act from our perspective. Whether such an action was a planned attempt at social influence, or an oversight, may matter very little to the outcome.

Second, the authors choose to talk about mechanisms for "transmitting" leadership. One might argue that *interaction* is a more appropriate concept for understanding the ways in which leadership is accomplished. The idea of transmission reflects a mechanistic view of the influence process—one that is associated with early views of the communication and influence process, but a perspective that has evolved significantly, as will be detailed in the next chapter. In more contemporary theories, communication is understood to be meaning centered rather than transmission centered. Moreover, influence outcomes are viewed to be coconstructed, resulting from interaction and collaboration.

As we explore in detail in subsequent chapters, the process and outcomes of social influence are defined as much by followers and their interpretations and responses as by leaders and their intentional choices. Moreover, as is apparent, the perspective on leadership presented here draws heavily on communication—both verbal and nonverbal behavior. In each of these respects, the framework and strategies in this view reflect a communication-centered understanding of leadership created in and through leader–follower relationships.

Conclusion

What is the value of being familiar with classic and contemporary concepts and theories of leadership for the current or aspiring higher education leader? How might this knowledge be useful in everyday leadership situations, such as recruitment and hiring, making and communicating decisions, dealing with interpersonal conflict or other sensitive matters, or evaluating one's own or others' performance as a leader? Quite often, the recruitment and hiring process for new leaders begins with identifying the desired academic or technical qualifications and credentials. Generally, the assumption is that these qualifications are the most critical attributes necessary for effective leadership. It can be argued, however—and this topic will be explored in greater depth later in the book—that an individual's leadership philosophy and approach are as important, and sometimes more important, to a leader's success. Each of the perspectives discussed in this chapter provide a particular way of thinking about what leadership is, and by implication what a leader does—or should do. Reviewing the concepts and approaches presented in this chapter offers a reminder of the range of ways of enacting leadership roles, the potential strengths and limitations of various approaches, and the potential match or mismatch of these approaches to particular leadership context and needs.

In the case of selecting and hiring a leader, for instance, attention to conceptualizing leadership provides an important complement to attention focused on disciplinary or technical needs. Each of the perspectives on leadership reviewed in this chapter can provide practical guidance for the recruitment, interviewing, selection, and retention process. When it comes to describing the capabilities desired in a director, chair, dean, or vice president, the trait approach points to quite different characteristics than does an authentic leadership theory. Similarly, distinctions between the skills or situational approach might well suggest a different line of questioning during the candidate interview process than would be implied by the transformational or servant approach.

Likewise, in many other typical leadership tasks—such as making and communicating decisions, dealing with interpersonal conflict, or deciding whether and how to evaluate the performance of leaders—there is likely considerable variation depending on the theory of leadership that guides one's thoughts and behavior. The approach suggested by the path-goal theory, for example, would likely be quite different from that implied by the authentic leader framework or that of the servant leader.

These theories are lenses—ways of seeing and thinking about the nature of leadership and the role and practices of leaders. The more we understand their underlying assumptions and can see their principles in action, the broader the array of insights and choices available to make sense of and address the full range of leadership challenges that arise.

For Further Consideration

1. Critical incidents in leadership

   Think back and identify an experience in higher education in which you were a participant or an observer that provided an example of outstanding or poor leadership. The situation could be one that was quite recent or in the distant past, one that occurred in your current organization or elsewhere.

   Describe the situation, taking care to change the names of individuals, institutions, departments, or other identifiers. As you consider this vignette, explore the following questions:

   • What made this a memorable and significant leadership example?
   • What leadership theories could be applied to further explore the dynamics represented within this situation?
   • What do you believe to be the reason for the leader's actions?
   • What were the interpersonal or organizational consequences of the leader's behavior?
   • What could and should have been done differently?
   • Can any general leadership principles be drawn from this scenario?

2. Case study analysis

   Choose two of the theories discussed in the chapter. Analyze the case study scenarios in this section through these two distinct theoretical perspectives. If theories are understood to be both a way of seeing and not seeing, what do each of these leadership theories allow us to see, and in what ways do they limit or restrict our vision in the selected case? What are the implications for leadership action based on each theory? What are possible positive and negative consequences from each course of action?

   • You have been asked to head a committee whose task is to identify, recruit, and interview candidates for the senior administrator role in a new department within your institution. Considering each leadership theory you have selected, what characteristics would be judged to be particularly important? Would the two theories point to the same or different criteria? What guidance might these theories offer in terms of how to describe the new position in job advertisements, the questions to ask of candidates, and ways to assess candidates who apply for the position?

- You are a department head and are called to a confidential meeting with the person to whom you report. At the meeting, you and a number of other leaders are told in confidence that a hiring freeze and institution-wide budget cut will be announced in 3 weeks. You are asked to keep this information in confidence. You have a search under way, and meetings are currently scheduled with the leadership team of your department this afternoon and a full department meeting the next day. What would the two leadership theories you selected advise you to do relative to sharing or acting on the information you have with colleagues? What are the probable consequences of those choices?
- You have a growing dissatisfaction with the work of a long-serving and highly regarded member of your administrative team. In your mind this person should be thinking about retirement. Your frustrations are building on a weekly basis as you note a growing number of errors and what seems like decreasing motivation. You are getting increasingly convinced of the need to do something to improve the situation. You have been keeping extensive notes on the problems, but you have not discussed your concerns or any of the particulars with the individual in question or with the person to whom you report. What are your options for dealing with the problem, and what are the potential benefits and liabilities of each option? What types of guidance are provided by the two leadership theories you selected?

Notes

1. The summary of theories was created by Kate Immordino and Ralph Gigliotti, based on the framework provided by Northouse (2019). The overview of theoretical perspectives, including the summary of strengths and critiques, reflects many of the central ideas from Northouse's work.

2. A number of other texts offer additional summaries of these seminal leadership theories, including, but not limited to, Gill (2012), Johnson and Hackman (2018), and Yukl (2012).

9

THE COMPETENCY APPROACH

Integrating Leadership Knowledge and Skill

In This Chapter

- What is the competency approach to leadership, and in what ways is it an appropriate approach for exploring leadership in higher education?
- What are the differences between the vertical and horizontal approaches to leadership competence?
- What are the critical competencies needed for effective leadership in colleges and universities?
- In what ways might an integrated competency framework be used to prepare leaders in higher education?

The term *competency* is an increasingly familiar one in the leadership literature. One useful definition of the term is offered by Marrelli et al. (2005), who explain that competence is "a measurable human capacity that is required for effective leadership" (p. 534). The term is generally understood to suggest that a competency has both a knowledge and a skill component. *Knowledge* refers to leaders' understanding of a concept. *Skill* refers to leaders' effectiveness in operationalizing the knowledge they possess and their strategic ability to effectively act on this information (Gigliotti, 2019; Ruben, 2012, 2019; Ruben & Gigliotti, 2019a; Ruben et al., 2021). Thus, theory and practice converge in conceptualizations of competencies, recognizing that understanding and proficiency in applying that understanding are both relevant. Leadership issues may arise because of the gap that often exists between these two facets of competency—between knowing and doing (Pfeffer & Sutton, 2000).

Competency-based approaches to leadership emphasize the ability of successful leaders to acquire a portfolio of knowledge and skills that they can apply strategically in a particular context or situation. Some leadership competencies are position specific, but many others are more general in their applicability. Position-specific skills that are important for effectiveness in particular sectors, disciplinary areas, and situations can be referred to as *vertical leadership competencies. Horizontal competencies* are cross-cutting or generic capabilities that have relevance and applicability that transcend various situations.

Many popular approaches to leadership in higher education are built around a focus on competencies, and this perspective holds great promise for the enhancement of leadership practice at all levels in colleges and universities (Gigliotti, 2019; Smith, 2007; Teniente-Matson, 2019; Wisniewski, 1999). As explained by Smith (2007), the competency approach "provides a valid and relevant context for understanding the knowledge, skills, abilities, and attributes necessary to effectively lead people and organizations" (p. 27).

The competency approach has the following attributes that make it particularly useful:

- integrates varying concepts and approaches to leadership
- focuses on factors over which leaders can exercise control
- accommodates connections between communication and leadership
- recognizes the need for leaders to exhibit an array of capabilities
- provides the basis for self-assessment and personal development
- presumes leadership abilities can be developed and learned
- can be applied to varying situations/sectors and at varying levels of generality
- offers a foundation for leadership development programming

These attributes offer a useful foundation for understanding and practicing effective leadership in higher education and also provide a helpful guide in leadership development efforts.

The Vertical and Horizontal Views of Competency

As noted earlier, the literature on the topic of competencies casts two distinct views (Ruben, 2012, 2018, 2019; Ruben & Fernandez, 2013; Ruben & Gigliotti, 2019a). What we refer to as the *vertical* view focuses on those leadership competencies that are specific to a sector, setting, context, work environment, or position. This view emphasizes the importance of context- and position-specific experience, knowledge, and skill as critical ingredients for effective leadership. The *horizontal* view highlights those general leadership competencies that are presumed to transcend work environments and positions—capabilities that are viewed as essential to outstanding leadership regardless of the sector or setting (Gigliotti, 2019; Ruben, 2012; Ruben & Gigliotti, 2019b; Ruben & Fernandez, 2013).

The Vertical View

In the context of higher education, the vertical approach begins with the assumption that a unique set of disciplinary, technical, and college-and university-specific competencies is needed for effective leadership. According to this view, outstanding leadership is provided by individuals who have superior technical, disciplinary, and job-specific knowledge and skill—a topic addressed in earlier sections of this book. This view plays out regularly in higher education. For example, when considering candidates for program director, department chair, dean, or provost, the outstanding teacher or scholar is a likely candidate for academic leadership based on the vertical view. In information technology (IT) units, the most technically knowledgeable individuals are regarded as particularly strong candidates for roles in leadership, just as those with the most expertise related to issues in student affairs are often considered prime candidates for the role of senior student affairs officer (SSAO). Figure 9.1 depicts the vertical approach in higher education leadership competencies.

An early example of the vertical approach was provided by Gilley et al. (1986), whose work identified the following competencies as essential for working effectively with college and university board members:

Figure 9.1. Vertical approach in higher education leadership competencies.

Effective leadership requires knowledge and skills specific to higher ed and to a particular discipline/ technical area and position.

This approach begins with the assumption that a unique set of competencies and specialized disciplinary or technical training is a defining characteristic of effective leadership in higher education.

- Exhibit dogged persistence in pursuit of goals.
- Keep antennae extended.
- Demonstrate a sixth sense about opportunities.
- Take unexpected actions.

Another higher education–specific approach to delineating competencies was developed through a collaborative effort between university presidents and vice presidents and former American Council on Education (ACE) fellows and the Texas A&M University Center for Leadership in Higher Education. In selecting specific core capabilities to address in their leadership program, Donathen and Hines (1998) identified the following competencies as being closely associated with effective senior academic leadership:

- communication
- decision-making
- use of systems
- professional ethics
- team development
- supervision
- planning
- teaching and counseling
- creativity and innovation

While some of these competencies may be viewed as applicable across a variety of roles, Donathen and Hines focused specifically on academic leadership in their study.

There have been several other more recent efforts to identify competencies associated with leadership effectiveness in higher education in general, and in particular college and university leadership roles, including competencies required for the roles of president (Dwyer, 2019), senior leadership (Agnew, 2019), chief business officer (Teniente-Matson, 2019), and student affairs professional (Smith, 2007; Wisniewski, 1999).

A vertical approach to leadership in higher education is appealing for many reasons. First, the perception that each position and each department possesses its own knowledge and skill requirements makes sense in a sector and within specialization areas that traditionally have viewed themselves as unique. It also aligns well with the siloed separation of college and university departments based on disciplinary, operational, or technical specialization. In addition, familiarity with one (often, one's own) area, along with the ability to focus in-depth in one area, makes the vertical approach a compelling topic for research. Credibility among peers and followers in colleges and universities requires relevant technical/disciplinary experience and knowledge—again, a reality that aligns well with a vertical orientation. Finally, the ease of access to studying leadership in a distinct area, along with the corresponding difficulties associated with studying leaders across disciplines and areas, adds to the appeal of this approach.

Despite these benefits, a number of limitations are associated with this perspective. Most notably, a vertical viewpoint fails to benefit from the extensive and potentially relevant leadership literature found in other fields and sectors. Furthermore, the vertical approach reflects a time when higher education was typified by the detached, ivory tower view of colleges and universities, as compared to the increasingly dominant marketplace model, which recognizes commonalities with other types of organizations and the importance of a broad range of leadership competencies. Additionally, recent efforts to recruit leaders from other sectors reflect an understanding that a focus on higher education–specific vertical leadership competencies may reproduce practices that have come under increasing scrutiny and criticism in recent years (Ruben & Gigliotti, 2017). Finally, a vertical approach may be criticized for failing to identify more generalized leadership knowledge and behaviors that are essential but not job, position, or sector specific.

The Horizontal View

The horizontal view, a generic approach to understanding higher education leadership competencies, is depicted in Figure 9.2. This perspective begins with the assumption that a general set of competencies is needed for effective leadership across a range of sectors, positions, and settings, of which higher education is but one example. Based on this view, effective college and university leadership requires generic knowledge and skills that transcend particular disciplines, technical areas, or positions. In this section, we describe four examples of horizontal studies that explore the diverse, nonsector-specific

Figure 9.2. The horizontal approach to higher education leadership competencies.

Effective leadership requires generic knowledge and skills that transcend particular disciplines/technical areas or positions.

This approach begins with the assumption that a general set of competencies is critical for effective leadership in any range of sectors, disciplinary/technical areas, or institutional settings or positions.

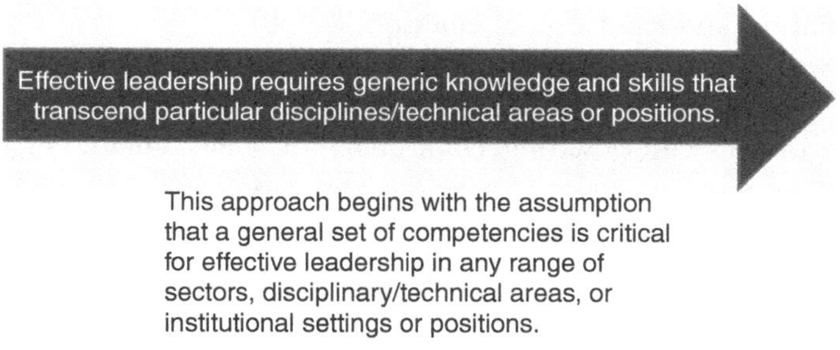

competencies needed for effective leadership. One can identify any number of additional leadership studies that reflect this approach.

As one example, in his work on the topic of leadership development, John Maxwell (1993) identifies 10 capabilities he regards as fundamental. These qualities—what we would describe as horizontal leadership competencies—are as follows:

1. Creating positive influence
2. Setting the right priorities
3. Modeling integrity
4. Creating positive change
5. Problem-solving
6. Having the right positive attitude
7. Developing people
8. Charting the vision
9. Practicing self-discipline
10. Developing staff

A second horizontal approach to leadership is provided in the ongoing work on emotional intelligence. Numerous scholars have contributed to current thinking about this topic, many building on Goleman's (1998) and Salovey and Mayer's (1990) work in this area. According to Goleman (1998), *emotional intelligence* is "the capacity for recognizing our own feelings and those of others, for motivating ourselves, and for managing emotions well in ourselves and in our relationships" (p. 317). Others have defined emotional intelligence as "the ability to perceive and express emotion, assimilate emotion in thought, understand and reason with emotion, and regulate emotion in the self and others" (Mayer et al., 2000, p. 396) and "the ability to purposively adapt, shape, and select environments through the use of emotionally relevant processes" (Gignac, 2010, p. 131). As Cherniss (2010) explains, success in work and life often depends on more than one's cognitive abilities; "it also depends on a number of personal qualities that involve the perception, understanding, and regulation of emotion" (p. 184).

These three definitions capture the reasons emotional intelligence aligns with the horizontal competency approach. In order to excel as a leader, regardless of the sector or setting, emotional intelligence theories suggest that one must demonstrate an understanding of self, other, and context in order to effectively manage and express emotion across a variety of organizational settings. Related to the process of social influence, Goleman (1998) describes emotional intelligence as "the *sine qua non* of leadership. Without it, a person can have the best training in the world, an incisive, analytical mind, and an endless supply of smart ideas, but [they] still won't make a great leader" (p. 5). (See Figure 9.3). Intellect alone does not predict effective leadership, which is an important point to consider as we think through the development of leaders in American higher education—a sector that includes some of the world's best thinkers and subject matter experts.

Much writing exists on the topic of emotional intelligence, and a comprehensive review of this literature is beyond the scope of this chapter. For our purposes, however, it seems useful to identify the four primary skills that constitute emotional intelligence: self-awareness, self-management, social awareness, and relationship management, as depicted in Figure 9.3 (Goleman, 2000). These four components each include a number of related competencies, as shown in Table 9.1. As is made clear by writings in the field, the characteristics of emotional intelligence represent a horizontal, or generic, approach to leadership competencies that transcend sectors, disciplines, professions, special areas, and departments (Cherniss & Roche, 2020).

Another approach to leadership and leadership development that reflects the horizontal perspective is the strengths-based approach introduced by Don Clifton and currently in use by Gallup (2021). This framework focuses on identifying and reinforcing a leader's assets rather than concentrating efforts on deficiencies that might be improved. Gallup's research notes that leaders who emphasize their strengths rather than liabilities tend to be more engaged and report a more satisfying quality of life. Based on the work of Donald Clifton, the framework identifies 34 cross-cutting competency themes,

Figure 9.3. Emotional intelligence: The Goleman model.

We each have developed certain emotional intelligence capabilities, and we can strengthen our competency in these areas through through persistence, refelctive practice, and feedback from colleagues or coaches.

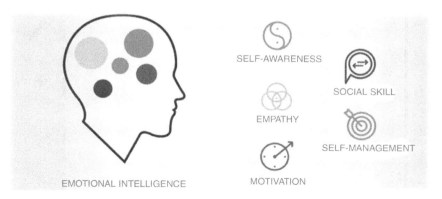

TABLE 9.1

Goleman's (2000) Emotional Intelligence Competencies

Four major skills make up emotional intelligence, with competencies in each quadrant:

- self-awareness
- self-management
- social awareness
- relationship management

	Self (Personal Competence)	*Other (Social Competence)*
Recognition	<ul><li>Self-awareness Social awareness</li><li>Emotional self-awareness</li><li>Accurate self-assessment</li><li>Self-confidence</li></ul>	<ul><li>Empathy</li><li>Service orientation</li><li>Organizational awareness</li></ul>
Regulation	**Self-Management**<ul><li>Emotional self-control</li><li>Trustworthiness</li><li>Conscientiousness</li><li>Adaptability</li><li>Achievement drive</li><li>Initiative</li></ul>	**Relationship Management**<ul><li>Developing others</li><li>Influence</li><li>Communication</li><li>Conflict management</li><li>Visionary leadership</li><li>Catalyzing change</li><li>Building bonds</li><li>Teamwork and collaboration</li></ul>

which are potential areas of greatest talent for a leader, and through a self-administered inventory, individuals are able to identify their unique profile relative to these competencies.

Broadly stated, the strength-based model suggests the following:

1. The most effective leaders have an intense, intentional focus on the positive, natural potential and tendencies of their mentor/mentee.
2. The most effective leaders know that their colleagues do not have to change who they are to be successful. Instead, they strive to help one another become better at being who they naturally are.
3. The most effective leaders spend more time studying success than failure.
4. The most effective leaders understand that focusing on strengths does not mean ignoring a person's weaknesses (Gallup, n.d.).

A fourth example of a horizontal approach is presented in Ruben's (2012, 2019, 2021a) leadership competency framework (see Figure 9.4). Based on a review and thematic analysis of approximately 100 academic and professional writings on the topic of leadership, Ruben created a competency framework and scorecard that identifies five thematic areas, or leadership competency clusters, each composed of a number of more specific competencies (see Figure 9.5). This framework incorporates the vertical and horizontal perspectives, reflecting the assumption that the knowledge and skill sets are complementary.

As indicated in Figure 9.4, one competency cluster designates the specialized, vertical view of leadership. Termed *disciplinary* competencies in

Figure 9.4. Leadership competencies scorecard (LSC 3.0): Major competency themes.

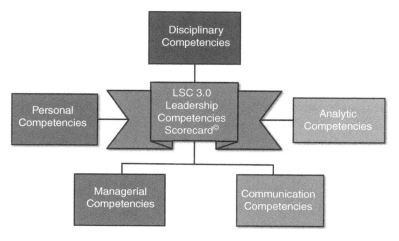

Figure 9.5. Specific competencies within each competency theme area.

Disciplinary	Personal	Analytic	Managerial	Communication
Education	Character, personal values, and ethics	Self-assessment and self-reflection	Planning, vision-setting, and strategy development	Credibility and trust
Experience	Cognitive ability and creativity	Problem-definition	Finance and law	Influence and persuasion
Technical and specialty expertise	Enthusiasm	Stakeholder analysis	Information/knowledge management and boundary spanning	Interpersonal relations and team-building
Knowledge of field	High standards	Systems, organizational, and situational analysis	Technological capability	Listening, attention, questioning, and learning
Knowledge of organization	Personal conviction and persistence	Analysis of technology to support leadership	Collaborative decision-making and engagement	Organizational, social, and public media and messaging
Familiarity with work	Self-discipline and self-confidence	Problem-solving	Mentoring and coaching	Diversity and intercultural relations
Professional development	Role modeling	Data analysis and interpretation	Change, risk, and crisis management	Facilitation, negotiation, and conflict resolution

LSC 3.0, this area refers to knowledge and skills related to the particular type of work, discipline, technical area, setting, or context. As noted earlier, in the section on the vertical view, these positional competencies include field-, discipline-, profession-, and sector-specific education, experience, and knowledge, as well as organizational knowledge, familiarity with the work, and professional involvement. Disciplinary and technical competencies are certainly helpful for leadership, but in and of themselves, they are unlikely to provide a sufficient foundation for those who aspire to become truly exceptional leaders.

The four additional thematic competency areas depicted in Figure 9.4 reflect the generic, horizontal view of leadership and include personal, managerial, communication, and analytic competencies.

As shown in Figure 9.5, *personal* competencies include standards, character, and the expression of values, including ethics, personal character, cognitive ability, creativity, enthusiasm, maintenance of high standards, personal conviction, persistence, self-discipline, self-confidence, and role modeling.

Managerial competencies are the administrative capabilities necessary for leadership in organizations of varying purpose, function, and size, including vision and strategy development, finance and law, information and knowledge management, and boundary spanning; use of appropriate information and communication technologies and strategies, collaborative decision-making and engagement, mentoring and coaching; and change, risk, and crisis management.

Communication competencies include the knowledge and skills necessary for effective interaction in interpersonal, group, organizational, and public settings. Among them are credibility and trust; influence and persuasion; interpersonal relations and team-building; listening and attention; question asking and learning; organizational, social, and public media and messaging; diversity and intercultural relations; and facilitation, negotiation, and conflict resolution.

Analytic competencies refer to thoughtful reflection on one's own and others' behaviors, careful consideration of the consequences of one's own leadership style and strategies, and alternative leadership options and approaches, including self-assessment and reflection; problem definition; stakeholder analysis; systems, organizational, and situational analysis; analysis of technology; problem-solving; and data analysis and interpretation.

The horizontal approach is appealing for several reasons. First, although sector- and discipline-specific knowledge and skills can be important, more general competencies are likely to distinguish truly exceptional leaders across contexts. Second, because general competencies are cross-cutting, a focus on these capabilities allows for the identification and development of leaders likely to be successful in any number of settings. Third, a horizontal approach allows leaders in higher education to benefit from the vast general leadership literature that is available. And fourth, it is a reminder that leaders from other sectors with generic competencies maybe able to excel in many higher education leadership roles. As with the vertical perspective, this generic approach has limitations, and position-specific competencies that may be essential to success in a particular position or institution would be overlooked.

A Two-Dimensional Competency Approach for Effective Leadership

Conceptual and practical advantages and disadvantages are associated with both competency approaches. What may well be most useful is a competency framework that integrates both the general and unique nature of higher education organizations and higher education leadership. A blending of vertical and horizontal approaches allows one to identify those capabilities that may be uniquely important within a specific position or setting, while also recognizing the value of competencies that are characteristic of outstanding leadership across diverse sectors and positions.

An integrated competency model, as illustrated in Figure 9.6, offers a way of thinking about and preparing leaders by integrating the richness of both perspectives. This model provides a framework that emphasizes the

Figure 9.6. An integrated competency model.

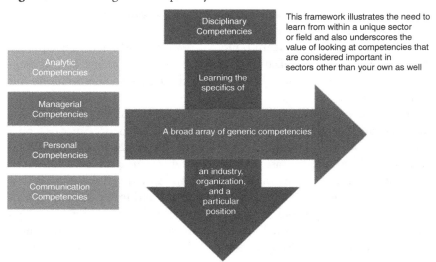

importance of understanding the landscape of higher education and the particular institution, discipline, profession, technical area, or position. At the same time, an array of horizontal competencies—such as those associated with personal, analytic, managerial, and communication knowledge and skill—are identified as essential for outstanding leaders, regardless of their specific roles or the institutions, disciplines, or specialties in which they work.

One of the greatest virtues of the competency concept is the emphasis placed on the relationship between knowledge and skill (Gigliotti, 2019; Ruben, 2012, 2019). Having a baseline knowledge of core competency areas as well as the ability to effectively enact that understanding in social, professional, or academic contexts is so often critical to the success of a leader. The blend is equally important in social, professional, and academic contexts. This ability to integrate conceptual knowledge with practice can be termed *translational competency*. Pursuing a mastery of this higher level *meta-competency*, and with it an alignment between purpose and person, is often one of the distinguishing qualities of outstanding leaders in higher education and other settings.

Conclusion

We believe the practical implications of the topics explored in this chapter are incredibly important. Higher education is not wholly unique as an organization, and neither are the requisite capabilities for college or university leadership. There may have been a time when a case for uniqueness could be made in a compelling manner, but that is no longer true in most contexts. If our idealized conception of leadership focuses too much on disciplinary and technical competence in the selection, preparation, and recruitment of leaders, it works to the detriment of higher education—particularly if that attention comes at the expense of an emphasis on horizontal capabilities. Increasingly important for leaders in colleges and universities at all levels are the general knowledge and skill sets necessary for communicating effectively with a broad array of internal and external constituencies, working collaboratively with colleagues from a diverse array of personal and cultural identities, building productive teams and fostering successful teamwork, anticipating and dealing constructively with crisis and conflict, and excelling in hiring and development efforts.

Higher education—like other sectors—benefits most from reflective leaders who embody an unwavering commitment to the integration of knowledge and skill, and to a balanced array of position-specific and cross-cutting competencies. Thinking broadly about these issues, we believe that many of our institutions could benefit from some rethinking and recalibration to give greater attention to personal, communication, managerial, and analytic competencies in their recruitment and development efforts. No doubt, further research will also be helpful in clarifying the ideal competency balance for various positions.

For Further Consideration

1. Reflection on recruitment in your institution

    Thinking in terms of your unit and institution, what competencies are typically the focus in the recruitment, selection, and/or promotion of faculty or staff to leadership positions? Would you characterize these as primarily vertical or horizontal competencies? In what ways might increased attention to the two-dimensional framework be a useful model for developing faculty and staff for future leadership positions?

2. Search committees

    How should members of search committees determine what competencies are needed for particular leadership positions? How might members of the committee assess the competencies of candidates throughout the search process?

3. Training and development

   Imagine that as director of a specific unit, you have become aware of concerns about morale. Which of the competencies presented in this chapter should be a logical focus for you to leverage to improve the productivity and attitude of members within the department? How might you use the proposed two-dimensional approach to leadership competencies to address the needs of the department over the short and long term?

4. An exemplary organization

   Identify a noneducational organization or institution that you greatly admire. It could be a large corporation, a mission-centered nonprofit, or a government-related association.

   Drawing on the ideas from this chapter, consider the following questions based on this exemplary organization:

   - What, in your opinion, makes this organization excellent?
   - How would you describe the leaders and leadership within this organization?
   - Which of these characteristics does the organization share with your college or university?
   - What can colleges and universities learn from the best practices of this organization?

LEADERSHIP AND
COMMUNICATION

Principles and Pragmatics

In This Chapter

- What is the strategic value of communication?
- What is the difference between the informational and relational dimensions of communication, and why is this distinction important?
- What principles of strategic communication are particularly relevant for leaders in higher education?
- How can strategic communication provide a foundation for a leadership problem analysis and problem-solving rubric?

Communication Basics: The Foundation for Strategic Leadership

Communication is an essential human process—what Lee Thayer (2003) describes as the *sine qua non* of social life. As he observed, "The essence of being human is . . . communicating-to and being communicated-with" (Thayer, 1968, p. 18). Communication is so natural and fundamental—not unlike breathing—that we think of it as a very simple process, if and when we think about it at all. Communication may be verbal or nonverbal, face-to-face or mediated, accidental or intentional, planned or unplanned, and it plays a central role in interaction between people—in interpersonal, group, organizational, community, as well as international contexts. An analysis of communication dynamics and outcomes across settings provides a wealth of evidence regarding how important but also how difficult the process can be. Some might go so far as to suggest that there is no greater challenge in life—personally, professionally, organizationally, and internationally—than effective communication.

American colleges and universities provide myriad examples of the wonders and the difficulties of human communication. Higher education institutions bring together a collection of bright, highly educated, and independent thinkers, all equipped with interests and expertise in a wide variety of fields and professional affiliations. The success of the institution and fulfillment of its varying missions all depend on communication—with students and colleagues and members of many vital external constituencies. Any thought that communication would be easier for particularly bright and well-educated people is quickly dispelled by observing a few months of campus life. In fact, it sometimes seems that precisely the reverse is true: One's technical and disciplinary expertise often increases the difficulty in sense-giving and sensemaking, particularly when interacting with those who have different disciplinary orientations, educational experiences, cultural identities and affiliations, work roles, or situational goals.

Across any number of higher education contexts, as in so many other personal and professional settings, communication problems can be costly, often leading to one or more of the following outcomes:

- confusion and misunderstanding
- mismatched expectations
- errors
- wasted time and resources
- personal conflicts
- blame and defensiveness
- loss of confidence in colleagues and leaders
- disengagement and low morale
- dissatisfaction and reputational damage among external constituencies

Because communication is such a basic and pervasive activity, it is uncommon to be deliberate or methodical when engaging in the process. In this chapter, we advocate doing just that as a way of attempting to minimize undesirable or unintended outcomes, and we urge leaders to engage in what can be termed *strategic communication*. We use the word *strategic* in this context to imply thoughtful, goal-oriented planning and implementation in communication efforts, and also thorough "after-action" analysis as to what worked as planned, what didn't, and what lessons can be applied in future situations. After an exploration of some basic principles of leadership communication, we will describe a pragmatic rubric and step-by-step process designed to help leaders become more strategic in communication.

The Perfect Laboratory

Colleges and universities offer a great setting for observing a broad range of individual, social, and organizational activities, and there may be no more interesting laboratory for those interested in learning about the dynamics of leadership communication.

Consider the following example:

> After a yearlong search to fill one position allocated to the department by the dean, the unit is informed that it can hire two individuals from the finalist list instead of just one. The dean was expecting joy and jubilation from members of the department. Contrary to this expectation, however, the dean's unanticipated sharing of this news at a department meeting is not met with delight or celebration, but rather with silence and indifference.

An outcome that one would presume to have been quite logical, and that would have led the department, search committee, and chair to express gratitude, evoked quite different reactions. Moreover, what might be an occasion for celebration and gratitude for the validation of the good work and future needs of the department instead became an incident that drove a deep wedge between the dean and members of the department and its leadership. How and why did this happen?

The explanation for this seemingly improbable outcome can be traced to inadequacies in leadership communication strategy. While leaders at all levels are elected or selected to guide and coordinate an expansive array of interests and perspectives of individuals and groups for which they have responsibility, this is seldom a simple assignment, and almost never one in which the outcome can be achieved without careful planning and attention to the details of communication in execution. In the pages ahead we explore some of the factors that explain outcomes such as those reported in the vignette and then revisit the example in some detail after reviewing key issues related to communication and leadership strategy.

Considerations in Formulating and Implementing Strategy

Use of the word *strategic* is meant to underscore a point made earlier in this volume: Effective leadership is not about being authentic or intuitive, acting instinctively, or simply "being yourself." No matter how small, each of the many leadership moments and challenges matters, and an element of strategy can be critical to one's leadership during these circumstances. Think of strategy not as a deceptive or manipulative practice, but rather as a thoughtful decision about how best to handle a particular situation employing the most appropriate approach available from among the many one might consider. The selections one makes are not simply about what will work or produce the desired outcome, but also about relationships and values. The way each situation is handled makes a statement about who you are and what matters to you. Each creates precedents, strengthens or diminishes the quality of connections with others, and shapes the history and legacy in terms of which your future actions will be judged.

The Importance of History

A leader's impact is fundamentally shaped by the ways in which messages, actions, and behaviors are understood and responded to by followers. The most fundamental component of strategic leadership in an organizational setting, therefore, is the formulation and enactment of communication behaviors that simultaneously take account of the perspectives of the leader and their goals, and also those of their colleagues. For this to be done effectively, it is essential to pay attention not only to the present moment and the purposes at hand, but also to the history of communication among those involved.

Communication events consist of a sequence of verbal and nonverbal messages, behaviors, and actions and responses to them. The sequential message sending and receiving between individuals creates a process, and that process, over time, creates a history—one that often has a profound impact on the delivery, reception, and interpretation of any event. Simply stated, communication history shapes the way individuals attend to, interpret, and react to particular messages. Given this reality, in addition to being ethnographers, leaders must also be historians, and leadership strategy must focus on the current communication events and challenges *in the moment*, but in a manner that also takes account of the background relevant to the situation at hand. Doing this effectively requires an awareness of the current circumstance and perspectives at play, an understanding of the relevant history, and a clear sense of how one's actions will contribute to the evolving history of relationships and the organization.

From the perspective of leadership strategy, the following three points about communication are particularly important: First, while communication events are far more tangible and visible than communication histories, an understanding of the latter is essential to making sense of the former.

Second, current actions contribute to an unfolding history that will affect future encounters as well as the evolving culture of a group, organization, or community with which future members and leaders must contend. Third, every decision or action contributes to the perceptions of a leader and the broader context in which that individual's leadership actions will be understood and remembered.

In the faculty hiring vignette described earlier, the history of interaction between the chair and department members and the dean played a central role in the way the "good news" to create an extra position for the department was interpreted. Very salient to that history from the perspective of the chair and department members was the fact that the candidate the department recommended as its first choice—pursuant to an extensive search, interviews, and multiple meetings devoted to comparing candidates—was initially rejected by the dean with the explanation that he did not feel the candidate was as strong as some others. No detail was provided.

Without meeting with the department chair, search committee, or members of the department to discuss his thinking or to hear the rationale for their preference, the dean went ahead and extended an offer to another candidate—the one he most favored. The department and chair were left wondering about the rationale for the dean's decision and action and were annoyed at not having been involved in a discussion with the dean on any of these issues. Did the dean have a vision of what was needed that differed from that of the department? Was the job description that had been collaboratively developed and approved by the dean and department now deemed no longer relevant? Did the dean mistrust the ability or motives of the department in its analysis or recommendation process? All these questions were being discussed among department members.

Of significance is the fact that this series of events closely followed two previous search cycles where the dean's role in the final selection process had also been viewed by the department and chair as mysterious, intrusive, dismissive, and disrespectful to the department chair and its faculty. This concern had been brought to the attention of the dean, who seemed puzzled by it but assured all involved that the process would be improved as they headed into the current search. So, quite clearly in this instance, the message as received by the chair and faculty about the news of an additional hire was not the message that the dean expected. Rather than speaking to the dean's generosity or desire to reaffirm his regard for the department by offering a second position, it was interpreted as yet another insult to the faculty, a challenge to their ability to render meaningful personnel judgments, and an affront to traditions of shared governance, leadership transparency, and collegial decision-making.

As the example so clearly indicates, the ways in which leadership messages are interpreted depends on a great many factors, over which a skilled leader has some control, many of which are historical, and all of which can be enhanced by thoughtful reflection and analysis. In this case and others, enhancing the predictability of communication outcomes requires one to begin by taking account of the current perspectives and relevant history of all key parties, establishing and conveying clear expectations for the present situation, monitoring communication as it progresses, maintaining open lines for feedback, and being prepared to refine messages, processes, strategies, and structures as may be necessary in pursuit of the intended outcome as events unfold.

Leadership Communication Principles and Pragmatics

Translating communication theory and core concepts into practice is a fundamental challenge for leaders. In the following section, six principles that help with this process are presented, and the implications of each are discussed.

- Information Flow and Relationships
- The Antigravity of Information Flow
- Process and Content
- Arrows and Waves
- Leadership and Followership
- Hearing What You Want versus Hearing What You Need

Information Flow and Relationships

"Communication is important" is a familiar refrain in many organizational settings and circumstances. But what does that mean, exactly? Write and speak clearly. Choose words carefully. Be succinct in presenting the main point of the message. Repeat key points but avoid being overly repetitive. Listen attentively. Ask questions for clarification. Pay attention to nonverbal as well as verbal messages. All of these tactics are important and helpful to the effectiveness of communication in any setting. However, these considerations are really just the tip of the communicative iceberg.

It is easy for a leader to assume communication is effective—and strategic—as long as messages are articulately delivered. Thinking of the example of the dean who conveyed the positive news about the two faculty hires, for instance, it is likely that the dean assumes his communication was clear, appropriate, and effective. However, as discussed previously, in addition to the personal and organizational factors that are involved in any communication situation, history, content, and relational dimensions of communication are also important to the process and outcomes (Watzlawick et al., 1967).

Every communication encounter has the potential to convey information and also to shape or be shaped by relationships. As a leader, it is therefore critical to continually remind oneself of the informational–relational duality in communication planning, action, and analysis. Thinking about what to say is only the beginning; in addition, one needs to consider how and when to say it, to whom and in what setting to say it, and how the message is likely to be interpreted and reacted to. A second category that needs careful planning and analysis relates to how this communication event is likely to influence and be influenced by the relationships and histories among those involved. All of these questions serve as a reminder that the interpretation and impact of leadership messages are fundamentally shaped by recipients and the communication context. As a consequence, much of one's success in leadership communication depends on effective strategy. The goal of this planning is to enable the leader to better understand and predict, and to guide their messaging and actions such that they have an increased likelihood of resonating in intended ways with colleagues and potential followers (Ruben & Gigliotti, 2019b).

Efforts to convey information involve the negotiation and coordination of meaning among the parties involved. Successful outcomes require an iterative process with a number of vital steps, including establishing goals, creating and transmitting messages, listening to and observing whether one's messages are attended to, discerning how these messages are interpreted, noting what actions result, and carrying forth this process while making necessary adjustments along the way. Thus, when a leader's purpose is to promote the sharing of knowledge, an idea, a perspective, or a point of view, the steps identified in Figure 10.1 can be helpful: Introduce/state purpose, explain, check for understanding, clarify and restate, and summarize the intended takeaways. The goal, of course, is to increase the likelihood that the message sent equals the message received, or, put another way, that the sensemaking outcomes for potential receivers match the sensemaking intentions of message initiators. The linear progression from the statement of purpose to the summary of intended takeaways may seem to be a simple enough prescription for effectively sharing new information; in practice, however, the dynamics and outcomes involved are complex, not necessarily sequential, and neither the process nor the outcomes are as predictable as the model might seem to imply.

An important theoretical insight—alluded to in the previous discussion— is that every interactive event involves not only *information*-related, but also

Figure 10.1. Focusing on the information dimension.

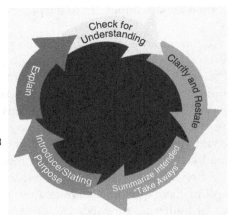

Goal: Increasing the likelihood that MS = MR sensemaking will match sense-giving

relationship-related dynamics. Every message that is sent and received has the potential to initiate, reaffirm, or change the relationship between individuals involved. And as they are formed and evolve, relationships influence the interpretations of messages, reactions to new ideas, and also the emergence, reinforcement, or decline of trust and credibility. More generally, relation-building aspects of communication are vital to the creation of what might be termed *leadership capital*—which translates into support and respect for a leader that are accumulated when things are going well and a willingness to be more patient, tolerant, and supportive of a leader when difficulties arise.

The relational aspect of any communication exchange is often more difficult for leaders to understand and analyze than the content—or information—dimension. Several points are helpful in this regard: First, most relationships are formed initially based on self-interest. Second, first impressions can have a significant impact on the way relationships are likely to develop. Third, and perhaps most important for present purposes, relationships must be nurtured and maintained over time.

The relational communication cycle involves a sequence of steps, as depicted in a simplified form in Figure 10.2. The process includes the following elements: establishing rapport, showing interest, demonstrating empathy, respecting point of view, and acknowledging/thanking. These stages do not necessarily occur in a linear sequence, nor are all present in every communication encounter. The model is not intended to be prescriptive; rather, the depicted stages capture some general dimensions of communication focus when one's explicit goal is creating, shaping, and reinforcing relationships.

Figure 10.2. Focusing on the relationship dimension.

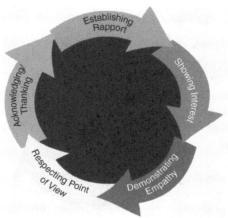

Other beneficial communication behaviors, which generally contribute to relational—and, often, also to informational—goals include the following:

- listening attentively
- clarifying/establishing common goals
- conveying mutual respect and support
- valuing diverse perspectives
- clarifying expectations and boundaries
- maintaining consistency
- being transparent with information, ideas, and processes
- displaying empathy and perspective-taking
- promoting a sense of teamwork—sharing the glory and the pain
- recognizing the accomplishments of others
- using inclusive thought and language ("we," "us," "our," vs. "I," "me," and "my")
- avoiding self-preoccupation and self-promotion—the "it all began when I became your leader" syndrome—and the temptations of "narcissistic leadership" (Chatterjee & Hambrick, 2007)

Other behaviors, such as those listed in Box 10.1, generally detract from and weaken relationships bonds.

In the hiring vignette discussed previously, there seems little doubt that relationship dimensions of the communication process were critical to the eventual outcomes. Absent any information on the dean's rationale or

BOX 10.1
Communicative Acts That Weaken Relationship Bonds

Just as relationships may be enhanced through communication strategies, relationships may also be weakened through communication. Porath's (2015) research on incivility in the workplace captures various communication behaviors that are regarded as "rude" and potentially damaging to relationships in the workplace. Porath identified the following as among the most often cited rude behaviors by bosses, in descending order of frequency:

- interrupting people
- being judgmental of those who are different
- paying little attention to or showing little interest in others' opinions
- taking the best tasks and leaving the worst for others
- failing to pass along necessary information
- neglecting to say "please" or "thank you"
- talking down to people
- taking too much credit for things

When asked to consider the rude behaviors that people most often admit to seeing in themselves, the following items were frequently cited:

- hibernating into e-gadgets
- using jargon even when it excludes others
- ignoring invitations
- being judgmental of those who are different
- grabbing easy tasks while leaving difficult ones for others

thinking about the process or candidates, and coming on the heels of other problematic search processes in previous years, faculty members felt ignored and disrespected, and the chair felt undermined—all outcomes that were quite predictable from a relational perspective. This situation led to faculty meetings and multiple email exchanges that questioned the dean and the dean's motives and contemplated an appropriate response. Although the hiring decision had already been made, the department decided to demand a meeting with the dean to discuss the process and its consequences.

The dean agreed to meet after a number of requests from the chair and senior faculty. When he arrived at the meeting, he assumed the role of meeting chair and began with a speech, explaining that a dean always knows things by virtue of their position that often can't be revealed to chairs or faculty. He then indicated that it had been his intention all along to hire the person the department recommended in addition to offering a position to the candidate he preferred. So, the "good news" was that the department was receiving an extra faculty line, and he went on to announce that he had already extended an offer to the department's preferred candidate.

The dean expressed his unhappiness at the way the chair and faculty had disrespected his authority and failed to understand that he was operating in the best interests of the department throughout the entire process. The chair and faculty sat rather silently in disbelief. The chair had had no prior knowledge of the decisions or the decision-making, nor did the search committee. The dean seemed quite surprised that there was anything short of jubilation within the group.

The meeting ended on a somber note. The vignette provides a classic example of a leadership failure—a failure that could have been a significant success, adding to the dean's credibility, respect, leadership capital, and leadership legacy, had the dean understood and applied basic concepts of strategy and focused on both informational and relationship dimensions of the communication process.

The Antigravity of Information Flow

Process complexity and outcome unpredictability are increasingly problematic as the number of individuals involved in the communication process increases. This is the case, for example, when a communication flow begins with a senior leader in one part of the university and progresses to a series of other leaders in other units, such as a dean, chair, committee chair, graduate program director, faculty members, and perhaps in some cases eventually to students. The message initiator may mistakenly assume that information will flow logically through the formal channels of the organization. Unfortunately, the flow from the top level to others in the organization is problematic in many cases. This can be a particularly difficult circumstance if individuals in some units receive the intended information or reports while others do not. Similar communication dynamics can occur across units, leading some individuals to feel they are valued and connected and others to be frustrated or resentful because they are out of the loop. Even when the conduit works reasonably well, the message received may well be lost or distorted through negligence or by uninformed, recalcitrant, or oppositional colleagues—or simply as a consequence of the multiple handoffs among the many involved individuals in the communicative chain.

Referring once again to the hiring vignette, discussing expectations relative to the candidate search and the selection process was a critical but neglected activity for the dean and the chairs of the department and search committee. Issues that could have been clarified through more carefully designed information dissemination and follow-up discussion include the following: Was it the expectation that the department would put forward one candidate or several? Should finalists be ranked by the department in order of preference? Was the dean committed to following the department's recommendations, or did he view these merely as advisory? Particularly given the troubled history relative to recruitment and hiring, endeavoring to be as clear as possible about the process was a critically important step. The department thought they had addressed these issues thoroughly, having discussed and agreed on the type of faculty member needed, collaboratively developing the job description within the department and soliciting the dean's input and approval, engaging the dean fully during campus visits of candidates, and chatting informally with the dean after each visit. In none of these information events had members of the department or chair come away with a sense that there were major differences of opinion or brewing problems.

In situations where multiple individuals are involved in the review and approval process, as is typically the case with new employee recruitment and selection, intentionality, careful planning, and thoughtful follow-through are vital from the perspectives of both information flow and relationships. In this case, as in so many others, effective leadership requires formalized communication planning along with attention to message clarity, repetition, careful selection of channels, appropriate dissemination, and feedback loops to help ensure the fidelity of messages as they flow through the organization.

Process and Content

In any communication situation, the focus is most naturally on the intended message and its content. This is the "what" of communication. Equally important, however—often even more important—is the "how." *Process issues*, as they are often termed, relate to how the message content will be conveyed, what organizational channels will be employed, who will be engaged in the event and in what sequence, what will be documented and in what form, and how this process will be monitored and refined as needed.

Particularly in higher education contexts characterized by relatively loosely coupled systems and personal autonomy, the way things are done is as important as substance. As a result, even great ideas may not be accepted if ample opportunities are not provided for colleagues to be engaged in review, discussion, and decision-making. This is a helpful reminder that being taken account of, included, listened to, valued, and respected can matter as much as achieving one's preferred outcome.

From a leader's perspective, there is often a concern that extensive engagement and analysis will be time-consuming, and of course it certainly does require more time and energy than simply making a decision on one's own. However, it is also often the case that one either dedicates the necessary time up front for an appropriate level of engagement and consensus-building or pays a higher price later in dealing with a predictable array of questions, challenges, and resistances.

Not only is the "pay-later" approach often more time-consuming in the end, but it also increases the risks of failing to garner the support necessary for acceptance and successful implementation. Any veteran college or university administrator can point to a number of great ideas or initiatives that ran into significant roadblocks from faculty, staff, students, or other stakeholders. In many cases those impediments could have been avoided with more balanced attention to the communication process as well as content. These topics will be discussed in greater detail in chapter 15, which focuses on organizational change.

Arrows and Waves

Communication is not like archery. That metaphor suggests an activity that involves skillful crafting of a message, taking careful aim, and then sending it on its way toward the intended target hoping—expecting, really—that the message sent will be the message received. In this view, communication situations are instantaneous and well-bounded events, potentially very predictable and controllable based on the skills of the archer. Unfortunately, due to the complexity and nuances of human communication, the most carefully crafted arrows, sent by the most skilled archers, aimed at precise targets, often fail to land as intended, and more often than not the outcome does not coincide particularly well with the archer's intentions.

A better metaphor to capture the nature of human communication is that of waves rolling in and breaking against a coastline—well-defined cognitive and emotional personal coastlines shaped over many years for each of us by the constant ebb and flow of messages. Over time, these messages, like waves against a beach, shape the contours of our individual shorelines. It is unlikely that any single wave will have a dramatic impact, as it is unlikely that any single message will have a transformative effect on a message recipient. In the case of shorelines and communication there are exceptions to this rule, as with a tsunami or a single life-changing message, but these are rare.

The implication is not that communication and message sending are without value or impact. Certainly, this is not the case. But the wave metaphor helps us shift our thinking to a more constructive view of communication and the dynamics of influence. It helps to explain why a single communiqué about a great new idea may well have less impact than the initiator of the message anticipated—if the great new idea even makes it to the cognitive shoreline rather than dissipates as it rolls in. As one poignant example, think about cigarette usage and the numerous messages about the risks of smoking through various channels, from multiple sources, often over many years, that generally are required to change the behavior of a long-time smoker. Another example has been provided by the relatively slow uptake and resistance to social distancing and mask wearing in spite of extensive communication efforts advocating the importance of these behaviors.

The implications for a leader are many. These are particularly profound when it comes to communication about new or changed decisions, policies, ideas, or directions. They are also important for a leader in thinking about and planning routine day-to-day communication. The wave and shoreline metaphor also offers the following guidance: Anticipate the impact of individual cognitive and emotional factors, along with the cultural, historical, and relationship dynamics discussed previously; don't expect any single message to achieve the effect you hope for; recognize the need for multiple messages, redundancy, and the use of numerous message sources and channels; and be prepared to draw on your leadership competencies related to patience and perseverance, among others.

Leadership and Followership

As critical as leadership is, various authors note (Collinson et al., 2017; Ruben & Gigliotti, 2019b) that there is a risk in overly romanticizing the concept and attributing too much power to leaders when it comes to controlling outcomes. It's important to remind ourselves that leaders have limited influence (Ruben & Gigliotti, 2019b). Indeed, as Benjamin Hooks and others have stated, "If you think you are a leader, and turn around to find no one following, you're just someone taking a walk." In point of fact, a great deal of influence over "leadership outcomes" rests with the choices made by "followers." Followers decide who and when to follow, support, work with, and/or endorse, or they may choose to do none of these. It is in the act of choice to engage as a follower that the leader has the power of influence bestowed on themselves (Platow et al., 2015; Ruben & Gigliotti, 2019b).

A critical implication of these perspectives is that aspiring leaders need to pay close attention to the sensibilities, sensitivities, needs, and goals of potential followers. These insights also point to the importance of creating messages, strategies, processes, and structures that advance the aspirations of a leader but will also resonate positively with would-be followers (Ruben & Gigliotti, 2019b).

Hearing What You Want Versus Hearing What You Need

Hearing how effective one is as a leader and the extent to which colleagues support and agree with your ideas, plans, and approach is always reassuring. But those messages are only helpful if they are authentic, and for the leader the consequences of "fake news" can be very problematic.

The most important feedback consists of information that you *need* to hear—information that candidly and constructively speaks to potential risks, barriers, or problems related to your plans and intentions, along with suggestions for how to best address these concerns. The key point is that what a leader genuinely *needs* is not commentary that simply complements them or reinforces presumptions about the wonders of their leadership, but rather information that will help them be successful in their role.

As a leader, one's goal should be to create a culture of trust and nondefensiveness, where openness to candor, critique, and constructive criticism is always welcome when these options support core values and the greater good of the organization. Toward this end, it is vital to personally display an openness and receptivity. The goal is to cultivate the understanding that to you, loyalty is about colleagues who will share information that will make the organization more effective and feedback that will help you become a better leader.

A Rubric for Strategic Leadership

Colleges and universities, as noted throughout this text, are incredibly dynamic and complex places. The multiple missions, stakeholder concerns, decision-making processes, and potential areas of strategic focus present faculty and staff leaders with a seemingly endless number of choices as they endeavor to translate challenges into opportunities. For all these reasons, leadership extends beyond doing what comes naturally. It is not simply about being yourself. Rather, strategic leadership and communication involve systematic and intentional planning and execution.

All leaders encounter a number of challenging circumstances on a daily basis: Some are complicated and nuanced, such as the case study discussed in this chapter; others may be more routine and easily addressed. Every leadership action—no matter how significant or insignificant it may seem—is an important one in many respects. Each has consequences for the organization, for the leader and for colleagues. Each action sets precedents, contributes to an impression of the leader, and strengthens or diminishes the quality of the leader's relationships. Each decision also contributes to the foundation in terms of how a leader's future actions will be judged, and each will ultimately contribute to their lasting legacy. The following rubric for strategic leadership outlines five critical steps that can be extremely helpful in addressing the multiple challenges a leader faces:

1. Analyze the situation.
2. Define the audience(s).
3. Clarify goal(s).
4. Select and implement a plan of action.
5. Debrief.

Using this framework, as described in the next sections, requires conscious effort initially. Over time, however, its use becomes a matter of habit—one that can greatly enhance one's effectiveness across a variety of circumstances. Each leadership situation can be viewed as a teachable moment and an opportunity to apply, test, and further refine one's skills.

Analyze the Situation: Determine What Is at Stake

The first step involves a careful assessment of the circumstances confronting a leader. The critical questions to ask are these: What is at stake in this particular situation? Is the issue related to a program, department, or the institution as a whole, or to students, faculty, or staff members? Alternatively, is what's at stake the credibility, identity, or reputation of the leader? Being clear on the nature and significance of the issue(s) involved and what is at stake provides a necessary starting point for developing a thoughtful strategy. Keep in mind that a leader's handling of mundane as well as challenging situations can be important in the short run and can also shape the long-term identity of an individual or organization.

The following list should be helpful in identifying issues that may be at stake in any situation.

For the program/department/institution:

- core purposes or aspirations
- critical values or principles
- a problem to be addressed

- consistent practices
- organizational climate, culture, or morale
- critical regulations or policies
- fair and equitable treatment
- personal and professional standards and practices

For others in the organization:

- resources
- status
- pride
- recognition

For you as a leader:

- clarifying your role
- establishing your voice
- upholding personal values or principles
- setting or maintaining a precedent
- maintaining your credibility
- defining your personal/leadership style
- demonstrating consistency in how you treat colleagues, students, or problems

Define the Audience(s): Who Needs to Hear From You if You Decide to Respond, and Why?

This step allows the leader to determine the intended audience(s). It is far too easy to omit careful consideration of who you need to reach with a particular message, thereby missing an important stage of the strategic communication process. The following are some possible audiences to include:

- a specific individual or individuals
- broader groups
  - the individual(s) directly involved in a situation
  - all those present or aware of the situation
  - the entire department
  - the individual(s) to whom you report
  - specific groups (students, a committee, alumni)
  - senior colleague(s)
  - a friend, partner, or confidant
  - others

Clarify Goal(s): What Exactly Do You Hope to Accomplish?

The third step calls for a leader to clarify goals. Building on your assessment of what is at stake and your decisions regarding those with whom you should communicate, it is essential to determine *exactly* what you want, need, or hope to accomplish. Recognize that it is impossible to determine what would be an effective or ineffective plan of action—the next step—without deciding what your intentions will be. A strategy that is perfect for one goal can be problematic or disastrous when viewed in terms of other goals. Perhaps the most obvious examples are the potential problems that occur if you are not clear as to whether your objective is listening to and learning what others are thinking versus informing or persuading them of your point of view.

A myriad of communication goals may be appropriate in any situation, including, but not limited to, any of the following:

- gathering information
- providing input
- clarifying facts
- solidifying relationships
- persuading or influencing
- assuring that your position, reaction, or perspective is clear
- soliciting input for decision-making
- being on the record
- conveying interest/concern
- displaying expertise

Select and Implement a Plan of Action: What Do You Do, When, and How?

The fourth step involves reviewing options and selecting a plan of action. The issues to consider here are as follows:

- What *action* should be undertaken—if any—and what is the most appropriate *timing*, and why?
  - Do nothing special (e.g., when not much is at stake, benefits versus costs of response are not clear, the problem will likely take care of itself).
  - Respond immediately, addressing the most pressing issue(s).
  - Think further about the situation (e.g., give the matter more thought, then revisit options).

- What is the *message* to be conveyed, and why?
  - informative (e.g., historical, factual, defining/clarifying problem, or citing other sources)
  - persuasive (e.g., evidence-based, values-based, vision-based)
- What *channel(s)* or *venue(s)* will be most effective, and why?
  - one-to-one (e.g., "spontaneous" informal or scheduled appointment)
  - group (e.g., meeting, town hall gathering, or focus group)
  - mediated (e.g., telephone, email, text, or social media)

The first decision is whether it makes sense to respond to the situation at all, and if so, what timing is most appropriate. This decision requires leaders to carefully identify the potential costs, benefits, barriers, and sources of resistance before selecting a course of action. This stage is often where leaders are inclined to begin. It should be apparent, however, that moving to action without first being clear about what's at stake, who the appropriate audience is, and precisely what the goals are is a mistake.

A second decision involves determining precisely what message you hope to convey and how best to frame that message. Finally, decisions need to be made about the best way to deliver the message. Is a one-to-one discussion best? Or perhaps a group meeting? Or a mediated interaction using phone, email, text, or possibly social media?

Debrief: How Did It Go?

The final stage of this process, and perhaps the most frequently overlooked, consists of personal reflection and "after-action" debriefing and analysis. This stage leads one to consider how well the plan and execution worked, using feedback when it is available. The following questions can be useful in this stage:

- Did your strategy achieve the outcome you intended? Were there unanticipated consequences?
- How would others involved in the process describe the way things went?
- Is further follow-up needed? (If so, repeat previous four steps iteratively.)
- What might you do differently in the future to *address* this kind of problem if it were to occur again?
- How could you *prevent* this kind of situation from developing (e.g., set clearer expectations, stay closer to the process, request periodic progress reports, or assign several people to collaborate on the task)?
- What personal and/or professional leadership lessons can you take away from the situation?

The decision to address a particular situation—and how to do so—often carries enormous consequences. This model for making strategic communication choices can be useful to all leaders in approaching the numerous challenges they encounter. The model emphasizes the value of moving systematically through the first four stages prior to developing a strategy and taking action. In so doing, the rubric provides a structured approach to help leaders apply the assessment and communication competencies discussed in the chapter to evaluate a situation, clarify their goals, and focus on individuals with whom they will be interacting. The overall aim is to consciously select a strategy that is best suited to the circumstance at hand.

While a strategic leadership rubric does not guarantee desirable outcomes, the framework can certainly increase their likelihood. The discipline required to employ a strategic approach might be cumbersome at first. When implemented regularly, however, it will become quite natural. Like other topics presented in this book, this framework is intended to be applicable across a broad range of settings and circumstances. In applying the rubric in any particular context, a leader should give consideration to relevant nuances and subtleties, but the basic steps and their purposes remain constant.

Strategic Communication Insights

This chapter concludes with a set of tips and tactics related to strategic communication. These thoughts highlight a number of the leadership communication principles offered throughout the text. In particular, leadership is a process of social influence that is achieved through communication that might be verbal or nonverbal, planned or unplanned, intentional or unintentional, used for good or for evil. Importantly, the messages, processes, strategies, and structures are enacted by a leader in collaboration with colleagues, supporters, or followers. As noted, leadership is not possible without followership, and social influence is possible only with collective buy-in. These principles, like others offered in this chapter, are not meant to be a prescriptive list for influencing others; rather, they are offered as helpful guidance for leaders endeavoring to enhance their strategic competencies.

Nothing is more important than being clear on your communication goals, your audiences, and your messages. The five-step strategic communication rubric allows you to enhance your analysis of problems and strategies available for addressing them. Emphasis is placed on defining what is at stake in a situation, identifying relevant audiences, thoughtfully selecting goals and messages, and methodically implementing the plan of action. Once these steps have been implemented, debriefing and reflecting on what transpired in order to learn from your successes and failures is a final step. This model emphasizes the importance of clear communication goals, which we view as one of the most essential facets of strategic leadership and communication.

Colleagues won't know or care as much about your plans, priorities, or rationales as you do. Remember how long it has taken you to reach a point of understanding and a readiness to act on a major initiative, and the many experiences that brought you to your present view of what needs to be done. To help others reach this same place, you need to recreate a similar process or set of experiences for them, recognizing that these steps will need to be more compressed than those you went through. As a part of this instructional process, leaders must do all they can to create a compelling and descriptive vision of challenges and opportunities, what is possible, what should be done, and why, tailoring messages to the various goals and interests of the specific audience. Asserting one's authority to advance a particular position might work in the short term but will not build a base of trust and understanding, nor necessarily motivate action.

A single message seldom has much impact. Remember that effective communication requires repetition. As discussed previously but is worth repeating in this list of key principles is the idea that one message seldom motivates a change in behavior or opinion. Recall the metaphor related to the waves on the shoreline, whereby communication and social influence are understood to be parts of an ongoing process through which messages wash over individuals—roughly analogous to waves repeatedly washing against a shoreline. Over time these messages shape the sensibilities and responses of receivers, much as waves shape the contours of a beach. In practice, do not count on your messages (meeting minutes, comments at meetings, etc.) to flow downward to colleagues in your organization in a logical, unadulterated way. Plan for and learn to appreciate the need for repetition. Expect to be bored with your messages before they get to the people you are trying to reach.

The simple message is the one that is remembered and retold. Let the elevator ride be your guide. Have a simple story about vision, benefits, and challenges ready to share—one that can be told on an elevator ride going up or down three or four stories. The use of concise but powerful language can help to leave a memorable impact on those with whom you interact in your formal and informal leadership roles. Be prepared to elaborate if questions are asked and if you can be certain there is a genuine interest in learning more.

Don't count on getting agreement on what really happened in the past, who did what, who's to blame, or why it was done this way and not that way. Each of us has a huge stake in our perceptions and interpretations of events and their significance. Communication events have a history— one that is important to reflect on and understand—but public discussions aimed at clarifying that history often serve as a trap or obstacle to forward movement. Effort is generally better spent going forward than dissecting history to determine who did what that led to what problem.

In communication, less is sometimes more. More communication is not necessarily better communication. Flooding channels with too many messages—including social media posts, texts, and emails, and engaging in too many meetings and interpersonal interactions with colleagues and others—can be problematic when it comes to ensuring your contributions receive close attention. Related to this strategy, it is essential for leaders to invest substantial time in activities that allow colleagues to share their views and feel listened to and valued.

Finally, in some instances, clarity and full disclosure are not the intended goal of communication; rather, ambiguity can be used strategically and purposefully by a leader to avoid making a definitive commitment on a particular issue or course of action at an inopportune time or circumstance (Eisenberg, 1984). All of these observations point to the potential importance of making strategic choices about what's at stake, and given that, how much information to share and with whom.

Think carefully about the best leadership architecture in any situation. There are a number of alternatives for structuring a leadership team. Give careful consideration to the design and appropriate use of leadership architecture, taking into account the circumstances, goals, leader's communication style, the capabilities of colleagues, the unit culture and climate, and other relevant factors.

The following information sharing models are available:

Mass communication (top-down, one-to-many) model: With this model, the leader deals with everyone in public, through shared forums, or through publicly shared messages to the entire organization. The advantages include the following: Everyone has equal access to information and the approach takes less time, less customized messaging, and less investment up front in communication activities. However, this approach can overload individuals with information that is not pertinent to all, lead to inattention to particularly important messages, and result in messages being directed to everyone when only certain individuals need to receive the information (e.g., rules pertaining to particular programs, individual reprimands, or new procedures).

Interpersonal (one-to-one) model: The leader communicates directly and personally with each individual on a one-to-one basis. This model, which is only viable in smaller organizations, or in work groups within larger units, allows for spontaneous, interactive, and customized communication. The interpersonal model allows leaders to gather personal perceptions, build coalitions, and plan strategy without public commitments. However, the lack of a systematic approach results in the uneven dissemination of information, leading to some individuals' perceptions and reality being privileged and others marginalized.

Intermediary/mediated (gatekeeper) model: Using this model, a leader forms and uses a layered architecture. This model allows a leader to form structures based on particular needs or interests, such as program-centered or topical area committees, communities of practice, or task forces, or the formation and utilization of an executive committee. Note that this model may be used in a way that purposefully includes or excludes particular formal or informal leaders or individuals. Considerations include time available, the effectiveness of existing communication channels, appropriateness of group segmentation, or levels of resistance or support, needs for customized and topically focused interaction. Limitations include the potential exclusion of interested individuals from particular groups and the challenges of effectively conveying information across groups. These limitations can be overcome to some extent through formalized and systematic planning and follow-up.

Combinations: Each of these designs can be used in any combination for particular purposes or for specific periods of time.

A leader won't be successful with everyone—nor with any one person all the time. Leadership roles in higher education can be incredibly consuming and exhausting. To avoid burnout, always keep in mind the institution's best interests and consider changing messages, processes, strategies, and structures in a way that makes sense for your audience, your institution, and for you. Be persistent, but remain grounded and open to concluding that you have reached a point of diminishing returns in your efforts with some potential message recipients.

Do not underestimate the power of powerless language. Leaders are often taught to use assertive and direct language; however, leaders must also recognize the value of powerless language in certain situations. Expressing vulnerability, asking questions, talking tentatively, and seeking advice are all communication tactics that can allow one to influence others. As Grant (2013) acknowledges, what is often described as powerless language can be incredibly influential in building rapport and trust and gaining the admiration of others.

Plan to be pleased and surprised when colleagues acknowledge or thank you for your work or accomplishments as a leader. Some colleagues can be counted on to notice and express their appreciation for your efforts on behalf of the organization; many others cannot. More likely than praise or complements are messages that identify problems, failures, or gaps colleagues identify in your leadership, pointing to ways you can better meet their needs. This is especially true for those who have not occupied roles similar to yours. Despite this predictable and sometimes frustrating pattern, there is likely to be useful information in the complaints and suggestions of your critics. Also, because of their scarcity, compliments and expressions of appreciation and support will be particularly appreciated.

It may be useful to structure a periodic organizational debriefing session, where colleagues are asked to list and discuss things that are going well and things that can be improved. These discussions can provide useful information on organizational and leadership needs and can also remind colleagues that it is important to focus on strengths as well as areas for improvement.

Conclusion

The importance of strategic leadership communication cannot be overstated. It is far too easy to assume that one has become an effective communicator based on life experiences or professional or educational accomplishments. In reality, the demands of academic and administrative leadership in higher education can present a host of challenges for even the most accomplished faculty and staff leaders. For everyone, becoming a skilled strategic leader is a work in progress. The five-step rubric presented in this chapter, along with the related principles and insights related to strategic leadership and strategic communication, focus a spotlight on communication behaviors that will be particularly helpful in each of these endeavors.

For Further Consideration

Vignettes

Read through the following vignettes. For each, consider how the five steps in the strategic leadership communication rubric, and the insights, tips, and tactics discussed throughout the chapter, apply. Specifically, how might the rubric and insights from the chapter be helpful in addressing and potentially preventing each of these situations.

1. A particular staff member on a committee you lead is consistently resistant to points you raise and initiatives you propose at meetings. The pattern has become quite predictable. It seems to you that whatever ideas you introduce, the individual finds problems with the suggestion, and the problems are generally voiced in meetings in a way that stalls discussion. What guidance would the rubric provide?

2. A colleague in your department went over your head as chair and obtained from the dean additional resources for teaching that you denied based on equity considerations. You were unaware of the meeting between the dean and faculty member. How might you best deal with the situation at this point?

3. A student comes to you to express confidential concerns about what he believes is a romantic relationship developing between one of your faculty members and a student in the class. He reports that this is extremely awkward for others in the class and requests that you address the problem immediately. How should the situation be handled?

4. In your capacity as department chair, you assigned a faculty member the task of developing a core course for the department, based on input from everyone who would like to contribute. A semester has passed, and the deadline for the approval of new courses is fast approaching. Three days before the faculty meeting at which new courses are to be reviewed and approved, the colleague assigned to the task of developing the course distributes what looks like a final draft of the syllabus. At the meeting, various faculty members complain that this was supposed to be designed with broad input to reflect the perspectives of the entire faculty, but clearly this approach was not taken. The author of the syllabus explains that he had been disappointed to have received no input or suggestions during the

previous semester. No one recalls any input being sought. What should you do?

5. You are one of four members appointed to a committee to develop a first draft for a new program to be implemented within your department. No committee leader was appointed, and you find yourself adopting the leadership role. One of your colleagues seldom attends meetings, and when she does, she has only negative input. Clearly she is opposed to the idea of the new program and does not seem to appreciate your efforts to move the group forward. How might you best handle the situation?

6. Your school, composed of four departments, was formed based on some common interests and what the central administration viewed as interdisciplinary potential. To most faculty, however, the merger was understood to be a matter of administrative convenience. In the 4 years since the unit was formed, there have been some grassroots efforts to develop a unifying rhetoric and future vision, but none of these have been enthusiastically supported. Word has come to you that the administration believes it has becoming essential for the school to develop a unifying narrative and a more collaborative rather than divisive attitude. You have been asked to head up the group to develop this shared narrative. What principles and pragmatics from this chapter will be particularly helpful?

11

CONFLICT AND DIFFICULT CONVERSATIONS

A Leadership Competencies Laboratory

Brent D. Ruben and Christine Goldthwaite

onflict is an inevitable aspect of organizational life within colleges and universities, and one of our greatest tests as leaders is the way we think about and respond to conflictful situations. Problems related to conflict occur in relationships, workgroups, teams, departments, and schools and at the institutional level. Many definitions of conflict have been offered. One general and quite useful classic description is "an incompatibility of interest between two or more persons giving rise to struggles between them" (Simons, 1974). Recognizing that "incompatibilities" may be "real" and tangible, or symbolic and conceptual (Ruben, 1978), we suggest modifying the definition to "any perceived incompatibility of interest between two or more persons giving rise to struggles between them." Conflict can be triggered by competition over scarce resources, contradictory points of view about organizational priorities, conflicting values, differing perspectives on particular ideas, contentious responses to future plans, disagreements about aspects of day-to-day operations, reactions to a written or spoken message, or any of a number of other events, circumstances, or perceptions.

One of the particular challenges for leaders with regard to conflict pertains to the tendency to view conflict in negative terms, as a struggle, fight, incompatibility, or problem that must be solved or eliminated (Ruben, 1978). Indeed, conflict can "feel" uncomfortable depending on the way it is understood in a particular situation. But even when conflict seems and feels negative, it can have many positive qualities and can lead to beneficial long-term outcomes if leaders allow themselves to approach these circumstances with a neutral, even positive outlook and a commitment to find benefits in the situation. These benefits could be a more informed solution to a problem, more constructive collaboration among colleagues, an enhancement in perspective, or personal learning by the parties involved. The point is simply that neither the conflict nor potential outcomes are inherently negative or positive, but rather ultimately depend on the way a leader frames and addresses the situation (Ruben, 1978).

As is so often the case, determining whether to attach a positive or negative valence to a particular circumstance is very much a matter of interpretation and sensemaking. Without becoming overly philosophical, we can say that neither problems nor their interpretation exist fully formed or defined in the world; rather, we define them as we make personal sense of the events we encounter. Just as communication processes play a role in determining what we will regard as a potentially positive or negative circumstance, communication is also extremely important in the way we interact with others in these situations.

Much of what has been written under the heading of "difficult conversations" deals with circumstances that are potentially conflictful, potentially negative, and often emotionally charged, where the challenge as a leader is to constructively frame the situation and to address it in a way that results in positive and productive outcomes.

In formal and informal situations of all kinds, topics emerge that may be difficult for leaders and colleagues to address. This difficulty may be attributed to the sensitivity of the topic, strongly held opinions, intense emotions, or a history of challenging or conflictful communication. The core difficulty may also arise from recognized power differentials among the individuals involved, the high stakes surrounding a particular issue or set of issues, and often some combination of these factors.

Difficulty in Personal Interactions

It has become a widely accepted truism that conversations regarding topics such as religion and politics can be problematic, especially among individuals with strong convictions or competing perspectives on the subject. These topics can even become contentious among close family and friends.

One remedy often suggested is to avoid controversial topics altogether. Avoidance can be an effective strategy, but it seems unfortunate that otherwise close friends and colleagues cannot have constructive conversations on such topics and that the selected approach for dealing with these difficult matters is to avoid them entirely. In these and other circumstances, a strategy of avoidance can contribute to a context that is superficial, unproductive, and uncomfortable for all involved. Take for example a situation where friends of opposing political orientations are in the same room watching news programming on a channel recognized for partisan reporting, or when colleagues in a group discussion at work begin to exchange views on a senior leader who is liked and admired by some of those present yet disliked and disrespected by others. Predictably, messages will resonate in a confirming way with some but lead to a strong negative reaction by others, and vice versa. One person's truths may be another's fiction, and efforts to discuss controversial or contentious topics have the potential to easily spiral out of hand and lead to troublesome outcomes.

Difficulty in Professional Interactions

Difficult communication situations are relatively common in workplace contexts, and often issues arise that *must* be addressed; avoidance may not be a viable option. Such situations may occur in one-to-one conversations, group meetings, and organizational settings. The classic example of a difficult conversation arises when an individual must share information that is likely to be regarded as negative or potentially upsetting. This can occur, for example, where unwelcomed test results must be discussed with a patient or student, or when, as a leader, bad news about a hoped-for promotion must be conveyed, a critique is needed to address a pattern of deteriorating performance, or behaviors judged to be inappropriate or unprofessional must be confronted.

Analogous situations arise when a leader needs to communicate difficult messages to a workgroup or department, such as when a leader judges the performance of the unit to be substandard, or when that leader has been told by superiors that matters of concern must be addressed with the workgroup or department. Conflicts that a leader must address may also arise due to interpersonal incompatibilities, task disagreements over what needs to be done, or process disagreements related to responsibilities for completing work within groups or teams (Jehn, 1997). More broadly, leadership challenges also occur when delivering difficult messages regarding significant organizational issues. These may include topics such as anticipated mergers, budget cuts, plans to outsource core services, or other changes that affected parties will likely find troubling.

Thinking in terms of educational and academic health care environments in particular, if left unaddressed—or addressed in a less than ideal manner— these kinds of situations can damage the educational climate, employee morale and engagement, and workplace productivity, and may ultimately have an adverse impact on organizational effectiveness or the experiences of beneficiaries (Overton & Lowery, 2013).

Preparing for Difficult Conversations

There are concrete steps leaders can take in preparing for difficult conversations that will help to improve the chances for a positive outcome. The principles of strategic communication can be helpful for engaging in these types of discussions (Ruben et al., 2017). The model that follows, adapted for the context of engaging in difficult conversations, is one such guide that might be useful for formal leaders or those seeking to influence the outcomes of a difficult conversation.

What Is at Stake?

First, for the individual contemplating how to approach a difficult conversation, it is important to determine what is at stake for the organization and the individuals involved. How might a difficult conversation advance important organizational aspirations, standards, and principles? How might the conversation affect employees' dedication to the organization and their work? In what ways will the interaction influence the employees' perception of the leader? What precedent does the selected approach set for addressing future difficult topics in a candid and constructive manner? Are there personally sensitive or identity issues that may be playing a role in the situation for one or more individuals? How might the handling of sensitive matters affect the experiences of beneficiaries—students, patients, or visitors, for example— and their view of an organization or its faculty and staff? Gaining clarity on what is at stake will provide a rationale for the discussion and serve as a guide in preparing for a difficult conversation.

Who Is the Audience?

A second step is to consider who should be included in the conversation. Is this a matter that should be taken up with one individual, several individuals, a workgroup, or an entire department? What benefits and liabilities may result from engaging a larger group in the discussion, and in what ways should the presence of a broader audience influence one's approach to the conversation? Is there a relevant history of communication with this individual or group that should be considered? What power or role differentials exist, and how should one take account of these factors in preparing for and engaging in the conversation? How important is the cultivation of long-term relationships with this individual or group? Each of these considerations can be important to the way one thinks about and prepares for a challenging conversation and to the short- and longer term success of the communication event.

What Is the Goal?

Goals provide an essential guide for difficult conversations because they have the potential to shape the way the interaction unfolds. It is therefore critical to clarify goals and desired outcomes prior to the start of the conversation and to continually remind oneself of your intentions as the conversation progresses. Particularly when problematic topics are being addressed or when emotions are heightened, having clearly defined goals and predetermined outcomes in mind can contribute to the ways in which one navigates the conversation.

While the goals may seem rather obvious, there are often many nuances to consider. For example, initiating a conversation intended to solicit input and gain an understanding of a topic of concern to the other party would be quite different in approach and messaging than one where the aim is to share a list of concerns with others. Regardless of the purpose for the conversation, it is important to remind oneself that every communicative interaction has both a relational and informational dimension (Watzlawick et al., 1967), and both require consideration. While the primary goal may be to deliver a difficult message that involves a series of facts, a no less important goal may be to preserve or strengthen—or at least not further damage—a relationship. In an organization where many legal or regulatory considerations are in play, upholding policies or procedures may need to take priority. Even in highly regulated environments, however, the longer term foundation for a commitment to policy adherence is reinforced through attention to relational communication.

Thinking through one's goals prior to every difficult encounter can be challenging or time-consuming, but this stage is particularly critical when planning to engage with individuals who may be reluctant to speak candidly on a given topic, or with those who have lesser or greater positional power. In addition, an important secondary goal is for leaders to handle difficult conversations in a way that models an approach to leadership communication that would hopefully be emulated by colleagues when they are dealing with comparable situations.

What Is the Plan of Action?

Step 4 focuses on the actual planning of the conversation. Formulating the action plan requires a determination of one's intended message and the selection of an appropriate venue or medium for the conversation given the identified goals. For example, should the message be primarily informative, simply conveying the facts related to a decision, or should the message also explain the underlying rationale? Should the message include a persuasive appeal designed to influence listeners to change their perspectives or behavior? Is the message designed to solicit information, or is a two-way exchange of perspectives most appropriate given the identified goals?

This stage also involves a consideration of the most effective channels for the circumstance, whether it be an email, an informal, spontaneous hallway conversation, a town hall meeting, or a formally scheduled one-on-one meeting in one's office. For example, if a message is likely to stir emotions, a face-to-face setting is generally most appropriate, despite the potential for triggering open conflict and the need to respond more quickly and extemporaneously than might be required if the conversation took place via email or memo. If the matter is likely to be highly contentious or potentially litigious, it may also be important to follow up with written confirmation of key points from the conversation and to consider having a designated witness or security personnel present to provide a third-party account of what transpired in the meeting, and in extreme cases to assist with tensions that may arise in the moment.

How Did It Go?

An important step often overlooked by leaders is to reflect on the outcomes of the discussion. Important questions to consider during this stage are as follows: How would you describe the process, tenor, and outcome of the meeting? How would others involved in the process summarize the conversation? What follow-up steps are required? How should this discussion be documented in cases of potential grievances or litigation? What might be done differently in the future to address this kind of problem if it were to occur again? How can this kind of situation be prevented from developing (e.g., set clearer expectations, stay closer to the process)? What personal and/or professional leadership lessons can you take away from the situation? Identifying a colleague who can be a helpful sounding board, coach, or mentor with whom to confer in this debriefing stage can be extremely beneficial.

These five steps can be valuable as a guide for leaders. The fast-paced nature of the contemporary workplace is such that we may have the tendency to move immediately into difficult conversations without adequate planning related to the rationale, goals, or most appropriate communication infrastructure for the encounter. As Ruben et al. (2016) are careful to note, "While strategic communication practices do not guarantee the absence of undesirable outcomes for leaders, such practices certainly lessen their likelihood of occurrence and their severity if and when they do occur" (p. 202).

Communication Strategies for Difficult Conversations

There are a number of specific communication strategies that can be helpful in addressing and managing conflicts and other difficult situations in a productive manner. Various authors (Dowling, 2008; The Ohio State University, 2019; Stone et al., 1991) offer advice and suggestions, such as the following:

- **Create a positive climate**. At the outset of a difficult conversation, endeavor to create a climate where all parties feel comfortable sharing their thoughts and feelings without fear of being immediately criticized or attacked. Be proactive and clear in expressing your desire to have a constructive interaction. Demonstrating mutual respect and taking a problem-solving stance helps to create a positive environment (Patterson et al., 2002).
- **Focus first on areas of potential agreement**. Promote shared respect and a sense of mutual purpose. Identify values, perspectives, and "high-level" themes on which all parties can agree that will serve as the foundation for the conversation prior to engaging in the specifics. Focusing first on shared values and goals generally provides a useful point of entry to the discussion. From those areas of shared perspective, the conversation can move to topics where there will be predictable differences of opinion or sources of potential conflict or concern. To the extent that these difficult topics can be described in relation to common values or goals, there is often a greater likelihood of mutual understanding and, ideally, increased receptivity.
- **Listen carefully and actively**. An effective and nonjudgmental focus on the ideas and words of others—rather than your own reactions—is essential, though often quite difficult to achieve. Helpful techniques include asking clarifying questions, paraphrasing, and summarizing what you think you heard the other person say before offering a response of your own.
- **Focus on perspective-taking**. Engage in listening efforts with the goal of understanding the situation from the other person's point of view. How do they see it? What information and arguments are they incorporating into their perspective? How do they construct their point of view and arrive at the conclusions they do? This understanding is important in its own right for clarifying others' viewpoints, and it can also be helpful in formulating the most effective response to the situation. Moreover, the act of listening conveys a level of respect that fosters the best possible climate for the subsequent discussion of points of disagreement.

- **Avoid accusations, defensiveness, generalizations, and attributions of motives or implied blame**. Rather than engage in a discussion of one another's motives or the history of disagreements about a given problem, it may be more productive to focus instead on goals, current topics, and a path forward for the future. Consciously avoid tendencies to overreact verbally or emotionally to particular "hot-button" or trigger phrases that may be used by others. Often the best approach is simply to ignore potentially annoying words or phrases (Cherniss & Roche, 2020). Endeavor to steer clear of personal sensitivities and concerns that are not central to the issue at hand.
- **Distinguish between facts and stories**. Focusing on facts, while minimizing personal accounts, narratives, and stories that refer to feelings, perceptions, and attitudes, tends to keep the conversation on track and helps to steer clear of emotional responses and reactions.
- **Minimize the use of contentious words and phrases**. Avoid using words or terminology that might be lightning rods and that could trigger a knee-jerk reaction in others. Also, suppress your own tendencies to react to particular words of others in a reflex-like manner, focusing instead on the more general concepts behind the words.
- **Adopt "Yes, and" rather than "Yes, but" framing**. Often the simple decision to use "and" rather than "but" can help to create constructive conversations rather than generating defensiveness. For example, a much more positive climate is established by a phrase such as, "I can understand and agree with your first point, *and* I would like to hear more about your thinking about the second point" rather than "I like your initial point, *but* the second point is unclear."
- **Expect the unexpected**. Assume that the conversation may not proceed exactly as you had hoped. Anticipate points of possible difficulty while also developing contingency strategies and alternative messages. For example, think about how to deal with silence or hostile responses. Generally, the best approach is to remain respectful, be mindful of your goal(s), stay on message, and remember that you always have the option to defer parts of the discussion to a later time if you choose. If you decide to select this option, you create an opportunity to gather additional information or consider alternative approaches, messages, or venues/media. There may be times when remaining respectful and calm is particularly difficult, especially when others are not exhibiting these same behaviors. Indeed, it may even become necessary to indicate that a person's comments and manner are inappropriate and to reschedule the conversation to provide the individual an opportunity to collect their thoughts

and moderate their emotions to ensure the session will be more constructive for all involved.

- **Plan how you will close the conversation**. Generally, this should include a summary and an expression of appreciation for others' willingness to have a constructive/civil discussion of the situation or problem, acknowledging that you understand it was not necessarily easy to do, and indicating your desire for positive future interactions on this and other subjects. There are situations where achieving one's goals will not be possible, and it may be necessary to step away, defer final action, or plan to continue the discussion at a future time. Also, be prepared to revisit the conversation in the future of a problem persists. If extreme personal sensitivities, allegations, and concerns surface, and particularly if they may have regulatory or legal or implications, it may be important to put the conversation on hold and defer follow-up until there has been an opportunity to consult with individuals who are appropriately trained or who occupy official university-assigned roles in human resources or other responsible departments.

Helpful Openings

Beginning a difficult conversation can be particularly challenging. Author Judy Ringer (2019) offers a number of possible opening lines that may be useful, modeling an approach that emphasizes the use of "I" statements:

- I have something I'd like to discuss with you that I think will help us work together more effectively.
- I'd like to talk about _____ with you, but first I'd like to get your point of view.
- I need your help with what just happened. Do you have a few minutes to talk?
- I need your help with something. Can we talk about it (soon)? If the person says, "Sure, let me get back to you," take the lead in getting back to them if they do not follow-up.
- I think we have different perceptions about_____. I'd like to hear your thinking on this.
- I'd like to talk about _____. I think we may have different ideas about how to _____.
- I'd like to see if we might reach a better understanding about _____. I really want to hear your feelings about this and share my perspective as well.

Communication Style and Style Flexibility

Over the course of a lifetime of experiences, each person develops a unique communication style—a customary, preferred, and natural approach for relating to the many situations and people they encounter (Ruben, 2021b; Ruben & Stewart, 2020). Communication styles are habits of practice. They serve as default guides in our interactions in social and professional settings.

Typically, communication styles operate in the background of our experiences. As such, they are seldom a subject for reflection. This lack of conscious attention can be a problem for leaders—actually, for anyone striving to be as successful as they can be in social and professional situations. If individuals could assume that their default communication styles were always effective and well-received, regardless of the goals, situations, or persons with whom they were interacting, there would be no problem. As discussed in the previous chapters, however, so often personal, social, and professional effectiveness depend on an individual's ability to apply analytic and communication competencies to evaluate a situation, their own goals, and the communication styles of those with whom they are interacting, and then to select their approach accordingly. Various tools and techniques, including many of those related to emotional intelligence, are available to assist with the self-reflection and awareness-raising for leaders (Cherniss & Roche, 2020). One tool designed specifically for this purpose is the Communication Style Inventory (Ruben, 2021b).

While a reflective and strategic approach to communication style can always be an asset to leaders and others in professional settings, it is particularly essential when dealing with conflict and difficult conversations. Some leaders, for example, naturally use an outgoing, highly verbal style in their dealings with others, while others may customarily use a more passive and restrained interpersonal style, due either to preference or apprehension about speaking in social situations. Each approach has its assets and liabilities, depending on the situation at hand. In a low-stakes situation, a reserved, moderated response may be a very reasonable approach, enabling one to avoid conflict and solidify a foundation of goodwill for future situations. On the other hand, an emergency or crisis is likely to call for greater expedience, assertiveness, and tenacity. That said, an overly expressive and assertive approach in a crisis situation can exacerbate tensions and may trigger unhelpful emotional responses. Developing the ability to analyze situations, determining how others with whom you are interacting are likely to deal with particular events, and being well-informed about your own communication style—and then consciously selecting an approach based on that knowledge—can be extremely helpful for preparing for difficult conversations. While generalizations can be problematic, it is helpful to be mindful that some common responses to challenging and conflictful situations should be avoided if at all possible. These include (a) avoiding and failing to engage with the issue; (b) passively yielding to another's position; (c) accepting an outcome that is wholly incompatible with one's goals; and (d) remaining overly rigid in one's position. Every effort should be made to prevent these outcomes.

Each person's communication style is highly individualized, falling somewhere on a spectrum that ranges from an internalizing approach at one end to an externalizing approach at the other (Ruben, 2021b; Ruben & Stewart, 2020). Each end of the spectrum defines an extreme. An internalizing style is characterized as being less verbal, reserved, and indirect, and an externalizing style is highly verbal, blunt, and dominating. While there are assets associated with both styles, each also has liabilities (Ruben & Stewart, 2020). For example, someone with an internalizing style might be perceived as sensitive to others' needs and wants, an effective listener, and willing to compromise. Their style might also be interpreted as avoiding important issues and being slow to respond and overly sensitive, with the result of potentially limited or diminished impact. Someone with an externalizing style might be viewed as articulate, outgoing, and able to take charge, but also may be less aware of nonverbal cues, too quick to respond, or insensitive, with the result being damage to one or more relationships.

Leading difficult conversations requires individuals to be aware of their natural approach and to recognize another's style in order to develop flexibility, particularly when extreme styles intersect in difficult conversations. For example, if two individuals with an externalizing approach are engaged in a difficult conversation, escalating conflict may be likely, while at the other extreme, inaction may be the result of difficult conversations among two individuals with dominant internalizing styles. Knowing one's own natural or "default" style and making an effort to assess the style of others who will be engaged in a discussion is an important first step. More generally, striving to develop flexibility in one's own style as a way of adapting to the varying needs of situations and the styles of others becomes a very useful leadership competency to acquire.

Building a Facilitative Culture and Climate for Difficult Conversation Success

Difficult conversations are made more problematic in organizations or relationships with a dysfunctional communication climate, or situations where there exists a culture devoid of mutual respect and shared purpose. Difficult conversations are far more likely to be productive when all involved parties feel that it is safe to engage in dialogue, particularly when there are opposing opinions, strong emotions, and high stakes (Patterson et al., 2012). These realities point to the benefits of ongoing efforts to create a congenial, respectful, and supportive relational and organizational climate.

It is also the case that a climate characterized by defensive, demeaning, or destructive interactions will make it even more difficult to achieve positive outcomes when difficult conversations are needed. In a toxic communication climate, people are reluctant to engage and avoid candor in order to protect their identity and self-esteem. Armed with this insight, it is important that leaders continually work to create a climate where employees feel valued and "psychologically safe" (Edmonson, 1999). While this phrase has a variety of meanings, some associated with pejorative or politically oriented perspectives, the basic dimensions of the concept are quite important for leaders to keep in mind. As Edmondson (2019) notes,

> Psychological safety is broadly defined as a climate in which people are comfortable expressing and being themselves. More specifically, when people have psychological safety at work, they feel comfortable sharing concerns and mistakes without fear of embarrassment or retribution. They are confident that they can speak up and won't be humiliated, ignored, or blamed. They know they can ask questions when they are unsure about something. They tend to trust and respect their colleagues. When a work environment has reasonably high psychological safety, good things happen; mistakes are reported quickly so that prompt corrective action can be taken; seamless coordination across groups or departments is enabled; and potentially game-changing ideas for innovation are shared. In short, psychological safety is a crucial source of value creation in organizations operating in a complex, changing environment. (p. xvi)

Edmondson also offers three strategies leaders can use to create a psychologically safe climate. These include creating shared expectations, encouraging individuals to voice their perspectives and concerns, and supporting and motivating continuous learning. For leaders, the implications are clear: Strive to be open, encouraging, respectful, constructive, and nonjudgmental in communication and encourage colleagues to do the same.

Conclusion

There are no magical formulas that assure success in difficult conversations. Nonetheless, thoughtful planning, focused engagement, and careful reflection following these conversations are strategies that can help to increase the likelihood of productive and satisfying outcomes. As a leader, it is essential to be able to acknowledge and respond to disagreement and conflict in a constructive manner. Often, expressions of concern, criticism, or complaint can provide insights about ways to improve leadership and organizational practice. Those who give constructive voice to their concerns can be among one's most dedicated, well-intentioned, and helpful colleagues—rather than being troublemakers or sources of problems as one might assume. While difficult conversations are seldom a favorite pastime for leaders, they represent opportunities to clarify standards of performance, develop employees, promote candor, and most importantly, advance the quality of the organization, its culture, and its work.

For Further Consideration

How would you handle the following situations based on the ideas and suggestions presented in this chapter?

1. A memo outlining a new performance review and evaluation process was distributed to all leaders. The impact of this new program will be significant, and you expect it will cause great concern among your colleagues when they learn about it. You also have concerns and personally do not fully support the change as it is currently structured. The topic is an agenda item for the next meeting. How do you, as program director, introduce and handle the discussion at the meeting?

2. A junior faculty member in your department has complained to you about what is described as bullying behavior of a senior faculty colleague. As the department chair, you have informally discussed the issue with the senior faculty member, but he does not see that his behavior is a problem and instead suggests that his junior colleague should "toughen up." Recently you have observed his hostile criticism of others in a faculty meeting, prompting the need for you to raise the issue of his behavior again. How would you handle this second communication that you expect to be "difficult"?

3. You are a recently recruited leader in a major unit within the institution. You were promised support of various kinds, and based on those commitments you have shared information with members of the unit and newly recruited faculty members. Nine months have

passed and only a few of these commitments have been realized. You are becoming deeply concerned about your ability to meet the expectations established when you were hired, the declining morale of new and continuing colleagues, and what you see as the very real possibility that you will fail through what seems like no fault of your own. You decide you must have a candid conversation with the person to whom you report, because the time to turn the situation around is limited. What is at stake, what are your goals, and what are your key talking points? What trigger words and phrases should be avoided? What is the ideal outcome from the conversation?

12

LEADERSHIP SELF-ASSESSMENT AND REFLECTIVE PRACTICE

Always a Work in Progress

In This Chapter

- How does one translate theories of leadership into personal leadership practice?
- What differentiates personal leadership development from organizational leadership development?
- Why is personal leadership development important for the individual leader as well as the unit, department, or institution that one leads?
- How can the five-step model for becoming a more effective leader presented in this chapter be useful to one's growth and development?

The pursuit of leadership excellence is a personal matter, one that must begin with an individually defined and personally relevant sense of purpose. The developmental process of becoming a better leader is ongoing and enduring, and this is certainly the case within colleges and universities, which are dedicated to continuous learning. As detailed in this chapter, there is great value in applying the principles of continuous improvement to one's own development, especially when situations are challenging and desired outcomes are elusive.

The concepts of learning and change are both critical for facilitating the development of successful leaders (Day et al., 2004). As described by Kegan (1982), Luthans and Avolio (2003), and others, leadership development is a process that occurs over the course of one's life. An individual's commitment to development requires a continuous process of learning, discovery, and self-awareness. The metaphor of a journey is often used to describe this life-long activity. Like many personal and professional journeys, the terrain can be rough, the conditions are often unpredictable, and the destination quite often is uncertain. Despite variables that lie beyond any individual's control, the decision to develop as a leader must be made with clarity of intention and purpose.

The aim of leadership development is not necessarily identifying a specific plan of action; rather, the more significant challenge is engaging in a deliberate commitment to a plan and maintaining momentum. Continuing with the metaphor of a journey, this chapter lays out a series of concepts and guides individuals can choose to take with them when engaging in leadership development. The concepts, tools, strategies, and models presented in the following pages are designed to be useful for academic and administrative leaders in strengthening overall leadership performance and in their sense of efficacy.

Personal Leadership Development

Individual or personal leadership development is sometimes termed *leader development*. Here, we use "leadership development" and "leader development" interchangeably. These concepts are distinct from the expansive concept of institutional or organizational leadership development, which will be addressed in chapter 18. Leader development, as defined by McCauley, van Velsor, and Ruderman (2010), is "the expansion of a person's capacity to be effective in leadership roles and processes" (p. 2). In leadership development, an emphasis is placed on cultivating human capital, or the "individual-based knowledge, skills, and abilities associated with formal leadership roles" (Day, 2001, p. 585). We focus here on self-assessment and self-improvement for individual leaders in higher education, with a goal of having readers better understand the expectations and requirements associated with academic and administrator leader roles.

As noted throughout this book, leaders in higher education face complex and multifaceted challenges, and these challenges show no signs of subsiding. Across the academy these positions require proficiency in a wide array of competencies. Many of the decisions leaders make will directly affect the short- and long-term future of the institution. Thus, an investment in personal leadership development is an investment in the very future of the organization. McCauley, Van Velsor, and Ruderman (2010), editors of the *Center for Creative Leadership Handbook of Leadership Development*, provide a list of areas that might be positively influenced by leadership development:

Leading oneself

- Self-awareness
- Ability to balance conflicting demands
- Ability to learn
- Leadership values

Leading others

- Ability to build and maintain relationships
- Ability to build effective workgroups
- Communication skills
- Ability to develop others

Leading the organization

- Management skills
- Ability to think and act strategically
- Ability to think creatively
- Ability to initiate and implement change

Each of these topics is relevant to the work of higher education. Investments in leader development can improve both individual and collective capacity, contributing to significant improvements in effectiveness, quality, and morale across the college or university.

The Path to Becoming a Better Leader

As noted, developing one's skills as a leader occurs over time and can be thought of as a process of continuous (self-)improvement. The model presented in Figure 12.1 outlines key steps one may choose to consider when engaging in leadership development over the course of one's career. This model takes account of personal reflection, the articulation of a clear rationale for why one leads, feedback provided from self-assessment tools and the feedback of others, and the generation of and ongoing commitment to a purposeful plan for development.

The first step in the learning and change process involves defining your leadership philosophy and the standards to which you aspire. The second stage is determining where you stand relative to those standards. Gaps between current performance—in general or in particular situations—and

Figure 12.1. The path to becoming a better leader.

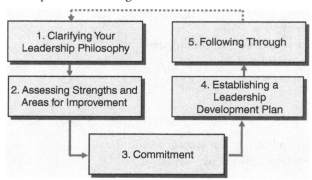

the defined standards represent potential areas for improvement that can only be addressed through a genuine and systematic commitment to change. The next step is translating that commitment into the development of plans and strategies for improvement, followed by the final step of ensuring follow-through on those plans. As the dotted line in the figure implies, the learning and change process is ongoing and involves a recursive cycling through the steps. This model of learning and change is applicable in a wide range of contexts, including personal, social, and organizational situations, and it is particularly relevant for leadership development.

Existing leadership styles and skills should not be regarded as permanent fixtures of one's life. On the contrary, it is important to continually monitor and refine one's approach to leadership, building on insights from personal reflection and the formal and informal feedback provided by others. The learning and change model presented in Figure 12.1 provides a tool that outlines the process by which that can occur.

Clarifying Your Leadership Philosophy

A sound approach to leader development begins with gaining clarity in terms of personal and professional aspirations. This initial phase involves the identification and clarification of a leadership philosophy. By thinking about the type of leader you want to be, you engage in a process that allows you to move forward with intentionality and purpose. Identifying role models and reading the leadership literature—including professional and practical advice and biographies of respected leaders—are helpful actions at this stage. Four questions seem especially important:

1. What are your aspirations as a leader—your *vision of leadership*?
2. How would you like to be viewed by others—your *leadership identity*?

3. For what will you be uniquely known as a leader—your *leadership brand*?

4. What would you like your lasting contribution to be—your *leadership legacy*?

Taken together these four aspects comprise one's leadership philosophy. The process of developing your personal view of leadership is akin to what Stephen Covey (2013) describes as "beginning with the end in mind"—a rich opportunity to reflect on who you are and imagine the possibilities of who you intend to be. This initial phase challenges you to reflect on your own leadership goals and aspirations while considering the expectations, perceptions, and attitudes of the many stakeholders with whom you might engage in your work as an academic or administrative leader.

Despite the multiplicity of leadership concepts and roles, several fundamental questions can be particularly helpful in clarifying your personal philosophy and vision. Perhaps the most basic of these questions are described by Perez (2015), as follows: "Before you take a job as an academic administrator, know what issues you are willing to resign over and what you are willing to be fired for. If you don't know the answers to these questions, you shouldn't take the position." Considering the various guideposts presented in Table 12.1 can help you further clarify your leadership philosophy.

TABLE 12.1
Formulating Your Personal Leadership Guideposts

How does your ranking of these various leadership dimensions inform your brand as a leader? What are you known for, and what would you like to be known for in your unit, department, or institution?

How would you rate the following in importance to you personally?
(very important: "1"; somewhat important: "2"; not important: "3")

__ Thought of as an honest and candid colleague
__ Respected for your intellect and insight
__ Admired for your contributions to your discipline or professional area
__ Remembered for your contributions to the department and institution
__ Thought of as a competent leader
__ Known as a supportive and accommodating leader
__ Seen as someone who is forceful in voicing your opinions
__ Seen as an inspirational, transformative leader
__ Building a reputation among senior administrators as an effective leader

(Continues)

TABLE 12.1 (*Continued*)

___ Leaving a significant legacy
___ Regarded as a champion of student rights
___ Respected for your dedication to teaching/learning
___ Developing the next generation of leaders
___ Admired for your dedication to the well-being of your colleagues

Assessing Strengths and Areas for Improvement

The next step on the path to becoming a better leader involves the assessment of strengths as well as areas that need improvement. This phase allows you to understand where you stand relative to the aspirations and philosophy identified in the previous step. Leaders in higher education come from many disciplines and technical areas, often with little familiarity with the issues in higher education beyond their own areas, and with little or no background in leadership, management, or organizational theory and development. Assuming a formal leadership role in a college or university requires a candid assessment of strengths that can be leveraged and of areas most in need of improvement.

One structured approach to self-reflection involves a consideration of the various competencies needed for effective leadership, using a tool such as the Leadership Competencies Scorecard—the LCS, discussed in chapter 9. The LCS outlines various competencies useful for successful leadership, including positional competencies, analytic competencies, personal competencies, communication competencies, and organizational competencies (Ruben, 2006, 2019, 2021a). Using this model, the self-improvement process involves several steps:

- identifying competency areas of strength and also areas of needed improvement via self-reflection
- asking colleagues to complete the inventory with you as the target
- comparing self- and colleagues' assessment to identify specific competencies that must be enhanced to attain your stated leadership philosophy
- practicing the application of competencies identified for improvement
- documenting progress in areas for improvement (e.g., keep a journal, ask for feedback from members of your leadership team, your peers, or your superiors)
- engaging in an ongoing reevaluation of areas of strength and potential improvement, and continuing a process of feedback solicitation, practice, and progress documentation

TABLE 12.2

Summary of Relevant Behavioral and Leadership Inventories

Inventory Tool	Description	Key Metrics	Website
Campbell Leadership Descriptor	A self-assessment designed to help individuals identify characteristics for successful leadership, recognize their strengths, and identify areas for improvement	Vision Diplomacy Personal styles Management Feedback Personal energy Empowerment Entrepreneurialism Multicultural awareness	www.ccl.org/leadership/assessments/CLDOverview.aspx
DiSC personality test	A self-assessment of personality and behavioral style intended to improve work productivity, teamwork, and communication	Dominance Influence Steadiness Conscientiousness	www.discprofile.com/what-is-disc/overview
Emotionally Intelligent Leadership Inventory for students	A 57-item evidence-based assessment that measures how often students engage in behaviors that align with emotionally intelligent leadership	Nineteen emotionally intelligent leadership capacities categorized into three domains: • Consciousness of self • Consciousness of others • Consciousness of context	www.wiley.com/WileyCDA/WileyTitle/productCd-1118821661.html

(Continues)

TABLE 12.2 (*Continued*)

Inventory Tool	Description	Key Metrics	Website
Leadership Competencies Scorecard 2.0	Provides a competency-based framework that identifies and integrates a diverse array of characteristics described in scholarly and professional writings as being important for effective leadership	Analytic competencies Personal competencies Communication competencies Organizational competencies Positional competencies	www.nacubo.org/Products/ Publications/Leadership/ What_Leaders_Need_ to_Know_and_Do_A_ Leadership_Competencies_ Scorecard.html
Leadership Practices Inventory (LPI)	A 30-item self-report measure that assesses leadership behaviors based on the five practices of exemplary leadership model	• Model the way • Inspire a shared vision • Challenge the process • Enable others to act • Encourage the heart	www.leadershipchallenge.com/ leaders-section-assessments. aspx
Leadership Style Inventory (LSI)	Designed to assist in the reflective learning process to help people explore and better understand their own approach to leadership by distinguishing two leadership style preferences	• Directive style • Consensual style	www.nacubo.org/Products/ Organizational_Development_ Series/Organizational_ Development_Series_The_ Leadership_Style_Inventory. html

(*Continues*)

TABLE 12.2 *(Continued)*

Inventory Tool	Description	Key Metrics	Website
Myers–Briggs Type Indicator (MBTI)	A self-report questionnaire that indicates personality types based on the psychological preferences identified by Carl Jung. These preferences are indicative of how individuals perceive the world and make decisions.	• Sensation • Intuition • Feeling • Thinking	www.myersbriggs.org/my-mbti-personality-type/mbti-basics
Clifton Strengths Finder	Based on a 40-year study of human strengths, Gallup created a language of the 34 most common talents and developed the Clifton Strengths Finder assessment to help people discover and describe these talents.	Thirty-four strengths, including but not limited to the following: • Achiever • Belief • Consistency • Empathy • Includer • Strategic • Woo	strengths.gallup.com/default.aspx
True Colors personality test	A self-assessment of personality traits identifying individual strengths and challenges across four personality types	• Green = independent thinkers • Gold = pragmatic planners • Orange = action-oriented • Blue = people-oriented	truecolorsintl.com

This competency approach to personal assessment and improvement is one of many available in the leadership literature. For a sample of other leadership inventories, descriptions of the tools as offered on their websites, and the various metrics that they seek to assess, see Table 12.2.

Making use of any of these inventories has a number of benefits: First, each of these tools encourages reflection in responding to the various inventory questions. The very act of completing these inventories may enhance one's understanding of self, other, and context. Next, the potential leadership inventory findings are broad enough to be made relevant to the leadership work needed in higher education. For example, admissions counselors, associate professors, and public safety professionals, despite their different work requirements and institutional responsibilities, may use the findings from these inventories to inform their approach to work and leadership. Finally, the listed inventories present a series of metrics for what is understood to be effective leadership practice.

Tracking your scores on these various inventories over time may help further clarify your strengths and areas of improvement. Note that inventories and self-ratings are always subject to the limitations of our self-report and self-perception. The way we see ourselves and the way we believe we are behaving are often inconsistent with how others perceive us. For this reason, there is value in gaining the perspectives of others on our leadership performance, needs, and strengths. Mentoring and assessment methods that allow for colleagues or friends to constructively share their perspectives—methods such as 360-degree feedback—can be most helpful in this regard.

Committing to Reflective Practice

As described in chapter 9, the idea of enhancing one's leadership competencies is particularly compelling because of the relationship between knowledge and behavior. Competencies have both a knowledge and a skill component. *Knowledge* refers to leaders' understanding of a concept. Skill refers to leaders' effectiveness in operationalizing the knowledge they possess and their strategic ability to act effectively on this information (Ruben, 2006, 2019). Both an understanding of the competency and a proficiency in enacting the skills and behaviors associated with each competency are important.

It is also the case that an understanding of a leadership theory or concept does not naturally translate into action. Often, in our self-assessment we blur the distinction between knowing and doing, and leadership issues may arise because of the gap that often exists between theory and practice (Pfeffer & Sutton, 2000). Feedback and evaluations from others are critical to reflection and leader development. Without such input, it becomes very difficult to separate one's knowledge and good intentions from the way these play out in practice. Reflection is essential to connecting knowledge and practice. Simply put, reflective practice involves a commitment to consciously monitor and review your actions as a leader, the understandings that guided those actions, and the outcomes that result (Dewey, 1933; Lewin, 1952; Schön, 1984). Schön (1984) describes this practice as follows:

> The practitioner allows himself [sic] to experience surprise, puzzlement, or confusion in a situation which he finds uncertain or unique. He reflects on the phenomenon before him, and on the prior understandings which have been implicit in his behavior. He carries out an experiment which serves to generate both a new understanding of the phenomenon and a change in the situation. (p. 68)

In essence, the idea is to apply the scientific method to your own performance as a leader—to become, in effect, a leadership researcher—where the focus of study is your own understanding and behavior, the outcomes that result, and the lessons learned that can inform how you might more effectively approach future leadership situations.

Continuous improvement requires ongoing experimentation and reflection, similar to the research traditions of higher education. Through reflective practice, one can revisit both the leadership philosophy and self-assessment findings as a way of assessing continuing gaps, tracking progress on these areas of improvement, and identifying new areas in need of attention. As noted previously, and important part of this process includes receiving feedback from those who observe your actions and reactions in specific contexts and situations, which provides a check on self-assessments that may be overly self-critical or self-congratulatory.

Committing to reflective practice implies that time will be spent debriefing at the end of interactions, meetings, or events—reviewing and rethinking the leadership concepts that guided your actions, reexamining the way those understandings were put into practice, and reflecting on outcomes. The following are some key questions to use in the reflective process:

- What was I trying to accomplish?
- What understandings—theories or concepts—guided my actions?
- How effective was I at translating my understanding into practice?
- Was the outcome what I expected or hoped for? If not, why not?
- What options should I have considered?

- What refinements should I consider for the future in my understanding and my actions?

By focusing on individual leadership behaviors as a specific unit of analysis, demonstrating a commitment to solicit and use feedback, and treating every leadership situation as a learning opportunity, you can continue to experiment with and learn from various approaches to leadership that best meet the needs of the unit, department, or institution. As highlighted throughout this book, the context(s) within which one leads, coupled with the needs, expectations, and history of the followers, shape the approach to leadership that might be most effective.

Establishing a Leadership Development Plan

The three previous steps eventually lead to a point where you can begin to establish a clear, realistic, thoughtful, and action-oriented leadership development plan. Such a plan might include the following elements:

- Commit to becoming a student of leadership theory and practice.
- Identify role models from whom you can learn.
- Make every situation a learnable moment and an opportunity to become a better leader.
- Look for informal and formal opportunities to lead and learn both within and beyond your unit, department, or institution.
- Establish goals and develop a plan for how to achieve these goals in every influence situation.
- Monitor your behavior.
- Debrief to assess your effectiveness, perhaps by comparing your goals and the outcome that was realized.
- When possible, seek third-party assessments from others.

McCauley, Kanaga, and Lafferty (2010) offer a wide array of approaches to individual leadership development, organized into five broad categories:

Developmental relationships

- Mentors
- Professional coaches
- Manager as coach
- Peer learning partners
- Social identity networks
- Communities of practice

Developmental assignments

- Job moves
- Job rotations
- Expanded work responsibilities
- Temporary assignments
- Action learning projects
- Leadership roles outside work

Feedback processes

- Performance appraisal
- 360-degree feedback
- Assessment centers

Formal programs

- University programs
- Skill training
- Feedback-intensive programs
- Personal growth programs

Self-development activities

- Reading (books, articles, online resources)
- Speakers and colloquia
- Professional conferences and trade shows
- Fireside chats, town hall meetings, all-staff meetings (p. 45)

Your institution may offer any number of these opportunities for leadership development, depending on the organization's "climate for development" (McCauley, Kanaga, & Lafferty, 2010, p. 50). This idea reappears in chapter 18 on collective leadership development initiatives. For now, it is most important to recognize the need for articulating a personalized plan for development— one that bridges the theories, concepts, and ideas to emerge from self-reflection and self-assessment with the concluding step of following through.

Following Through

The final step on one's leadership development journey is follow-through. The plan, along with the various methods of self-assessment and self-reflection, are only worthwhile if they are put into action to improve one's own leadership practice and to strengthen the unit, department, or institution that one leads. This emphasis on action is consistent with what Ibarra (2015) identifies as the outsight principle, which she describes as follows: "The only way to think like a leader is to first act: to plunge yourself into new projects and activities, interact with very different kinds of people, and experiment with unfamiliar ways of getting things done" (p. 5). These new ways of acting change not only how we think, according to Ibarra, but also who we become along the way. She continues by acknowledging the following important point about leadership development, one that is especially relevant in higher education:

> Who you are as a leader is not the starting point on your development journey, but rather the outcome of learning about yourself. This knowledge can only come about when you do new things and work with new and different people. You don't unearth your true self; it emerges from what you do. (p. 5)

For Ibarra, it is through action—and what we would describe as following through on the plans that you initially set for yourself as a leader—that you can begin to learn how to lead. As she suggests, "Knowing the kind of leader you'd like to become is not the starting point on your development journey, but rather the result of increasing your outsight" (p. 186).

The value of following through and acting on these leadership plans cannot be underestimated. A commitment to personal leadership development—like any personal change—is challenging. Changing one's leadership behavior and practices can be particularly difficult for higher education personnel. As mentioned throughout this text, our education and socialization as faculty and technical staff members provide preparation for *individual* success. Faculty members, in particular, learn to be independent and self-directed. While these characteristics may be important for our success as individuals, they are generally unrelated—sometimes even antithetical—to those necessary for effective leadership. As we learn to develop an independent point of view, argue on behalf of specific claims, and defend our perspective, these same criteria may pose potential liabilities for leadership development, where careful listening; encouraging feedback, negotiation, and compromise; asking for help; cultivating interdependent relationships; and developing a base of support are critical.

Finally, trained as creative thinkers, faculty and technical professionals tend to be very effective at developing plans—which is certainly an important capability for leaders. However, implementing those plans with others often requires a different knowledge and skill set. Without effective implementation, our efforts can easily contribute to stereotypes associated with the slow pace of change within higher education.

Conclusion

The most proactive and constructive approach to enhancing leadership competencies and behaviors is much the same as it would be for improving musical or athletic competency: Maintain a commitment to further development and broadening of knowledge and skills, devote serious attention to reflective practice, seek opportunities and helpful tools to aid in genuine self-reflection, solicit others' evaluations and improvement suggestions, identify and learn from others who possess the desired knowledge and skills, pursue opportunities to practice and improve, and stay the course. A lifelong dedication to leadership development is at times arduous, unpredictable, and complex, yet maintaining a commitment to ongoing reflection and improvement of one's competencies is a defining value of individuals who come to be recognized as outstanding leaders.

For Further Consideration

1. LCS
   Download and complete the LCS—available at https://ol.rutgers.edu/leadership-competencies-scorecard/ (Ruben, 2021a) and ask a friend or colleague to complete the same inventory with you in mind. Focus particularly on the results for your ratings for "effectiveness in practice," compare your self-assessments with the assessments from the other person, use the results to develop a profile of leadership strengths and areas in need of improvement.
2. Personal leadership plan
   Complete one of the self-assessment inventories listed in Table 12.2. If you choose to complete more than one of these inventories, develop a profile that integrates the findings from the various assessments. Create a personal leadership plan that aligns with your personal and professional goals. Based on the findings of the self-assessment tool(s), determine your core strengths and areas of improvement as a leader. Identify, also, specific actions you can take to enhance your leadership effectiveness. Place these intended actions on a timeline that you can revisit periodically as part of your personal leadership plan.

PART THREE

APPLIED TOOLS FOR LEADERSHIP AND ORGANIZATIONAL EFFECTIVENESS

13

THE EXCELLENCE IN HIGHER EDUCATION MODEL

An Integrating Framework for Envisioning, Pursuing, and Sustaining Organizational Excellence

In This Chapter

- What do we mean by excellence in higher education?
- How does organizational excellence differ from and relate to academic or professional excellence?
- How can the concepts of organizational excellence be helpful for envisioning and achieving outstanding performance in colleges and universities?
- How can the excellence in higher education framework be used to guide planning, assessment, and improvement?

The pursuit of excellence is often mentioned as a core value by administrators across a variety of institutions and fields. But what exactly is meant by excellence, and what tools are available to help leaders conceptualize and pursue this vision? Hearing the word *excellence* used to describe a university, department, or program quite naturally evokes an image of academically and professionally distinguished faculty and staff, whose collective expertise makes it possible to create exceptional educational, research, and outreach programs. While certainly an important ingredient of excellence, the talents and achievements of individual academics and professionals are often not particularly good predictors of the overall performance of the program, department, school, or college of which they are a part. The reason is simply that the excellence of individual faculty and staff is but one component of organizational excellence.

While there are clearly defined criteria and procedures for evaluating individual academic and technical excellence, unfortunately, comparable criteria, rubrics, or tools to help leaders identify elements of organizational excellence, or to assess the effectiveness of higher education organizations, are not readily available. This chapter is devoted to exploring this gap, and to describing excellence in higher education (EHE)—one framework designed specifically to address this critical need.

Assessment, planning, and improvement are familiar concepts within colleges and universities, and every campus has administrators, faculty, and staff who are committed to employing these activities within their units. What is often lacking, however, is a systematic and integrated approach to organizational excellence that can be applied consistently within the varying units of the institution and one that is also appropriate for bridging differences among academic, professional, administrative, student life, and service organizations.

Conceptualizing and Pursuing Organizational Effectiveness

In much the same way that common evaluative frameworks and rubrics are useful in conceptualizing and assessing faculty qualifications or course design and learning outcomes across multiple disciplines, comparable templates can be extremely valuable for designing, planning, assessing, and improving organizations across an institution. The EHE framework (Ruben, 2016a), inspired by the Malcolm Baldrige approach (Baldrige National Quality Program, 2021), is one such tool.

For leaders throughout a college or university, the EHE framework can be helpful for addressing a variety of common challenges, such as the following:

- Your division has undergone significant transitions over the past several years in response to changing environmental demands. There is now a need to step back and take stock of where the division stands, how well the unit is functioning, whether current programs and services are effectively serving their intended constituencies, and whether there are important unaddressed needs.
- As a recently appointed dean, you feel the need to get a quick but comprehensive sense of your leadership team and staff and to identify strengths and priorities for improvement.
- Your supervisor has asked you to conduct a full review of your administrative unit with an eye to considering where significant improvements might be made in the services offered.

- Preliminary discussions are underway to consider the merits of launching a new program, and there are widely differing opinions as to the viability of such an effort.
- In anticipation of accreditation, you want to begin a systematic review of your department and its programs that will meet the requirements of accreditation, but also be of ongoing value to the unit and its faculty and staff.
- You are on the leadership team of an interdisciplinary initiative that was launched 3 years ago with participants from multiple disciplines and services, and you think it is now time to evaluate the effort and develop a list of priorities for the next 3 years.

For leaders confronted by any of these or comparable situations, the EHE framework can be helpful. What follows in this chapter is a description of EHE, the rationale for its use, and the steps involved in implementing the model within any unit in a college or university—or for the institution as a whole.

The Baldrige Framework

Of the various approaches to systematic organizational review, planning, and improvement, none has been more successful or more influential than the Malcolm Baldrige model (Baldrige National Quality Program, 2020).[1] The Malcolm Baldrige National Quality Award (MBNQA) program was established by the U.S. Congress in 1987, named after U.S. Secretary of Commerce Malcolm Baldrige, who served from 1981 until his death in 1987.

The intent of the program was to promote U.S. corporate effectiveness by providing a systems framework and national awards program for organizational assessment and improvement. The model represents a blend of scholarly concepts of organizational theory and behavior, principles from the professional literature, and successful organizational and leadership practices. The framework and program accomplish the following: (a) Identify the essential components of organizational excellence; (b) recognize organizations that demonstrate these characteristics; (c) promote information sharing by exemplary organizations; and (d) encourage the adoption of effective organizational principles and practices. As such, the program provides a useful conceptual framework and helpful guide for leaders as they envision and pursue organizational excellence in a variety of contexts and settings.

Central to the model are the following characteristics:

- a clear and shared sense of purpose (mission) and future aspirations (vision)
- effective leadership and governance processes
- strategic planning, clear priorities, and shared goals
- high-quality programs and services
- strong and reciprocally valued relationships
- qualified and dedicated employees and a satisfying work environment
- systematic review processes and the assessment of outcomes
- comparisons with peers and leaders
- documenting outcomes information for evaluation and improvement

Each of these concepts is pertinent to organizational excellence, and as we shall see, each can be an important guide for leaders in their efforts to achieve and sustain a high level of effectiveness within their programs, departments, schools, or institutions. More specifically, these factors are useful in reviewing and improving the quality of one's organization, responding to the numerous challenges posed by the changing landscape, and assuring that higher education organizations are able to take full advantage of the talents of faculty and staff members.

Baldrige Categories

The Baldrige framework includes seven categories, illustrated in Figure 13.1. Each of these represents an important component and contributor to organizational effectiveness. The connections between the elements of the model suggest that these components are important in their own right but also interact in significant ways in the ongoing functioning of any organization. Internal processes and interactions between the organization and stakeholder communities contribute to a dynamic system in which the whole is significantly more than the simple sum of the component parts. Although the language and definitions used to describe the framework have changed over the years, the seven basic themes have been constant.

In addition to the national Baldrige program, parallel programs were implemented in many states, and versions of the Baldrige framework were also created for the health care and education sectors, as will be discussed later. Beyond the more than 1,500 organizations that have applied for Baldrige review and recognition (Baldrige National Quality Program, 2020), the National Institute of Standards and Technology (NIST) estimates that thousands of additional organizations have used

Figure 13.1. Baldrige view of organizations: A systems perspective.

The Malcolm Baldrige* framework consists of seven categories or themes that are viewed as critical to the effectiveness of any organization—small, large, manufacturing, sevice, health care, education.

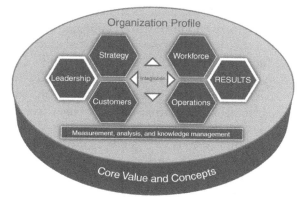

From Baldrige Perfomance Excellence Program. (2015). *2015–2016 Baldrige Excellence Framework: A Systems Approach to Improving Your Organization's Performance.* Gaithersburg, MD: U.S. Department of Commerce, National Institute of Standards and Technology. http://www.nist.gov/baldrige.

the criteria for self-assessment. The framework has also had a significant international influence.

There are numerous case studies, professional endorsements, and leader testimonials that speak to the benefits of the Baldrige model in advancing organizational insight and practice (American College of Healthcare Executives, 2015; Baldrige National Quality Program, 2015d; Dawson, 2016; Furst-Bowe & Bower, 2007; Leist et al., 2004; NACUBO, 2011; Sorensen et al., 2005; Weeks et al., 2000). In addition to these qualitative reports, quantitative studies also provide evidence of the value of Baldrige criteria for improving organizational effectiveness. Organizations rated highly in terms of Baldrige criteria have been shown to outperform other organizations financially and also report improved work processes and performance, improved quality in mission-critical areas, increased employee engagement, reduced turnover, heightened job satisfaction, improved customer and patient satisfaction, fewer complaints, and increased customer retention rates. Additional benefits identified include reduced costs, greater reliability, increased on-time delivery, fewer errors, greater market share, and improvements in a range of other sector-specific indicators (Baldrige National Quality Program, 2015c; Heaphy & Gruska, 1995; Jacob, 2004; Jacob et al., 2012; NIST, 2016; Przasnyski & Tai, 2002; Shook & Chenoweth, 2012; Sternick, 2011).

Baldrige in Higher Education: The EHE Framework

In 1995, customized versions of the Baldrige framework were developed for education and health care, and these were implemented initially in 1999. The education criteria (Baldrige National Quality Program, 2021) were intended to be broadly applicable to school and educational settings at all levels—public or private—but were not crafted specifically for institutions of higher education. The EHE approach and model (Ruben, 2016a) was developed to meet this need. EHE represents a translation of the general organizational principles provided in Baldrige to address the distinctive missions, stakeholders, structures, language, and cultures of colleges and universities.

The first version of EHE was published in 1994 and has been revised through a number of subsequent editions.[2] The 2016 version (Ruben, 2016a) is structured to be appropriate for use by higher education institutions of all types, and also by a full range of specialized units within colleges and universities—business, student affairs, and administration, as well as academic and professional disciplines.

EHE serves a number of purposes. The framework

1. offers a systemic vision of the components of organizational excellence and performance
2. defines standards of excellence and effectiveness based on the mission and aspirations of an institution and its academic, administrative, student life, and service departments and their programs and services
3. provides a strategy for highlighting current strengths and areas in need of change
4. serves as a tool to inventory, organize, and integrate existing assessment, planning, improvement, and other change initiatives
5. offers a blueprint for designing new or reorganized institutions, departments, programs, or services
6. provides dual focus on approach and execution

Efforts to address organizational renewal challenges arising from the COVID-19 pandemic have also revealed the value of the EHE framework for thinking through ways to review and reset organizational functions in the wake of a crisis, as detailed further in chapter 20.

Paralleling the Baldrige framework, EHE is built on a foundation that underscores the importance of the following fundamental organizational principles within higher education:

- effective leadership that provides guidance and ensures a clear and shared sense of organizational mission and future vision, a commitment to continuous review and improvement of leadership practice, and attention to social and environmental consciousness
- an inclusive planning process and coherent plans that translate the organization's mission, vision, and values into clear, ambitious, and measurable goals that are understood and effectively implemented throughout the organization
- knowledge of the needs, expectations, and sources of satisfaction/ dissatisfaction of the groups served by the organization; operating practices that are responsive to these needs and expectations; and processes in place to stay current with and anticipate the changing needs of these groups
- focus on mission-critical and support programs and services and associated work processes to ensure effectiveness, efficiency, appropriate standardization, documentation, and regular evaluation and improvement with the needs and expectations of beneficiaries and stakeholders in mind
- a workplace culture that encourages, recognizes, and rewards excellence, engagement, professional development, employee satisfaction, and pride and provides strategies for synchronizing individual and organizational goals
- implementing measures, methods, processes, and systems for the assessment and analysis of organizational progress and outcomes and ensuring the sharing of this and other information of concern to the institution
- documenting and using information on organizational outcomes to monitor and report on progress, stimulate innovation, guide continuing improvement, and inform future-oriented strategy and planning

EHE Categories

The EHE model, illustrated in Figure 13.2, includes seven categories that are considered necessary components of excellence in any educational enterprise at any level—a program, department, center, school, college, or university (Ruben, 2016a). In the context of the model, each such enterprise is viewed in systems terms. The overall performance and the sustainability of that system are seen as consequences of the quality of the seven

Figure 13.2. Excellence in higher education: The framework and categories.

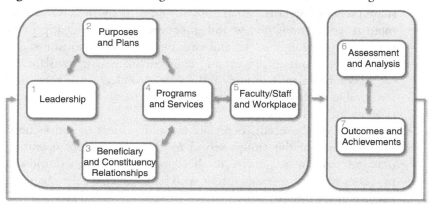

components and of the interactions and alignment among them (Ruben, 1995, 2004, 2021).

EHE has a number of attributes that make it a particularly appropriate and useful tool for organizational review and improvement. The model

- provides a foundation based on widely accepted standards of organizational effectiveness
- facilitates systematic review and creates baseline measures
- utilizes terminology and approaches that are adapted to the culture of higher education
- aligns with accreditation frameworks and standards
- applies to academic, administrative, student life, and service organizations
- scales to departments, programs, centers, advisory councils, or governing groups of any size, or an entire institution
- offers a tool to inventory and integrate ongoing assessment, planning, and improvement initiatives
- promotes the sharing of information and best practices across institutions, departments, and programs
- facilitates alignment across critical functions and inputs that contribute to and predict desirable outcomes
- broadens participation in leadership and problem-solving
- enhances organizational and leadership knowledge and understanding

What the Seven EHE Categories Address

The seven categories of the EHE framework reflect and elaborate on the foundational principles discussed earlier.

Category 1: Leadership

Category 1 focuses on the effectiveness of leadership approaches and governance systems in advancing the purposes, priorities, and plans of the institution, department, or program; how leaders establish and communicate aspirations; how leaders set goals; and how leadership and leadership practices and performance are reviewed and evaluated. Also addressed are issues related to how leaders and leadership practices encourage innovation and attention to stakeholder needs and expectations and how leadership practices and governance structures are reviewed and improved.

Category 2: Plans and Purposes

Clarifying and building consensus on organizational mission, aspirations, and goals and developing and implementing plans are the central themes of category 2. The category also focuses on the importance of environmental scanning, benchmark comparisons with other organizations, and the alignment and coordination of plans and action steps throughout the organization. Also addressed in this category is how faculty and staff and other relevant stakeholders are engaged in defining aspirations and goals and in creating and implementing plans.

Category 3: Beneficiary and Constituency Relationships

The focus of category 3 is on the external stakeholder groups that benefit from, influence, or are influenced by the work of the organization. Among the groups that are considered—depending on the unit being reviewed—are current and prospective students, employers, alumni, local communities, regulatory agencies, members of relevant disciplinary or professional communities, and collaborators or suppliers in other academic or administrative units within the institution. The category includes questions about how the institution or unit is perceived by critical stakeholder groups, how the organization learns about the needs and satisfaction/dissatisfaction levels of individuals in those groups, and how this information is used to enhance the organization's reputation and working relationships with these key constituencies.

Category 4: Programs and Services

Establishing and maintaining the quality of academic and administrative programs and services that are critical to the fulfillment of the organization's mission and aspirations is the primary theme of category 4. The nature of the mission, aspirations, programs, and services will vary substantially depending on whether the work of the unit involves academics, administration, student services, facility services, or other functions. This category focuses on how an organization identifies, documents, evaluates, and regularly improves each mission-critical program and service. Also considered in each case are important operational, support, and administrative services. Additional questions relate to how, and how often, reviews are undertaken to determine if particular programs are candidates for expansion, restructuring, or discontinuation.

Category 5: Faculty/Staff and Workplace

The quality of the faculty and staff and the nature of the organizational culture, climate, and workplace are the topics of category 5, which considers how the program, department, or institution being reviewed recruits and retains faculty and staff, assures excellence and engagement, creates and maintains a positive and inclusive workplace culture and climate, recognizes and rewards accomplishments and superior performance, promotes and facilitates personal and professional development, and provides career development guidance.

Category 6: Assessment and Analysis

Category 6 focuses on the criteria, processes, systems, and internal communication channels through which assessment and analysis take place. The category emphasizes the methods and mechanisms through which an organization assesses, integrates, analyzes, and shares information regarding current environmental conditions, progress and outcomes regarding organizational continuity and renewal efforts, and other issues of concern. Also considered are the processes through which information on trends and peer and leading organizations is assembled, organized, and made accessible to leaders.

Category 7: Outcomes and Achievements

This category focuses on outcomes, with an emphasis on documenting and using evidence provided by the metrics, processes, and systems identified in category 6. Also considered are how outcomes compare to peers and leading organizations. The category calls for information and evidence to highlight, communicate, and celebrate progress and achievements and to focus attention on areas where change is needed. Documented outcomes information is particularly essential for internal monitoring and external reporting and accountability, which are critical to continuing organizational improvement.

Baldrige, EHE, and Accreditation

The broadly stated purposes of Baldrige and EHE have a good deal in common with regional and program accreditation processes, and there is clearly a complementarity among these frameworks. As described in the standards of one of the regional accrediting associations, the goal of the accreditation process is to "stimulate . . . evaluation and improvement, while providing a means of continuing accountability to constituents and the public" (Southern Association of Colleges and Schools Commission on Colleges, n.d.). These same goals are central to Baldrige-based frameworks.

As with accreditation, the Baldrige and EHE approaches emphasize the need to broadly define excellence; value leadership and planning; establish clear, shared, and measurable goals; create effective programs and departments; conduct systematic assessments of outcomes; and engage in comparisons with peers and leaders.[3] The frameworks also share in common the position that review, planning, and continuous improvement are essential to institutional effectiveness and should be thoroughly integrated into the fabric of every institution aspiring to excellence (Baldrige National Quality Program, 2015a, 2015b; Middle States Commission, 2014; North Central Association of Colleges and Universities, Higher Learning Commission, 2015; Western Association of Schools and Colleges, 2013).

The most fundamental characteristic of the Baldrige, EHE, and accreditation frameworks is a commitment to an iterative process of mission-based goal-setting, assessment, and improvement, as illustrated in Figure 13.3. By emphasizing the importance of clear purposes and aspirations, the evaluation of departmental and institutional effectiveness, and the use of this information for continuous improvement, the Baldrige and EHE frameworks promote the integration of the core values and standards emphasized through accreditation into the day-to-day activities of the organization. While these approaches are not a substitute for accreditation, and vice versa, EHE reinforces purposes of accreditation in a number of useful ways.

Figure 13.3. Common themes across frameworks.

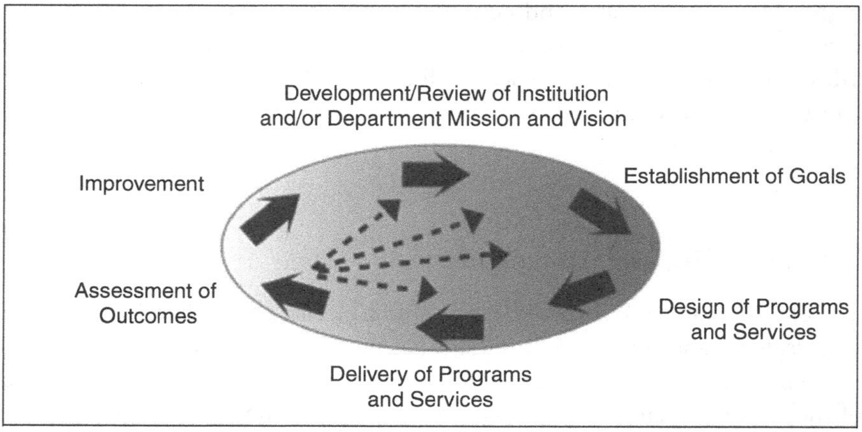

The EHE Process

The EHE process, as it is typically employed, involves self-assessment by members of the organization being reviewed. There are other assessment strategies that can be used. Engaging members of the organization directly in the assessment process, however, has the advantage of creating a common understanding of various perspectives on the performance of the unit and is also beneficial for creating a shared view of the needed improvement priorities and ensuring the buy-in necessary to mobilize the group to focus on these improvements at the conclusion of the assessment process. This helps to address the familiar complaint that organizations dedicate too much time reviewing and discussing possible improvements but too little time following through to make changes.

Used in the self-assessment mode, the process consists of the following steps in reviewing each category:

- Discuss the basic themes and standards.
- Brainstorm a list of strengths and areas for improvement for the organization within that category.
- Review exemplary practices in the category as implemented by leading organizations.

While not a requirement, a very helpful step is to ask participants in the process to score the current practices of the organization on a 0 to 100% scale to capture organization member perceptions of the extent to which the unit is fulfilling the standards of the category. Guidance for scoring is provided in the EHE *Workbook and Scoring Instructions* (Ruben, 2016b).[4]

To illustrate how this overall process works, consider category 2—purposes and plans. The category focuses on developing and implementing organizational directions, aspirations, goals, and plans (see Table 13.1). Typically, the assessment for this category begins with the session leader or facilitator discussing with members of the organization whether current statements of mission, vision, and/or values, and a planning document exist, and more generally how these documents are created, reviewed, and/or refined. The discussion transitions to questions about how faculty and staff have been involved in the development of the plan and whether and how these organizational directions are translated into priorities and action steps and implemented in a coordinated manner to foster continuing innovation and improvement. The discussion then shifts to other concepts addressed within the category (Ruben, 2016a, 2016b).[5]

The next step is for the participant group to create a list of strengths and areas for improvement for the category with the help of a facilitator, noting the ways in which the program, unit, or institution is effectively

TABLE 13.1
Purposes and Plans: Guiding Questions

**An Example:
Category 2 - Purposes and Plans**

Focused on the planning process, and how mission, aspirations and values are developed and communicated, how they are translated into goals and action steps engaged in these processes.

- Is there a formalized planning process?
- How are faculty/staff engaged in developing and implementing plans?
- Does an up-to-date, written plan currently exist?
- Does that plan effectively translate the mission, vision, and values into priorities, measurable goals, and action steps with specified roles and responsibilities?
- How does the plan take account of current strengths and areas in need of improvement, innovation, or elimination?
- Does the plan consider resource needs?
- Are the plans and goals synchronized with those of the larger organization or institution?

addressing—or failing to address—the themes in each category. The discussion and documentation of strengths and areas for improvement continue until participants feel they have covered all questions and criteria included in a particular category.

The next step is a review of "exemplary practices" in the category being discussed (see Table 13.2), followed by the scoring stage (assuming the rating process is being used). At this point, scoring guidelines, provided in Table 13.3, are distributed and explained, and participants complete individual ratings of the effectiveness of the unit in the category under discussion based on their personal assessments of how fully their program, department, or institution addresses the standards for the category.[6]

The ratings are done individually and without consultation. Ratings are collected and aggregated, physically or electronically, and displayed on a spreadsheet (typically projected on a screen in real time), and the distribution of scores is discussed, maintaining the confidentiality of individuals' ratings. The average rating for the category is calculated and discussed in comparison to results from previously scored categories.

TABLE 13.2
Purposes and Plans: Exemplary Practices

- A clear and shared sense of the organization's purpose and aspirations
- Formal planning process in place and understood by all
- Plans built fully synchronized with the mission, vision, and values of the organization *and* institution
- Plans include short- and long-term goals
- Sufficient time and resources allocated for benchmarking/peer review research, environmental scanning, and the development and pilot testing of innovations
- Plans include clear, measurable, ambitious goals and action steps and a strategy for monitoring progress to completion
- Plans identify possible programs and services that should be improved, as well as programs and services that are candidates for major renovation or discontinuation
- Resources, climate, culture, and peer comparisons integral to the planning process
- Anticipate and allow for addressing strategic opportunities and unexpected events'and "crises"
- Plans, goals, and action plans broadly communicated and enthusiastically supported and pursued throughout the organization

TABLE 13.3
Percentage Rating Guide

Rating	Approach and Implementation
100% to 90%	• A superior approach; systematically addressing all dimensions of the category • **Fully** implemented without significant weakness or gaps in any area • Widely recognized leader in the category/item • Systematic approach and commitment to excellence and continuous improvement **fully** ingrained in the organization and its culture
80% to 70%	• A well-developed, systematic, tested, and refined approach in **most** areas, addressing **most** dimensions of the category • A fact-based assessment and improvement process throughout **most** of the organization with few significant gaps • Recognized as an innovative leader in the category • Clear evidence of effectiveness, innovation, and ongoing improvement throughout **most** areas of the organization and its culture
60% to 50%	• An effective, systematic approach, responsive to **many** dimensions of the category • Approach well implemented in **many** areas, although there may be unevenness and inconsistency in particular work groups • A fact-based, systematic process in place for evaluating and improving effectiveness and efficiency in **many** areas • Clear evidence of excellence, innovation, and continuous improvement in **many** areas of the organization and its culture

(*Continues*)

TABLE 13.3 (*Continued*)

Rating	Approach and Implementation
40% to 30%	• An effective, systematic approach, responsive to **some** dimensions of the category • Approach implemented in **some** areas, but some work areas in the early stages of implementation • A systematic approach to assessing and improving effectiveness and efficiency in **some** areas • Evidence of effectiveness, innovation, and ongoing improvement in **some** areas of the organization and its culture
20% to 10%	• The beginning of a systematic approach to **a few** dimensions of the category • Category criteria addressed in **a few** programs, services, activities, and processes • Major implementation gaps that inhibit progress in achieving the basic purpose of the category • Evidence of effectiveness, innovation, and ongoing improvement in **a few** areas of the organization and its culture
0%	• **No** systematic approach to category; anecdotal information on approach and implementation; not part of the culture of the organization

The various steps discussed previously are repeated after each category, and a review of the aggregate ratings takes place after all categories have been considered. See Figure 13.4 for an example of the completed ratings profile for a hypothetical institution, department, or program.

Once these steps have been finished for all seven categories, the list of strengths and areas in need of improvement captured in notes (ideally on a computer file or flip charts) are reviewed and discussed further. Duplicated or similar items may be combined, and any items mentioned in one category that might have been more appropriately listed in another can be shifted.

The next step is to identify a list of priorities for attention. This can be done by participant multivoting to rank order improvement priorities across all categories.[7] Suggested criteria for use in the ranking process include potential impact and feasibility. This process can take place in a group setting immediately following the assessment or at a later time via an anonymous online voting process. Alternatively, the selection of action priorities can be completed by a leadership team or executive council. This approach streamlines the process but reduces engagement and, in many cases, participant enthusiasm and buy-in. In either case, the goal is to identify four to five priorities for improvement, which will become the immediate focus of attention and action by the unit and its leadership.

Next, action planning templates can be completed for each highly ranked improvement priority. Typically, these include a summary statement of the project mission, a list of key steps, identification of the individuals or roles that should be involved in the project, a proposed team leader, a project

Figure 13.4. A sample profile.

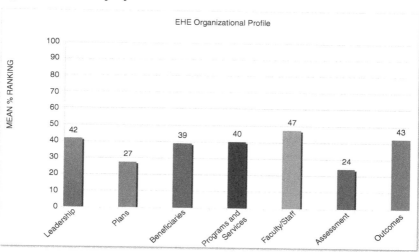

timeline, an estimate of resources, and a listing of important outcomes and measures (Ruben, 2016b). The work on specific initiatives often takes place in the weeks and months ahead, with leadership coordination and periodic progress reporting, as shown in Figure 13.5. As these projects are completed, the group could return to the list of other areas for improvement to select another group of action items. Ideally, the entire assessment-improvement cycle is repeated on an annual basis.

As noted, the most common method for presenting the EHE program is a retreat or workshop with members of the leadership team, a cross section of faculty and/or staff within the unit, or the entire organization. A workshop might last from one-half to one and one-half days, depending on whether the activity focuses solely on assessment or also includes priority setting and planning. Alternatively, the program can be presented in a series of half-day sessions or in any of various other formats.

The Value and Impact of the EHE Program

Having a single organizational framework that can guide systematic review, planning, and improvement activities across an institution is a unique and important attribute of EHE. Within academic units, the process naturally focuses on how the college or department may function more effectively to fulfill its academic mission and aspirations, evaluate its accomplishments and improvement needs, and introduce program and service innovations.

Figure 13.5. The EHE assessment, prioritization, planning, improvement cycle.

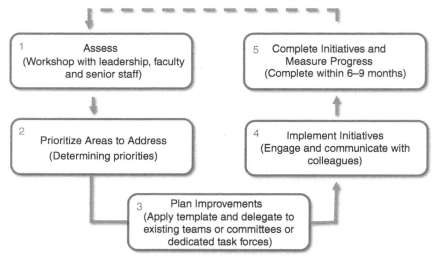

In addition, the model is useful for academic units to address student learning and service needs, identify departmental processes that can be streamlined, focus on faculty and staff needs, and enhance day-to-day operations. Within administrative or service units, the benefits include clarifying mission and aspirations, refining core programs and services, enhancing work processes, and enriching service relations with external constituencies.

Using the same model within academic, student life, administrative, and service units creates a common, institution-wide vocabulary for conceptualizing, assessing, planning, and improving organizational effectiveness. It also fosters the sharing of approaches and strategies across units and promotes the vision of each being an important and interdependent part of the campus system as a whole. Perhaps most important, it encourages alignment among goals, priorities, and plans throughout an institution.

For any organizational assessment or improvement program—accreditation, Baldrige, or the EHE process—the question that always arises is whether the initiative has the intended value and impact. While important, positive perceptions and enthusiasm among participants are not necessarily decisive indicators of value when weighed against the substantial investment of time and talent that is required in any assessment or planning activity.

Two studies were undertaken at Rutgers to assess the organizational benefits of the EHE assessment process beyond immediate participant reactions following the program (Ruben et al., 2004, 2007). Findings from these studies point to the impact of the process in the acquisition of a knowledge and theory base, in the clarification of organizational strengths, and in the pursuit of critical improvement needs.

With support from the Lumina Foundation, the National Association of College and University Administrators conducted a national research initiative to study Baldrige/EHE in 2010–20011 (NACUBO, 2011). The study focused on initiatives at eight U.S. colleges and universities where Baldrige/EHE was introduced. At each institution, the framework was employed to address one of three specific goals: (a) improving and strengthening core functions (financial planning, accreditation, and IT); (b) creating and implementing new practices (space measurement and planning, human resources, and performance management); and (c) promoting multicampus and system-level change (organizational change, innovation, and operational process improvement). The NACUBO–Lumina study confirmed earlier findings relative to the value of the Baldrige/EHE framework to guide and motivate organizational improvement, to introduce new and innovative practices, and to facilitate multicampus alignment and change (NACUBO, 2011).

From our own experience and available evidence, it seems clear that the EHE program can be helpful to leaders in developing a conceptualization of organizational excellence, identifying components that are important to realizing that vision, acknowledging current strengths and improvement needs, and providing a framework and tool to guide and support organizational change efforts across the institution.

To date, more than 65 academic and administrative departments at Rutgers University have participated in the program. Roughly 60 other colleges and universities in the United States and internationally have also found this program helpful in their assessment, planning, and improvement efforts. Additionally, the EHE model has been applied in various research and training contexts in Botswana, Canada, Chile, China, Greece, Iran, Northern Ireland, Qatar, Saudi Arabia, and Thailand, and the EHE guide has been translated and published by Wuhan University Press for use in China.

An adaptation of EHE—named excellence in higher education-renewal (EHE-R)—has also been developed. The aim of this version of the model is to guide colleges and universities in addressing review, strategy formulation, and planning challenges in times of crisis and disruption (Ruben, 2020a, 2020b, 2020c, 2021). This framework is discussed in some detail in the final chapter of the book.

Conclusion

The specific aim of the EHE assessment process is to establish ways of tracking progress, gauging effectiveness, and promoting meaningful and ongoing improvement in the quest for excellence. As noted, the approach can be extremely useful as a guide for organizational design, assessment, planning, and change throughout a college or university—in administrative, service, and student life organizations, as well as in academic and professional programs, departments, centers, or entire institutions. It can be usefully applied to guide the development of a new organization or the ongoing refinement of existing units, or to assist with organizational review, reprioritization, and reset following a crisis.

In addition to identifying institutional needs, the EHE process has value in promoting self-reflection, enhancing interdisciplinary and interdepartmental communication, and establishing clearer and more comprehensive standards of organizational excellence. EHE also establishes a foundation for using evidence to document and track performance, and it encourages benchmarking as a strategy for innovation and change. Finally, participation in the EHE process contributes to leadership and professional development for faculty and staff and enhances a sense of teamwork and a shared recognition of strengths and improvement priorities and possibilities for all involved.

For Further Consideration

1. Personal reflections

Consider the seven EHE categories. In which of those categories would you rate your unit and your institution the highest and the lowest? Do you think your colleagues would agree with your assessment?

2. Case scenarios

Review the cases that follow and consider the guide questions for each of the scenarios:

- You are a new leader of your unit, recently appointed as director/dean. You see a need to get a quick but comprehensive sense of your leadership team and strengths and areas for improvement in the unit.
- You have been asked to conduct a full review of your administrative unit with an eye to considering where significant changes might be made in the services offered. This could include creating new initiatives or discontinuing existing programs or services.
- Your unit is thinking about launching a new program, and you recognize the need for a systematic approach to planning.
- In anticipation of accreditation, you want to begin a systematic assessment of your department and its programs.
- An interdisciplinary unit has been in existence for 3 years, with participants from multiple disciplines and services and collaborators from various administrative and service units. You want to take stock of where things stand and develop a list of priorities for strategic planning in the next year.
- You are heading into a recovery period following a major disruptive crisis and see the need for a framework to guide assessment of current strengths and improvement needs and to help with the identification of short- and longer term priorities going forward.

Scenario guide questions

- How would you decide whether EHE was appropriate?
- What goals would guide your thinking, and what outcomes would you hope for?
- How might EHE be helpful conceptually? Operationally?

- What questions or concerns might you have?
- Which criteria would you be most interested in analyzing throughout the process?
- If you decided to use EHE, who would you involve in the process?
- How would you prepare for EHE?
- How would you conduct the EHE process?
- In what ways would you follow up with the group at the conclusion of the session?
- What leadership challenges could the EHE process present before, during, and after the assessment process?

Notes

1. For further information on the Baldrige National Quality Program, visit www.nist.gov/baldrige/.

2. The first version of this model was called tradition of excellence and was published in 1994 (Ruben, 1994). Revised and updated versions were published under the current name, excellence in higher education, in 1994, 1997, 2000, 2001, 2003, 2005, 2009/2010, and 2016a.

3. For a comparative analysis of educational goals and outcomes identified by the regional and professional accrediting associations, see Association of American Colleges and Universities (2021).

4. In some instances, because of time restrictions or participant resistance to the idea of quantitative rating, the scoring process can be omitted. While eliminating the scoring detracts from the precision of the rating process, the possibility of quantifying the extent of similarity/difference in perceptions among participants, and the establishment of a quantitative baseline, it does not seem to materially alter the process or its value in other ways.

5. A detailed discussion of the elements of the category is provided in the *Excellence in Higher Education Guide* (Ruben, 2016a). Outlines and discussion guides providing details of the step-by-step process can be found in the *Workbook and Scoring Instructions* (Ruben, 2016b), a typical page of which is shown in Table 13.1. Slides and facilitator guidance are provided in a facilitator's guide. The guide also includes additional information and structured exercises that are helpful for encouraging fruitful discussion of the core concepts in each category.

6. The ranking could be done in two stages, beginning with rankings within categories and then proceeding to an overall ranking across categories.

14

STRATEGIC PLANNING

Translating Aspirations Into Realities

Sherrie Tromp and Brent Ruben

In This Chapter

- What is strategic planning and what purposes does it serve?
- What are the key steps associated with successful strategic planning initiatives within higher education?
- What options exist for engaging in strategic planning at the unit, departmental, or institutional level?
- Why is the process of planning as important as the plan's substance?

While strategic planning has become increasingly popular within colleges and universities in recent years, the concept is not a new one for higher education. One of the first meetings of campus planners was held at the Massachusetts Institute of Technology in 1959, and approximately 25 individuals were present (Dooris et al., 2004). The meeting was centered on the need for facilities planning during an era of rapid expansion. Massive changes in the second half of the 20th century led to the expanded adoption of strategic planning initiatives, and by the 1980s strategic planning had emerged as an influential practice throughout higher education (Keller, 1983). Interest in strategic planning has grown dramatically. An estimated 70% of colleges and universities in the United States engaged in some form of strategic planning in 2000 (Sevier, 2000), and that number continues to grow steadily, with efforts often linking planning to assessment, budgeting, and generalized management initiatives (Flynn & Vredevoogd, 2010).

The growth in popularity of strategic planning can be traced to a variety of internal and external influences. Among the benefits typically attributed to strategic planning efforts are the following:

- stimulating meaningful dialogue about the unit, department, or organization's mission, aspirations, values, and priorities
- establishing shared and energizing goals and strategies for progress toward those aspirations
- identifying environmental influences that are important to organizational advancement
- defining necessary action steps and fostering the broader commitment required to successfully execute these steps
- identifying critical audiences and stakeholders for the organization and developing key messages and a persuasive communication, marketing, and financial development plan
- analyzing the directions and approaches of peers and leaders
- adopting effective practices that align with the goals of the organization

With its range of missions, multiplicity of stakeholders, and distinctive shared governance structures, higher education serves as a unique setting that requires special considerations with regard to planning. In his seminal work on academic planning, Keller (1983) set the stage for a new approach to planning in higher education when he pointed out the importance of such questions as "What business are we really in?" "What is most central to us?" and "How shall we proceed?" (p. 72).

This chapter describes strategic planning, discusses the multiple purposes for which it is appropriate, and focuses specifically on the implementation and use of strategic planning as a tool for leaders in higher education.

What Is Strategic Planning?

As summarized in Immordino et al. (2016), *strategic planning* is defined by Allison and Kaye (2005) as "a systematic process through which an organization agrees on—and builds commitment among key stakeholders to—priorities that are essential to its mission" (p. 1). Rowley and Sherman (2001) define it as "a formal process designed to help an organization identify and maintain an optimal alignment with the most important elements of its environmental set" (p. 328). Bryson (2011) characterizes strategic planning as "a deliberate disciplined effort to produce fundamental decisions and actions that shape and guide what an organization (or other entity) is, what it does, and why it does it" (p. 26). Although definitions differ, most share in common the depiction of strategic planning as an intentional leadership tool for setting future directions (vision) in a dynamic environment through a process that takes account of—and ideally engages—key stakeholders and applies basic planning principles and practices. As Keller explains, unlike other forms of planning, *strategic* planning focuses on determining and guiding outcomes rather than falling victim to myriad external forces that bombard organizations on a daily basis—reactions to which result in ad hoc or activity-based planning.

Successful strategic planning efforts carefully consider the two fundamental—and fundamentally different—processes, *ideation* and *implementation*. Ideation, or idea generation, is the process through which directions, strategies, and initiatives are developed. Implementation refers to the steps involved in moving an idea from the pages of a planning document to the reality of campus life. As central as ideation is to strategic planning, it alone yields little benefit if insufficient attention is devoted to follow-up implementation. Implementation typically draws heavily on concepts from change leadership, discussed in detail in the next chapter. It is mentioned here, because any effort at strategic planning is incomplete unless it takes account of both the development of ideas and plans and their implementation. The process typically includes the following steps:

- articulating organizational aspirations in a coherent and compelling manner
- offering ideas and goals that are ambitious yet achievable
- taking account of the national and local contexts and regulatory considerations, as well as institutional and organizational strengths, weaknesses, opportunities, and threats (SWOT)
- giving attention to needs, expectations, and perceptions of stakeholders and collaborators—groups that use, benefit from, influence, or are influenced by the organization
- providing comparisons to peers and leaders
- providing a foundation and context for decision-making, action planning, operational priority setting, and resource allocation
- developing a disciplined approach to moving ideas that are advanced in a plan through to implementation

Why Strategic Planning?

Academic leaders face many challenges and are also presented with many opportunities for which strategic planning can be helpful. Among these are the following:

- diminishing resources
- complacency and low aspirations among members of the organization

- inconsistency between the way insiders and outsiders view the organization
- a lack of shared perception of priorities or goals
- individuals and groups focused on priorities that detract from the mission of the organization as a whole
- a changing political or economic landscape
- an absence of a clear or shared set of criteria or measures of progress or success
- a need to redirect the organization toward new opportunities—new programs, initiatives, or areas of focus
- insufficient attention devoted to innovation, change, and out-of-the-box thinking

In considering how best to address these sorts of circumstances, any number of leadership approaches come to mind, and strategic planning may not initially be among them.

In approaching such situations, there is an understandable tendency to focus directly on what seems to be the particular issue at hand—to launch a program to reduce expenditures, increase revenues, strengthen teamwork, enhance marketing, initiate measures, and so on. Often, however, what may look like a very specific and narrowly defined challenge that could easily be addressed through marketing, team building, skills training, measures training, improved internal communication, or a new incentive structure as a manifestation of a larger set of issues that would be more efficiently, effectively, and lastingly addressed through comprehensive approaches. Strategic planning can be a particularly valuable tool in these contexts.

Strategic planning can be implemented as a standalone activity or pursued in conjunction with other institutional assessment activities, such as preparing for accreditation (e.g., Dodd, 2004; the Middle States Commission on Higher Education, 2014), award applications (e.g., the Malcolm Baldrige National Quality Award program; Jasinski, 2004; Ruben et al., 2007), and other institutional initiatives. At the University of Wisconsin–Madison, for example, strategic planning was infused throughout the organization during two accreditation cycles (Paris, 2004). At Pennsylvania State University, an integrated planning approach utilized strategic planning to integrate budgeting, enrollment management, and human resource planning (Sandmeyer et al., 2004). At Northwestern University's Feinberg School of Medicine, strategic planning efforts have been linked with changes in the medical school's budgeting structure in order to better align activities with the institution's mission and resources (Haberaecker, 2004).

The Components of Strategic Planning in Higher Education

While strategic planning approaches used in higher education may vary in some respects, most include as a central component the need to develop, clarify, and promote a shared understanding of mission, vision, and values of an institution and within each of its academic, administrative, student affairs, or service units. Once defined, the aim is to develop and implement plans and strategies that translate these organizational perspectives into a well-defined blueprint for collective action (Tromp & Ruben, 2010). Often, this collective action involves change, and more specifically, it allows for the identification of "the means by which . . . organizations establish priorities and goals and coordinate their efforts to anticipate, direct, and manage change" (p. 7).

A typical strategic planning framework for higher education consists of a series of major planning phases (Tromp & Ruben, 2010): (a) reviewing—and in some cases drafting or clarifying—the organization's mission, vision, and, often, values; (b) determining the list of key stakeholders and their perspectives; (c) conducting an environmental scan, including benchmarking; (d) establishing themes/goals; (e) identifying and prioritizing strategies and action plans; (f) drafting the planning document; and (g) specifying intended outcomes and achievements, as illustrated in Table 14.1 and described in the following sections. We use a hypothetical Center for Online Learning to illustrate the application of this model.

TABLE 14.1
Purposes and Plans: Guiding Questions

Making the Plan Work		Mission, Vision and Values	• **Reference Points:** What needs, aspirations, and values does the plan support or advance?
	A. Leadership	Stakeholder Perspectives	• **Active Consideration:** Whose opinion matters to us, why, and what do they expect or need?
	B. Communication	Environmental Scan and Benchmarking	• **Taking Account:** What are the relevant strengths, areas for improvement, and comparison data?
	C. Assessment	Themes/Goals	• **The Big Ideas:** What we need to do to fulfill the aspirations of the plan?
	D. Culture	Strategies, Priorities and Action Plans	• **The Work:** How will we achieve our goals, and who does what when?
	E. Follow-Through	Plan Creation and Implementation	• **Documenting, Implementing, and Tracking Progress:** How will we pull the pieces together to realize desired results, measure success, and ensure-in buy and support?
		Outcomes and Achievements	

Note: Adapted from: Tromp (2010).

Mission, Vision, and Value Statements

Thoughtful mission, vision, and value statements are a reminder to members of the organization and other stakeholders of the organization's core purposes, aspirations, and fundamental principles. They provide an important communicative function for internal and external audiences and can offer a useful guide for day-to-day actions and decision-making within the organization. Of particular importance to leaders in higher education is the role these statements play in guiding programs and services, along with the leader's ability to communicate support for the organization's mission and vision for the future with existing and potential stakeholders.

Strategic planning typically begins by drafting, refining, or reviewing existing documents that address the issues of mission, vision, and values. In many organizations, statements on these themes already exist and may only need to be reviewed and reaffirmed. In other cases, some refinements and updates may be appropriate, and in still others, statements need to be created.

As discussed in chapter 4, a mission statement provides a description of an organization's primary purpose and reason for existence. It focuses on the current state and articulates what others can expect from the organization.

The mission statement should provide a clear and enduring description of the work of the organization, yet it can also be general enough to allow for change and growth. For example, a typical mission statement for a Center for Online Learning within a college or university might be "To serve as a center for training in online instruction and research for university faculty and staff and to provide students with increased options for learning."

The mission statements listed in Table 14.2, some of which have been copied from chapter 4, each provide a foundation for planning efforts at the unit, departmental, or institutional level.

Organizational Vision and Values

Vision statements describe aspirations and are generally considered—drafted, refined, or reviewed—after the mission statement. A vision statement for the hypothetical Center for Online Learning might be "To be a nationally recognized center of excellence in advancing online learning, education and research."

Some organizations may also have—or wish to create—statements of values or principles. If so, these should also be considered at this early stage in the planning process. Organizations operate in a manner that reflects particular values—whether explicitly stated or not. Values play a role in daily work practices, interactions, and relationships, which make focusing

TABLE 14.2
Examples of Departmental and Institutional Mission Statements

Public Research Institution

University of Michigan (n.d)
"The mission of the University of Michigan is to serve the people of Michigan and the world through preeminence in creating, communicating, preserving, and applying knowledge, art, and academic values, and in developing leaders and citizens who will challenge the present and enrich the future."

Private 4-Year Institution

Kalamazoo College (n.d)
"The mission of Kalamazoo College is to prepare its graduates to better understand, live successfully within, and provide enlightened leadership to a richly diverse and increasingly complex world."

Public 2-Year Institution

Westchester Community College (n.d)
"Westchester Community College provides accessible, high-quality, and affordable education to meet the needs of our diverse community. We are committed to student success, academic excellence, workforce development, economic development, and lifelong learning."

Medical School

Georgetown University School of Medicine (n.d)
"Guided by the Jesuit tradition of Cura Personalis, care of the whole person, Georgetown University School of Medicine will educate a diverse student body, in an integrated way, to become knowledgeable, ethical, skillful, and compassionate physicians and biomedical scientists who are dedicated to the care of others and health needs of our society."

Academic Department

Northern Arizona University (n.d) Social Work Program
"The mission of the Northern Arizona University Social Work Program, grounded in the history, purpose, and values of the profession, is to educate competent, generalist social workers for practice with diverse populations and multi-level social systems in local, regional, and global contexts. The generalist practice for which we educate is based on social work knowledge, values, and skills; geared to practice with rural and Indigenous populations of the Southwest; and focused on addressing poverty, structural racism, and oppression. This practice provides leadership in promoting human rights and social and economic justice, and service with vulnerable and underserved populations locally, regionally, and globally."

(Continues)

TABLE 14.2 (*Continued*)

Administrative Department
Loyola University (n.d) Division of Finance and Administration "The Division of Finance and Administration is responsible for preserving, enhancing, and supporting the University's financial, physical, and human resources. The Division provides consultation, support, and services to the University. In order to achieve these goals, the Division must challenge the actions of all University units to ensure the activities proposed and resources requested refl ect sound business judgment and support the overall goals and mission of the University. The Division's staff works closely with all areas of the University to • Responsibly manage the University's resources ensuring its sound financial condition for this generation and those that follow; • Deliver quality services expeditiously; • Enhance the physical infrastructure of the campus; and • Create conditions in which students and employees can do their best work."

on them an important consideration if organizational culture and climate are being considered as a part of the planning process. While values are not always included as a part of the planning framework, a statement that captures such aspirations can be an important element in both planning and guiding the day-to-day activities of the program, department, or institution. The values for the Center for Online Learning, for example, might include "collaboration, inclusion, professionalism, and integrity," as well as "appreciation of diverse perspectives and backgrounds, respect for all points of view, and a commitment to enhancing the value and uses of technology within the academy."

Determining Key Stakeholders and Their Perspectives

Achieving clarity on the list of those who benefit from and collaborate with any program, department, or institution—the second step in this planning model—is a critical dimension for general organizational practice and for strategic planning efforts. The Johnson & Johnson Credo (n.d.), for instance, identifies doctors, nurses, patients, employees, communities, and stockholders —in that order—as the company's key constituencies. A deliberate and explicit prioritization of key stakeholders can be very helpful for defining aspirations, developing plans, establishing specific goals and strategies, and guiding individual employee decision-making and behavior. Leaders and colleagues within colleges and universities can similarly benefit from clarifying their key stakeholder groups and identifying their current and future needs and expectations related to potential priorities—topics that were discussed in general terms in chapter 3.

Environmental Scanning and Benchmarking

Environmental scanning is another critical step in strategic planning. Also known as a SWOT analysis, this stage in planning calls for a careful consideration of the social, health, economic, political, regulatory, technological, and cultural environments in which an organization functions, particularly those factors that could impinge on potential plans or the planning process. Depending on the context, and the time and financial resources available, the extent and sophistication of data collection and analysis can vary considerably—involving some or all members of the organization; representatives of key external stakeholder groups; and relevant regional, state, national, and perhaps international information sources. A decision may also be made to draw on external expertise to assist with this analysis. Regardless of how this stage is conducted, it is vital to afford a central role to members of the program, department, or institution who may have useful insights and perspectives.

Benchmarking—gathering information from comparable organizations within and beyond the institution—is also an important step in planning. In nearly all cases, there exist relevant peer or aspirational institutions or units to which comparisons can be made. In combination, environmental scanning and benchmarking contribute to a leader's knowledge of potential challenges and opportunities and can also allow for the adoption of innovative ideas from other institutions, and sometimes other sectors.

Goals/Themes

Building on the foundation of an organizational mission, vision, and values, a well-defined list of stakeholders and stakeholder perspectives, and pertinent information from environmental scanning and benchmarking activities, the strategic planning process focuses next on establishing themes (broad areas of interest or focus and/or goals)—more specifically, desired results related to each theme. *Goal-setting* is a commonly used term in strategic planning, but in some cases the term *theme* is used. While not identical, themes and goals are both helpful organizational devices for identifying the means by which a vision can be pursued. Identifying goals or themes is a core activity in strategic planning.

Goals/themes should be broad and far-reaching in scope and should describe what the organization needs to do to achieve its high-level aspirations. In establishing goals/themes, it is important to resist pressures to create a catalogue of projects that might be undertaken. While the formulation of an expansive list of suggested activities is a logical step for later in the planning process, it is important to first clearly formulate and articulate goals/themes that represent the broad critical needs and aspirations of the organization, the focus of which will guide efforts to determine the particular projects that make sense. It is also important to express these goals/themes in terms that allow for tracking progress and measuring outcomes (Tromp & Ruben, 2010). In the case of the hypothetical Center for Online Learning, for example, a central goal or theme may be "Faculty affordability: To make high-quality, affordable education available for higher education faculty who wish to further their online education design, delivery, and evaluative capabilities."

Strategies, Priorities, and Action Plans

The next step in the process is the formulation and implementation of strategies and action plans. Strategies or statements describe *how* the themes/goals will be addressed, and action plans specify *what will be done*, *by whom*, and *when*. At this stage, many project ideas that may have surfaced in earlier discussions can be considered, and those that have the greatest potential impact and return on the investment of time and resources can be adopted as priority strategies.

Plan Creation

When these stages have been completed, the strategic planning document can be drafted. The plan is, by design, a visible and public document—one intended to be a clear statement of direction, a leadership tool, and a communication vehicle. In creating the content and format for the planning document, consideration should be given to audiences for the plan and expectations as to how the plan will be used (Tromp & Ruben, 2010). Once completed, it is a leadership responsibility to disseminate the plan; promote the value and importance of its content within and beyond the program, department, or institution; and track and share information on progress.

Outcomes and Achievements Documentation

Achieving and sustaining the intended outcomes is, of course, the overriding purpose of strategic planning and the fundamental goal for organizations and leaders alike. Ironically, if there is one area in which higher education organizations fall short, it is in measuring and tracking progress over time, documenting achievements related to goals/themes, and making the necessary adjustments to maximize the probability of fulfilling the aims of the plan and planning process. Although listed as the final step in the planning process, considerations relative to this stage should begin early and continue throughout the implementation and follow-through stages.

Implementation and Progress Monitoring

To be successful in this effort, leaders need to ensure that the organization has identified critical indicators of success for the plan as well as the planning process, determine the appropriate methods for monitoring progress at each stage, and decide how information regarding progress toward the intended outcomes will be organized and shared. The aim of such an effort is to develop an approach for using this information that will assure follow-through for the plan and promote alignment and coordination of efforts across the organization.

Table 14.3 highlights specific elements to emerge from the planning process for the Center for Online Learning.

While the content of the individual phases of the strategic planning process is essential to creating the plan itself, it is no more important to a successful outcome than is the *process* by which the plan is developed. Five process considerations, listed in Figure 14.1—leadership, communication, assessment, culture, and outcomes monitoring—are particularly important considerations (Tromp & Ruben, 2010).

Figure 14.1. Steps to facilitate the success of the planning process.

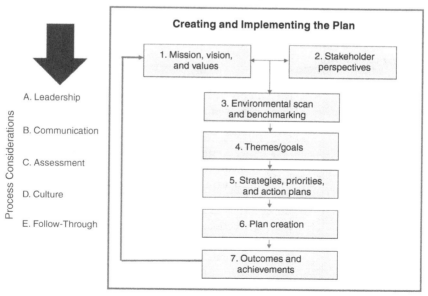

TABLE 14.3

Planning Components for a Hypothetical Center for Online Learning

Mission, vision, and values	Mission
	To serve as a center for training in online instruction and research for university faculty and staff, and to share information and materials with comparable centers at other institutions
	Vision
	To be a recognized center of excellence in online learning education and research within the university, regionally, and nationally
	Core values
	• Collaboration • Professionalism and integrity • Tolerance for diversity in levels of knowledge and experience in technology
Stakeholder perspectives	The following stakeholders are a sample of those constituents who have an interest in the center:
	• Online instructional faculty and staff • Students • Partner colleges and universities • Learning management system providers • Online accreditation associations
Environmental scan and benchmarking	Strengths
	• A strong reputation for being a national leader in online learning education and research • Highly productive research and training center
	Weaknesses
	• Limited staff compared to other research centers • Inadequate resources for conducting advanced qualitative and quantitative data analysis
	Opportunities
	• Predictions for extensive growth in online education nationally and internationally • Corporate donors who are interested in contributing to the work of the center

	Threats
	• Growing number of critics of online education • Potential for universal budget cuts across the university
Themes/goals	*Goal #1:* To make high-quality, affordable education available for higher education faculty who wish to further their online education design, delivery, and evaluative capabilities *Goal #2:* To expedite participant progress toward instructional program completion
Strategies, priorities, and action plans	*Corresponding strategy #1:* Seek creative funding alternatives that will expand available resources for instructional programs *Action plan:* Identify current available corporate, government, and educational grant options
	Corresponding strategy #2: Identify areas of primary impact on completion rates compared to peers *Action plan:* Survey current faculty in the program to determine facilitators and barriers to completion
Plan creation/ implementation	The strategic planning leadership team for the center created a full-color document highlighting the details of the plan. The plan was printed for in-house audiences, posted on the center's website in an accessible format, and distributed to key external stakeholders who are familiar with the work of the center.
Outcomes and achievements	At the conclusion of the 1st year of the program, the center hosted a forum to highlight some of these notable accomplishments: • Based on survey data and benchmarking with peers, funded two new technology support people to assist with training about online platforms • Implemented a program completion audit application that allows participants to track their progress toward completion and entertain what-if scenarios about class choices • Obtained two grants used to provide additional course offerings each semester so that participants do not have to wait months for a needed course to be offered

Key Considerations in the Planning Process

Leadership

Of the many leadership themes and capabilities important to higher education, several are especially valuable in assuring a successful strategic planning process. Knowing and leveraging the competencies of those who will design and guide the overall leadership process is fundamental. Also critical is designing a leadership architecture that assures representation from varying levels of the organization and its key internal constituencies to guide the various phases of the planning process. Members of the core planning leadership team should possess subject matter expertise and should also be able to adopt a collaborative style. Members of this team might also serve as leaders of subcommittees designated to coordinate particular aspects of, or stages in, the planning process and to ensure multidirectional communication.

Communication/Stakeholder Engagement

Communication is fundamental to formulating appropriate and agreed-on plan themes/goals, selecting priority projects, and framing messages and selecting media and delivery methods for each audience at each planning stage. Communication, in this context, does not refer solely to the dissemination of top-down messages through varying channels—although this is one aspect of the process. What is critical is to approach communication as a process of *engaging with* key stakeholders—supporters *and* critics.

Identifying and engaging key stakeholders in strategic planning efforts at multiple stages is critical to success. Often, the ultimate aims of strategic planning are not realized if there is insufficient engagement of faculty and staff—and other stakeholders—in the effort. Engagement is important for gathering relevant information, creating and testing preliminary plans, improving details of the plan, promoting commitment, and ensuring that the plan will have the support necessary for successful implementation. As suggested by the Society of College and University Planning (n.d.), "Strategic planning is generally considered an executive responsibility, but in higher education, all levels of the organization need to [be engaged]."

The traditions of shared governance, the customary pattern of relatively loosely coupled units, and the typical levels of autonomy in which higher education units and their members often operate, all point to the importance of faculty and staff engagement. As Woodhouse (2015) notes,

> As more and more faculty resolutions against strategic plans and administrative actions surface, nearly all of them have a common thread: concern over not only the proposed changes, but how those changes are

communicated. Often faculty members decry a lack of transparency or consultation. Sometimes their concerns are as simple as the vocabulary administrators use.

Achieving meaningful and satisfying faculty and staff involvement can be quite challenging, and it is not difficult to understand why short-circuiting this step so often occurs. While faculty and staff generally express a desire to be actively involved in developing plans—and express dismay if not included—leaders often find that in practice, this may not be easy to accomplish, may require a substantial amount of time, and can result in contentious deliberations along the way. That said, meaningful engagement of stakeholders—and particularly faculty—is a vital step in a successful planning process.

Additional complexities result from efforts to consider the perspectives of students and other key external stakeholders, to draw on comparisons with peer organizations and leaders within and outside the institution, and to focus attention on relevant environmental and economic factors. Meaningful engagement of all groups that have a stake in the planning effort often requires the development of innovative strategies and some persistence. Likewise, gathering information on relevant environmental and economic factors can require special effort, but information derived from these sources enhances the likelihood of developing a sound plan that will be broadly embraced and supported during implementation.

Culture

Taking account of the cultural orientations of faculty, students, and staff groups, and especially the relevant history, traditions, and sources of natural support and resistance for planning initiatives, can be very helpful. Most fundamentally, leaders need to identify and consider the multiple occupational and cultural orientations and traditions within the organization. This knowledge is useful in all phases of plan development and implementation and is particularly critical for determining who needs to be engaged in the planning process, at what stages, and in what ways.

Cultural awareness can be helpful in identifying potential facilitators and impediments to planning efforts and can also help in predicting and developing communication and engagement strategies to predict and address likely reactions to specific goals, strategies, and action plans. If the institution is unionized, for example, the history of relationships between the administration and unions can be an important consideration in planning and implementation. Similarly, attention to campus cultures may provide insights that are helpful in the selection of appropriate language for mission, vision, values, theme/goal statements—even the name for the overall planning process—increasing the likelihood that the terminology resonates in the best possible ways with key audiences.

Outcomes Monitoring and Follow-Through

Establishing indicators and methods for monitoring progress and documenting outcomes in the planning process and its implementation is another important consideration. Tracking efforts allows leaders to monitor process outcomes related to the planning effort, such as stakeholder comprehension and engagement, as well as progress related to the alignment of plan elements to assure that themes/goals and strategies mesh with one another and support the mission and vision.

Follow-through is probably the most difficult yet most important factor in successful strategic planning. Academic and administrative units are often very adept when it comes to envisioning what might be, and in posing creative possibilities for the future. In following through on the details necessary to realize the planning vision and goals, the results are often less stellar. Given this reality, a significant leadership and communication challenge is keeping faculty and staff engaged throughout the implementation stage of strategic planning efforts.

Toward this end, it is often helpful to establish mechanisms and methods for addressing this potential problem. One tactic is to create an implementation task force to monitor, guide, and regularly report on this critical stage in the process. Creating accountability mechanisms, consistently reiterating the importance of the implementation process through regular communication efforts, publicly recognizing achievements, and celebrating those involved all help to sustain energy and engagement. Helpful leadership actions during the follow-through phase include the following:

- Ensure that each program, project, or initiative has an assigned "owner" who is responsible for moving the initiative ahead and seeing it through to completion.
- Hold periodic group meetings to share progress and identify areas for collaboration as well as potential delays or problems.
- Maintain engagement of multiple stakeholder groups using their preferred communication channels.
- Create and meet an expectation for periodic updates to critical audiences.

Many of the concepts and techniques from change leadership—the topic of chapter 15—apply to successful strategic planning. The factors discussed in the foregoing section in relation to strategic planning are also applicable in leading and implementing organizational changes of all kinds.

Varying Approaches to Strategic Planning Initiatives

Generally, the ideal approach is institution-wide planning that sequentially integrates all units of a college or university to create a unified plan for the institution as a whole—one that articulates how the current and aspirational purposes, goals, and action steps of each unit fit within the larger institutional context. If, instead, the planning is to be implemented within a single division, school, or unit, here too the recommended approach is to first develop a plan that defines and clarifies the overall unit directions and plans and then move to planning within individual departments and units that are part of the larger organization. This kind of cascading methodology increases the likelihood that the broad purposes, goals, and strategies provide a foundation that is carried through in the plans of units within the organization.

In the top-down approach, the process begins at the highest level of the organization, and the broad framework of purposes and aspirations can guide planning efforts undertaken subsequently within individual constituent units. Alternatively, the planning sequence can begin with units that constitute the larger organization (for instance, programs or departments within a division or institution) completing unit-based plans. These plans could then be synthesized to create higher level plans for the organization or institution as a whole. A combination of the two approaches, where a plan is created through multiple iterations of reciprocal drafting, reviewing, and fine-tuning at multiple levels, has the potential to be maximally inclusive of the range of perspectives within the organization. Multiple iterations often provide the richest opportunities for engagement by faculty and staff at all levels, leading to few surprises and broader support when the final plan is completed. At the same time, the approach of considering and integrating multiple iterations can be time-consuming and may lead to the emergence of conflicting goals that require resolution.

As there are various options for sequencing efforts, alternatives also exist regarding how to design and coordinate the process. One option is to assign all phases of planning to internal leaders, taking advantage of available talents and resources that reside within the institution. Typically, in this model, a strategic planning leadership team is formed, headed by senior leaders, and includes content experts from the institution. This team has responsibility for designing, developing, coordinating, and implementing the planning initiative with others selected to participate from within the unit.

Another approach is to procure the services of consultants who may be contracted to design and oversee part or all of the strategic planning process.

Intermediate possibilities are also available. For example, the unit's leadership team may oversee some aspects of plan design, development, and implementation while also securing the support and guidance of external consultants or individuals from elsewhere in the university who have expertise in one or more aspects of the planning process. The role of the external experts can be highly visible, or their role may be to offer behind-the-scenes support, essentially serving as coaches, with the unit leaders providing the public face of the planning effort.

When it comes to making choices among these varying options and approaches, there are obvious trade-offs to consider, based on such factors as the capability and experience of unit leaders and others who might serve as consultants or coaches, the culture and previous practices of the organization, available resources, time considerations, the real and perceived benefits or liabilities of having internal or external expertise, and validation for the process and the final report. One possible strategy that provides a way to manage the trade-offs is to vary leadership strategies for different stages in the process. For instance, if an expansive and detailed environmental scan is required, it might be better accomplished by external consultants. External resources might also be used to conduct interviews, focus groups, or surveys of various stakeholder groups, and to analyze resulting themes. Further, external expertise might be used to design and produce the completed planning document. Internal leaders, consultants, or coaches might then be utilized for integrating the consultant's input at appropriate stages, reviewing and clarifying the mission and vision, developing core themes and goals, identifying and prioritizing strategies, and designing the publication of the document drafted by the leadership team, as illustrated in Table 14.4.

Another option to consider is the use of pre- and post-planning activities, including meetings with leaders to establish goals for the planning process; the development, distribution, and analysis of preplanning surveys to faculty, staff, and other stakeholders that become the basis for issue identification; facilitated planning sessions or retreats with various groups; the solicitation of feedback from others on a preliminary draft of the final strategic planning report; post-report debriefing with leaders; and follow-up. The value of any of these options depends, of course, on the circumstances at hand, including available resources and attitudes toward the use of internal or external consultants.

Conclusion

Approaches to strategic planning tend to include many of the following steps: the clarification of mission, vision, and values; analysis of internal and

TABLE 14.4
A Hypothetical Approach to Facilitating a Strategic Planning Effort

Plan Component	Suggested Approach
Mission, vision, and values	Develop internally (with or without facilitation by others from outside the institution or unit).
Stakeholder perspectives	Inventory the available information internally and develop strategies for gathering additional needed information.
Environmental scan and benchmarking	Conduct an internal SWOT analysis involving faculty and staff (with or without facilitation by someone from outside the institution or unit). Consider additional research and consulting support for gathering and analyzing national data if that is necessary to the scope of the planning process.
Themes/goals	Develop internally (with or without facilitation by others outside the unit).
Strategies, priorities, and action plans	Develop internally (with or without outside facilitation).
Plan creation/ implementation	Develop draft internally. Consider consulting support for professional-level editing, layout, and publication of the plan.
Outcomes and achievements	Develop an internal monitoring group (with or without outside facilitation).

external needs, expectations, and influences; identification of core organizational issues; assessment of internal and external strengths, weaknesses, threats, and opportunities; development and selection of strategic imperatives; implementation of strategic goals; and assessment of outcomes and achievements (Burkhart & Reuss, 1993; Immordino et al., 2016; Pfeiffer et al., 1986; Roberts & Rowley, 2004; Tromp & Ruben, 2010).

The success of a strategic plan can be judged not only on the quality of the document and specifics of the formal plan, but also on the inclusivity of the process and engagement and shared sense of ownership of the goals, plans, implementation, and outcomes and commitment to future planning efforts. These efforts can help to clarify organizational purposes and aspirations, promote the development of broad and high-level goals, guide the allocation of resources, energize the organization to address key issues, and assist in the articulation of clear measures of success. Use of follow-through, periodic progress checks, and ongoing communication allows leaders to ensure that strategic plans become living, adaptive documents that serve as helpful and energizing guides for the institution and its multiple constituencies. More generally, planning provides the essential foundation for organizational change, a process to be discussed in detail in the following chapter.

For Further Consideration

1. Residential learning community
   Senior leaders from academic affairs and student affairs would like to design a residential learning community for undergraduate students organized around the themes of sustainability and environmental leadership. Based on your understanding of student and academic affairs, along with your commitment to the environmental focus of the learning community, you have been asked to oversee the planning effort for the new community. The overarching goal of planning is to engage collaborative partners from various academic and student life areas to think through the mission, structure, and general curriculum of the residential learning community. You recognize that there will be many individuals with an interest in the topic; however, like many institutions, collaboration across the traditionally siloed departments is not common.
   - What are the critical considerations in designing the planning process?
   - With whom would you engage throughout the process, and how would you facilitate the sharing of ideas across collaborative units?
   - What challenges might you expect to encounter—and how can you strategically design the planning effort to best address these challenges?
   - Given the graduate structure, how will you ensure continued collaboration and engagement across the institution within the implementation process?

15

ORGANIZATIONAL CHANGE

A Matrix Approach

In This Chapter

- What is organizational change, and what makes change complex in both a personal and organizational context?
- What are the predictable sources of resistance to change in organizations—particularly change in higher education?
- Why is resistance to change both a problem and an opportunity?
- What are the common stages associated with the acceptance or rejection of change efforts?
- Which strategies are most useful for leading change efforts in higher education?

Each New Year's Eve, millions of people make resolutions about things they need, want, and intend to change—in their outlooks, their behaviors, and their lives. Examples include wanting to lose weight, manage finances more effectively, exercise more, spend more time with family, complete a project, travel more, and so on. These kinds of resolutions are familiar to all of us as adults. Moreover, as we think back to our early school experiences, many of us can probably remember making well-intentioned pledges to ourselves each fall. "*This* year, I'm going to be a better student. I will get new and better notebooks, be more organized, devote full attention to my studies, and pay closer attention in each class. I won't put off working on assignments or studying to the last minute. *This* year will be different!"

When it comes to change, optimism reigns supreme, and bookstores sell a vast array of self-help guides that nourish our optimism. However, in so many cases—despite our resolutions, book purchases, and best intentions—we find it extremely difficult to implement meaningful change.

The challenges associated with change are inescapable; they exist at all levels of life. Immune systems resist intrusions that threaten our physical well-being, our psychological system resists perceived threats to our emotional and cognitive stability, and organizations, communities, and societies resist threats to existing patterns (Bertalanffy, 1968; Ruben, 1975). Weight control is one area in which many of us engage in change efforts, and the statistics on the success of those efforts across the population are quite revealing. Ayyad and Andersen (2000) found that in an analysis of 17 comprehensive studies, including a total of more than 3,000 dieters, only an average of 15% were successful in effecting change, defined in that analysis as losing and maintaining a weight loss of at least 20 pounds for 3 years or more. So often our hopes and plans for weight control and other change efforts are dashed, as we slip back into old habits and patterns that have been, and will continue to be, influential forces in our lives.

Our disappointments lead to frustrations, but they also teach a powerful and important lesson: Hope and good intentions, in and of themselves, are generally not effective strategies for change. This lesson provides the foundation for one of the most fundamental concepts of behavioral science—and an especially relevant topic for those engaged in leading change in American colleges and universities: The single best predictor of what we are likely to do in the future is not what we say, intend, hope, or plan, but rather what we have done in the past and what we are doing in the present. Simply said, *behavior is the best predictor of behavior.*

None of this implies that people and circumstances do not change. Changes of various kinds are occurring continuously—within our bodies, relationships, workplaces, and the world at large. Some changes are triggered by what are considered natural forces—health, financial, or environmental factors. Others are the result of purposeful efforts to promote planned change. No doubt we can each point to examples of successful changes in our own lives and those of friends and colleagues; in relationships, social processes, and organizations; and at national and international levels. The changes can involve the adoption of new ideas, innovations, technologies, structures, or behaviors, and in many cases, they occur in spite of significant resistance when a proposed change is initially introduced.

At the national level, an interesting example of successful planned change in the face of considerable resistance is the decrease in cigarette smoking that has occurred in the past half century. In 1965, 42.4% of the U.S. adult population smoked. Through ongoing, systematic, and multifaceted change efforts, this rate has dropped consistently—to approximately 14% in 2019 (Centers for Disease Control and Prevention, 2019). Even though this decrease is substantial, the challenge continues with each new generation of potential smokers, as various sources of resistance—and new innovations, such as vaping—continue to inhibit the change. Another notable example of a behavioral change process—which occurred over a period of days and weeks rather than months and years—included new norms of handshaking, frequent handwashing, and the maintenance of social distance in the immediate aftermath of the COVID-19 pandemic.

Purposeful Change in Organizations

The focus of this chapter is on planned organizational change within higher education. Organizations have habits, traditions, and histories—and similar to their impact on individuals, these factors reinforce past and present practice and impede efforts to stimulate progress and innovation. The barriers one encounters with change planning and implementation are particularly daunting in colleges and universities, where organizations are loosely coupled, decision-making is often decentralized, and attention to the perspectives of multiple stakeholders is essential to successful change. A 2015 survey conducted by *The Chronicle of Higher Education* asked college and university presidents to identify one strategy they would use to cut costs or raise new revenues at their institutions if they did not have to worry about the consequences among their constituents. Of the respondents, 16% did not choose any of the options presented. As Selingo (2013) noted, "Even when given a pass from the potential consequences of their actions, presidents remain reluctant to initiate major changes on their campus" (p. 12). This hesitation is likely shared by academic and administrative leaders across higher education, reflecting their challenging firsthand experience with such efforts in the past.

Personal change is difficult, but it involves only one individual, and we can arguably exercise some direct control over ourselves. Organizational change involves many people—all with their own personalized agendas, hopes, fears, and sensemaking frameworks. As Machiavelli (1532) wrote in *The Prince*, "There is nothing more difficult to take in hand, more perilous to conduct, or more uncertain in its success, than to take the lead in the introduction of a new order of things." Offering convincing contemporary support for Machiavelli's caution are studies of the success rate of organizational change efforts, which indicate that as few as 30% of these initiatives are considered successful (Aiken & Keller, 2009; Kotter, 1996a; Smith, 2002). Technical and resource considerations are often the first to be blamed for a high failure rate, but as we shall discuss, failures to recognize and address personal, cultural, and communication issues generally are more fundamental sources of the problem. These factors are especially problematic in complex organizations such as colleges and universities.

Lemons to Lemonade: Resistance to Organizational Change

Understanding resistance is critical for understanding the change failure rates and the many difficulties associated with leading change. Resistance to personal as well as organizational change results from any number of factors. For example, a proposed change

- may not be deemed necessary;
- requires a substantial investment of time, when there is already too much to do;
- comes as a surprise;
- calls for new routines, knowledge, or skills;
- assumes resources that may not be forthcoming;
- undermines our sense of self and our identity;
- threatens our present status, stature, or roles;
- may introduce mistrust and lack of confidence in leaders; or
- implies a criticism of the present systems, processes, or structures.

The expression of resistance can take many forms—some quite obvious, some much less so. Depending on the organizational culture, climate, and other factors, expressions of resistance may include avoidance, questioning, challenging, redirecting, delaying, withdrawing, or sabotaging—overtly or covertly.

Because resistance is recognized as an impediment to planned change, it is commonly regarded as a problem. A leader's first instinct is to mitigate resistance when it surfaces. But it is important to recognize that resistance can also have benefits, and the determination of its valence generally depends on its advocate's role or goal. People advocating change tend to view resistance in negative terms—as an impediment to achieving the intended outcome—while those who are the intended targets of change efforts may view it positively.

Even when resistance hinders a change agenda, it has the potential to be helpful. Resistance may point to insufficiencies in the way advocates have explained the need for change, or to a timeline that fails to provide sufficient time for affected individuals to integrate the proposed ideas and innovations in their thinking. In such cases, resistance may point to a need for further revision or consultation, which ultimately may lead to a better plan and broader acceptance by stakeholders. In his book about the Olympic champion rowing team from the University of Washington, Daniel James Brown (2014) shares a relevant quote by George Pocock, a leading designer and builder of racing shells:

It is hard to make that boat go as fast as you want to. The enemy, of course, is resistance of the water, as you have to displace the amount of water equal to the weight of men and equipment, but that very water is what supports you and that very enemy is your friend. So is life: the very problems you must overcome also support you and make you stronger in overcoming them. (p. 53)

As with racing shell design, the ways that leaders respond to resistance have the potential to translate into more constructive, appropriate, and broadly sustainable outcomes.

Stages of Change Acceptance or Resistance

The process of accepting or rejecting proposed changes of new proposals, ideas, technology, or behaviors is complex, and as many authors have suggested, when change initiatives are successful, they tend occur through a series of stages (e.g., Kotter, 1996b; Lewis, 2010; Ruben et al., 2008, 2017; Ruben & Goldthwaite, 2021). The number of stages identified, and the labels attached to each, vary among authors. Ruben et al. (2008, 2017) described five such stages.

As illustrated in Figure 15.1, the first stage in the model is *attention* and relates to gaining an awareness of and perceiving a need for change. Clearly, if one is unaware of proposed changes, or sees no need for the change, nothing can happen. Once an individual becomes cognizant of the need, the next step in the change process is *connection*.

Connection occurs as individuals begin to give serious consideration to specific change initiatives, develop personalized ways of thinking about the prospect of a change, and engage in discussions with others about these possibilities. With this investment of time and effort come conceptual and emotional linkages that enable the change process to move forward. If these

Figure 15.1. Stages in the change process.

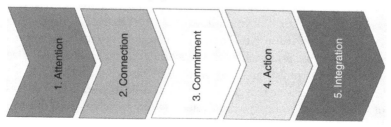

connections do not develop, it is unlikely that an individual will be motivated to expend the effort needed to move to subsequent stages in the change process. Particularly in colleges and universities, where dialogue, analysis, and engagement are so highly valued, meaningful connection is critical to both the quality and likelihood of acceptance of new initiatives. It is important to keep in mind, however, that the penchant for extensive conversation and analysis can lead to loss of momentum, causing the change process to stall at this stage.

Commitment and the acceptance of a new direction, idea, or behavior progresses if commitment translates into *action*. In the final stage, *integration*, either proposed changes are incorporated into the lifestyle of an individual or the culture of an organization or society, or they gradually fade from practice.

The model provides a macro-level view of how change generally works—when it does. In doing so, it oversimplifies some important dimensions of this process. First, the model does not capture the many stakeholder groups that must move through this change process if the goals of an initiative are to be realized. Second, the model implies a linearity and sequential progression through stages that is likely to vary from one situation and individual or group to another. While successful change generally requires a progression through all five stages, this progression may well include iterative looping and reversals, and as noted, it can stall at any point.

Consider an example of how these dynamics play out in health practices. Suppose you visit a doctor, and you learn based on exam results that your blood pressure is up from your last visit, that it is "borderline, tending toward the high side." Your physician tells you that you need to significantly reduce your sodium intake and increase exercise, and you should return for a recheck in six months. If you are not successful in these efforts, medication or other intervention strategies will be necessary. Does this news grab your attention? Is it sufficient to foster a personally relevant connection and motivate behavior change? If it is, you may have questions for the doctor or a nutritionist, and you will likely want to do some reading and research about elevated blood pressure, sources of sodium, and approaches to lowering sodium intake—and about exercise and other lifestyle strategies for lowering blood pressure. Will you commit to a low-sodium diet and increased exercise? If so, will you follow through with the actions necessary to implement that commitment? Finally, will you incorporate these actions into your behavior to the point where they become routine, leading to the change advocated by your physician—and ultimately resulting in lower blood pressure? And, if you achieve this goal, will you be able to sustain that success? At any of these stages, you may resist, reject, falter, or delay—and fail to move to the next step in the advocated direction. Unless all stages are completed, the physician's planned change goals for you—and yours for yourself—will likely be unsuccessful.

An examination of the pattern of efforts to promote the adoption of new personal practices to limit the spread of COVID-19 provides another example of the dynamics of change. Initial messages warning of the dangers of the virus and the advocation of specific changes relative to masks, social practices, and physical distancing to stem the tide of virus spread were adopted by some, but also ignored by many others, including a number of national leaders. "It's not a problem here." "Just use common sense and you'll be fine." "I'm not in the demographic group that's likely to be affected." All of these were manifestations of resistance to initial warnings and were largely overcome by waves of evidence-based messages from various leaders, published evidence and medical advice on the mechanisms that promote or inhibit viral spread, mounting social pressure, the imposition of regulations, and in some cases, personal experience with the consequences of the virus. Even in the face of a deluge of messages of many months from many sources and mounting evidence, change efforts were not fully successful.

Strategies for Stage 1: Capturing Attention

Managing organizational change is an area of increasing importance for academic as well as administrative leaders. As with the examples from other contexts, the aim of change leadership is to guide others successfully through the stages described. As implied in the model and foregoing discussion, the first consideration involves gaining the attention of those who need to understand and support the change initiative. While this undertaking may seem simple and straightforward, capturing the attention of others in a world with so many messages and people competing for time and interest can be a significant challenge. This is particularly the case if the topics do not signal the need for urgent response, such as predicted enrollment changes over the quarter century, evolving potentials for the use of new technology, anticipated changes in health care and retirement options, or projected changes in the demand for residential housing expected in 2030. Additionally, the loosely coupled nature of higher education institutions adds to the complexity of leading and mobilizing attention to particular initiatives, especially when the impact of changes may differentially impact individuals, programs, departments, and services across the institution.

As noted, gaining attention involves clarifying the importance and need for the advocated change. This attention-gaining process should generate a sense of importance or urgency. Ideally, this stage should create a *burning platform*—conveying a sense of urgency and the notion that continuing with the present course of action (or inaction) will soon result in highly undesirable outcomes. Gaining attention for one's agenda and issues is essential, but avoiding the *attention paradox* is also a consideration. While the use of dramatic, fear-inducing, or shocking message strategies will likely gain attention, if overdone they may actually lead to denial and alienation and may trigger resistance among intended supporters because of the anxieties they evoke.

Strategies for Stage 2: Promoting Connection

Strategies that heighten awareness and receptivity should be followed by efforts to connect individuals with the issues at hand and encourage discussions of the need, challenge, or problem(s) and potential solutions. A key prior consideration in this stage is identifying individuals (and groups) who need to be actively engaged. This list would include key stakeholders—individuals and groups with a direct or indirect stake in the proposed change or its consequences. Depending on the circumstances, these stakeholders might include board members, administrators, faculty, staff, alumni, students, donors, the media, and perhaps the local community. This stage also involves determining whether specific individuals within those groups are especially important to engage because of their insight or influence, or the resources they control. For example, along with faculty and staff, members of advisory boards, high-level donors, or political officials might wield extensive influence relative to a change such as a major construction project or organizational changes threatened by anticipated financial shortfalls to the institution. As noted, the primary goal at this point in the process is facilitating personal engagement and dialogue among internal and external stakeholders in order to generate a shared understanding of the rationale for the proposed change, what the change will involve, and what it will mean for them.

Strategies for Stage 3: Developing Commitment

Developing commitment or resolve relative to the advocated change is the third step. This stage includes identifying and focusing on areas of agreement and also identifying, addressing, and working through obstacles. Typically, these goals include ensuring the availability of needed resources, providing opportunities for engagement and influence, and ultimately building consensus, working coalitions, and a readiness to act.

Strategies for Stage 4: Motivating Action

Motivating action is the fourth task. Success at this stage involves clarifying intended change outcomes, promoting the desired behavior, and identifying specific tasks or actions that need to be implemented. The ultimate aim is to enlist the desired actions, which often requires providing the necessary resources and training identified in the previous stage. The goal is to support the necessary behaviors, remove obstacles to action, facilitate activities that move the initiative in the desired direction, and continue these efforts until the intended change outcomes are realized.

Strategies for Stage 5: Assuring Integration

Once the envisioned goals have been achieved, the final challenge—and by no means a minor one—is sustaining the change. The passage of time, waning attention, continuing background resistance, or a change in leadership can result in a gradual backsliding and an undoing of the many gains achieved through the prior steps. In this final stage, strategies should aim to mitigate these tendencies by showcasing and celebrating changes, publicly recognizing and rewarding innovators, developing reinforcing processes and structures, and implementing mechanisms for regular review and improvement.

Whether in personal or organizational contexts, unless these and other reinforcing steps are initiated, it is likely that recent advances will gradually regress to the older patterns, traditions, or behaviors. So it is, for instance, with weight loss, as discussed earlier, where evidence suggests that losing weight, while difficult, is far easier than maintaining the lower weight. Undoubtedly, we can all think of any number of personal and organizational examples where these same dynamics are quite familiar. The strategies noted can help diminish these undesirable outcomes.

Five-by-Five Matrix of Organizational Change

In the preceding discussion we provided an overview of the dynamics and stages of change, the potential liabilities and benefits of resistance, and considerations for negotiating through the five stages. Five additional factors are critical in guiding organizational change efforts. Each of these is *cross-cutting*—that is, each plays a vital role in the tasks associated within each of the five stages of change. These factors include leadership, constituencies, communication, culture, and outcomes, and as we shall explain, each of these requires planning.

- *Leadership* is concerned with defining and designating appropriate individuals or teams to guide the change initiative through each of the five stages.

- *Constituencies* involves identifying stakeholders to be included in planning and implementation efforts in each stage of a change initiative.
- *Communication* refers to information sharing, information gathering, and collaboration with those involved with, knowledgeable about, or affected at each stage of the change effort.
- *Culture* involves taking account of the organization's language, history, norms, rules, and traditions that may influence the dynamics of change.
- *Outcomes* relates to developing and implementing a systematic approach to monitoring progress and outcomes as the change process progresses at each stage and overall.

Overlaying these five cross-cutting success factors (listed horizontally) across the five stages of change (listed vertically) produces a 5 × 5 matrix for organizational change, as shown in Table 15.1. The matrix displays the five stages of change as columns and the five cross-cutting success factors as rows. Each cell represents a point of intersection between the two sets of considerations, and each interaction highlights an important area for

TABLE 15.1
The Five-by-Five Matrix for Planned Change

STAGES	1. Attention (Gaining Attention of Key Individuals and Groups)	2. Connection (Involving Stakeholders in Design and Planning)	3. Commitment (Securing Responsibility, Dedication, and Resources)	4. Action (Developing and Implementing)	5. Integration (Evaluating, Reinforcing and Refining)
FACTORS					
1. Leadership: • Coordinator • Team members • Architecture					
2. Constituencies: • Key stakeholders • Supporters • Resistors					
3. Communication: • Messages • Channel(s) • Audiences					
4. Culture: • Barriers • Resistance • Facilitators					
5. Outcomes: • Assessment • Methods • Metrics					1

attention by academic and administrative leaders as they plan and implement a change initiative.

The 5 × 5 matrix provides a useful framework for developing and implementing those efforts. Successful organizational change requires a foundation of systematic planning. As discussed in the previous chapter, the essential goals of planning are to provide a foundation for organizational change, achieve a shared understanding of the purpose and intended outcomes of the project, and coordinate action in the implementation of a plan during each stage. If the planning is done in an inclusive way—as opposed to by one individual—the process can also contribute to the quality of decision-making and to the morale and enthusiasm of those involved with or affected by the change. Using the 5 × 5 matrix helps to guide this effort and can place these goals in the larger context required for implementing a plan.

A key first step is to clearly and succinctly define the purpose(s) of the planned change initiative or project and why it is needed. A second step involves the identification of all groups that are directly affected by or have an interest or stake in the change initiative. Formulating specific goals that will describe the needs and purposes of the initiative is another important task. Determining the best strategies for each goal—how each goal is to be accomplished—comes next. These decisions provide the background for the development of an organizational change plan. The 5 × 5 matrix provides a systematic approach that takes account of the stages in the change process in general, plans for a particular change initiative, and identifies the five factors that help to ensure successful outcomes.

Factor 1: Clarifying Leadership Roles and Structure

Leadership is indispensable to the success of every stage in the process of planned change, as it is for planning in general. Key questions include the following:

- Who needs to be involved in championing the change initiative in each stage of the process?
- What leadership structure or architecture exists to support this effort during each stage?
- Who will have overall responsibility for coordinating the effort during each stage of the change process?

The knowledge and skills of individuals selected to play leadership roles in the change process are very important. Senior leaders who are well-informed about the rationale and need for a particular change, and who are credible and adept at presenting this information, can make an especially valuable contribution in stages 1 and 2, and again in stage 5. In stage 2, and even more so in stages 3 and 4, other leaders and peers who can clearly articulate the need, goals, plans, and details of the initiative play vital roles. Beyond specific knowledge, leaders in these stages must also be credible and respected, effective in face-to-face and virtual modalities, and also highly competent in other analytic, managerial, and communication competencies, as described in chapter 9. In stage 5, a senior leader's role in recognizing the accomplishments of change leaders and highlighting positive outcomes can be very significant for reinforcing and sustaining gains from the change process.

Another facet of leadership is the establishment of an appropriate leadership team and the broader leadership structure or architecture necessary to facilitate the process. The leadership structure may consist of one or several teams and possibly subteams. Depending on the specific nature of the initiative, it may make sense for the composition of the leadership team or teams to match the needs of particular stages. The appropriate size, composition, and responsibilities of the leadership structure will vary greatly from initiative to initiative, depending on the complexity of the organization, the scope of the project, the number of constituencies involved, the extent of resources committed, and the length of time available to complete the project.

The strengths and limitations of those who will be asked to play a role in the effort should be carefully considered when forming leadership teams. Generally, it is a good strategy to select participants whose competencies, knowledge, and skills augment those of the senior leader. It is also important to identify and involve individuals who understand and can effectively represent the perspectives of the various groups that the proposed change will affect, who will understand and help to champion the planned change, and who have the competencies necessary to facilitate success at a particular stage in the process. Different team members might serve as coordinators of different tasks in different stages, with the goal of matching leadership knowledge and skills to the objectives of each stage.

Table 15.2 provides an example of a template for the identification of a leadership group and/or architecture to guide planned change through each of the five stages. The guide focuses attention on the analysis and decisions regarding who (person or leadership team) will need to complete what task(s), during what time frame, for each stage in the planned change process.

TABLE 15.2
Leadership Architecture Guide

Stage	Leader (Person/team)	What the leader/ team should do	Time frame
1. Attention			
2. Connection			
3. Commitment			
4. Action			
5. Integration			

Factor 2: Identifying Key Constituencies

Efforts to identify all individuals, groups, and organizations affected by the envisioned change, and determinations as to which of these groups should be the focus of attention in each stage, is a second key activity. Guiding questions include the following:

- What individuals, groups, or organizations are most directly impacted by the change, and how should they be most appropriately involved as collaborators or partners in planning and implementation?
- What groups or individuals are likely to be indirectly affected, how should they be involved, and in which stages?

Depending on the specifics of the situation at hand, devoting additional attention to identifying constituency groups that may be particularly supportive, and those that are likely to be resistant, and at what stages, can also be a useful step in planning. As Lewis (2011) notes, stakeholders are at the center of any change initiative. They can contribute to the successful adoption of a change, stall the process, or block the effort entirely. Lewis identifies four roles stakeholders may play in the change process: *Opinion leaders* are persuasive individuals who can influence other stakeholders' attitudes and behaviors about a change. *Connectors* are individuals who serve as boundary-spanning links between and among various stakeholder groups; they are important because they are able to disseminate either positive or negative information or forge alliances across stakeholder groups. *Counselors* are a source of social support for those impacted by a change, and *journalists* collect and share information about a change initiative, reporting on successes and failures, the veracity of rumors, reactions to the change, and supporters or detractors of the change, for example (Lewis,

2011). Remaining mindful of these roles, and individuals who may occupy them, can be an important element of strategy for leaders of planned change.

Factor 3: Developing Communication Strategy and Framing

Along with planning and leadership, communication is a key contributor to the successful execution of the five stages of change. Communication can seem like a simple and straightforward activity. Someone has an idea for an organizational change that makes sense to them. The individual creates a message (orally, visually, or in writing) and conveys it to others in the organization or to persons they would like to inform or persuade. However, as we know from previous discussions, differences in experience, needs, perspective, motives, knowledge, roles, and a number of other factors contribute to a situation where messages sent and the meanings intended by leaders or others are often not received and interpreted as desired.

As noted previously, it is easy to assume that everyone else is as knowledgeable and concerned about the issues that matter as is the leader, but this is typically not the case. With regard to understanding the purpose and need for change, for instance, those who have been intimately involved in the thought and preparation processes have already recognized the significance of the effort. But many others whose understanding and support are needed are unlikely to initially share that understanding or enthusiasm. To move them to the desired point of insight and interest requires a systematic, time-release communication process that makes it possible for others to work through and digest the information in the way a leader did. Then, ideally with the opportunity for discussion and engagement, others will reach conclusions similar to those of the leader.

In addition, a single message is seldom likely to be sufficient to create change, as discussed previously. Telling someone, "This change is needed and important," will not get the job done; rather, considerable repetition and reframing will be required to bring about attention, connection, commitment, action, and integration. Viewed from the perspective of senior leaders, repetition can be agonizing and may begin to seem wasteful; however, the primary goal is not for the leader to feel good about their communication effort. Rather, the goal is to reach all important stakeholders so that they can understand, endorse, and support the initiative. Leaders are likely to become quite bored with the specific messages and the communication process long before everyone who needs to be familiar with and supportive of the effort has been engaged.

It will not be possible to be equally successful with everyone with whom a leader must communicate during the change process. In any communication situation, some receivers are relatively easy to reach through well-crafted messages. These individuals will be willing to listen to the proposed change, and they are likely to develop a basic understanding of the rationale for change.

There is always a fraction of the audience that is not easy to engage. They may lack interest in the initiative or simply not be able to relate to the new perspectives, purposes, goals, or needs as described. It is nonetheless important to attempt to gain the attention, connection, and commitment of this group. At some point, however, it becomes reasonable to conclude that the investment of time and effort directed toward particular individuals is no longer useful. Instead of contributing to progress toward the intended outcome, the efforts create frustrations and drain energies that could be better invested elsewhere.

Perhaps the most important place to invest effort is with members of the target audience who are uncommitted and thus likely to become either supportive or resistant depending on the quality of the communication effort. As these individuals come to understand and support an initiative, they become part of the de facto leadership team and can be particularly influential agents of change with other stakeholders. Indeed, they often make up a group that is effective in explaining why they reached their conclusion because they are regarded as relatively objective parties, with no personal stake in the outcome.

Communication efforts relative to change are easier if the message is simple and brief and can be conveyed in about the same amount of time that it takes to ride several floors in an elevator. Imagine a situation where a colleague says, "Can you tell me about that project you're working on?" What do you say? A very unpromising start would be, "Well, let me begin by giving you some background. In October 1987 . . . ." This is not a good beginning for a succinct explanation, and one that likely will not get beyond the early-1990s before the elevator door opens and your colleague (gratefully) departs, with little or no understanding of the key points of the project and probably very little interest in inquiring further.

People attend to, remember, and retell messages that are simple and to the point. Longer messages with many details are more difficult to understand, harder to remember, and more likely to be misinterpreted and distorted in retelling. "Elevator stories" intentionally provide very few details. If the person you are talking to asks for additional information, that may be your cue to provide historical context or current details.

Framing is another relevant concept in change communication (Fairhurst, 2004; Fairhurst & Sarr, 1996). There are many ways to describe a particular situation, change initiative, or project, and framing choices can have considerable influence on whether a message is noticed, how it is interpreted, whether it is remembered, and how it is conveyed to others.

As discussed in chapters 9, 10, and 11, communication concepts are translated into action through the communication strategy a leader employs to support the change process. Key questions to consider include the following:

- Who are your internal and external target audiences (affected parties)?
- What are your intended outcomes?
- What are the probable sources of support and resistance?
- What are the appropriate messages for each audience?
- What are the most effective channels for reaching each audience with your message?
- Who is the most appropriate messenger?
- What impact are you expecting from your messages?

Clear goals, thoughtfully tailored messages, and purposefully selected channels that are appropriate for a particular stage and a specific audience are vital components in change communication. Many potential goals may be adopted, as shown in Table 15.3. Messages should be created to achieve the selected goals, paying attention to the messages' substance, language, length, framing, and tone.

Channel selection can also be a significant strategic variable. There are many different means of communication, depending on the goals, audiences, and situation. In some instances, the potential for immediate, face-to-face interaction is desirable. In these circumstances, one-on-one sessions and focus groups are appropriate. At other times, a large group setting such as a town hall meeting, teleconference, or production video may be a better choice.

TABLE 15.3
Possible Communication Goals

• Gain attention	• Increase awareness
• Listen and understand	• Provide information
• Clarify	• Encourage
• Reinforce a point of view	• Persuade
• Engage	• Motivate
• Create buy-in	• Prompt action
• Heighten commitment	• Promote sustainability

There may be other stages or situations where the possibility of spontaneous and immediate reactions could interfere with specific goals or be difficult for leaders to handle spontaneously. In these circumstances, asynchronous channels—email exchanges, blogs, or website FAQs—may be more appropriate, because they provide the opportunity for leaders to think through their responses before reacting.

Other considerations in media selection are relative to the issue of how public and permanent you want messages to be. Face-to-face conversation is fleeting, while emails, blogs, and other media-based documents are far more permanent and portable. The extent of permanence can be a virtue or a liability, depending on factors such as the stage of the project, level of support, assessed need for communication flexibility and adaptability, the comfort and skill level of the communicator, and especially the goals.

As illustrated in Table 15.4, leaders may utilize many communication options, and in each case, the assets and liabilities of unique channels suggest a need for careful analysis and decision-making relative to their selection. Quite likely, different messages and channels will be best suited for differing internal and external audiences—and perhaps differing subaudiences within each of these broad categories. Consider a plan to purchase and tear down a number of local homes to expand a campus. In such a situation, members of the community, media, homeowners, local government, faculty, staff, and students might each require their own communication approaches to address the specialized priorities and media preferences of each group.

TABLE 15.4
Communication Strategy Guide: Stage 1—Attention

Communication . . . in order to connect to what audiences, to achieve what goals/outcomes, to overcome what anticipated resistance (e.g., needs, questions, concerns), with what message, through which channels, coming from whom?					
Audience	*Goal*	*Resistance*	*Message*	*Communication Channel*	*Message Source*

Note: Adapted from Tromp, S. A., Ruben, B. D. (2010). *Strategic planning in higher education.* National Association of College and University Business Officers, p. 77.

One additional and important consideration is the selection of message sources. Is the president, an area vice president, a dean or director, one or more faculty or staff members, or an alumnus of a student group the appropriate source for particular messages in the change process? Depending on the initiative and the culture of the organization, individuals in each role may bring particular strengths and liabilities, and these points should be factored in when choosing who will serve as message sources.

Communication planning should take account of each stage in the change process, along with goals, messages, and channels. Generally speaking, a distinct strategy is required for each stage. Table 15.4 provides an illustration of a template for planning a communication strategy during stage 1. Individuals and groups can complete similar templates for each stage; collectively, the templates will provide a systematic, sequential, and comprehensive guide to communication planning and implementation for any initiative.

Factor 4: The Role of Organizational Culture

Change initiatives have the potential to reinforce or disrupt particular cultural traditions. Because of the differential impact proposed changes may have, attention to culture, how various groups and traditions may be affected, and how best to take account of these factors are important issues to consider in the planning process.

As discussed previously, cultures are stable and naturally resist change, and the more a particular cultural group is affected directly or indirectly by a proposed change, the more thoughtful attention, creativity, and persistence will be required for successful outcomes. The two largest and most critical employee groups within higher education institutions—each with their own cultural traditions—are the staff/administrators and the faculty. As we know, fundamental and predictable differences exist between these two employee groups, and these differing orientations can become quite significant during organizational change.

Suppose that a university with a tradition of decentralized and collegial decision-making decided to consider enacting new approaches to its online course offerings. Imagine that the innovations would include establishing new university policy, a new university office, and a new centralized system through which all online courses from all academic departments would be designed, approved, and managed. Imagine further that a joint committee of faculty and administrators/staff was formed to consider this idea and make recommendations about the advisability of moving in this direction. In designing or leading this committee or the change effort more generally, a number of cultural issues are likely to come into play. For example, administrative and staff members could be expected to focus attention on issues related to operations, cost, system needs and capabilities, regulatory concerns, and legal matters, while academics would be likely to begin discussions with consideration of the impact of potential changes on faculty autonomy and academic freedom, intellectual property, and appropriate inclusivity in the process of considering any change in the traditional approach.

The following questions are helpful when considering the role of culture in organizational change:

- What elements in the history of the organization may affect each stage of the change initiative?
- In what ways will this change align or conflict with organizational traditions?
- In what ways should various organizational cultures be considered in each stage of the change initiative?

As we know, faculty, staff, administrative, and student groups are clearly not the only stakeholder groups for which culture and identity issues are important, and thinking carefully about who will be affected by proposed changes, and how, is most essential in change planning and implementation. The essential point to keep in mind is that effective change leadership requires what we characterized earlier as ethnographic and intercultural competencies that take account of, respect, and benefit from the strengths and insights of each group's point of view in moving forward.

Table 15.5 provides a template that can be used for thinking through the issues related to culture that are relevant to a particular change initiative.

TABLE 15.5
Culture Guide Worksheet

Stage	Group/Cultural Issue	What Needs to Be Done
1. Attention		
2. Connection		
3. Commitment		
4. Action		
5. Integration		

The first column calls for a listing of the various groups and issues to consider at each stage. The second column asks for details of what needs to be done. For example, if strategic planning activities have been conducted in a way that created resistance or planning fatigue, this could be noted as a "group/ cultural issue." Leaders might then decide to eliminate some of this "cultural baggage" by labeling and describing the new initiative in ways that are less likely to bring up past negative associations—an item to be discussed and noted in the "What Needs to Be Done" column of the worksheet. Framing the work as "State College: Our Priorities for the Decade Ahead" might avoid some of the knee-jerk response that could be associated with "A Strategic Plan for State College."

The worksheet allows space for comments and plans for each stage. Depending on the initiative, the number of groups involved, and overall complexity, it might make sense to create separate sheets for each stage in the process. Leaders could also perform a more granular analysis of the cultural groups involved and the issues that must be considered. For instance, if a change to online instruction using anatomical simulations was being contemplated, one could predict that faculty members with minimal experience with interactive virtual methodologies would likely be more reticent than colleagues who have more familiarity with asynchronous virtual platforms. For each group, different strategies and approaches might be appropriate.

Similarly, it might make sense to engage staff and administrative subgroups differently. Staff members who would have direct responsibility for technical support of a new system might represent one group; deans and unit business managers might be another, and so on. In this example, students represent an additional cultural group to be considered, and within that group there are many distinct subgroups—residential and commuting students, majors and nonmajors, undergraduate and graduate students, students who have and do not have easy access to personal computers, and so on. In situations such as this, plan development and implementation decisions should be made in a manner that takes account of the distinctive perspectives and needs of the groups involved.

Factor 5: Assessment—Monitoring Progress and Outcomes

With regard to organizational change outcomes assessment, the goal is to adopt and use measurement approaches that help to monitor progress and results in as simple and straightforward a manner as possible. Assessment is a critical factor with change initiatives; without attention to this issue, it may be impossible to determine whether an initiative is progressing as intended, until it is too late to revise, refine, or redirect the approach. Moreover, in the end, assessment is critical to documenting final outcomes.

The basics of assessment are straightforward. The key questions include the following:

- How do we assess progress at each stage of the change initiative?
- How do we assess the effectiveness of the overall process and outcomes of the effort in relation to our goals?
- How can our knowledge of progress during each stage be used to enhance the overall success of the change initiative?

Table 15.6 provides an example of a template that can be used to guide the assessment process through each of the five stages of change.

An Integrated Approach

In this chapter, we have reviewed the major components of the 5 × 5 matrix—the five stages of change and the five cross-cutting key success factors. There is no magic bullet or foolproof formula that assures success in all situations. However, a disciplined approach using the model in planning and implementing change initiatives can certainly enhance the quality of the innovation or change being introduced, facilitate acceptance and recognition, reduce risk and resistance, and decrease the time it takes to achieve each of the desired outcomes.

TABLE 15.6
Assessment Guide Worksheet

Stage	To Accomplish What?	What Will Be Assessed?	How Will You Assesss?	How Will Info Be Used?
1. Attention				
2. Connection				
3. Commitment				
4. Action				
5. Integration				

This approach is helpful because it addresses many of the reasons change initiatives fail, which include the following:

- The importance of each stage in the change process is not understood.
- Factors that are essential to change at each stage—planning, leadership, communication, culture, and outcomes assessment—are overlooked.
- Key constituencies are not engaged in appropriate ways and at appropriate times.
- An effective leadership architecture is not designed or implemented.
- The need for buy-in is underestimated.
- The dynamics of learning and change for individuals and organizations are misunderstood.
- There is insufficient senior-level support.

Principles of Organizational Change

In thinking broadly about successful organizational change, it is helpful to keep in mind the following relevant principles of leadership:

- No change is so small or insignificant that you can ignore issues of planning, leadership, constituencies, communication, culture, or outcomes assessment.
- Assume that you know and care much more about the change initiative—and reasons for it—than those at other levels or other parts of the organization, and plan the steps in the change process accordingly.
- Create and engage a cadre of people who understand, support, and will help to champion the change.
- Seek the perspectives of those who have insights, experience, and outlooks that you do not have.
- Realize that all change has both temporary and longer term effects on members of the organization and other stakeholder groups.
- When it comes to understanding dynamics and consequences of change, try to see things from the point of view of the affected parties and apply the golden rule.

Conclusion

Rapidly changing environments call for organizations that are flexible and adaptable. As Blumenstyk (2015) noted,

Leadership in higher education today requires a delicate balance: a posture that prevents both knee-jerk reactions to the latest trend and flat-footed reluctance to go after real opportunities. . . . Whatever the model, it's clear that cruise-control leadership is no longer an option, even for colleges that don't face immediate financial threats.

The concepts, principles, and tools offered in this chapter are intended to help leaders effectively guide their institutions through times of turbulence and change and to transform these challenges into meaningful opportunities to innovate and advance the work of higher education.

For Further Consideration

1. Personal change reflection
   As a personal thought experiment, recall examples in which efforts were made by a family member, friend, or colleague at work to encourage you to make a significant change in your life—for example, to spend more time with family, learn new skills at work, or undertake a lifestyle or behavioral change. Was that effort successful? Why or why not? Did you resist the change? Were you able to overcome that resistance? If resistance did occur, at what stage or stages in the process did it intervene? Can you analyze and explain the outcome of the planned change effort based on the five stages in the change model?

2. Postmortem analysis
   Identify one or more failed change initiatives within your institution. Conduct an informal postmortem analysis using the 5 X 5 template as a resource to determine exactly where in the process and why, the change initiative broke down. Consider what might have been done to avoid the failure.

3. Recruitment and selection at Corwin College
   Traditionally, each search committee at Corwin College developed its own search process for recruiting and selecting new academic and administrative directors and deans. Several administrators have discussed the idea of creating a single search process or procedure and supporting materials for all senior leader searches across the college. At this point, the idea is very much in its infancy, and the president

has asked you to chair a committee to develop a framework for planning and implementing the new campus-wide search process. Recognizing the complexity and array of issues involved, the recommendation is to use the organizational change matrix as your guide. You also have been asked to annotate the suggestions in your plan with the rationale guiding your recommendations. The president looks forward to meeting with your committee when the proposal is complete.

16

OUTCOMES ASSESSMENT

Creating and Implementing Measurement Systems

In This Chapter

- What are the origins of the widespread interest in measures, metrics, evaluation, and assessment in higher education?
- What are the potential advantages and disadvantages associated with the use of metrics?
- What are the central elements of a mission-to-metrics framework, and how can the model be helpful for higher education leaders?
- How can establishing measurement systems help to clarify the institutional, departmental, programmatic, or project mission, vision, and goals?
- How can academic and administrative leaders use measurement systems to create shared understanding of and commitment to organizational aspirations?

There is no mistaking the growing national, state, and local emphasis on measuring outcomes. These efforts have never been more apparent than in the period of the COVID-19 pandemic when the graphs and tables presenting data on new cases, rate of transmission, and mortality rates have been featured prominently in presentations by medical, political, and organizational leaders at all levels, and in trend analysis and comparative analyses used by organizations of various kinds. The pervasive use of metrics and data analysis is emblematic of the recognized value of this approach for describing a situation, capturing and displaying changes, and identifying potential areas where attention is needed. At the same time, these approaches for reporting measures highlight some of the inevitable controversies that occur when metrics are used to track progress and report on outcomes. Questions arise as to what markers and measures are most appropriate, what methods should be used to gather necessary data, how often data reporting should take place, how to compare data from one setting to another, and how past data can be used to project future events. Also of interest are questions about how to predict and account for the lag between early warning signs and subsequent developments, how data are best displayed, and perhaps most important, how to assure that measurement data are accurate, reliable, useful, and used to analyze situations, address problem areas, and guide leadership and decision-making and behavior.

Assessment is a topic of increasing emphasis in higher education. Markers and measurements for assessing student learning, faculty productivity, job placement, institutional finances, diversity and inclusion, workforce trends, and recruitment and enrollment patterns are becoming ubiquitous throughout most institutions. And, as in other sectors, measurement efforts play an important role for leaders in colleges and universities in the recovery and renewal processes made necessary by the COVID-19 pandemic.

The Assessment Trend in Higher Education

The ways in which markers are selected and used in higher education have evolved over the years. Historically, the most critical considerations in evaluating the quality of colleges and universities were factors such as the stature of faculty and staff, the quality of the programs offered, the level of distinction of students selecting and attending particular institutions, the extent of library holdings, and the adequacy of financial and physical assets. Within this tradition, there was a notable emphasis on the quality of resources and the richness of opportunities provided by the institution. Today, as noted previously, that traditional emphasis is matched, if not surpassed, by efforts to assess the benefits that stakeholders, especially students, derive from these institutions—most particularly, what they learn, how they progress through the institution, and how their education benefits them following degree completion. This shift in emphasis has led to increasing efforts to assess outcomes related to all elements of an institution, department, or program's mission, aspirations, plans, and goals, not only those relevant to teaching and student learning, but also to research, scholarship, service, and outreach.

Assessing outcomes, rather than inventorying inputs, institutional resources, and attributes, reflects a major shift in thinking, one that seems to have captured the attention of most, if not all, of higher education's external stakeholders—parents, employers, state and national educational organizations, accrediting and regulatory agencies, and the general public. The 2006 Report of the Commission on the Future of Higher Education—more widely known as the Spellings Commission, named after a former U.S. Department of Education secretary Margaret Spellings, who subsequently became president of the University of North Carolina system—may have been the single greatest factor in creating momentum for more rigorous and systematic measurement of the effectiveness of higher education.

Representing a broad range of constituencies and perspectives, the 19-member commission focused broadly on the challenges facing U.S. higher education, voicing concerns about what was believed to be a pressing need for enhanced accountability and significant reform in many areas (Miller, 2006; Ruben et al., 2008; Schray, 2006; Spellings Commission, 2006). The preamble of the report, titled "A Test of Leadership: Charting the Future of U.S. Higher Education," acknowledged the many accomplishments of colleges and universities, but was also unequivocal in expressing concerns about the risks of complacency:

> This Commission believes U.S. higher education needs to improve in dramatic ways. As we enter the 21st century, it is no slight to the successes of American colleges and universities thus far in our history to note the unfilled promise that remains. Our yearlong examination of the challenges facing higher education also brought us to the uneasy conclusion that the sector's past attainments have led our nation to unwarranted complacency about its future. It is time to be frank. Among the vast and varied institutions that make up U.S. higher education, we have much to applaud, but also much that requires urgent reform. (Spellings Commission, 2006, pp. ix–xiii)

Although the substance of most of the issues raised in the Spellings Report was not particularly new, the strident language and broad distribution of the commission's reports and communiqués, coupled with the official status of the group and concerns about increased external regulation, prompted vigorous reactions from many quarters (Berdahl, 2006; Lederman, 2006, 2007; McPherson, 2006; Spellings Commission, 2006; U.S. Department of Education, 2006; Ward & American Council on Education, 2006). A fundamental issue in the report and subsequent reactions to it reflect what Kennedy (1997) described as a "kind of dissonance between the purposes our society foresees for the university and the way the university sees itself" (p. 2), and what Ruben (2004) characterized as a tension between the traditional values of the academy and the values of the contemporary marketplace.

The report included six specific recommendations. Of greatest relevance to this chapter, the commission recommended the following:

To meet the challenges of the 21st century, higher education must change from a system primarily based on reputation to one based on performance. We urge the creation of a robust culture of accountability and transparency throughout higher education. Every one of our goals, from improving access and affordability to enhancing quality and innovation, will be more easily achieved if higher education embraces and implements serious accountability measures. (Spellings Commission, 2006, p. 21)

Of the specific recommendations outlined in the report, this one was most controversial (Ruben et al., 2008): Greater focus on accountability and transparency—taken to imply more attention, and perhaps mandates, to measure performance and effectiveness—triggered emotions ranging from unbridled enthusiasm (most generally among external stakeholders and critics of the status quo) to acute anxiety and strong resistance among many college and university faculty and administrators and higher education organizations. For higher education, the recommendation signaled an increased focus on outcomes measurement, particularly the measurement of classroom learning, institutional effectiveness and efficiency, and functions of colleges and universities presumed to be value-adding. Many within higher education believed that the recommendation threatened the avowed purpose(s) of American higher education, including the tenets of academic freedom. In the midst of the fray, the terms *assessment* (along with *measurement, metrics,* and *accountability*) sometimes carried rather toxic connotations for members of the academic community (Ruben et al., 2008).

Ironically, when assessment is described in generic and academic terms, it would be difficult to find anyone inside or outside higher education to argue with its value. Who would disagree with the assertion that it is essential to determine, document, and ensure the quality of the work within colleges and universities and the benefits derived by individuals and groups served by these institutions?

Not everyone within higher education reacted negatively to the increased pressure for assessment. A number of individuals had long seen the need for a more explicit focus on the scholarship of education and on the application of higher education's research and professional expertise to examine and improve its own practices.

Origins and Evolution of Measurement in Other Sectors

Outcomes assessment had its beginnings in the business world, where the approach has long been used for the evaluation of accounting and financial performance, reporting, and the comparison of performance across multiple organizations or divisions. Particularly for complex organizations with multiple units geographically dispersed and remote from management, quantitative measurement methods became an attractive alternative to narratives and anecdotes, which had been the traditional tools used for accountability. Measurement techniques also offered a tool for making comparisons in performance over time and across organizations.

More recently, measurement methods—variously termed *performance metrics*, *key performance indicators* (KPIs), *scorecards*, and *dashboards*—have become increasingly popular. Figure 16.1 provides an example of the ways in which assessment data can be displayed using graphics of various kinds. Figure 16.2 illustrates a hypothetical dashboard of the sort that might be used to display financial performance results. The dashboard concept draws its name from the analogy to the dashboard of an automobile, which aggregates and displays a few critical measures that can be easily monitored without diverting attention from the fundamental task of driving—or, in the case of an organization, leading.

Performance measurement was also widely adopted in health care, where measurement and reporting systems are used in emergency situations, but also more routinely to track performance in areas such as treatment outcomes,

Figure 16.1. Displaying assessment results.

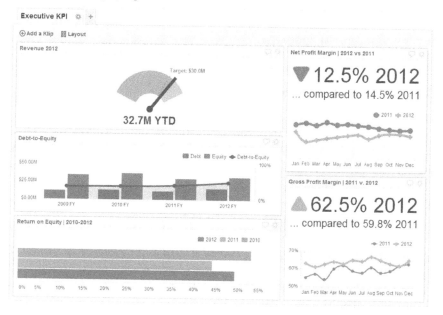

Figure 16.2. A sample financial performance dashboard.

hospital occupancy, emergency room wait times, average length of patient stays, lab turnaround time, and patient satisfaction (Healthcare Dashboards, 2015). In public sector organizations, dashboards are used to document and communicate levels of performance of civic and governmental agencies, such as city planning, parks and recreation, public health, and roads and highways (Government Dashboards, 2015). The application of performance measurement has been particularly extensive in community policing. The CompStat measurement system, originally developed for use in New York City, has since been widely adopted nationally and internationally (Bratton, 1998, 1999; Weisburd et al., 2004).

Benefits and Limitations

The continuing popularity of organizational measurement across sectors is not difficult to understand. In addition to their original uses for documenting and reporting performance and facilitating comparisons across organizations over time, measurement systems offer a number of additional benefits, including the following:

- energizing the discussion and clarification of aspirations and goals
- encouraging more fine-grained specification of intended outcomes
- helping to clarify what markers constitute evidence of successful or unsuccessful outcomes
- providing the basis for tracking performance over time and offering comparisons to peers and leading organizations

- contributing to the development of predictive models—identifying upstream factors that lead to downstream outcomes
- reinforcing a focus on behavior and activities that contribute to key plans and priorities

On the other hand, critics such as Brancato (1995) point to various potential limitations. Because measures are historical, they may lack predictive power. This is particularly the case if measurement methods fail to capture internal and environmental changes until it is too late for the information to be incorporated in modeling and planning. Moreover, measures may have limited value if they are too granular, overly localized in scope, or fail to capture critical markers and predictors of the desired outcomes. Also, some factors can be difficult to define and assess, for example, intellectual capital, leader effectiveness, employee motivation and satisfaction, or changes in environmental conditions. These measurement challenges can inadvertently lead to bypassing measures of important but difficult-to-measure processes or behaviors. Finally, some important markers are best assessed using qualitative analysis and tools, and such data are not always easily integrated with quantitative measurement systems.

Notwithstanding these concerns, measurement systems are widely used and can be extremely valuable, not only for the data they provide but also for the value of the process that is required to identify, establish, and create consensus on the list of key markers and metrics. Conversations associated with this process are often as valuable as the decision about specific metrics that result. Ideally, the markers and metrics are informed by organization-wide discussions of organizational purposes, aspirations, and goals as a prerequisite to selecting specific key measures on which to focus primary attention. Kaplan and Norton (1996, 2001, 2004, 2006), authors who have written extensively about what is termed the *balanced scorecard*, and others who have written on this subject list the following benefits related to the development and use of metrics:

- guiding leadership strategy
- clarifying and gaining consensus about vision and strategic direction
- communicating and linking strategic objectives and measures throughout the organization
- aligning individual and organizational goals and plans
- establishing and aligning targets
- conducting strategic reviews
- obtaining feedback and responding proactively to accountability and performance measurement pressures

- creating a culture of ongoing and integrated self-assessment, planning, and improvement
- motivating constructive conversations about organizational purposes, aspirations, plans, and goals.

Measurement in Higher Education

The assessment of the quality of the work within higher education has always been important in concept and practice; however, what is assessed, how it is assessed, and the terms used to describe the activity have evolved considerably over time. As noted previously, we have seen a noticeable shift in focus away from the educational opportunities, resources, and facilities *provided*, to an emphasis on those outcomes or benefits *derived from* the contributions of the institution, unit, or program. So, while assessment is not a new topic for higher education, the growing challenge is to extend assessment models to include greater attention to the benefits and outputs created as well as the benefits derived, rather than exclusively to organizational and resource inputs.

The primary push for outcomes assessment has been in teaching and learning, with increasing attention now being devoted to evaluating what is being learned and how that learning is beneficial to students, rather than solely emphasizing what is being taught and the goals of faculty. A second area in which assessment is increasingly emphasized is the evaluation of institution, department, program, and service performance outcomes. The focus in this regard is shifting from what is provided and delivered in the way of resources and opportunities to what the intended beneficiaries receive and use. The additional challenge is to usefully link these activities to planning and improvement so that assessment does not occur in a vacuum and is part of an integrated effort to increase the effectiveness of programs and services. This effort has led to an increased popularity of programs such as the Baldrige and Excellence in Higher Education model, as discussed in chapter 13; strategic planning methodologies discussed in chapter 14; and continuous improvement programs, initiatives, and tools focused on efficiency and quality improvement, such as Six-Sigma and Lean.

Measurement systems can be used to benefit any or all functions and services of higher education institutions. Among others, the list of functional areas where measurement can be usefully employed includes administration, research, media relations, student affairs, human resources, facilities, finance and budgeting, and athletics. Broadly speaking, these systems can be implemented for any program or office that provides services to students, faculty, staff, or any other stakeholder groups.

Assessment concepts are also flexible in terms of the level at which they can be applied. Measurement frameworks may focus on the effectiveness of the institution as a whole, or of a specific department or program. In addition to their value for monitoring the work of continuing units, they may also be applied to track and evaluate initiatives or projects that have a fixed beginning and ending point.

The appropriateness of particular markers and measures of effectiveness will, of course, differ based on the level of assessment. In the case of institution- or campus-level organizational assessment, a question such as "What are the university's primary goals?" initiates the conversation. At the general education level, one may ask, "What are the educational or learning goals of our core requirements, or what core knowledge and capability do we expect graduates of a particular institution to possess?" At the department level, the process may begin with the question that links to mission areas, such as "What are our primary goals: organizational, educational, research and service?" And at the program or service level—which could be, for example, an academic or administrative program, or a service program or student life initiative—one would ask, "What are the goals of our program or service?" One can also use the assessment framework to define and measure the effectiveness of strategic planning or other campus projects in fulfilling their intended purposes and goals.

Regardless of the terminology, setting, or level of analysis one chooses, the fundamental questions are the same:

- What are we trying to accomplish?
- How will we evaluate our progress?
- How effective or successful are we in our efforts?
- How will we use this knowledge to improve what we do?
- How will it move us closer to our vision/aspirations?

The Mission-to-Metrics Process

How does one go about creating a measurement system? The illustration in Figure 16.3 depicts the mission-to-metrics process, including the components and flow involved in moving from the selection of the *focus for assessment* to the *identification of a set of specific measures* that are used in the formalization of a measurement system. In this process, the mission and vision of an institution, department, program, or project provide the essential focus and serve as the initial point of reference.

Figure 16.3. Assessment: Mission to metrics framework.

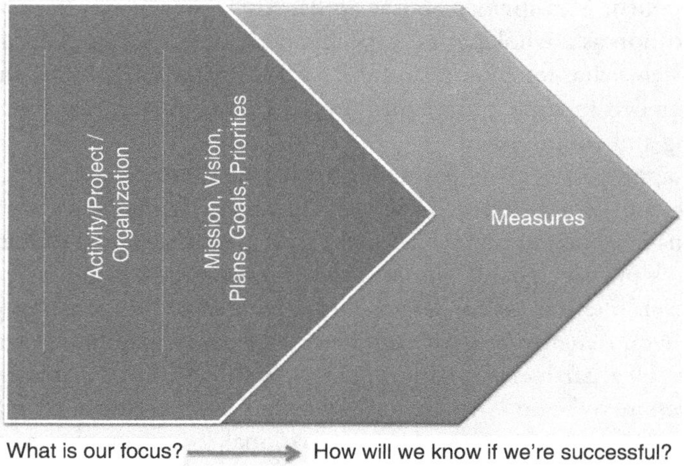

Step 1: Clarify the Focus of Assessment

The process begins by clarifying the focus of assessment. Will the assessment concentrate on an entire institution, or a particular department, program, strategic plan, project, or some other activity? The next step is to determine if a statement describing the mission, vision, values, plans, or goals exists. Clear and shared statements of purpose and aspiration—in the form of mission and vision statements—are basic to the development of a measurement system, and identified priorities and goals are also helpful. If these have been established previously, they may simply be reviewed and reaffirmed. If these do not exist, then creating them is a necessary foundational step in establishing a measurement system. (See the discussion of mission, vision, and goals statements in chapters 4 and 14.)

Step 2: Selecting Appropriate Metrics

The next step is to identify—and to reach agreement on—the most appropriate indicators or metrics to track in order to evaluate the organization's effectiveness relative to the assessment. Ideally, the mission, aspiration, or project goal statements incorporate concepts that can be easily translated into markers and measures. This can be a challenge, particularly when abstract terminology is used in the statements; the more abstract the concepts, the greater the difficulty in deciding on the most appropriate markers and measures.

In the creation of mission and goal statements, there is great benefit in using language that points to tangible markers that can be observed, measured, and tracked. Bringing this level of precision to statements as they are created is very helpful for progress and outcomes tracking later. As an example, assume that the focus for assessment is a departmental strategic plan and that our objective is to develop metrics to measure outcomes of the various goals of the plan. Suppose that one of the goals is "to establish new and productive partnerships with other campus units." The next question to be addressed is "What indicators will be the most appropriate measures of progress toward fulfillment of this goal?" One obvious metric would be the number of *new* partnerships established. As we discuss later, various other indicators in this case also might be selected as useful—perhaps most obviously, one or more indicators that would be helpful in measuring the more abstract concept of *productive*.

A more complex example of the challenge of operationalizing concepts is provided by an aspiration or goal such as "enhancing diversity, equity, and inclusion." On the one hand, it is easy to assume that the terms *diversity*, *equity*, and *inclusion* are widely understood. From a measurement perspective, however, questions arise as to what, exactly, these words are intended to mean in a particular organizational context, and to the specific activities and behaviors that are considered relevant markers for these meanings. Also important are decisions regarding what measures and measurement approaches should be used for translating these understandings and markers into metrics and outcomes information that can be tracked, shared, analyzed, and used to address gaps, maintain focus, and recognize progress and accomplishments. A list of potential markers and measurement methods associated with the goal of "enhancing diversity, equity, and inclusion" might include some or all of the items detailed in Figure 16.4, depending on the setting and circumstances.

Step 3: Collecting and Organizing Information

Once markers and measures have been selected, a process is needed for collecting and organizing data associated with these measures. In some cases, as with elements of the suggested diversity and inclusion markers and measures listed in Figure 16.4, some relevant information may already exist in particular areas. With the strategic planning example, it is unlikely that the information about partnerships is available. In each instance, and in most others, it will be necessary to develop a method for the collection, storage, and analysis of information. In the case of the strategic planning example, it will be necessary to track the number of partnerships being established—as

Figure 16.4. Possible diversity and inclusion markers and measurement methods.

Faculty, staff, and student diversity profile (created to align with diversity definition)

- Recruitment (statistics, trend and peer analysis)
- Retention (statistics, trend and peer analysis)

Curriculum and academic programming (content addressing diversity-related topics)

- Core/foundational courses (descriptions, statistics, trend and peer analysis)
- Elective courses (descriptions, statistics, trend and peer analysis)
- Campus-wide reading program (descriptions, statistics, trend and peer analysis)
- Discipline-specific offerings (descriptions, statistics, trend and peer analysis)
- Antibias/diversity and inclusion training for faculty, staff, and students (descriptions, statistics, trend analysis)

Cocurricular and student life (organizations and activities responsive to diversity needs)

- Clubs and organizations (descriptions, statistics, trend and peer analysis)
- Events and seminars (descriptions, statistics, trend and peer analysis)
- Guest speakers (descriptions, statistics, trend and peer analysis)

Faculty, staff, and student inclusion (created to align with inclusion definition)

- Mentorship (peer- and senior-level) programs (descriptions, statistics, trend and peer analysis; interviews, focus groups)
- Participation in activities and organizations (descriptions, statistics)
- Formal leadership roles in activities and organizations (descriptions, statistics)
- Perceptions of climate and culture (survey ratings by faculty, staff, students; interviews, focus groups; hiring/exit interviews)

Recognition and support (created to align with diversity and inclusion goals and definitions)

- Financial merit- and needs-based support for students from underrepresented groups (descriptions, statistics)
- Recognition of leadership, research, engaged scholarship, and service advancing diversity, equity, and inclusion in reappointment and promotion consideration of faculty and staff (descriptions, statistics)
- Resources dedicated to diversity, equity, and inclusion advancement by faculty and staff (descriptions, statistics)
- Recognition of individual and unit-based diversity, equity, and inclusion achievements (descriptions, statistics)

Pipeline initiatives (created to align with diversity definition)

- Engagement of diverse candidates for future faculty and staff positions at the K–12, high school, and community college levels (descriptions, statistics, trend and peer analysis)
- Investment of resources in pipeline ventures (descriptions, statistics)
- Programming for future diverse candidates at the K–12, high school, and community college levels (descriptions, statistics, trend and peer analysis)
- Enrollment and retention in pipeline programs (statistics, trend and peer analysis)

Assessment, monitoring, and analysis

- Development/refinement of a measurement system at the institutional and unit levels (descriptions, peer analysis)
- Development/refinement of reporting systems to enhance information access, sharing, and use for diversity, equity, and inclusion-related goal-setting and improvement planning (descriptions, peer analysis)
- Identification and comparative assessment with peer and national leaders
- Trend analysis

Policies, processes, symbols, and infrastructure (with attention to issues related to diversity and inclusion definitions and goals)

- Review and update university policies with attention to issues of diversity, equity, and inclusion (description, statistics)
- Review of financial, salary, rank, and promotion data with attention to issues of diversity, equity, and inclusion (description, statistics)
- Identification of structural and symbolic barriers to diversity, equity, and inclusion goals (description, statistics)

Sources: Branch, A. (2020). *In pursuit of excellence: Understanding the aims of the university equity audit.* Rutgers University; Tomlinson, B. (2020, July 13). Faculty members propose an anti-racist agenda. *Inside Higher Ed.* https://paw.princeton.edu/article/faculty-members-propose-anti-racism-agenda; Nevin, J. (2020, April). *Student diversity measures.* Rutgers Center for Organizational Leadership.

well as the most appropriate way to define what is meant by "productive" and how these determinations will be captured and recorded. For instance, is productive meant to refer to generating resources, engaging faculty/staff, engaging students, enhancing the reputation, or all of the above?

Data collection and analysis is a much more complex challenge with the diversity, equity, and inclusion example. Particular markers must be selected, along with measures and measurement methods, and it is unlikely that a measurement system would include all these potential measures, at least initially. Moreover, as noted earlier, the effort to define appropriate measures inevitably requires useful discussions that typically lead to much greater clarity about goals. The discussion and clarification process is critical for the establishment of a measurement system and is also likely to create a greater shared sense of the purpose of the venture and to guide individual and group actions in pursuit of these purposes.

Step 4: Displaying, Disseminating, and Using Information

The final step involves the display, communication, and use of the information provided by the measurement system. More specifically, this includes documenting outcomes, communicating outcomes information internally and to relevant external stakeholders, and using the results for monitoring and improvement. Outcome information can be collected and monitored during periodic intervals, aggregated to track trends, and used to establish improvement targets. In interpreting measurement data and its implications, setting performance targets, or identifying gaps or deficiencies, outcomes can be compared to previous results and to pertinent data from peers, aspirants, or leaders at one's own or another institution. Periodically, the measures and overall measurement system should be reviewed to ensure that they continue to be appropriate for evaluating progress toward fulfillment of the mission, aspirations, priorities, and/or goals.

In summary, the key steps in developing an assessment system are as follows:

- Clarify the focus for assessment and review or develop clear statements of purpose, aspiration, and goals for the institution, program, service, strategic plan, or project on which assessment will focus. This process should include a clarification of the definitions of key concepts to be measured and should identify appropriate metrics.
- Develop a system for capturing and communicating progress and outcomes information and identifying appropriate internal and external audiences for this information.
- Assess outcomes and achievements relative to these purposes, aspirations, plans, and goals, as appropriate.
- Include comparisons of outcomes over time and with peers and other institutions and organizations.
- Track, monitor, analyze, and use results to document outcomes and achievements, reinforce the shared sense of priorities, inform day-to-day decision-making and resource allocation, improve programs and service offerings, establish performance targets, and generally enhance quality, effectiveness, and efficiency relative to the focus of the assessment.

Figure 16.5 provides an example of one way to present a snapshot of key assessment outcomes for an academic unit.

A number of factors should be considered in the selection of metrics to incorporate into a measurement system. To be useful, the metrics selected should be

- valid—accurate and objective, measuring what you set out to measure;
- reliable—consistent and dependable; and
- useful—able to be easily understood and used.

Figure 16.5. A summary performance "scorecard" for the Rutgers School of Health Professions considerations in selecting measures.

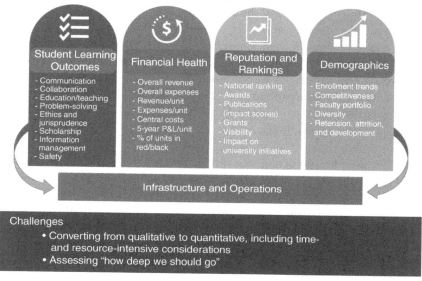

The selected measures should also have the following characteristics:

- *Strategic.* Measures should be chosen carefully to be useful in monitoring the organization's success in pursuing the mission, aspirations, plans, goals, or projects that are the focus for assessment. The aim is to select a few metrics that are useful for documenting key outcomes, setting improvement targets, guiding strategy and improvement efforts, and communicating a view of the work of the institution and/ or unit to internal and external audiences.

- *Aligned with those of the larger organization.* Measures should take account of the mission, aspirations, plans, and goals of the larger units of which they may be a part, and those of the institution as a whole. Ideally, the selected measures will be useful in demonstrating how the focus for assessment fits with and contributes to the institutional directions and aspirations.

- *Appropriate.* To the extent possible, metrics chosen for use should reference factors over which the organization has control and that reflect its mission. Measures should also capture the priorities or concerns of constituents and beneficiaries—those in the position to evaluate performance and whose judgments are important to the organization's success and standing.

- *Sustainable.* Measures should be able to be supported over time. Consider at the time it is created what it will take to sustain a measurement system. Outcome information that is inexpensive and easy to gather is the ideal. Take care not to commit to an overly elaborate system of measurement and dissemination that may be costly or difficult to sustain. Adding additional metrics to a system over time based on need and capacity is preferable to overreaching in an initial system design.

Note that the purpose of this assessment process is not usually to conduct the kind of rigorous research that is necessary for publication in academic journals, but rather to develop useful operational tools that are helpful guides for planning, decision-making, evaluation, and monitoring and documenting outcomes.

Types of Measures

In selecting measures, the preferred approach is to identify various types of measures to capture the different sorts of information that may be most helpful. To this end, consider including a combination of activity, professional standards, benefits/satisfaction, and impact measures.

- *Activity measures.* The most common type of metric consists of a count of the number of activities, tasks, events, or participants associated with the organizational mission, aspirations, plans, or projects that are the focus of assessment. Returning to the earlier example involving strategic planning goals, the *number of partnerships established* is an example of an activity measure. In the case of diversity, inclusion, and equity measures hiring, retention, and salary data are among the most obvious measures.
- *Professional standards measures.* Evaluating the caliber of organizational activities in terms of professional or disciplinary standards employed by peer or aspirant organizations or based on third-party evaluations, is a second approach to measurement. Thinking in terms of "productive partnerships" or the effectiveness of diversity and inclusion programs in the examples discussed previously, professional standards measurement would call for the use of metrics that would compare the nature and character of partnerships and diversity and inclusion

programs established by your organization with those at peer, aspirant, or leading departments or institutions. This information can be acquired in various ways, including exchanging comparative data with other institutions, from national higher education associations, or from the literature. Importantly, these measures help to ground local assessment within a framework that has broad standing within the higher education community. Beyond the credibility associated with such measures, they also facilitate benchmarking and comparisons of outcomes with other institutions.

- *Benefit and satisfaction measures.* Assessing the benefits and satisfaction levels of constituents or beneficiaries provides a third useful source of information. The perceptions of those involved provide the basis for these measures. In the case of a strategic planning goal related to establishing productive partnerships, judgments by a leader or members of the departments involved regarding the effectiveness and value of newly established partnerships would provide the basis for this type of measurement. When assessing diversity and inclusion, perceptions of the climate and culture of a unit or institution overall, and personal comfort within the community as a student, faculty, or staff member can provide a helpful component of a comprehensive assessment of progress on diversity and inclusion goals.

- *Impact measures.* These measures gauge the impact of focal programs, services, projects, or goals in relation to overall organizational or project purposes, aspirations, plans, and goals. Although these measures are generally the most difficult to capture, they are often the most meaningful. Impact measures extend beyond activity, professional standards, and benefit or satisfaction criteria to directly assess the ultimate impact of an initiative. In the case of establishing productive interdepartmental partnerships, considerations of objective evidence related to the productivity of newly established partnerships would be appropriate. Examples might include measures related to joint publication, collaborative grant applications, interdisciplinary events or programs, or interdisciplinary course offerings, depending specifically on the overarching goals envisioned for particular partnerships. In the case of the diversity, equity, and inclusion example, measures such as 5-year retention, promotion to tenure, and progression to significant leadership roles are examples of potential impact measures.

Each of these types of measures has value, and each is also limited in some ways. In most cases, activity, professional standards, benefit or satisfaction, and impact metrics complement one another, collectively providing a useful portfolio of measures that offer a comprehensive profile of the effectiveness of a project, program, department, or institution. Depending on the particular focus for assessment, *efficiency measures*—focusing on resource utilization of time, money, or human capital—might provide a useful fifth category of metrics.

Gathering Measurement Data

Most organizations already have access to some of the information needed for assessment. Thus, it makes sense to determine, first, what relevant information is currently available and only then to think about how to collect additional information that may be needed. For instance, if attendance, participation, hiring, retention, salary information, or other such data are available, and there is confidence in their accuracy, these can serve as useful activity measures. An organization might also make use of information that had been gathered for some other purpose, such as a report by an accreditation review group.

Instituting new methods will likely be necessary to collect some of the needed information. For instance, it may be useful to conduct focus groups or surveys or enlist the services of mystery shopper groups composed of students or alumni who could provide useful feedback based on their experiences with a program, department, or institution. A variety of sources are available for the information required to establish and support the chosen measures, including the following options:

- *archival*—information that already exists within the organization but may need to be located, reformatted, and analyzed
- *unobtrusive*—information derived from observing behaviors
- *solicited*—information collected through interview, focus groups, surveys, or other intentional information-gathering activities

Assessment may utilize measures that are direct, indirect, or inferential. The classic example of *direct* measurement in the case of learning outcomes is administering a test before and after taking a course as a direct measure of what a student learned. Another direct measurement is the results from licensure exams after completion of a specialized program designed to prepare students to pass an exam. Direct measures are believed to provide the most desirable form of evidence. *Indirect* measures are considered good but less than ideal. *Inferential* metrics are sometimes helpful but of less value. Each of these measures could shed light on the effectiveness of an institution, department, or program in fulfilling its mission; direct measures are most persuasive because they measure behaviors that are most clearly related to the desired outcomes. Direct measures of learning are considered more useful, for example, than those that would result from surveying students at the end of the course about how much they had learned, which is an *indirect* measure. Whether the student recommends the course to friends represents an *inferential* measure of learning. If the goal was to measure *satisfaction* with the course as opposed to *learning*, asking for an individual's opinion would be a direct measure. If the student or faculty recommends the course or institution to friends, that could be considered an inferential measure of satisfaction.

There are no perfect measures. Each has strengths and limitations, and the aim is to use the best and most appropriate measures available for each situation depending on the questions being asked, the purposes of the measurement system, and the desired outcomes intended for gathering and assessing these metrics.

Measurement System: Planning, Displaying, and Sustaining Assessment

Measures alone are not an assessment system. As discussed, a viable system requires a well-defined focus for assessment; clear statements of purpose, aspirations, plans, or goals; a list of appropriate indicators or measures; identified measurement methods; techniques for gathering and analyzing evidence; and a systematic approach to displaying, disseminating, and using the resulting information. A planning matrix such as that provided in Figure 16.6 can be valuable in providing a framework for the development of such a system.

Displaying Assessment Results

There are numerous ways to display assessment results, including standard report forms, tables, charts, dashboards, and other forms of graphic display. For example, consider the strategic planning process used at James Madison University.[1]

Following an 18-month process, JMU developed 11 of what it calls "core qualities," the key nonnegotiables that were central to the plan. Each core quality was supported by four to seven university goals, which in turn are supported by objectives. In order to add critical levels of assessment, evaluation, and accountability to its plan, the university developed a performance measures dashboard—a relatively short list of key measures that could provide at-a-glance tracking of JMU's success in living out its

Figure 16.6. Measures planning matrix: Sample.

Focus of Measurement	Measure	Measure Type	Data Collection Method	Process for Data Analysis/ Dissemination	Desired Outcome
❶ University resources	• Solicitations for consultation and assistance	QS, I			Enhanced reputation and utilization of materials
❷ National resources/ leader	• Peer inquiries, invitations, and adoptions, selected and bench marking	QS, B/S			ROI and ROM
	• Peer reviews			Search staff will collect,	
Core Programs				interpret,	
❸ Organizational effectiveness	• Satisfactions of beneficiaries and constituents with programs and services	B/S	• Survey ratings on a 1–5 scale by program participants	and distribute the infromation	Engagement in institutionally strategic initiatives
❹ Innovation and change	• Long-term value added		• Research on impact	on a quarterly basis	Increased requests for collaboration and assistance
❺ Academic leadership	• Participation levels	A	• Enrollment stats and repeats	for all measures	Utilization of materials
❻ Senior administrative leadership	• Appointments/ promotions	I	• Follow-up interview and tracking individuals		Influence of program on current practices and new directions

*Activity, quality standards, benefit/satisfaction, impact

new plan. While a lengthy list of hundreds of key performance measures was already in place, the dashboard created a short list of quality measures that would provide a succinct story of the plan's progress with a few carefully chosen metrics. The resulting dashboard was a combination of existing measures (e.g., student-to-faculty ratio and 6-year graduation rate) as well as new ones (e.g., percentage of undergraduates involved in research and student involvement in civic engagement). The measures are tracked consistently, either affirming performance for elements of the plan or suggesting improvement in one or more goals or objectives. A similar model can be found in the Georgia Tech 2020–2030 Strategic Plan, with six priority focus areas, each of which include focus aspiration statements, action items, and indicators of progress.

Other examples are provided in Table 16.1, which includes three goals of the Purdue University Engagement (2015) initiative, and Figure 16.7, which provides an example of a way to display outcome results associated with those goals using graphics.

Dissemination

The way in which data are displayed and communicated can influence how internal and external constituents understand and use these results. They are also important for documenting outcomes, setting future targets, and telling

TABLE 16.1
Engagement at Purdue

Mission

To design, guide, and lead collaborations that drive innovation, prosperity, and an improved quality of life throughout Indiana and beyond.

Engagement Goals

- Connect and collaborate with businesses, communities, and regions to leverage talent, innovation, and resources to address current and emerging real-world issues and opportunities.
- Promote, facilitate, and reward faculty and student engagement including the scholarship of engagement as a recognized channel for faculty advancement.
- Identify and deliver innovative programs and strategies to meet the informational, educational, and technical needs of the current and emerging workforce, businesses/industries, and communities/regions.

Figure 16.7. Engagement at Purdue: Fast facts.

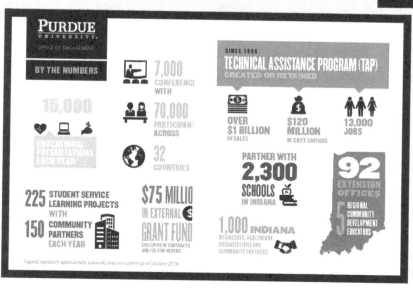

internal and external groups one's story of accomplishments, progress, and future aspirations.

A closely related decision pertains to the list of who should receive assessment results. This list, of course, depends on the focus of assessment and the overall aims of the process. It is generally useful to create a list of internal and external groups with whom to share results as a part of the early planning process. Under some circumstances, it may be useful to separate groups into segments and to customize the distribution based on interests, relevance, and other factors. Not all audiences will be equally interested in all outcomes data, and some results may be designated for internal use only. A planning guide to help think through these communication issues is illustrated in Table 16.2.

Outcomes information can be used to assess performance by comparing current outcomes with results from previous years and with the results from peer, aspirant, or leading institutions. Measurement information can also be used to guide strategic planning: to review, refine, and update goals, to identify resource allocation priorities, and to inform day-to-day decision-making. Outcomes information from a project, program, or department can be integrated with university assessment results and used to document progress and effectiveness to external audiences, or to identify opportunities for improvement. Particularly as it relates to the internal uses of outcome results, a well-documented system of displaying and communicating outcomes enables an organization to maximize the value of the system in support of improvement, planning, and decision-making. Communication and information technology can be extremely important to the effective use of assessment information for analysis, improvement, and reporting.

Sustaining the Measurement System

Sustainability refers to the goal of maintaining the viability and usefulness of the measurement system over time. As noted earlier, from the perspective of sustainability a good practice generally is to develop a measurement system slowly and resist the temptation of trying to measure too much at the outset. A better approach is to identify all relevant measures, but to collect data for only a few critical indicators initially, adding more over time.

Identifying and addressing key issues and barriers to the sustainability of the measurement system can be a challenge. To achieve this goal, it is critical to develop a plan that will keep measures relevant, which requires regular review to ensure that the system is responsive to current purposes, aspirations, plans, and goals. It is also important to periodically validate the

TABLE 16.2

Communication Planning Matrix

Communication Goal *What do we hope to accomplish? (Desired outcome)*	Target *For whom? (Key audiences)*	Audience Needs and Expectations *What matters to this group? What potential needs, questions, concerns exist?*	Content *What message is appropriate?*	Messenger *Who is the best person to deliver the message?*	Method Used *What vehicle to deliver message?*	Pros and Cons *Chosen message, messenger, vehicle*

relevance and usefulness of the measures for key internal and external constituencies. Finally, reviews of the assessment process should assure that results are displayed and communicated in a timely and easily accessible manner.

Conclusion

The assessment process is critical for evaluating the effectiveness of an organization's work, clarifying and building consensus on aspirations and goals, sharing information about outcomes internally and externally, establishing targets, and continuing improvement. Despite the limitations associated with the use of metrics, a culture that emphasizes evidence over anecdotes and narratives of personal experience is increasingly required by external stakeholders and also increasingly useful to members of any organization. Monitoring outcomes is essential for ensuring accountability; guiding strategic planning; identifying the need for change and innovation; and promoting, advocating, and championing accomplishments of one's unit, program, or department. Through the use of measurement, academic and administrative leaders are also able to demonstrate a willingness to be transparent and accountable, establish priorities to advance the aims of the organization, and clarify how the work of faculty and staff throughout the institution contributes to these aspirations.

For Further Consideration

1. Development of measurement system
   You have been asked to develop a measurement system for a priority initiative within your school/administrative unit. Select a hypothetical but personally relevant school, program, or project, develop a draft of measures, and complete a first draft of a measurement system matrix using the worksheet provided in Table 16.3.
   - What questions do you have about this method for developing measures?
   - What organizational challenges surfaced that need to be addressed as you develop measures within your organization?
   - What could help make the selection of measures for your organization easier, more productive, or more useful?
   - How would you disseminate outcomes information, and how might technology be helpful in this process?

- What challenges might you anticipate in assuring that the information is used?
- How might you go about gaining buy-in and engagement in the assessment process?
- What are the probable challenges to sustaining the effort?

TABLE 16.3
Measures Planning Matrix Sample

Focus of Measurement	Measure	Measure Type*	Data Collection Method	Process for Data Analysis/ Dissemination	Desired Outcome

* Activity, quality standards, benefit/satisfaction, impact, internal effectiveness

Note

1. We are grateful to JMU's president Jon Alger and associate vice president Brian Charette for their assistance in providing this brief overview of the JMU planning and dashboard development process.

17

CRISIS LEADERSHIP

A Values-Centered Approach to
Crisis in Higher Education

Ralph A. Gigliotti and John A. Fortunato

In This Chapter

- What is crisis leadership and how does the subject draw upon concepts from crisis prevention, management, and communication?
- In what ways can academic and administrative leaders engage in a values-centered approach to crisis response and prevention?
- How can leaders better detect crisis severity and the types of crises that are most likely to impact a college or university?
- Which communication strategies associated with crisis leadership are most relevant for academic and administrative leaders?

eadership and communication principles and strategies are generally developed and executed during periods of normalcy. In an ever-increasing and wide-ranging number of situations, however, leaders in higher education are being confronted with crises of various kinds—

> events or situations of significant magnitude that threaten reputations, impact the lives of those involved in the institution, disrupt the ways in which the organization functions, have a cascading influence on leadership responsibilities and obligations across units/divisions, and require an immediate response from leaders (Gigliotti, 2019, p. 61).

Crises can create havoc for an institution of higher education, especially for its key internal stakeholders, students, faculty, and staff. Given the impact on multiple stakeholders, crises garner focused and immediate attention from the leaders of an institution who seek to minimize the impact on the institution and return to "normalcy." Leaders' actions, including strategic

314

communication, are fundamental to the goal of preserving the integrity of the institution when it is beset by a crisis.

As this chapter was being developed, leaders were faced with multiple issues that had the potential to emerge or reemerge as crises: the short- and long-term implications of the global COVID-19 pandemic, the national reckoning on race and social justice, events triggered by climate change (e.g., wildfires in California and the Pacific Northwest), the culture of free speech on campus, the perceived decline of the value of higher education, and long-standing challenges to higher education business models that have become increasingly unsustainable on many campuses. In addition to these complex issues that impact large segments of or even the entire sector, leaders of institutions of higher education face an array of issues that arise all too often and have the potential to develop into crises. Among these are on-campus violent crimes, including shootings and sexual assaults; cybercrimes; allegations of discrimination based on race, gender, sexual orientation, and other "identity" categories; athletic and Greek hazing scandals; academic integrity violations; fraud and misconduct by faculty or staff members (e.g., the 2019 college admissions scandal); natural disasters; faculty or administration public disagreements with governing board decisions; and violations of federal and state antidiscrimination laws, among other recurring issues. Unfortunately, this list only skims the surface of recent issues and crises to impact American colleges and universities. Engaging with issues that can become or immediately present themselves as crises is now fundamental to the work of academic and administrative leadership (Gigliotti, 2019, 2021).

The history, stability, and culture of the institution along with the tangible actions taken by leadership during and in the aftermath of a crisis help to determine both the extent of the disruption brought about by particular crisis events and the consequences to the institution that ensue. Of course, the nature of the crisis is determinative as leaders may face unparalleled and sometimes unprecedented challenges that require them to make quick, appropriate, timely, and highly consequential decisions.

A leader cannot hope to be successful in these situations without a systemic understanding of the nature of organizational crises, a well-rehearsed and well-informed set of principles for approaching crisis situations, and perhaps most important, a clear sense of how institutional values should guide one's decisions and actions. Each of these topics will be explored in this chapter. It begins with an overview of relevant background information on the topic of crisis and continues with a breakdown of the types of crises that may directly influence leaders in higher education. In the remainder of the chapter, prominent characteristics and principles for effective crisis leadership during these challenging moments will be considered.

Crisis Management and Crisis Leadership

Like leadership development more broadly, formal preparation in crisis management and crisis leadership is limited in higher education, particularly for those individuals who do not occupy the most senior roles at a college or university. At the same time, as Genshaft (2014) suggests, "higher education is particularly primed for poor handling of crises" (p. 10), in part due to this lack of preparation, the competing interests of multiple stakeholders, and an ongoing preoccupation with deliberation and consensus that might prevent agile and rapid responses. This perspective reflects the survey findings of Mitroff et al. (2006), who found crisis preparation in higher education to be extremely inadequate, and one may wonder if the recent convergence of crises might lead institutions, consortia, and external organizations to provide more dedicated professional development offerings on this topic moving forward.

With roots in the corporate sector, much of the scholarly and professional literature on the topic of organizational crisis has centered on the principles and practices of crisis management. These writings generally focus on specific strategies and tactics to deal with events that threaten, disrupt, or endanger an organization, those it serves, or its employees—and the threats to an organization's reputation that crises embody. Only recently have we seen an increase in writing on the topic within the context of higher education.

Managing a crisis is only one part of a leader's responsibility. The concept of crisis leadership shifts the focus from the mechanistic or tactical view of the leader's role during periods of crisis—often referred to as *crisis management*—to one that is systematic, anticipatory, proactive, and expansive—a perspective that is more appropriately labeled *crisis leadership* (Gigliotti, 2019). Crisis and risk prevention, management, and communication are all embedded in this broader view of crisis leadership. Leading during crisis hinges on a purposeful reliance on one's own values and those of the organization, an unwavering commitment to empathy and care for those one leads, and a dual focus on both the immediate short-term needs the crisis gives rise to and the long-term interests of the organization.

In addition to coping with and preparing for crises, the work of leaders involves a consideration of the ways in which crises are declared and the implications of using this label to describe a specific event or series of events. The process of defining and labeling a crisis is often subjective, and some might argue that the label is overused, leading to a mischaracterization of the circumstances of the moment. For example, leaders may use the invocation of crisis as a strategic opportunity to cut through red tape, skip particular processes, and move quickly—all of which are appealing within a context that is often characterized as slow moving, committee driven, and bureaucratic.

Additionally, others may describe an event or series of events as a crisis to accentuate the moment, expedite a formal institutional response, and generate increased public attention. Because the way any event is viewed lies in the eye of the beholder, it is incumbent on leaders to monitor how others view local and cross-institutional challenges facing an institution, appreciate the different ways in which a crisis situation can be interpreted by diverse stakeholders, and recognize the ways in which shared institutional values can help a leader and members of an organization reach common ground when facing these high-stakes situations (Gigliotti, 2020b).

Some events or situations are widely recognized as major crises for an institution, such as loss of life due to an active shooter or widespread destruction due to a natural disaster. In many other situations, however, a leadership challenge arises when different stakeholder groups offer competing perceptions. Thus, it is important to consider how one defines, views, and conceptualizes crisis, and the consequences that arise from those definitions. One of the major challenges facing leaders is to recognize the ways in which they and others in leadership roles—as well as stakeholders—play influential and often subjective roles in identifying and reacting to an event, incident, or state of affairs as a crisis.

While subjective, multiple, and sometimes conflicting, these perceptions often have tangible consequences that leaders will ideally consider when taking action and engaging in strategic decision-making. Consider, for example, the case of the statue of Silent Sam at the University of North Carolina at Chapel Hill in 2019 (Vasquez, 2019), where competing perceptions regarding the placement of a Confederate monument at the entrance of the flagship campus reflected polarized views of a situation. In this instance, the statue of Silent Sam continues to be the source of much debate—perceived by some as a symbol of racism, oppression, and an unfortunate reminder of the nation's ugly past; whereas, to others, the statue remains an important marker of state and national history that merits prominent placement on the campus (Vasquez, 2019). In this case, the leader's challenge is to understand all perspectives, analyze possible courses of action, and recommend decisions that respect and reinforce core organizational values—a critical topic to be discussed in greater detail later.

The History, Definitions, and Stages of Crisis

In the section that follows, we will review some of the key concepts related to the evolution of perspectives on crisis and the various definitions, stages, and taxonomies that are most salient to the context of higher edcation.

Crisis History

The term *crisis* has its roots in the Greek language, where it represents a "turning point," similar to the medical usage of the term in Latin to imply the turning point of an illness. The origin of the word maintains a positive connotation, referring to the turning point in sickness, tragedy, or peril (Ulmer et al., 2018). These turning points, often reflecting the choices and decisions that human actors influence, have the potential to fundamentally shape the future of an individual or organization (Shrivastava, 1993). Beginning in the 18th century, crisis evolved to mean a difficult situation or dilemma—a turning point oriented in a more negative direction. Ulmer et al. (2018) highlight the Chinese interpretation of crisis, *wei chi*, which translates to "dangerous opportunity." As we examine the many intersecting crises challenging colleges and universities at the present time, "dangerous opportunity" seems to be a useful way of recognizing the threat and fear posed by contemporary crises, and of the tremendous need and opportunity for repair, renewal, and reinvention that they also present.

Crisis Definitions

There are many different ways to define a crisis, but all converge on the idea that, distinct from more localized emergencies or incidents, crises have the potential to "disrupt the entire organization" (Pauchant & Mitroff, 1992, p. 3). Reviewing the many definitions, several themes stand out as being most important for leaders in higher education. First, crises present a disruption from normal activity that threatens the well-being of organizational stakeholders (Irvine & Millar, 1998; Weick, 1988). In the case of colleges and universities, crises often impact students, faculty, staff, alumni, and the local community in a range of dramatic ways. Additionally, crises may threaten the reputation of the organization and its leaders. As we have witnessed in the higher education response to the pandemic and national racial unrest, the scope and consequences of some crises are pervasive, and the impact extends well beyond a particular institution.

The substance, timing, and narrative created for a leader's decisions (e.g., whether to hold or cancel on-campus activities in fall 2020) may have immediate and lasting reputational consequences for an individual leader and the institution, and these decisions also serve as a potential model for other institutions. In all such cases, while crises present a substantial threat that must be addressed, they also present an opportunity for leaders to articulate, demonstrate, model, and reaffirm the core values and principles of the college or university—values such as transparency, truth, respect, and a commitment to the safety, dignity, and well-being of all members of the community—and to project those values beyond the boundaries of the campus. The ability to be guided by shared institutional values is not limited to the initial response to the situation, but rather precedes the crisis and is embedded in its aftermath. Crises test these core values—and also provide a venue to display and communicate them.

Finally, perception matters in moments of crisis (Benoit, 1995, 1997; Coombs, 2015; Gigliotti, 2020b; Mitroff, 2004). Institutions of higher education have an important role to play in establishing and maintaining high standards and core values in a way that instills confidence in the institution and demonstrates care for members of the institution. The challenge for leaders is negotiating the complexities of the situation itself, while also responding in a way that cultivates hope, trust, and safety for those one leads and that ensures a favorable reputation for the institution and its leaders (Gigliotti, 2019). As we describe in this chapter, reputational concerns, while important, are ideally addressed as a natural consequence of competent, effective, and values-based leadership.

Crisis Stages

The life cycle of a crisis is another important concept discussed in the literature. The idea here is that an underlying order and pattern generally exist within the disruption of crisis (Li & Yorke, 1975; Lorenz, 1963; Wheatley, 2006). One model divides crisis management into five phases: (a) signal detection, (b) probing and prevention, (c) damage containment, (d) recovery, and (e) learning (Mitroff, 1994). Coombs (2015) provides a model that features three general stages: precrisis, crisis event, and postcrisis. These phases are helpful in that they suggest the predictable order through which events unfold that can be helpful in addressing crisis dynamics, yet the caution is that crises by their very nature are unpredictable and require leaders to be prepared as well as flexible. In some ways, these models cast the crisis as a linear process and put forward a set of prescriptive strategies for best managing the isolated incident (Gigliotti, 2016).

The view of crisis leadership that is central to this chapter helps to better explain the broader array of factors through which crises unfold and can help leaders to better understand and sometimes shape the evolution of such events and situations at their institutions. For example, in the child sex abuse scandal at Penn State (Freeh Report, 2012), the public announcement of the many allegations against the former assistant football coach might be viewed as the commencement of the crisis. However, a somewhat different sequence of events is evident if viewed from a broader leadership perspective. As outlined in the Freeh Report (2012) commissioned by the Penn State Board of Trustees, critical facts relating to Coach Jerry Sandusky's child abuse were concealed from and by leaders across the university—a troubling finding that points to the many historical factors leading to the public components of crisis.

In the case of the global pandemic, it is hard to pinpoint the origin of the crisis in terms of when it began to affect a particular person or institution—for some, it may trace back to the sudden shift to a fully online teaching and working operation in March 2020, whereas others may view the disruption to the 2020–2021 academic year as the beginning of a major crisis. Both examples highlight the subjectivity involved with how we view such events and the difficulties in precisely defining its beginning and end points.

Crisis Taxonomies

There is an abundance of crisis taxonomies in the existing literature, several of which are depicted in Table 17.1. In consulting this list, one may notice that some are more salient to the context of higher education, such as natural disasters, technical breakdowns, and incidents of violence, which are becoming increasingly common for colleges and universities. As in other contexts, these crises in higher education may range in severity and breadth of impact from single, isolated events to those that trigger institution- or society-wide disruptions.

As the lists in Table 17.1 seem to suggest, there are numerous ways to categorize crises, one obvious method being based on whether they are man-made or natural disasters (Lindell et al., 2007). Cole et al. (2007) present the following list of man-made disasters that are most applicable to colleges and universities: sexual assault, stalking, campus dating violence, hate crimes, hazing, celebratory violence (riots), attempted suicides, suicides, murder/suicides, manslaughter, aggravated assault, arson, and attacks on faculty and staff. Man-made or natural disasters require different responses. For example, a college or university may be a "victim" of the forces of Mother Nature, yet culpable for neglecting to prepare for—or deal effectively with—the potential disaster. One might also consult this list of crises that emerged as most relevant for colleges and universities based on interviews with senior higher education leaders and a content analysis of more than 1,000 articles from a variety of news outlets (Gigliotti, 2019):

TABLE 17.1
Crisis Taxonomies

Lerbinger (1997)		
Natural	Technological	Skewed management values
Confrontation	Malevolence	Deception
Management misconduct	Business and economic	
Meyers and Holusha (1986)		
Public perception	Sudden market shifts	Product failure
Top management succession	Cash crises	Industrial relations crises
Hostile takeover	Adverse international events	Regulation/deregulation
Coombs et al. (1995)		
Natural disasters	Malevolence	Workplace violence
Technical breakdowns	Human breakdowns	Rumors
Challenges	Organizational misdeeds	
Mitroff and Anagnos (2001)		
Economic	Informational	Natural disasters
Human resource	Reputation	Psychopathic acts
Physical loss of key plants and other facilities		
Coombs (2007)		
Victim crises: Minimal crises responsibility	*Accident crises: Low crises responsibility*	*Preventable crises: Strong crises responsibility*
Natural disasters	Challenges	Human-error accidents
Rumors	Technical-error accidents	Human-error product harm
Workplace violence	Technical-error product harm	Organizational misdeeds
Product tampering/ malevolence		

Academic

- Crisis that disrupts or violates the core academic mission of an institution (e.g., widespread plagiarism or academic fraud)

Athletics

- Crisis that involves student athletes or the athletic enterprise of an institution (e.g., athletic hazing incident)

Clinical

- Crisis that involves patients, clinical research, or the health/medical institution of an organization (e.g., physician malpractice)

Facilities/technological

- Crisis that disrupts the physical or virtual infrastructure of an institution (e.g., chemical spill or cyberattack)

Financial

- Crisis that directly involves the business operations of an institution (e.g., significant decrease in state appropriations)

Human resources

- Crisis that directly involves the employees and/or employment practices of an institution (e.g., employee crime)

Leadership

- Crisis dealing with institutional governance and oversight (e.g., publicized conflict between state legislature and university leadership or an internal dispute between a leader and a subordinate)

Natural disaster

- Crisis resulting from the natural processes of Earth (e.g., hurricane or flood)

Public safety

- Crisis that threatens the well-being of the members of the institution (e.g., active shooter, coronavirus)

Racial/identity conflict

- Crisis triggered by racial or other social identity tensions within the institution (e.g., campus unrest resulting from one or more racist incidents)

Student affairs

- Crisis involving students or the student experience at an institution (e.g., student mental health issue)

Some crises, such as those we are dealing with today, including a global public health emergency or systemic racism, have far-reaching consequences that cut across several of the crisis types detailed. As such, they may require leaders to adopt approaches that address multiple crisis dimensions simultaneously or sequentially, raising important challenges regarding the content, timing, and dissemination of messages. Regardless of the taxonomy or scheme one uses, leaders must be prepared to look within and beyond the institution as they consider the types of crises that may impact the college or university.

Crises Can Test Core Values of an Organization

In very fundamental ways, crises test the core values of an organization—and by understanding the various dimensions, phases, and types of crises as outlined in the literature, academic and administrative leaders may better prepare for these potentially troubling, yet not entirely unexpected, situations. Furthermore, without preparation, leaders may find themselves acting in ways that violate either their own personal value system or that of the institution they lead, or even both value systems.

Two frequently mentioned cases in the literature provide valuable lessons for leaders across sectors. The response by Johnson & Johnson to the 1982 poisonings caused by Tylenol capsules that had been tampered with is one such classic case. The oil leakage associated with the Exxon *Valdez* provides a second. As some writers have noted, the juxtaposition of a positive response by Johnson & Johnson with the notoriously poor response to the Exxon *Valdez* oil spill in Prince William Sound in 1989 led to the emergence of crisis management as a field of study (Heath & O'Hair, 2009; Mitroff, 2004). Many of the leadership characteristics distilled from these classic cases remain relevant to today's higher education environment. In particular, there remains great value in approaching crisis leadership through a values-centered lens—an orientation that positions clarity, consistency, and congruency between the way that one leads during difficult times and those core values that are most critical to an institution (Gigliotti, 2019).

In the case of Johnson & Johnson, the company faced a situation that was devastating in its impact on the victims of the poisoning. Beyond the immediate effect on health and safety, organizational leaders were forced to take decisive action to prevent future injuries—and to act in a way that would restore trust in the good name of the brand. The bold decision to quickly recall Tylenol from every provider initially had a costly impact on the share price of the company, but it resulted in long-term financial and reputational benefits for Johnson & Johnson. This case demonstrates how addressing crises in appropriate and timely ways is a function of the nature of the organization and its core values—a function that goes beyond the tactical strategies used for protecting and managing one's reputation. Crises test the core values of an organization. The decision to pull the Tylenol product from all shelves is a response that so clearly embodies the values and priorities of the Johnson & Johnson (n.d.) credo, which gives priority to the health of patients.

This case is often compared with examples of organizations that failed to respond to crisis in a way that is consistent with their core values. Some examples include the failed response by Exxon and BP, respectively, to oil spills in Prince William Sound, Alaska, and the Gulf of Mexico; the Roman Catholic Church's lack of leadership during an ongoing child abuse scandal; and the lack of preparation for and ineffective response to Hurricane Katrina and the COVID-19 pandemic. A common thread runs through the core values of Exxon, BP, the Roman Catholic Church, FEMA, and the federal/local government: a stated commitment to the welfare and well-being of others. This value was tested by the aforementioned crises, and as we see time and time again, effective responses at one point in time may not guarantee effective approaches in future situations, and maintaining standards represents an ongoing challenge for an organization and its leadership.

Within the context of higher education, recent examples of crises testing core values might include situations that involve debates over academic freedom and free speech, protests dealing with issues of diversity and equity on the college campus, or the decision to furlough employees due to widespread financial challenges. Crisis leadership involves the alignment of decisions with the organization's core values. As these values are tested, the very mission of the unit, department, or organization provides a compass for decision-making when the stakes are exceptionally high.

Understanding Crisis in Higher Education

One does not have to look far to identify a full range of crisis examples in higher education, nor to see the relevance of the classic cases discussed in the previous sections. Higher education news outlets and general news outlets often report on the array of disruptive events that are affecting colleges and universities. It is difficult to pinpoint the complex and multifaceted causes for these events, yet a useful first step for academic and administrative leaders is to consider which events are most likely to impact one's institution and how the institution's values and purposes can serve as a useful guide in directing the actions of leaders at all levels. Whether the disruption is a flood, widespread health and safety concern, a single act or multiple acts of violence, a series of protests in response to acts of racial injustice, or a student hazing scandal, the mission, vision, and values of the institution provide a useful foundation for thinking about the appropriate ways to approach this situation—before, during, and after a crisis.

In November 1999, Texas A&M University continued with its autumn tradition of building and burning a bonfire as part of its rivalry with the University of Texas at Austin. During the construction of this bonfire, the logs—which weighed the equivalent of two 747 jumbo jets—collapsed, killing 12 students and injuring 27 more. In her reflection on this horrible event, the executive director of university relations at Texas A&M, Cynthia Lawson (2014), commented on the power of leadership during this dark period in the university's history. Consistent with the mission and values of the university, the priorities included the rescue and recovery of the victims at the site of the bonfire and the immediate support of students, parents, and other key university stakeholders.

The Texas A&M response is often recognized as one of the "best managed in higher education," due to the prompt reaction, the development and implementation of a process to investigate the cause of the accident, the emotional support from leaders across the institution throughout and following the incident, and the creation of a task force charged with identifying the university's vulnerabilities and risks (Lawson, 2014). When President Ray Bowen was asked about his expectations for media relations in the aftermath of the crisis, Lawson described his response accordingly: "'That's what I hired you for,' he said. And then, looking [Lawson] directly in the eye, he added, 'Just do the right thing, Cindy'" (p. 40).

This desire to "do the right thing" is consistent with other examples of effective crisis leadership in higher education, including Tulane University's response to Hurricane Katrina, the University of Oklahoma's reaction to racist chants by members of a fraternity, and Duquesne University's actions following an on-campus shooting incident. When core values drive the crisis leadership response, the reputation of the unit, department, or institution is not the primary area of focus. Rather, the reputation is upheld by the commitment to these articulated values, such as protecting the safety and well-being of students, staff, and faculty; taking responsibility for mistakes and oversights; and seeing that they are corrected. Like the Tylenol case, doing the right thing based on aligning behaviors with one's core mission and values is paramount (Gigliotti, 2019).

Effective leadership in these situations requires, first and foremost, an understanding of the importance of maintaining the core values of the institution, along with the context for crisis prevention, reputation management, and crisis management. The complexity of higher education institutions causes colleges and universities to be especially vulnerable, underscoring the need to manage and prevent crises and to engage in effective communication during these moments of organizational disruption.

In higher education and elsewhere, determining the right thing that needs to be done is another example of subjectivity, and the appropriate response from leaders may not be immediately clear, nor will one response receive praise from all impacted groups. In the face of the COVID-19 pandemic, for example, consider the varying responses from colleges and universities, the different approaches to reopening campus-based activities, the competing values that guide these decisions, and the messaging used to communicate these decisions to the campus community and external audiences. It is essential for both academic and administrative leaders to understand the complexity and nuances of crisis situations, recognizing the importance of ethics, integrity, and core values in guiding leadership behavior. We take up these topics in subsequent sections of this chapter.

Crisis Leadership: Beyond Public Relations

Much of the writing on crisis in organizations focuses primarily on the public relations implications—how to protect the reputation of the institution, maintain a favorable impression in the eyes of many stakeholders, and view and use communication as a tactic to shape public opinion. While these perspectives may be accepted as sufficient in organizations in some sectors, they provide a limited perspective when thinking about higher education and the leader's role and responsibility. Leaders at all levels, as discussed throughout the book, have the responsibility of establishing and sustaining a culture and climate where core values are maintained and practiced.

Crisis situations present major challenges that test the organization and leaders in their ability to think through and deal with multiple challenges simultaneously. These include analyzing the situation; mobilizing appropriate resources to attend to injury, the loss of life, or damage to the physical structure of the institution; and planning and executing appropriate internal communication with faculty and staff, as well as communication with students, safety and emergency personnel, media, the public, and other affected stakeholders.

As discussed in chapter 8, many leadership and social influence outcomes are often unplanned, unintentional, unpredicted, and unpredictable. The message sent by a leader, particularly during times of crisis, is not guaranteed to be received by those most affected by the crisis; in fact, the gap between message sent and message received is particularly likely to occur during these events. Single messages seldom have much impact on broader impressions. Furthermore, the historical context is significant in shaping the design, interpretation, and evolution of messages related to an organizational crisis. For example, when a crisis strikes, it is important to consider the organization's history with events of this type, the leader's past experiences in dealing with such events, and the susceptibilities and expectations of those stakeholders most impacted by the event. For these reasons, crisis management and crisis prevention are only part of the story. Leadership in times of disruption, particularly in higher education, extends beyond reputation management, prevention, and public relations–oriented management. Rather, leadership in such circumstances presents a broader framework for understanding what is most at stake during these periods of disruption (Gigliotti, 2019).

A summary of writings on organizational crises indicates that differing leadership competencies are important to specific stages, and collectively these competencies offer a remedy to some of the more problematic dimensions of a situation (Booker, 2014). These competencies include the detection of early warning signs in the environment; the strategic use of communication in preventing, preparing, and containing the crisis; and the promotion of learning throughout the process and at the conclusion of the crisis. This emphasis on learning and improvement in operating procedures and communication practices is especially relevant in colleges and universities that place learning at a premium—the characteristic situated at the core of their brand. This focus on risk assessment, learning from an event, and broader views of leadership reflects a more proactive and holistic approach to dealing with crises in colleges and universities (Mitroff, 2004).

DuBrin (2013) extends this summary of crisis leadership behaviors to include the following:

- Stay calm during a crisis.
- Plan before and during a crisis.

- Make good use of your team.
- Avoid stonewalling the problem.
- Reestablish the work routine.
- Exercise transformational leadership.
- Give recognition for accomplishments.
- Do not waste the crisis.

In addition to this list of behaviors, if core values become lived values, leaders may be more likely to maintain trust in order to more easily pursue each of these behaviors. If these values are violated, however, no communication strategies can be expected to offset the loss of trust in a leader.

In a time when more, rather than fewer, campus crises seem probable, leadership competencies become ever more indispensable. For example, the ability to adapt is understood to be a critical competency for leaders (Muffet-Willett & Kruse, 2008). The continuum depicted in Figure 17.1 highlights the unique demands on leaders during these difficult times. These demands call for leaders who can make appropriate and timely decisions and lead effectively in a complex environment.

Tactical (or persuasive) communication, clarity of vision and values, and caring relationships are critical components of crisis leadership (Klann, 2003). This emphasis on communication and relationships is also central to Muffet-Willett's (2010) summary of crisis leadership actions that are most relevant to colleges and universities, as illustrated in the model in Figure 17.2. As depicted in the model, communication and feedback mechanisms are situated at multiple junctures in the process, yet, as acknowledged in chapter 8, these processes are subjective and impacted by an individual's personal framing and sensemaking. Administrative decision-making is critical, but so too are those mechanisms for soliciting feedback from key stakeholders across the institution. Not surprisingly, this emphasis on creating dialogue

Figure 17.1. Crisis leadership continuum (Muffet-Willett & Kruse, 2008).

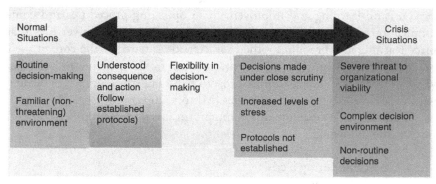

Figure 17.2. Higher education crisis leadership practical process model (Muffett-Willett, 2010).

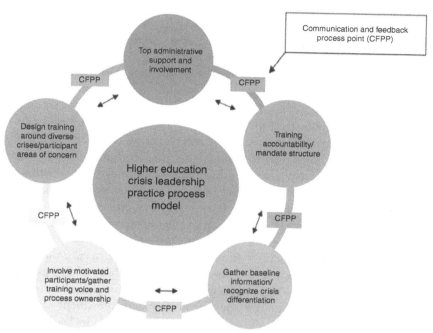

is a value shared across the higher education sector. The model also speaks indirectly to the inherent limitations of a focus on crisis management or prevention. Crisis leadership encompasses the communication that occurs at senior-level decision-making, in organization-wide training initiatives, and in the messages that occur before, during, and following an disruptive event.

Key Communication Considerations for Crisis Leadership Practice

Crisis leadership involves more than simply verbalizing the right messages to the right audiences at the right time to uphold the reputation of an institution in the face of crisis. Rather, it calls for a nuanced way of thinking through the "right" thing that should be done consistent with institutional values; a more expansive understanding of the types of risks that a unit, department, or institution faces; and a continual emphasis on personal and institutional learning.

Focusing only on the delivery of appropriate responses is a simplistic view of communication that violates much of what we currently understand about human communication. Rather, communication theory points to the importance of understanding the organization's history with crises, appreciating the diverse needs of one's stakeholders, and leading with integrity throughout the entire process (i.e., before, during, and after). Competent leadership in these situations involves prevention and management, consistency and clarity, trust and transparency—with communication playing a critical role during each phase (Gigliotti, 2019). By building and maintaining a reservoir of goodwill at the individual and collective levels, a foundation is set for authentic, values-centered dialogue when crises do occur. Specifically, it seems likely that the reputation and history that serve an individual leader and collective organization well during times of normalcy are essential for effective leadership and performance during difficult times. This reputation provides a solid foundation on which to stand when crises strike.

As discussed previously, recognition of the organization's history and an acknowledgment of future vulnerabilities are critical. This broader paradigm for understanding crisis does not diminish the importance of communication during the event itself. To the contrary, there is generally a need to use communication strategy to inform, educate, and inspire those most impacted by the situation—and to do so in a way that displays a commitment to organizational values and builds confidence in the institution and its leaders.

Crisis Prevention Strategies

Prevention is a recommended philosophy; however, it is naive to think that all crises can or will be prevented. And in the case of many environmental or expansive social crises, control is beyond the ability of any single individual or institution. In all such situations, however, a deep understanding of the situation and a sophisticated awareness of organizations, leadership communication, and culture allows for a richer and broader understanding of ways to prevent some of the disruptive situations confronting colleges and universities. If one considers first the array of events that might impact institutions, along with those areas of vulnerability across units and departments, we can begin to take an important first step in preventing some future crises from occurring and being better prepared to address social, economic, and environmental calamities that lie beyond one's limited scope of control.

If we consider the parallels between colleges and universities and local cities, the characteristics are similar. Colleges provide services to a diverse group of residents and commuters. They have a responsibility to care for these individuals—to provide food, shelter, security, and opportunities for fulfillment.

Just like cities, colleges and universities are also vulnerable to a host of traumatic events that could threaten this mission of protection, security, and fulfillment—such as the global pandemic that continues to threaten students, faculty, and staff. Tabletop simulations, crisis preparation training sessions, and the development of sophisticated preventions plan are all examples of ways we can proactively think through the nuances of specific crises—both learning from events that came before us and evaluating the vulnerability of the unit, department, or organization for potential future challenges. The crisis prevention plan should assess the unit, department, or organization on two dimensions—first, the probability of a specific event impacting the group, and second, the potential devastation created by particular events (Fearn-Banks, 2011). Based on the responses to these first two questions, leaders can then determine specific actions worth taking to most effectively prevent certain situations from occurring. In many instances an investment in planning and prevention can be less costly than the resources that would be needed to both manage tragic events and rebuild the organization's credibility. Furthermore, an investment of resources at this point in the process might also mitigate future litigation damages.

The development and refinement of protocols following crises is another useful strategy for preventing similar scenarios in the future. For example, learning about the strengths and weaknesses of past responses to natural disasters, active shooter situations, or hate crimes can strengthen the collective capacity of the institution to better prepare for future episodes of similar magnitude. Recognizing the frequency, complexity, and unpredictability of explosive or potentially explosive circumstances within higher education is leading a growing number of colleges and universities to craft "all hazards" emergency operations plans (McIntire, 2015).

In contemplating the design of these protocols, academic and administrative leaders must consider the following questions as a way of minimizing the severity of the crisis:

- In what types of situations is your unit, department, or institution most vulnerable?
- Depending on these vulnerabilities, which internal and external stakeholders are most at risk?
- Who needs to be engaged throughout the crisis response process?
- What communication is needed, to whom, and through which delivery method?

The goal of the protocol is to prevent these serious events from rising to the level of a crisis during and after the active situation has occurred. Other issues are more complex, such as student uprisings, misconduct by high-profile leaders, or unanticipated economic downturn. For these crises, along with others, it becomes especially important to privilege and emphasize learning across the institution as a way of creating a collective awareness about those issues that might lie on the horizon.

Internal and External Communication Strategies

As noted, communication is a critical component of crisis leadership. According to Gores (2014),

> When tragedy strikes, the campus community, stakeholders, and the local community look to leadership for direction and guidance. How leaders respond in the first several hours and in the days that follow offers tremendous opportunity to bring a campus together or put the campus at risk. It is not possible to predict or control a crisis, but it is possible to control the response and the way in which the institution reacts to it. (p. 147)

Leaders in higher education must grapple with the in-the-moment complexities in order to audit where things stand and to detect vulnerabilities for future crises. Adding to this complexity is the notion that there may be moments when the leader can be proactive and frame the situation for others, whereas in other circumstances crises may already have been identified and labeled as such by other stakeholder groups and, therefore, require immediate attention by the leader. In both instances, three critical questions need to be answered:

1. What happened?
2. Will it happen again?
3. What tangible actions has the organization undertaken to prevent the crisis from reoccurring?

These questions allow institutional leaders to consider short- and long-term issues while also encouraging broader communication and future planning and prevention efforts.

Communication in a crisis is especially important for its ability to either improve the situation or make it worse. One of the goals is for leaders to avoid escalating or compounding problems of the moment by their communication, recognizing Benson's (1988) point that crisis communication can significantly diminish or magnify the harm. Three fundamental concepts should guide communication during times of crisis (Coombs, 2006). First, *be quick.* A prewritten press release, for example, can demonstrate that the organization is aware of the crisis, understands its severity, is already address-ing the situation, and is working toward responding to the key question of what happened. This statement could express empathy toward the situation, if applicable. Social media have facilitated the speed with which an initial communication can be provided and have raised expectations of stakeholders to quickly receive communication from the organization. Second, *be consist-ent*. The presentation of conflicting responses can be especially problematic for the institution. Again, one of the goals is to avoid creating a secondary crisis due to poor communication surrounding the primary event. Finally, *be open*. Crises inevitably lead to information vacuums. It is necessary for the college or university to fill that vacuum with truthful information that reflects well on the organization. If higher education leaders are not address-ing that need, others might be—and they may be providing information that is detrimental to the organization.

The leader's response must align with the severity of the crisis and must be timely, frequently relayed, and accessible. Depending on the circum-stance, several core communication principles should be considered at the unit, department, and institutional levels (Nelson, 2014):

- Activate timely and early alert messages.
- Provide frequent updates.
- Incorporate a variety of tools and media.
- Leverage the university's, department's, or unit's website homepage.
- Educate and involve stakeholders such as parents, leadership councils, and alumni.

The design of crisis response messages requires careful consideration of the needs of those most affected by the situation, while also recognizing that as a leader you are simultaneously communicating with internal and external stakeholders.

Crisis communication should be tailored to the particulars of the situ-ation. With a thoughtful assessment of a crisis situation, leaders in higher education can take account of and make effective use of the different types of responses and media available; the unique vulnerabilities of one's unit, department, or institution; and the potential sensitivities associated with the culture of a college or university. This is especially the case as leaders con-sider crises that are self-imposed. For example, the decision to arm public safety officers or expand the number of surveillance cameras across campus may trigger different sets of reactions at various institutions—incidents that can be characterized as internal crises or can create the conditions for a per-ceived crisis. In such an instance, effective leadership involves the ability to forecast the anticipated reactions from campus stakeholders prior to major announcements and decisions.

Interactions With Media

Because of the significant role of a university as part of the geographic community in which it is located, the young adult population it serves, and the standing it has in society, a crisis at a university often becomes a local or national media story. For these situations, academic and administrative leaders are expected to interact with the media, taking on the roles of information providers and advocates and representing the organization at large. Through these roles, leaders may provide relevant information on behalf of the institution, both highlighting and emphasizing certain aspects of the issue at stake. Recognizing the critical role of stakeholders, communication is informed by the various audiences that will receive the message—with the media taking on the role of a conduit for the message itself. Doug Lederman, editor of *Inside Higher Education*, provides the following advice for speaking with the media:

> I can say that in a crisis, one should be honest and forthright. Don't ever try to hide the truth, because if the media believe you are covering up the truth, or if it is found that there were truths being covered up, there is a good chance that will be worse than the actual crisis itself." (as cited in Parrot, 2014, p. 171)

The media, an important stakeholder for any college or university, have the responsibility to make decisions about what becomes part of their coverage. Colleges and universities are often the target for media attention when crises strike. In some instances, events challenge or call into question the noble mission of higher education—leading many to criticize these institutions for failing to live up to their articulated values. As discussed in chapter 8, agenda-setting theory is important for understanding the communicative role of leaders. It is also a foundational theory for the study of the mass media's role during times of crisis. The theory suggests that the selection of stories—along with the selection of certain facts—increases audience salience of the issues as well as the facts themselves (McCombs & Shaw, 1972; McCombs et al., 2014). There is competition for media coverage and the need to present certain facts within the coverage of a story, so it is imperative for higher education leaders to have a plan in place for interacting with the media. There are a number of mechanisms through which to communicate with the media during crises, including prewritten press releases, spokesperson/spokespeople, press conferences, website updates, and the use of social media. Each of these approaches calls for an established chain of command, carefully calibrated plans, and sophisticated media training. Parrot (2014) offers additional advice for higher education leaders:

> Trepidation for working with the media is understandable, but fear should never delay the issuance of a response or participation in an interview. [Leaders] must model the highest levels of leadership possible by pro-actively sharing their institution's story—a story that must be rooted in truth and framed with engaging language—and providing a plan for future direction. (p. 179)

When interacting with the media, two crisis communication models are especially useful for higher education leaders. One approach is image restoration (Benoit, 1995). As summarized in Benoit and Pang (2008), there are five distinct approaches that one can use to restore the image of an organization during a crisis, several of which can be used simultaneously:

1. Denial—the organization claims there is no crisis and offers a simple denial that it did not perform the act in question.
2. Evasion of responsibility—the organization attempts to reduce respon-sibility for the crisis by claiming it was either forced into the crisis by another culprit, it did not have the ability to prevent the crisis, it made a mistake, or there were good intentions in its act.
3. Reducing the offensiveness of the act—the organization attempts to rein-force the good traits of the organization, thus creating a more complete context with which the organization should be evaluated.
4. Corrective action—the organization implements steps to solve the problem and prevent a repeat of the crisis.
5. Mortification—the organization accepts responsibility for the act and apologizes. (pp. 247–251)

Although various strategies are available, and can be implemented simultaneously, as is clear by now, we advocate for the selection of strategies that most honestly reflect where one stands as a unit, department, or organization. For example, an apology can show remorse for the crisis, and by reinforcing the positive traits of the college and university, this type of response can broaden the context through which to evaluate the organization. Corrective action, responding to the speculation as to whether the crisis will occur again, has the potential to enhance the organization's image and offers the potential for the institution to emerge as a leader in directly confronting the issue. Once corrective action measures have been implemented and communicated, the organization can build on these favorable strategies. It should be noted that these approaches are mitigated by two important factors: (a) the nature of the transgression—some acts are so egregious it is difficult and perhaps impossible to overcome regardless of the strategies implemented; and (b) stakeholders' loyalty toward the leader or institution—some consumers will be willing to overlook the transgression because of their unwavering support for and commitment to their college or university. For these reasons, higher education leaders will respond differently to an on-campus shooting or sexual abuse scandal than they will to a crisis of lesser magnitude. Furthermore, the effectiveness of these communication strategies relies on the integrity of the claims, the authenticity of the postcrisis actions, and the leadership and organizational behaviors that precede the event.

The second model outlines seven response strategies organized by their perceived level of acceptance on behalf of the stakeholders (Coombs, 2015):

1. Full apology—very high acceptance
2. Corrective action—high acceptance
3. Denial—no acceptance
4. Attack the accuser—no acceptance
5. Ingratiation (organization reminds stakeholders of past good acts)—mild acceptance
6. Justification (organization claims the damage from the crisis was minimal)—mild acceptance
7. Excuse (organization denies intent)—mild acceptance

The role of the leader is to understand the magnitude of the situation and its importance to various stakeholders. If the issue is widely viewed as a crisis, the organization must respond accordingly (Gigliotti, 2020b). Leaders at the University of Missouri, for example, were forced to resign for not recognizing the severity of a racial crisis and for failing to respond in a timely and appropriate fashion to the concerns of multiple constituency groups. Some have also criticized the university leadership for reacting to racial incidents without fully addressing the deeper systemic issues plaguing the campus community (Parker, 2015). Recognizing that the issue in many instances cannot be dismissed as irrelevant, higher education leaders must ensure not only that appropriate messages are being sent, but also that the right person is delivering the message, depending on the type and severity of the issue. This protocol will likely appear in a formalized crisis management plan—one designed by a collaborative crisis management team that outlines key individuals and policies for best responding to the situation at hand. Leaders must be willing to participate in media training, if needed, and during the crisis itself the leader must be visible to internal as well as external audiences. Finally, the college or university must be willing to invest resources in the crisis management process and any subsequent corrective action procedures in order to restore and rebuild trust from the many stakeholders who have an interest in the institution. Referring back to the University of Missouri example, and as others demonstrate, it was important for the appropriate university official(s) to respond to the racial incidents impacting the community; but as these cases have also demonstrated, effective leadership involves more than reacting to a problematic incident on the college campus. More fundamentally, leadership relies on a deep understanding of your own organization's values and the needs, expectations, goals, and attitudes of these stakeholders as university officials create communities of inclusivity, respect, and mutual understanding—with communication occupying a critical role.

Conclusion

The strategies and tactics discussed in this chapter are useful for crisis leadership in practice, yet they are only part of a much more extensive story—one in which ongoing adherence to core institutional values is central. If a college or university has a history with a certain type of crisis, or if there is a pattern of leaders not considering the needs of certain stakeholders, no right mix of tactical strategies can guarantee a satisfactory response. To think otherwise is indicative of a rudimentary understanding of communication theory. It is worth repeating that the message sent by a leader, particularly during times of crisis, does not guarantee that the message will be received by those most affected by the situation or interpreted in the intended way. Single messages seldom have much impact on broader impressions, yet akin to the ongoing crash of waves shaping the ocean shoreline, these tactical communication strategies during a crisis may help to manage expectations, ensure transparency, and provide a framework for collective sensemaking to occur.

Crisis leadership in higher education involves recognition of the critical role of communication, and the broader context and complexities that shape both what is expected and accepted by one's stakeholders. It is important to note that while reputation management is often regarded as a critical goal, it is of secondary importance to the broader aims of crisis leadership. In articulating this point, Scott Cowan, in the analysis of his time as president of

Tulane University during Hurricane Katrina, (2014) listed 10 core principles of crisis leadership:

1. Do the right thing.
2. Seek common ground.
3. Marshal facts.
4. Understand reality.
5. Aim high.
6. Stand up for your beliefs.
7. Make contact.
8. Innovate.
9. Embrace emotion.
10. Be true to core values.

In many instances, individual crises are isolated occurrences that can attract a great deal of attention. Cowan's principles reflect the importance of embodying an approach to leadership that prepares a leader for these rare moments, while also serving the leader and their unit, department, or institution well during periods of normalcy. As summarized throughout this chapter, crisis leadership in higher education—a broader term that embodies and goes beyond both crisis management and crisis prevention—involves a recognition of the needs, expectations, and values of the many stakeholders who have an interest in colleges and universities. Crisis leadership positions communication as a critical competency for navigating tumultuous terrain. Finally, crisis leadership extends the unit of analysis from the crisis itself to the culture, history, and leadership decisions that underlie the unit, department, or institution (Gigliotti, 2019).

Leadership in times of crisis is a timely and important area of focus for all current and aspiring academic and administrative leaders in preventing, managing, responding to, and recovering from the situations that may tear at the institution and that may dramatically impact the lives of those who live, learn, and work in American colleges and universities. At the time of this writing, we are witnessing the convergence of many such threats to our institutions—the pervasive impact of a pandemic, widespread protests regarding racial unrest, and continued financial stress on colleges and universities.

The emphasis on crisis leadership presented in this chapter highlights the critical role of communication, feedback, and engagement in responding to these many interconnected issues—and suggests a more holistic approach to leading during times of crisis that makes prominent our shared values. As will be emphasized in the final chapter of this book, the work of crisis leadership is imperative for leaders and is especially pronounced in this current moment as we deal with a convergence of difficult and challenging circumstances—where unknowns, pervasive consequences, and dramatic impacts to the higher education landscape challenge leaders at all levels to thoughtfully employ the concepts and insights from the crisis leadership literature, and to do so in the context of changing and uncertain future conditions.

For Further Consideration

1. Recent case analysis
   Select a recent case involving a college or university crisis. Review the messages delivered by university leader(s) in response to the crisis.
   - Using Benoit's (1995) approach to image restoration, which of the following strategies did the university leader(s) utilize: denial, evasion of responsibility, reducing the offensiveness of the act, corrective action, or mortification?
   - Were these strategies effective or ineffective? Why?
   - In what ways did the strategies align or fail to align with the severity of the crisis? Align or fail to align with stakeholder expectations? Align or fail to align with the institution's values?
   - Is there anything you would have done differently in responding to this particular crisis?

2. Crisis prevention inventory
   Conduct a crisis prevention inventory by determining the types of crises that are most likely to affect your unit, department, or institution and most likely to have the most devastating effect.
   - Have you encountered any crises that were sudden and took the organization by surprise—or others that have been present for some time but have now becoming increasingly problematic (Seymour & Moore, 2000)?
   - Are there any specific areas in which you find your unit, department, or institution most vulnerable?
   - In which phases of the crisis do you feel most or least prepared as a leader?

3. Crisis leadership training and development
   What areas of training are most important for the leader of your specific area (e.g., media training, understanding of organizational processes and protocols, tabletop simulations of potential crises)?

In what ways might these areas of training help that leader better respond to a crisis?

4. Core values in responding to crisis

Describe the core values of your unit, department, or institution.

- Can you think of examples where the core values of your specific unit, department, or school would help prevent crises from occurring?
- What role can these core values play in providing guidance for leaders during times of crisis?
- Core values can also provide guidance in suggesting what not to do when crises strike. In what ways might your core values inform how you will not respond to a particular crisis?

18

LEADERSHIP DEVELOPMENT IN HIGHER EDUCATION

Formal and Informal Methods

In This Chapter

- How do natural organizational dynamics influence leadership development in programs, departments, and institutions?
- What approaches are available for developing leadership capacity within colleges and universities?
- What are the characteristics of the following types of leadership development models: early intervention, institutional, multi-institutional, and association-based?
- What factors are important for successful leadership development in colleges and universities?

The need for leadership development initiatives has long been recognized in the military and business worlds. The Association for Talent Development (2018) continues to report an increase in per-employee spending on leadership development, indicating nearly $160 billion spent annually by American corporations on training and development programs. Within a health care context, we are also seeing an increase in formal leadership programs. According to a study by the George Washington University School of Medicine and Health Sciences and the AAMC, of the 161 AAMC member schools, 99% of the 94 responding institutions offered some form of leadership training (Lucas et al., 2018). Ironically, higher education institutions at large have been considerably more ambitious in promoting and offering leadership and management development programs to other sectors than in embracing these programs for their own use (Gmelch & Buller, 2015).

In general, the emphasis on leadership development within colleges and universities has been limited, perhaps due in part to the presumption that subject matter expertise and experience are sufficient for leading effectively in this context. While leadership programs have grown considerably in undergraduate and graduate education, the suggestion that a faculty or professional staff member would need training has sometimes been viewed as insulting. Why would thought leaders in colleges and universities need training? Are they not already outstanding leaders by definition?

With the growing recognition that subject matter expertise, in and of itself, is not sufficient to assure outstanding leadership, formal and informal leadership development efforts in higher education are receiving increased attention. As Gmelch and Buller (2015) point out,

> Through academic leadership programs, institutions benefit from making the most effective use of this resource, building connections across campus, promoting purposeful leadership diversity, tapping hidden talent, retaining campus talent, expanding people's potential, and ensuring institutional renewal, effectiveness, and dedication. (p. 198)

In any instance, creating successful leadership development initiatives is a complex undertaking, particularly when a goal is to address insufficiencies in current practice. As discussed in chapter 5, organizational cultures and climates exert a powerful and pervasive influence—and their influence on present and future leaders is no exception. Organizational cultures provide a source of influence in leadership development. For better or worse, through one's assimilation and emulation of current practices, members of a school, department, or center often adapt to the procedures and traditions of an organization. The education offered by organizational culture is informal yet extremely potent.

Culture influences an array of fundamental leadership practices, such as how future leaders relate to and interact with colleagues, how conflict is addressed, what behaviors are valued and rewarded, how decisions are made and implemented, if and how leadership performance is reviewed, and the ways in which superior performance and failures are handled. Culture also creates expectations regarding the tone and frequency of in-person and email communication, the ways that meetings are conducted, how candor and critique of leaders are welcomed or suppressed, and many other facets of organizational life. These informal leadership education moments take place on every campus, in every department, and in every meeting. In ideal circumstances, these institution-wide lessons are the ones we wish to impart to future leaders. When this is the case, the role of formal leadership programs is to reinforce and supplement informal leadership training. Often, however, dissatisfaction with some elements of current leadership practice and the perceived need for change provides the motivation for initiating leadership development programs. In such instances, the core themes and behaviors being promoted in the program must compete for attention and adoption with pervasive and sometimes contradictory elements of current practice. The greater the contrast between the state of current and ideal organizational and leadership practices, the more formidable the challenges that must be overcome in leadership development programming.

The important role of organizational culture in "shaping" leadership perspectives and expectations has many implications for leadership development programming. One implication is that programs for leadership development should begin with an assessment of the current organizational and leadership culture and practices, a clear formulation of program goals, and consideration of the various dynamics of personal and organizational change that must be addressed in order for the program to succeed. The next step is to review and select from among alternative leadership development programming approaches and teaching/learning methodologies—considering the influences of natural forces at play that may support, compete with, or potentially undermine the goals of the effort. McCauley, van Velsor, and Ruderman (2010) underscore the importance of organizational climate in this regard:

> The climate for development is established and reinforced through six organizational processes: priorities of top management, recognition and rewards, communication, efforts to track and measure, resource allocation, and skilled employees. These processes are a powerful part of a development system because they are the drivers and motivators of development within the system and therefore provide support for leader development above and beyond that provided by the methods of development. (p. 50)

Clearly, organizational dynamics should be an important influence in the design of formal leadership programs, and they are also a significant factor in shaping outcomes.

Approaches to Formal Leadership Education and Development

Any number of themes can be components in leadership development programs; many of potential value have been examined in this volume, including the following:

- higher education landscape
- theories of leadership
- the unique nature of higher education leadership

- the distinction between formal and informal leadership
- communication and influence strategies
- self-assessment of leadership styles, strengths, competencies, and areas for improvement
- the variety of tools that are most germane for academic and administrative leaders in higher education (e.g., organizational assessment, planning, change, the use of rubrics and metrics, and leadership in times of crisis)

More generally, in their research on the topic, Gmelch et al. (2011) found three broad perspectives that should be emphasized in all leadership development programs: (a) habits of mind (an understanding of concepts), (b) habits of practice (a demonstration of skills), and (c) habits of heart (a commitment to reflective practice).

In addition to the number of worthy program themes and cross-cutting perspectives, numerous leadership development philosophies, theories, and models are available. Each of these models highlights specific concepts and considerations that are important to successful leadership development programming. Two of these models will be summarized here. One leadership development model that serves as a template for designing and implementing programs of this type is the J-curve model (Bolea & Atwater, 2015), which is shown in Figure 18.1. The model consists of the following nine essential elements of leadership mastery:

1. Set direction.
2. Build a team of people.
3. Create key processes.
4. Steward structure.
5. Nurture behaviors.
6. Promote conversations.
7. Provide support.
8. Set boundaries.
9. Ensure space to deliver.

Through these identified elements, leaders develop their own capacities while also enhancing the leadership capabilities of people around them. Furthermore, as the model illustrates, leadership development emphasizes both mastery and skill acquisition, and programs dedicated to the enhancement of competences in both areas must consider both what leaders do and how they lead.

Another model for developing leaders was introduced by the Center for Creative Leadership (McCauley, van Velsor, & Ruderman, 2010).

Figure 18.1. J-Curve model for leadership mastery (Bolea & Atwater, 2015).

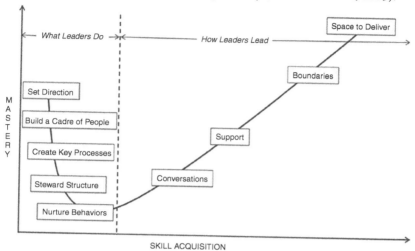

This two-part model consists, first, of a focus on the elements of assessment, challenge, and support, each of which has been shown to contribute to influential developmental experiences. The second part of the model describes the relationship among several aspects of the developmental process, including the opportunity to engage in a variety of experiences, a purposeful focus on individual leadership development, and the ability to learn—three factors that contribute to individuals' leadership learning. This model also considers the significant role of organizational context in leader development, which, as discussed at the outset of this chapter, is a source of considerable influence in leadership learning and development.

Using this model as a guide, leadership development efforts must integrate theory and practice in connecting central principles and concepts to the lived experiences of those participating in such programs. Additionally, as an ongoing and developmental process, individuals learn how to lead through practice—and leadership development programs can provide the space to support individuals as they navigate the inevitable challenges that might arise from one's experiences.

An emphasis in both approaches is placed on leadership development at the individual level and the collective level, with a recognition of the ongoing and fluid process of development. For example, as McCauley, van Velsor, and Ruderman (2010) note,

> Leadership development is an ongoing process. It is grounded in personal development, which is never complete. It is embedded in experience: leaders learn as they expand their experiences over time. It is facilitated

by interventions that are woven into those experiences in meaningful ways. And it includes, but goes well beyond, individual leader development. It encompasses the development of the connections among individuals, the development of the capacities of collectives, the development of the connections among collectives in an organization, and the development of the culture and systems in which individuals and collectives are embedded. (p. 26)

The developmental needs of individuals engaged in leadership vary as a function of the stage and level of one's position within an organization. Leadership development initiatives may be designed to support individuals who encounter differing circumstances, including (a) the level of leadership, (b) the leader's life-cycle stage, and (c) the leader's role-cycle stage (Guillén & Ibarra, 2009). For example, development efforts might focus on leadership at the project, unit, department, or institutional level. Considerations of the life-cycle stage differentiate the specific leadership needs and competencies for entry-level coordinators, midcareer professionals, and senior vice presidents. Finally, the role-cycle stage distinguishes the needs of those entering a specific leadership role in the institution as compared to those who are nearing the end of their formal leadership tenure. Both models highlight those elements that are most critical to the process of leadership development, focusing on specific tasks to enhance one's individual leadership effectiveness and also the broader context that allows for leadership growth and development.

As discussed in chapter 11 and earlier in this chapter, personal leader development is, of course, embedded in the processes, strategies, and structures of the organization's culture and in efforts designed for collective leadership education and development. Given this reality, personal leadership development ultimately must be an intentional process. The desired outcomes are only effective to the extent that individuals genuinely dedicate themselves to advancing their own leadership skills, and these behaviors are supported and reinforced by the organization and its culture.

Snapshots of Leadership Education and Development Models in Higher Education

Formal leadership development programs embodying these philosophies and concepts may be designed and offered by internal units within colleges and universities, external consulting firms, and professional associations. The remainder of this chapter offers snapshots of various approaches to leadership development in higher education, focusing particularly on four common approaches: programs that provide an early intervention model by integrating leadership preparation into graduate education; institutional or campus-based programs; a multi-institutional model illustrated by the Big Ten Academic Alliance; and cross-institutional programs offered by professional associations. The aim of this snapshot summary is to highlight various approaches to leadership development and to identify common goals, features, and areas of distinction.

Early Intervention Model

Many if not most leadership positions in higher education are eventually filled by individuals who have received graduate education. Thinking more specifically of academic leadership positions, current doctoral students across the range of academic disciplines will eventually occupy many if not most of these roles, yet leadership is not a topic that most disciplines explore, nor is it a primary focus for all but a few doctoral education programs. The PreDoctoral Leadership Development Academy (PLDA)[3] at Rutgers was developed to address this gap. PLDA is an early intervention approach to leadership education and development that cuts across academic disciplines and that is specifically geared for doctoral students who are recognized as both scholars and leaders in training (Gigliotti et al., 2016; June, 2010; Sacharow, 2010). The aim of PLDA is to better prepare doctoral students for future leadership roles through a year-long fellowship program. Since its inception in 2010, over 150 doctoral students representing more than 50 academic departments have participated in the program.

Upon being nominated, approximately 15 students are competitively selected across a number of academic disciplines at Rutgers for acceptance into the program each year. There is no additional cost beyond their normal registration and course fees. Students are required to enroll in two noncredit courses that are taught by an interdisciplinary team of faculty and administrators from across the institution. Students who complete the program receive a modest stipend and recognition of their participation as fellows in the program on their transcripts.

Recognizing that PLDA students enter the program with varying academic experiences, the program begins with an introduction to the broader context of higher education, along with an overview of relevant organizational and leadership theory and competencies.

The primary objective of the program is to provide students with foundational knowledge related to the study of higher education and to familiarize them with the concepts and current practices related to institutional types, missions, organizational structures, governance, finance, legal and regulatory issues, diversity and inclusion, and ethics (Rutgers PreDoctoral Leadership Development Academy, n.d.). By becoming familiar with the broader context of higher education, PLDA participants begin to think more substantively about the various leadership expectations and challenges in the academy, most of which cut across disciplines and institutional types. Additionally, the sessions are designed to introduce core concepts related to organizational leadership, culture, assessment, planning, communication, crisis, and change and to promote the development of enhanced personal and leadership competencies relative to each. Key readings, including scholarly articles as well as relevant news articles, present a broad overview of the state of American higher education, organizational and leadership practices, and underpinning concepts.

During these seminars, students have an opportunity to discuss issues and interact with current university leaders who deliver firsthand information about their approach to leadership in addressing challenges in their organizations. Classes also include case studies, role-playing, simulation, and other interactive experiential learning techniques. Students are expected to complete various assignments throughout the program, including an interview and shadowing experience with a campus leader of their choice and the development and presentation of a leadership development plan.

Existing assessment data point to the ongoing success of the program, including a deeper awareness of and appreciation for leadership and communication, a more nuanced understanding of the challenges facing institutions of higher education and the competencies and capabilities needed to lead these institutions, and the ability to learn about leadership and communication through interactive group exercises and mentorship offered within the program (Gigliotti et al., 2020). The PLDA program has been featured in *The Chronicle of Education* (Gigliotti & Qadri, 2017; June, 2010) and at invited presentations to the Big Ten Academic Alliance (BTAA), Council of Independent Colleges, Council of Graduate Studies, and Council of Academic Deans at Research Education Institutions.

Programs with a comparable framework have been implemented or are being planned at the University of South Florida, the University of Missouri, the University of Tennessee, Northwestern University, and Fordham University. These programs point to the importance of an early intervention approach to leadership in higher education—programs that begin to prepare doctoral students for the realities of higher education leadership.

Institutional or Campus-Based Model

Another approach to leadership education is to create campus-based programs for individuals who are current or aspiring leaders. An increasing number of institutions are creating programs of this type. In research on institutional or campus-based approaches to leadership development in higher education, Gigliotti (2017) identified the a number of initiatives offered by the 62 Association of American Universities (AAU) member institutions, as shown in Box 18.1.

BOX 18.1

- Roundtable conversations—structured meetings with peers, institution, and outside leaders on topics of interest among campus and community leaders
- Coaching sessions—one-on-one confidential executive coaching sessions for on-campus leaders
- Leadership/management assessments—self-assessment tools used to identify strengths and areas of growth, including but not limited to the CliftonStrengths assessment, Leadership Practices Inventory, Campbell Leadership Descriptor, Management Effectiveness Profile, Leadership Effectiveness Assessment, Myers–Briggs, DiSC, and Life Styles Inventory
- Leadership profile/individual career plans—electronic portals, typically organized by human resources offices, to track and monitor leadership accomplishments in current positions and identify the skills necessary to advance in a professional context
- Leadership certificate programs—formalized workshop series offered for current and/or aspiring faculty and staff leaders
- Leadership development courses—leadership workshops and programs, typically offered by human resources and talent development offices, for individual employees
- Executive leadership academies/fellowship programs—ongoing workshops for cohorts of aspiring leaders, which often include a mentor component and capstone presentation at their conclusion
- Onboarding opportunities—organizational socialization initiatives used to introduce new leaders to the knowledge, skills, and competencies required to succeed in the organization
- Speaker series—keynote presenters from on campus and the community who offer various perspectives on leadership in higher education

- Performance management programs—appraisal programs that assess individual performance in the institution
- Leadership webinars/self-directed online leadership resources—virtual seminars and resources on topics of interest for emerging leaders in higher education
- Mentor programs—formal pairing of emerging leaders with senior leaders from the campus offered to help individuals learn more about each other and to strengthen their organizational and professional knowledge
- Consultation opportunities—on-campus professionals with leadership and organizational development expertise available to assess and offer recommendations on individual and group performance
- Leadership libraries—collections of texts and resources related to leadership in higher education
- Succession planning resources—tools and materials for identifying and developing future leaders in higher education
- Coffee conversations/leadership lunches—informal meetings facilitated by presenters from across campus
- Group leadership forums—introductions to the complexities and nuances of leading project teams and workgroups in higher education, with an emphasis on managing group and organizational dynamics
- Leader assessments—method for collecting opinions from a wide range of coworkers and stakeholders related to one's leadership performance (e.g., 360-degree multiperspective feedback processes)
- Talent accelerators—incubators and other physical spaces used to encourage creativity and address areas of growth from leadership assessments
- Supervisory development labs/new executive officer training sessions—workshops and training programs offered for new and current supervisors within the institution
- Women's leadership initiatives—tailored experiential leadership programs for women in higher education, which often include female mentors from the campus community
- Leadership newsletters—bulletins issued routinely throughout the year to share information related to leadership in higher education and to formally recognize the accomplishments of campus leaders
- alumni leadership networks—formal and informal networking opportunities for graduates of on-campus leadership initiatives and new participants from the respective programs

TABLE 18.1
Toolbox of Instructional Methods

• Expert facilitation	• Case studies
• Models	• Simulations
• Negotiations	• Lecture case discussion
• Web-based learning	• Problem-based learning
• Action learning	• Service learning
• Mentorships	• Support groups
• Executive coaching	• Self-appraisals
• Evaluation and assessment	• Role-playing instruments
• Instructional games	• Shadowing current leaders
• Feedback mechanisms	• Personalized 360-degree evaluations
• Learning needs assessment	• Mental imaging
• Focused writing assignments	• Competency-based leadership training
• Formal socialization processes	• Teamwork exercises
• Structured interactions	• Outdoor initiatives (ropes courses, Outward Bound)
• Videos, films, multimedia	• Retreats
• Personal growth and planning	• Webinars
• Directed self-study	• Critiques

These instructional methods are consistent with the broader set of instructional methods that Gmelch and Buller (2015) provide, as shown in Table 18.1.

In addition to the review of AAU institutions (Gigliotti, 2017), inventories of campus-based leadership programs offered by the 14 member institutions of the BTAA were conducted (Gigliotti & Ruben, 2015b; Gigliotti et al., 2017; Ruben & Gigliotti, 2014). This synthesis of programs at AAU and BTAA member institutions highlights differentiated activities and services for academic and administrative leadership development that vary in size, duration, sponsoring departments, program themes, and targeted audiences—each of which is delivered through a variety of approaches and methodologies. Building on a review of campus-based leadership development programs completed by a graduate research team from Rutgers University,[2] Gigliotti (2020) synthesized the range of approaches to leadership development across the continua depicted in Figure 18.2, which could be useful in determining the specific features of a new program or initiative. The items listed in this figure are not mutually exclusive, and some programs may address each of the items noted.

The Academic Advancement Network at Michigan State University (MSU, n.d.), for instance, offers an array of programs and workshops for current and aspiring leaders, including conversations with MSU leaders, a leadership institute, focused lunches, executive seminars, and an awards program. Additionally, many of the publicized leadership development programs across the AAU and BTAA reflect the unique character of the university, with a stated focus on outcomes that are most germane to the institution. These direct linkages connect current and future academic leaders to the institution's mission, vision, and values. For example, the University Leadership Education and Development (U-LEAD) program at the University of North Carolina (n.d.) provides emerging leaders with an opportunity to

Figure 18.2. Continuum of approaches to faculty/staff leadership development.

Academic audiences	Administrative audiences
Individual capacity and development	Collective capacity and development
Fully online	Fully in-person
Small-scale applications (unit/department)	Large-scale applications (institution)
Skill-based	Concept-based
Nomination/application	Open enrollment
Targeted audience	Broadly promoted
Dedicated program faculty and administrators	Sponsorship and support from multiple existing units

gain the practical insight, knowledge, skills, and confidence needed for leadership effectiveness, through classroom sessions, active assessments of leadership characteristics, and participation in an intensive, practical project that addresses a major campus issue. Then they apply what they've learned in the real laboratory of the workplace—in the office the next morning.

Cultivating small communities of practice is another common theme among a number of these programs. For instance, the Rutgers Center for Organizational Leadership serves as a hub for academic leadership development, consultation, and research and sponsors a full portfolio of cohort-based leadership development programs that aim to build and enhance individual and collective leadership capacity, support university strategy initiatives, and cultivate a culture of leadership development across the institution (Rutgers University, n.d.). In many instances, participants of these programs are paired with mentors from within the organization for both guidance and support in their leadership development.

The programs variously include classroom instruction, workshops, experiential activities, self-assessment inventories, conversations with campus leaders, project team assignments, leadership coaching, and activities aimed at cultivating smaller communities of practice, in some cases including structured feedback and one-on-one mentoring experiences.

Multi-Institutional: The BTAA Model

The BTAA (n.d.)[4] is a collaborative organization that provides a unique and expansive approach to leadership education and development among its member institutions. The BTAA, formerly the Committee for Institutional Cooperation (CIC), was established by the presidents of the Big Ten Athletic Conference members in 1958 as the athletic league's academic counterpart. This consortium includes the 14 influential research universities that are members of the Big Ten Conference. The impact of this collaboration is reflected in the 1,100 patents issued this year to Big Ten schools, the $10.5 billion in combined research funding across the institutions, and the creation of OmniSOC, a joint cybersecurity operations center created by the Big Ten universities to rapidly respond to cyberthreats (BTAA, n.d.). These large research institutions have a substantial impact on a national and international scale, and one of the goals of the BTAA is to provide an infrastructure for enhanced collaboration that allows these institutions to save money, share assets, and create new opportunities that might not otherwise occur.

Peer-to-Peer Learning

Within the context of leadership training and development, the BTAA provides a range of formal and informal peer-to-peer and institution-to-institution programs, each of which promotes leadership networking and the sharing of practices among individuals who occupy comparable leadership roles in particular academic and administrative specialty areas. The BTAA provides the infrastructure for groups to assemble and collaborate. Many BTAA groups convene on a regular basis and typically fall into one of three categories: executive leadership, program management, and peer groups. The executive leadership groups include senior leaders at BTAA member universities who govern or make investments—or both—in BTAA activities. The program management groups are typically convened by an executive leadership group to engage in a collaborative analysis or manage a specific BTAA project or program, with support provided by BTAA staff. Peer groups are typically self-organizing peers from member universities who get together virtually or face-to-face, or both, to share ideas and best practices. Among all groups, knowledge sharing is a key benefit to their involvement.

Department Executive Officers Seminar and Academic Leadership Program

Two of the BTAA program management groups focus explicitly on faculty leadership development: department executive officers (DEO) liaisons and academic leadership program (ALP) liaisons. The groups are responsible for the development and implementation of the DEO seminar and ALP. Both are unique in that these consortium-wide professional development opportunities allow campuses to draw on talented speakers and facilitators who would not otherwise be brought to one individual campus each year because of fiscal feasibility. Additionally, the programs develop a talent pool of future leaders for the institution as well as all BTAA universities.

Launched in 1997, the DEO seminar is a leadership development program for newly appointed department heads and chairs at BTAA universities. Each institution invites five fellows to participate in the annual 3-day seminar. Individuals are selected by their respective campuses. The seminar focuses on topics involving departmental leadership skills, including but not limited to conflict resolution, time management, leadership style, and performance review of faculty. The objectives of the seminar are threefold:

- to hone the skills of the participants in key areas
- to develop a cadre of highly trained and motivated individuals who could be more effective in inculcating their skills and experience on their own campuses
- to develop an infrastructure of department heads and chairs who can communicate regarding key topics at BTAA institutions

The seminar serves as a venue to generate resource materials, network with colleagues across the Big Ten, and take part in group problem-solving. It provides a venue for sharing of best practices with best practitioners.

The ALP seminar is a yearlong, more extensive leadership development opportunity established 8 years before DEO. ALP is one of the longest-serving professional development programs that the BTAA offers. Although campus participation in ALP is voluntary, all 14 member institutions actively participate in the program. It is an intensive program that develops the leadership and managerial skills of participating faculty and provides participants with a better understanding of university-level academic administrative leadership and its challenges. The primary goal of the program is to help a select group of talented and diverse faculty further develop their ability to be effective academic leaders at all levels of research universities. Each institution establishes its own recruitment and selection process for identifying five fellows to participate in the program each year. Fellows are faculty or select executive-level professional staff who are recognized as emerging academic leaders.

The program consists of individual seminars that are designed to maximize interaction among participants. The program features guest speakers who address the group on identified thematic topics through case studies, workshops, and other group exercises, and participants engage in small group discussions and networking opportunities. Each seminar within the program focuses on a central theme: (a) contemporary issues in higher education, (b) internal and external relationships, and (c) money, management, and strategies. Table 18.2 provides a general framework for the three seminars.

Each campus chief academic officer appoints one or more institutional liaisons to serve as the central coordinator for the ALP, and the liaison also serves as the campus contact with the BTAA office. Liaisons usually hold positions in the provost's office, with responsibilities in areas such as academic leadership, faculty and staff development, and human resources, but also in a range of other academic administrative roles. They are responsible for supervising all aspects of the fellows' activities at their home institutions. Liaisons play an important role in recruiting and selecting fellows and are essential in the program planning and implementation of the seminars, as well as the on-campus enrichment programs that support the ALP experience.

To support the ALP fellows, each institution conducts its own series of on-campus enrichment programs. These supplemental programs often include scheduled discussion sessions between the fellows and a variety of campus senior leaders and, on occasion, external stakeholders. Among the leaders included are presidents/chancellors, provosts, regents/trustees, vice presidents (e.g., student affairs, development, general counsel, finance, and

TABLE 18.2
BTAA Academic Leadership Program Framework

Seminar I: Contemporary Issues in Higher Education	*Seminar II: Internal and External Relationships*	*Seminar III: Money, Management, and Strategies*
President and provost	President and provost	President and provost
Campus tour	Campus tour	Campus tour
Globalization	Faculty	Strategic planning
Diversity and inclusion	Staff	Financial planning/ budget models
Public engagement	Students	Philanthropy and advancement
Contemporary issues in higher education	External constituents/ stakeholders	Space/infrastructure
Teaching and learning	Research	Prioritization and time management
Academic leadership	Leadership values, styles, skills	Leading into your future

operations), athletic directors, deans, and so on. To ensure that the three campus seminars are as effective as possible, each campus is asked to coordinate a meeting between its fellows and campus officials whose portfolio includes topics to be discussed at the upcoming seminar. For example, before the seminar session that focuses on strategic planning and budgeting, ALP liaisons are asked to schedule a meeting with their campus budget officer.

ALP liaisons and BTAA staff design seminars and on-campus experiences to meet the specific program objectives with a balance of informational and interactive sessions and opportunities to network and socialize. By participating in the program, fellows may learn more about the organization, operations, finances, and structure of their own university and research universities in general. Additionally, fellows are able to think more deeply about the challenges and rewards of academic leadership while building relationships with other aspiring leaders from across the participating universities.

Program Evaluations
Topics and speakers for both programs are evaluated regularly. DEO participants are encouraged to complete a seminar evaluation, and ALP participants are encouraged to complete a preseminar questionnaire, an evaluation for

each seminar, and a postseminar evaluation. The survey responses provide critical feedback regarding the sessions, speakers, and logistics. Based on this feedback and the liaisons' recommendations, speakers and topics are adjusted and adapted to ensure that the seminar remains a progressive and innovative professional development opportunity.

BTAA completes program evaluations for all key programs on a rotating schedule. The program review is a process of refinement and an opportunity to reflect on what is working well and what improvements could be made based on feedback from the provosts, fellows, and liaisons. The most recent surveys for the programs indicate that both have a profound impact on the fellows' leadership development. Since its inception, more than 1,400 participants have completed the program. Many of them have gone on to serve with distinction as college presidents, provosts, and deans.

Association-Based Model

A number of external organizations offer training and development for higher education audiences, although their expertise and area of focus often extend beyond leadership programming. The types of organizations that might fall within this category include

- external consulting entities (e.g., McKinsey & Co., the Boston Consulting Group, IDEA Education),
- multi-institutional consortia (e.g., American Council on Education [ACE]; Association of American Universities; Higher Education Resource Services; National Association of Women Deans, Administrators, and Counselors; Harvard Institutes for Higher Education), and
- professional associations, research centers, and private training firms (e.g., Center for Creative Leadership; Higher Education Research Institute; International Leadership Association; ATLAS: Academic Training, Leadership, and Assessment Services; the Center for the Study of Academic Leadership, along with a myriad of sector-specific professional associations).

These organizations provide a wide array of services and resources for faculty and staff leaders in higher education, including program-specific support (e.g., crisis leadership consulting, assistance with strategic planning), a variety of online and in-person resources for navigating one's role as a leader, and extensive networking opportunities with other leaders in higher education. Additionally, many of these organizations provide specific programs and services for underrepresented groups. Some examples include the Women's Leadership forum and the Spectrum Executive Leadership program sponsored by the ACE, the Association of American Colleges and Universities Teaching to Increase Diversity and Equity in STEM (TIDES) initiative, and the numerous institutes sponsored by the Higher Education Resource Services (HERS).

There are certainly a number of advantages in pursuing the leadership services offered by these and similar organizations. Absent the constraints that may be present in campus-based programs, association-based training and development opportunities encourage candor and offer participants anonymity as they develop as leaders outside of their specific institution. Furthermore, these associations allow for learning from individuals who are often dealing with a host of similar challenges at peer institutions. The disadvantage, of course, is that the programs and services are often not tailored to the specific needs, values, goals, and culture of one's home institution. Additionally, upon returning from an impactful conference or leadership training program, the desire to initiate new practices at one's home institution is predictably met with the reality of the routine pressures facing college and university leaders and the absence of a setting specifically designed to support new leadership insights or behaviors.

In conceptualizing, designing, implementing, or adopting any program, it is important to begin with an assessment of organizational needs, as well as the knowledge and competencies required for effective leadership. Also important is a realistic assessment of the current organizational and leadership culture to determine the extent to which current practices are in line with organizational and leadership aspirations. When alignment is present, formal leadership programming is a far easier task than when more fundamental gaps exist. In either case, the design or selection of a program should reflect the sense of what is needed, and these same assessments should inform one's expectations of the outcomes.

Selecting an Approach to Leadership Development

When selecting an approach to preparing future leaders, we are reminded of the point made in chapter 11 that the development of leaders and leadership competencies is an ongoing and continuous process. Pointing to the inadequacy of onetime, short-term, and isolated workshops, Connaughton et al. (2003) note,

> It is unrealistic to expect that enhanced leadership capabilities can be developed in a 2-hour or even a week-long leadership workshop.

Rather, leadership competencies are best developed over time through a program that fosters personalized integration of theory and practice and that conceives of leadership development as a recursive and reflective process. (p. 46)

A highly focused, intentional, and multidisciplinary approach to leadership development seems to be the most desirable option, particularly those programs that align teaching methods with desired outcomes, encourage direct application and reflection, and offer various opportunities for learning about leadership (Connaughton et al., 2003; Prince, 2001).

To conclude, it is interesting to compare leadership development through participation in a onetime initiative (e.g., a program, workshop, or leadership book) with the leadership development that results from one's long-term socialization in an organization (e.g., through culture, process, a set of experiences over time, and ongoing role modeling). It is parallel to the difference between learning how to parent from attending a workshop or reading a couple of how-to books compared to the learning that takes place through the influence of the multitude of experiences, observations, and insights developed over years of learning from one's own and others' parents.

In all instances, communication is central to learning, and long-term leadership development involves an ongoing immersion in an environment filled with myriad verbal and nonverbal messages, strategies, processes, and structures, some provided intentionally and others unintentionally, that both shape and reinforce what is learned from any individual program or initiative. Clearly, leadership programs can contribute to leadership development and individual and collective efficacy, but it is incumbent on those involved in the design and delivery of such efforts to be mindful of the intended goals; to engage participants in meaningful opportunities for learning; to align these programs and initiatives with the strategic priorities of the department, school, or institution; to evaluate the impact of these programs; and to continually improve these efforts through robust longitudinal assessment, as described in this final section.

Implications for Evaluating Leadership Development Efforts

This final section focuses on considerations for evaluating the success and benefits of leadership development efforts. The ultimate impact of these initiatives, of course, depends to a great degree on the culture of the organization itself and the ways in which current institutional leaders model desired concepts, approaches, and strategies. Senior leaders, for example, serve as role models for others across the organization, and their insights, skills, perspectives, and support for leadership development is critical to the success of any formal and informal leadership development effort.

To be successful, leadership education programs and interventions must leverage the learning that occurs as individuals observe, analyze, and make sense of the practices demonstrated by others across the institution. Current leaders can cultivate a climate where effective leadership practice is prized and encouraged, and where meaningful leadership development is nurtured and supported. Often this approach involves welcoming change and supporting a reexamination of new approaches to leadership practices and styles. Borrowing from Maxwell (1995), if leadership efforts are to be valued,

> creating an environment that will attract leaders is vital. . . . Doing that is the job of leaders. They must be active; they must generate activity that is productive; and they must encourage, create, and command changes in the organization. They must create a climate in which potential leaders will thrive. (p. 17)

The onus is most certainly on current leaders to create this supportive environment for leadership development—an environment on which the future of our institutions depends. These points are amplified in chapter 19 on succession planning.

As institutions continue to take leadership development more seriously, questions and concerns will be raised regarding the impact of such efforts and the investment of time and resources into various types of programs. Evaluating the effectiveness of a leadership development program is not an easy task. There is no one right approach, but several options are available. Success or effectiveness indicators might include the number of participants who complete specific modules or the entire program, or completion of assignments or projects that are included in the curriculum of a leadership development program. Alternatively—or additionally—those involved with program design may look at the data from self-evaluations where leaders assess the knowledge or skills they believe to have gained from a program, or one might analyze evaluative feedback from multi-rater assessments of the leader completed by peers and colleagues. These quantitative and qualitative evaluation methods may focus on either the immediate or the long-term impacts the program has on an individual's leadership behavior.

The triangulation of various data sources is likely the best approach to assessing the ultimate impact of a leadership development initiative. In the end, the evaluative process must take account of the mission, aspirations, and goals of the program and the ways in which the program aligns with the priorities of the academic department or school, the administrative unit, or institution. In all cases, the evaluation of these efforts begins with a clear articulation and understanding of program goals. Predetermining what success might look like at the outset of a program or initiative can be a useful step in evaluating the impact of such efforts.

Conclusion

The programs and approaches highlighted in this chapter vary in scope, duration, intended audience, and outcomes, and when evaluating the impact of these efforts, one must consider the intended goals of such programs. These leadership programs might emphasize issues that are specific to the higher education landscape, or they may focus on leadership or organizational theory, research, or skills more generally. They might feature self-assessment tools or strategies for organizational assessment. Such leadership programs can include participation in team-building exercises or hands-on leadership projects as a component, along with a host of other methods for instruction and engagement. For higher education, as for leadership development programming in other sectors and contexts, no single approach to leadership development is likely to be fully satisfactory.

Enhancing leadership behavior through targeted training efforts is a daunting challenge, and one not simply accomplished through a few readings, discussions, exercises, or self-assessment inventories. No workshop, multiday program, or book alone can be expected to have a transformative effect on a person's leadership capability. As Gmelch and Buller (2015) suggest, "If we assume that it takes ten to twenty years for a highly intelligent person to become an expert in an academic discipline, why do we assume that we can train academic leaders in a three-day workshop?" (p. 8). An individual may learn new terms and concepts, hear about and practice newly acquired skills, and, it is hoped, come away with renewed motivation to make a difference as a leader, but even that may be a lot to expect from short-term workshops that are typical of so many leadership enhancement efforts. Clearly, the systematic improvement of leadership is a critically important, long-term process. Expecting otherwise invites disappointment.

Formalized leadership development programs occupy an increasingly visible, popular, and important role in higher education—nationally and on a growing number of campuses. The goals of these programs are easy to embrace as we face a growing array of challenges at all levels within higher education. Some programs are aimed at those in existing formal roles; others are designed to prepare participants for future positions. Still others have more general aims, seeking to enhance participants' informal leadership capabilities.

A comprehensive overview of leadership programs in higher education, provided by Gmelch and Buller (2015), along with their summary of strategies for academic leadership development, are presented in Table 18.3.

Drawing on various lessons learned from their academic leadership programs at Iowa State University, Gmelch and Buller (2015) go on to outline the following qualities that are characteristic of effective academic leadership programs:

1. Cohort groups can play a key role in most leadership development programs.
2. Leadership development programs should not serve merely as training programs; they should also act as support groups.
3. Leadership development must be an ongoing process.
4. Leaders can create and deliver their own learning opportunities.
5. Successful leadership development programs require a supportive culture.
6. Leadership programs tend to be most successful when they capitalize on small wins as they proceed.
7. Leadership development is most effective when it occurs within a specific context.
8. Setting aside time and space for the administrators' reflection is indispensable.
9. Regardless of institutional mission or personal beliefs, effective leadership development must have moral, ethical, and (in many cases) spiritual dimensions.
10. Leaders must leave campus occasionally to gain a broader perspective and vision.
11. Much of the value of leadership development is lost if institutions do not provide incentives for administrators to stay long enough to make a difference and sustain the change.
12. Leadership development programs work best when they are built around a single, well-delineated model of leadership development.

TABLE 18.3

Strategies for Academic Leadership Develop

Levels of Intervention	Leadership Development Component		
	Habits of Mind: Conceptual Understanding	Habits of Practice: Skill Development	Habits of Heart: Reflective Practice
Personal	• Higher education courses • Leadership conferences • Books and journals • Assessments and inventories • Exposure to new mental models	• External seminars (such as those offered by ACE and CASE) • Assessments and inventories related to skills • Support groups • Short commercial seminars • Executive MBA/MPA programs	• Journaling • Reflective practice • Facilitated peer mentoring • Executive coaching • Values clarification • Faith or other spiritual practices • Consultations with mentors or confidants
Institutional	• Orientation processes • Seamless socialization • Executive development • Administrative sabbaticals • Team-building activities • Professional stipends	• Campus leadership seminars • Internships and shadowing • Mentorships • Consultations with campus administrators • Consultations with colleagues off campus • Professional development projects	• Annual reviews • Leadership councils • Chair/dean or dean/provost one-on-one sessions • Campus support groups • Leader "therapy sessions" • Campus-based mentor programs

(Continues)

TABLE 18.3 *(Continued)*

Leadership Development Component			
Levels of Intervention	Habits of Mind: Conceptual Understanding	Habits of Practice: Skill Development	Habits of Heart: Reflective Practice
Professional	• Higher education organizations (such as ACAD, AACU, and AACSU) • New Leaders Council Institute (newleaderscouncil.org) • Higher education leadership organizations (such as the UK's Leadership Foundation for Higher Education and Australia's LH Martin Institute for Tertiary Education) • Personal networks • Former chairs, deans, and provosts	• Leadership and management books • Organizations designed for certain levels of administration (e.g., deans' organization, conferences for chairs) • Conference workshops • Skill-based training • Professional organizations • Disciplinary organizations	• Internet and intranet networks • Consortia • Regional, state, and national networks • National cohort programs

For Further Consideration

1. Leadership development culture and climate reflection
   Reflect on your own unit, department, or organization:
   - In what ways are leadership education and development encouraged or discouraged by your organizational culture and climate?
   - How might you describe this culture and climate to a new aspiring leader?
   - How does your organization incentivize, recognize, reward, or celebrate leadership development?
   - What can one learn about leadership as a result of observing the behaviors of leaders in your unit, department, or institution?

2. The design, justification, and evaluation of a campus-wide leadership development program
   As someone who is committed to leadership education and development, you would like to propose a new program for midcareer faculty and staff at your college or university. In talking to colleagues from other departments, you begin to recognize several troubling themes. First, there is a growing malaise across the institution, and many individuals lack the motivation for taking on formal leadership roles as department chairs or directors in major department or institutional committees. When you discuss the issue informally with colleagues, they report questioning their ability to function effectively in these roles and the value attached to this work by the institution.
   - How might you further assess the organization and leadership development needs within your institution in order to further clarify the dimensions of the problems, strategies for addressing the issues you discover, and the role a formalized leadership development program might play?
   - Given this context, what type of approach to leadership development (e.g., components, structure, duration, target audience, etc.) might be most effective or appropriate?
   - What themes or competencies would you emphasize in the curriculum of this newly developed program?
   - How would you evaluate the success of a leadership development program? What measures and methods might be most appropriate?

Notes

1. A more comprehensive collection of academic and senior leadership education programs offered by these institutions can be found in Gigliotti and Ruben (2018).

2. The authors wish to acknowledge the members of this research team who engaged in this benchmarking project: Stephanie Brescia, Maria Dwyer, Magy Gergus, Ralph Gigliotti, Christine Goldthwaite, Morgan Kandrac, Melanie Kwestel, and Bhargava Nemmaru.

3. PLDA is one of several Rutgers Center for Organizational Leadership programs, which have been supported by the university with additional contributions from Johnson & Johnson, AT&T, the Mellon Foundation, Anne Thomas, Francis and Mary Kay Lawrence, and the School of Graduate Studies, School of Arts and Sciences, the School of Communication and Information, and other Rutgers faculty and staff including Barbara Bender, Corrine Castro, Chris Goldthwaite, Jerry Kukor, Susan Lawrence, Barbara Lee, Courtney McAnuff, Dick McCormick, Francine Newsome Pfeiffer, and Morgan Kandrac, who currently serves as graduate coordinator for the program, and the many individuals who have preceded—and will follow her in this much appreciated role.

4. The authors wish to thank Big Ten Academic Alliance senior staff members, Barbara McFadden Allen, Amber Cox, and Charity Farber, for their contributions to this section of the chapter.

19

CONNECTING LEADERSHIP DEVELOPMENT AND SUCCESSION PLANNING

The Missing Link in Organizational Advancement?

In This Chapter

- What are the potential benefits of increased attention to leadership recruitment models and strategies?
- What are the connections between leadership development and leadership recruitment?
- What are best practices in leadership recruitment and selection?
- How can leadership succession and transition planning be most effectively utilized within colleges and universities
- How can leadership planning processes contribute to organizational advancement?

This chapter examines how colleges and universities recruit and select individuals for leadership positions and how these processes can be used most effectively to support leadership development efforts and to advance organizational effectiveness.

There are two major points of emphasis. First, *leadership succession planning* merits consideration as a means to develop candidates to fill leadership vacancies. In this approach, institutions invest time and money in leadership training with the idea that a strong bench of "homegrown" talent can be used to fill leadership vacancies as they arise. The costs and benefits of leadership replacement via succession planning versus other methods of leadership recruitment will be considered. Although some institutions do not have the bandwidth to adopt full-blown succession planning programs, the model provided later in this chapter presents a variety of options that institutions may choose to adopt.

The second major point of emphasis is that leadership selection outcomes are likely to be successful when they are informed by ongoing processes of organizational assessment and leadership development. What strategic goals does the college seek to realize? Is the institution seeking to adopt radical changes or a more continuous process of fine-tuning? Are leadership development programs preparing current faculty and staff with the knowledge and skill set necessary to provide effective leadership relative to these goals? Answers to these types of questions can and should shape decisions about leadership recruitment and selection. For example, a strategic plan might reveal that the institution is in need of both faculty and staff leaders with experience and proven competencies in fully online instruction and program development. Alternatively, a priority to create a more diverse and inclusive environment for students, faculty, and staff might result from the planning process. For the goal of increasing online instructional programming, depending on the time frame and sense of urgency at hand, the institution might decide to invest time and money to develop these competencies as a part of in-house leadership development programs with the aim of promoting individuals who successfully complete training into positions of leadership as vacancies arise. On the other hand, if the need for online expertise is pressing and immediate, searches for external candidates with the requisite competencies might make more sense. Similarly, for the goal of increasing diversity and creating more inclusive campus environments, a college might decide to use members of the leadership team who have increased the diversity of their local units by employing strategies that can be adopted by the wider institution. Such leaders might be promoted to higher levels of leadership to oversee these efforts. Absent local expertise, the institution should seek to hire from outside the institution to lead diversity and inclusion goals.

Generally speaking, as will be discussed in the pages ahead, leadership recruitment, selection, and transition processes work best when they connect with leadership development efforts and are driven by organizational assessments from which strategic goals are derived. Using continuous improvement and organizational assessment practices to inform leadership selection does not ensure that the candidate chosen will be successful in the long run. Moreover, the pool of available candidates—both internal and external—may be limited in number or comprised of candidates who are a poor "fit" with the needs of the department, school, college, or university. However, particularly when coupled with a commitment to leadership development programming to enhance the competencies of current employees, considering candidates from within the organization becomes a viable alternative to recruiting externally. This flexibility in approach to leader recruitment—considering both external and internal candidates—may well improve the chances that an institution will be better able to advance strategic goals and objectives.

Closing the Loop Between Leadership Development and Strategic Advancement

The connection between leadership selection and organizational advancement is determined, in part, by how senior leaders interact with leadership teams that are already in place. This section describes practices that connect leadership work with strategic advancement in a collegiate setting and offers suggestions that can help to create or elevate leadership as a core value within the institutional culture.

Strategic advancement usually represents change for an organization. The model of organizational change presented in chapter 15 highlighted the role of leaders in taking responsibility for leading change efforts. Here, we want to highlight the fact that organizational leaders such as deans, directors, and chairs, who are working to attain strategic objectives, often operate at a level below that of senior leaders who charged them with effecting particular changes. For example, a campus provost might assign deans to shift a percentage of their instructional programs from face-to-face to fully online formats or to diversify their faculty and staff. In this example, the provost would be viewed as the senior leader, and each dean is recognized as a leader with responsibility for implementing the change process.

According to the model presented in chapter 15, the change process begins with capturing attention (step 1) and ends with integration (step 5). The practical tips and suggestions offered next are designed to encourage senior leaders to make deliberate efforts to capture the attention of faculty and staff leaders and other internal stakeholders. These tips and suggestions also encourage senior leaders to promote the integration of desired changes by publicly acknowledging the accomplishments of leaders who report to them. The influence of recognition by the senior leaders is often overlooked in higher education, and its absence can hinder the change-integration process. It is important to note, also, that leadership recognition helps to ensure the sustainability of the change as positions of leadership become vacant.

The following lists offer suggested steps leaders can take to heighten attention to integration of leadership development and succession planning. A systematic approach that includes action steps such as these can be expected to make a great contribution to the advancement of a culture of leadership development at an institution, school, or program.

Capturing attention of leaders and other stakeholders:

- At the start of each academic year, campus/institutional leaders might report on progress toward institutional goals completed in the prior year, referencing measures/metrics that were shared when goals were initially developed and communicated and reporting on progress.
- Early in each academic year, campus/institutional leaders might host a breakfast or luncheon meeting for all unit leaders to reaffirm goals attained and those in progress, emphasizing the importance of leaders across the organization who are working toward these shared goals.

Promoting integration through public recognition of successes:

- Throughout the year, efforts might be made to promote leadership accomplishments across the organization, reminding the campus community of shared goals and exploring creative ways to engage faculty and staff leaders in sharing resources and best practices in organizational leadership.
- At the conclusion of each academic year, campus/institutional leaders might host a dinner meeting to recognize outstanding leadership accomplishments over the past year relative to established goals. Those selected might be recognized in institutional publications/ websites. Ideally, such public recognition would be accompanied by small grants or other infusions of resources to the leaders' units.
- At the end of each academic year, leaders and their supervisors should discuss accomplishments and plans for the future, including any refinements in goals or means of attainment. Both oral and written feedback should be provided to the unit leader from their supervisor.
- Campus/institutional leaders should be encouraged to expand the criteria used in reviewing and rewarding faculty performance to include leadership effectiveness. This is especially important for faculty members who are on the faculty promotion ladder at a midpoint in their careers and are serving in a formal academic leadership position such as department chair.

Bringing new leaders on board: Orientation to strategic goals:

- When considering leadership appointments, campus/institutional leaders should discuss and share views on current trends in higher education, important issues in the community and state, the college/ university, and the unit in question. Candidates should be asked about their views of the institution's and unit's strengths and weaknesses. If a strategic plan is in place, references to the plan are appropriate. In particular, candidates may be asked how the unit they hope to lead currently contributes to the college/university's standing and strategic objectives and what opportunities they see for further advancements that are possible under their leadership.

- At the time of appointment, candidates for leadership positions and the person to whom they report should discuss short- and long-term goals for the unit in question. If the new leader's supervisor has specific goals in mind, those goals should be discussed and an understanding reached about expectations and timelines for the year(s) ahead. The newly appointed leader's goals should align with institutional goals but need not be limited to them.

- At the time of an initial appointment and on an ongoing basis, supervisors should make clear their expectations about communication requirements when leaders under their supervision experience difficulties. For example, supervisors might request that leaders propose a cost-benefit analysis of two or more possible courses of action to address difficulties. The description of the problem and suggested action steps will help the supervisor clarify the nature of the leader's problems. Of course, supervisors can insist that a different course of action be chosen or derived.

Supporting leadership development:

- Senior leaders should encourage current and aspiring leaders to complete homegrown or external leadership development programs such as those discussed in the previous chapter.
- Senior leaders are open to advancing internal candidates for appropriate leadership positions within the organization as vacancies arise.
- Senior leaders support leaders taking appropriate positions of leadership at other institutions when such appointments represent growth for that individual. For example, a veteran department chair applies to become an associate dean or dean at another college or university, in part because an in-house vacancy is not on the horizon.

These steps underscore the important role all leaders can play in helping the college or university to realize leadership development and organizational advancement goals. The steps also reinforce the notion that leaders and leadership are important to the institution. Their work matters and is valued by and at the highest levels of the college/university. When it comes time to recruit candidates for leadership vacancies, a culture that values leaders and leadership development can be an important distinguishing feature of the organization.

Recruitment and Selection of Leaders in Higher Education

The following section will detail important recruitment and selection considerations at multiple levels of the institution, and when establishing transition plans and preparing for unplanned vacancies.

Top of the Leadership Organizational Chart

The responsibility and authority for the recruitment and selection of college and university leaders is vested in institutional governing boards and delegated to the appropriate level of leadership via the chain of command (e.g., president, provost, dean, etc., as described in chapter 5). Most often, college presidents/chancellors are recruited and hired from outside the organization. In a majority of institutions, the hiring of a new president almost always occurs through a lengthy search process directed by the institution's governing board and supported by a search firm that helps the college/university with recruitment and selection of candidates. Using a search firm has a number of advantages, such as the expertise of the firm in providing a structured process for assessing candidate qualifications with an emphasis on client specifications, the ability to recruit a robust pool of diverse and qualified candidates where it is possible to do so, and skill in providing a comparative perspective based on past searches conducted across the higher education landscape (Rodas, 2020).

Despite these advantages, the long-standing practice of using outside firms for presidential searches was called into question by Greenberg (2014), who argued that using a search firm to attract candidates for a presidency is unnecessary, since the pool of available candidates is almost always rather small due to the stratification of institutions. For example, a sitting president at a liberal arts institution is unlikely to make the short list of candidates at a research-intensive university. Greenberg (2014) also maintained that the typical list of desired characteristics in presidential job positions is so generic as to be unhelpful. Such qualifications often include the following:

- ability to articulate a vision
- a collaborative working style
- a capacity to lead and inspire diverse groups
- a commitment to excellence

- superb communication skills
- distinguished scholarly and professional achievement
- well-developed interpersonal skills
- an ability to work effectively with a wide range of constituents
- a commitment to diversity

In short, Greenberg (2014) questioned the assumption that search firms can do a better job than internal search committees because of the small size of the available external talent pool at peer or aspirant institutions and a lack of specificity about desired competencies. Both of these considerations are important in many leadership hiring contexts, not just those involving presidents/chancellors.

The major costs to the institution to fill leadership positions at or near the top of the organizational chart are the time commitments required of faculty and staff search committee members, the costs of advertising vacancies, and the costs of search firms. Also, a faculty or staff member, or leader assigned as chair or as a member of a search committee, may need to be released from other duties during the search process, and there may be costs associated with covering those duties with other personnel.

Costs of time and money aside, the challenge in a search for a senior leader is to identify candidates whose skill set matches institutional needs and who is a good fit for the institution. The selection of an individual from outside the institution runs the risk of introducing unnecessary or unwanted organizational discontinuities. If a department or institution is doing well, the introduction of change and the turbulence that inevitably accompanies an outside candidate who is unfamiliar with the organization may be unnecessary, wasteful, and potentially harmful. When perceived organizational weaknesses or urgent needs exist, the recruitment of external candidates with the appropriate knowledge and skill set to guide the change process is a potentially effective strategy, but even in those instances, attention to developing internal candidates who have an understanding of current strengths and improvements can be a viable approach.

Lower Levels of the Leadership Organizational Chart

Leadership positions in the middle to lower levels of the organizational chart, such as associate dean, department chair, or associate director, tend to be filled with internal candidates. Depending on the policies and procedures of the institution, the pool of eligible candidates might be small. For example, in chapter 5 we discussed how the growth of nontenure-track candidates has reduced the pool of available candidates for certain academic leadership positions for which tenure is a prerequisite. A dean or senior director might be forced to appoint an individual regardless of their enthusiasm or ability to lead, simply because they have not previously served and are eligible.

When internal candidates are selected, the time and financial costs to the institution are minimal. However, as discussed in previous sections of this book, these appointments often incur costs of a different kind, such as in those situations when the new leader may be ill-suited to lead those who were formerly peers. Learning leadership on the job can come with a price for the individual and the institution. While it may not have been his intention, when Greenberg (2014) referred to the limited pools of strong external candidates (in the case of presidential searches), he made a good case for institutions to engage in leadership succession planning, whereby a cadre of strong, internal candidates would be cultivated and available for consideration for a wide range of leadership echelons.

Transition Planning

One way to support leaders appointed from within the institution is to establish transition plans, which are feasible when the vacancy is anticipated with at least a one-semester time horizon. Many colleges and universities have become increasingly intentional about managing transitions into leadership roles when there is an employee in place to assume a new role either on an interim or permanent basis. For those faculty and staff leadership positions in which internal candidates are routinely selected, having a detailed plan for leadership transition is recommended (Mandelbaum, 2007).

To illustrate, an academic department chair vacating the position can document useful information (e.g., about operations, budget, and personnel issues), create a detailed timeline with to-do activities (e.g., for submission of course schedule and budget requests), and coordinate shadowing arrangements with the incumbent (Mandelbaum, 2007). This example can be generalized to higher levels of academic leadership, such as a dean. An associate dean or department chair who agrees to serve as interim dean, or who has been appointed as the next dean, can be invited to attend dean council or cabinet meetings with the existing dean. Using this approach, the new dean can develop an understanding of how the provost or vice president conducts meetings and can learn about the experiences and best practices of fellow dean participants. Similarly, the dean designate can accompany the existing dean to meetings with key donors and other important external stakeholders.

Transition plans can flatten the learning curve relative to both managing up and leading outside the institution—two key arenas that are often not visible to those who move into an interim role at a higher level than their present position. Staff managers and directors can engage in these same activities to ease the transitions for their successors.

Elements of transition planning can also be used when external candidates are appointed for academic and staff positions above the level of dean or director. For example, Jon Alger, president of James Madison University, reported that in the first several months after he assumed the presidency, the former president accompanied him to meetings with key external stakeholders in order to make introductions and ease the transition (J. Alger, personal communication, November 2, 2015).

Planning for a leadership transition must go beyond the workload and salary adjustments that are used to entice an individual to assume a leadership position. Such adjustments are important for the individual but are not educative or preparatory for the new leadership responsibilities. Mechanisms such as shadowing existing leaders, attending meetings with one's superiors and external stakeholders, and discussing these meetings can ease and facilitate the transition. Detailed "when-to" documents developed by the departing leader, manager, or director also put a fine point on general policies and procedures that may or may not provide helpful advice to an incumbent leader. Although documentation is difficult to obtain, many institutions engage in deliberate and thoughtful approaches to managing leadership transitions. Colleges and universities can build on these approaches to develop even more intentional approaches to leadership succession, as described later in this chapter.

Unexpected Leadership Vacancies

When leadership vacancies are anticipated, transition activities are useful to orient new leaders to their responsibilities and to support their work at the outset. Matters are more complicated when leadership vacancies are unexpected and occur with little advance notice. In these circumstances, internal candidates are almost always appointed on either an interim or permanent basis with little time for transition planning. Unexpected vacancies can be disruptive for the institution, as well as the faculty and staff employees (Calareso, 2013). In some cases, no suitable internal candidate is available to assume a leadership position, and an appropriate external candidate may not be readily found, recruited, or hired. This can create a serious and disruptive leadership gap for a semester, academic year, or even longer (Bennett, 2015).

Most individuals who have worked in higher education can cite examples like Bennett's (2015), in which the question "Who can we appoint to fill this vacancy, at least on an acting basis?" hits very close to home. Note that emergency appointments of internal candidates can have a domino effect, such that as higher positional vacancies are filled with existing leaders, vacancies are created at lower levels. For example, if a dean is appointed interim provost, who becomes dean? If a department chair becomes interim dean, who becomes department chair? Also, individuals promoted to acting positions with no real prospect of being selected permanently for the role run the risk of displacing a leader who may be well matched to the needs of their present role and may also create a lasting morale problem for the individual.

By developing a cadre of trained leaders within the institution via succession planning, institutions protect themselves from serious disruptions that may often result from unanticipated leadership vacancies. Unexpected vacancies—especially those that occur at higher levels within the organization—create vulnerabilities for an organization that pays little attention to leadership succession.

Colleges and universities routinely select candidates for leadership positions from within and outside the organization. A limiting factor in all searches is the size and robustness of the candidate pool. Outside search firms are often able to help an institution in this critical area. There are costs, benefits, and risks associated with conducting searches for external candidates; there are also costs, benefits, and risks associated with appointing candidates from inside the organization.

If radical changes are desired or needed, searching outside the organization probably has a better chance of success. If continuity in operations is desired, searching from within the organization can be a more appropriate strategy. Transition planning can support soon-to-be-appointed leaders before they assume their new roles. Leadership succession planning can enhance selection and appointment of leaders from within the college and university. Succession planning expands the candidate pool and provides a long runway of support and preparation for those ascending to positions of leadership for the first time.

Leadership Succession Planning Fundamentals

The U.S. Office of Personnel Management (2005) provides a succinct description of the purpose and process of succession planning. Succession planning is a systematic approach to

- building a leadership pipeline/talent pool to ensure leadership continuity;
- developing potential successors in ways that best fit their strengths;
- identifying the best candidates for categories of positions; and
- concentrating resources on the talent development process yielding a greater return of investment.

At its core, *leadership succession planning* is "the preparation to replace one leader with another" (Mamprin, 2002). Underpinning these practices is the view that some jobs are the lifeblood of the organization and too critical to be left vacant or filled by any but the best, most knowledgeable, and most qualified persons. From this perspective, "Succession planning is critical to mission success and creates an effective process for recognizing, developing, and retaining top leadership talent" (U.S. Office of Personnel Management, 2005, p. 1).

In corporate sector organizations, where succession planning is most widely practiced, an essential goal is to identify and develop new leaders from within the organization to succeed current leaders (Cascio, 2011). Typically, this preparation occurs long before the departure of the incumbent leader. Developing a detailed profile and description of a position can be part of the leader's portfolio of responsibilities, and in some instances incumbent leaders play a meaningful role in the review and selection of their successors. For example, as a part of the transition process, leaders might be asked to articulate a set of goals, describe general competencies required for the position, highlight pressing challenges and aspirations, and identify key markers that one would regard as critical for the next generation of leadership, given one's evaluation of the organization's current and future needs.

Succession Planning in Higher Education

College and university leaders typically engage governing boards, faculty, staff, and other stakeholders in systematic planning activities such as strategic planning (chapter 14), contingency/emergency planning (chapter 17), and planning for organizational change (chapter 15). Despite familiarity with and reliance on planning processes in these contexts, most colleges and universities do not engage in comprehensive leadership succession planning (Calareso, 2013).

In one of the few systematic studies on the topic, Richards (2009) identified three possible approaches to leadership succession planning in higher education.[1] The first and least sophisticated approach is labeled "back of the envelope." In this approach, an institution does not really plan for leadership succession but instead addresses immediate needs as they arise. The second approach is known as replacement planning. Here, a college or university might have backup charts for a few positions with one-to-one or single replacements specified. For example, in case of death or prolonged disability, the campus provost assumes the presidency on an interim basis. Within the replacement planning model, succession plans typically focus on a 1- or

2-year time horizon. The third and most complex approach to campus-based leadership succession planning, talent management, is characterized by four components: (a) consideration of long-term and future planning, (b) focus on key leadership positions, (c) emphasis on building management bench strength, and (d) adoption of a competency-based approach (Richards, 2009). Based on the limited research and writing on the topic, it appears that very few colleges and universities have implemented a talent management approach to succession planning, especially for academic leadership roles. More typical is the ad hoc, back-of-the-envelope approach or consideration of leadership successions on a case-by-case or replacement-as-needed basis (Calareso, 2013; Richards, 2009).

Approaches to succession planning on the staff–administrative side of higher education are more likely to align with dimensions of the talent management approach as compared with academic succession planning. For example, the College and University Professional Association for Human Resources (CUPA-HR) offers resources for leadership development and leadership succession planning. The information provided draws heavily on best practices from the corporate sector.

A number of factors—some historical, some philosophical, and others operational—help to explain the current state of affairs in higher education. Perhaps the most fundamental explanation can be traced to the lack of systematic processes for institutional assessment and evaluation of current leaders. Such assessment systems provide the foundation for rational and effective succession planning. Without a larger process of institutional assessment that includes ongoing and systematic evaluation of leaders, colleges and universities are not well positioned to engage in meaningful leadership succession planning, and this shortcoming also limits the potential effectiveness of leadership development programming.

Leadership development programs, as discussed in the previous chapter, are important for succession planning. However, even in situations where robust internal leadership development programs are in place, institutions must commit to promoting those who successfully complete these programs when open positions become available rather than routinely favoring external hires. For many institutions, this approach is countercultural. A traditional belief in the value of new perspectives being brought into the academy, particularly for academic leadership, represents another important impediment to the adoption of corporate-style leadership succession planning within higher education. We consider some of the costs and benefits of adopting or not adopting leadership succession planning in the next section of this chapter.

Why Engage in Leadership Succession Planning?

Many leading organizations in the corporate sector believe that the best approach to leadership succession is one that is proactive, focused on the development of an internal talent pool, and the result of carefully managed and coordinated transitions. For organizations that embrace leadership succession planning, the underlying belief is that the costs of leadership training for current employees who exemplify and contribute positively to the corporate culture often yield greater benefits than hiring candidates from outside the organization. No matter how thorough a search process may be, organizations are likely to be less certain of the capabilities, competencies, and experiences of external candidates than of employees already in residence. Moreover, even if strong external candidates are selected, under the best of conditions these individuals still require a good deal of time to understand the new organization and its culture. Well-prepared internal candidates are predictably more knowledgeable about the organization's strengths, weaknesses, and unique challenges and opportunities. For these and other reasons, approaches to succession planning that include thoughtful identification and training of the next in line for key leadership posts within the organization have many benefits.

With succession planning and leadership preparation as its standard approach, the corporate sector can, when deemed appropriate, pivot to filling positions with candidates from outside the organization. This might occur when it is determined that a cultural shift is necessary or the knowledge and competencies required are not resident within the organization. Thus, an investment in leadership succession planning gives such organizations two options for leadership succession: building strength from within and shopping the marketplace as necessary.

Juxtaposed with a corporate mindset, the identification and training of internal candidates for next-in-line succession is atypical in higher education. As discussed earlier in this chapter, the default approach for filling leadership posts at the middle-top echelon levels is an external search that relies on the marketplace—often with the assistance of search firms. Of course, internal candidates are often permitted to apply when external searches are conducted. Mrig and Fusch (2014) reported that 30% of responding institutions filled more than half of their VP-level positions with internal candidates, who may or may not have benefitted from leadership development activities or been selected based on careful succession planning.

It is important to draw a distinction between selecting an internal candidate who is either based or not based on systematic approaches to succession planning. For some academic positions, such as department chair, the selection of internal candidates is commonplace and external searches typically are not conducted. The next department chair is usually found from within the tenured members of the departmental faculty, often following a turn-taking or "sorry, you drew the short straw this time" approach. Although an internal candidate has been selected, this type of selection does not meet the criteria for the talent management approach to succession planning discussed by Richards (2009). Indeed, without prior training, a new leader selected in this manner—with little planning or preparation—is not necessarily well positioned or well prepared to lead, even though that individual is an internal candidate who possesses knowledge of the department and institutional culture.

A similar circumstance exists on the staff–administrative side. For entry-level leadership positions, current staff employees who meet and exceed expectations may be promoted. Although position descriptions from human resources make it clear that the new leader has the responsibility and authority to manage others or set strategic priorities, there is often little prior assessment of the person's suitability to lead. For many, the learning curve is very steep, especially if institutional leadership development programs are absent or ineffective.

The guiding philosophy, particularly as it relates to senior academic hiring, is built on the assumption that a change in perspective is important to organizational vitality. Regarding academic leadership, the thinking holds that so-called organization inbreeding can undermine growth and advancement. While this may be the case in some instances, continuity can often be of great value, as discussed. In either circumstance, the goal should be to select a candidate whose competencies best match the needs and aspirations of the department, college, or institution.

In an ideal circumstance, where a talent management approach is integrated with leadership development, assessment, and preparation, the preparedness of potential internal candidates and the needs of the organization are assessed over months or even years. In addition to being more sensitive to individual and organizational needs and capabilities, this approach has the advantage of providing more time and opportunity for greater in-depth analyses and preparation than do processes typically used to evaluate external candidates. This approach also increases the likelihood that both horizontal and vertical competencies—competencies associated with particular positions and those generally more necessary for effective leadership regardless of the technical or disciplinary area involved—can be taken into account. The benefits of institutional continuity and leadership succession planning when embedded in sustained organizational advancement efforts is nicely illustrated in the reflections offered by David Ward in Box 19.1.

BOX 19.1

Succession Planning

David Ward, University of Wisconsin–Madison

Leadership transitions in any kind of enterprise present so many opportunities and challenges that the process lies outside normal concepts of planning. Nevertheless, transitions are critical, and the search process is usually designed to consolidate continuity of mission and vision or to ignite some transformational process. Often this choice is linked to preferences for an inside or outside candidate. In the academic world, it is fair to conclude that there is very little succession management but there are always high hopes of transformational change. Yet the tempo and duration of change require consistency of direction that outlasts the tenure of individual leaders.

For about 20 years the University of Wisconsin–Madison did experience a consistency of direction under the leadership of three different chancellors—Donna Shalala, myself, and John Wiley. We were, I believe, quite different in our leadership styles, and while Donna was clearly an outside appointment invested with a mandate for change, John and I were long-standing faculty members who had previously served as provost. There was certainly no explicit succession plan, and each of us aroused different kinds of loyalty and commitments from different segments of the university community and its constituencies.

I believe that the continuity was rooted in the success of the self-study of the regional accreditation process in the late 1980s. The success of that study must be attributed to Donna's predecessors and in particular their choice of key faculty and staff who emphasized deeply the problems that needed to be addressed. This document was refreshed 10 years later by a similar self-study process, and the challenge of leadership was not the legitimacy of the issues before us but their willingness to address them.

All three leaders chose from these issues and addressed them—there were both common, high-priority issues and other issues more specifically identified with each of these leaders. The entire process of continuity was amplified by the high level of trust that each leader placed in the senior financial officer, John Torphy, who was both a critical and creative partner in the implementation processes. This mutual trust was not confined to the senior leaders but was also the basis of broad and flexible levels of implementation by the cabinet, deans, directors, and other functional and cross-functional unit leaders.

If leadership is embedded in a broadly supported set of goals rooted in the traditions and expectations of the university and its constituencies, leadership style is less critical, and the merits of inside or outside appointments matter less. An agenda rooted in a representative process greatly diminished the inevitable conflicts based on prior loyalties and unfamiliar personal styles of successive leaders.

Succession planning certainly helps develop leadership skills within an institution, but without some kind of campus commitment to issues and goals, no amount of succession planning or assumptions about the transformational capacities will work.

Succession Planning in Higher Education: Key Considerations

A general model of leadership succession planning in higher education appears in Figures 19.1–19.4. There are several considerations for effective leadership succession planning in a higher education context. First and most important, as discussed by David Ward in Box 19.1, planning for leadership transitions can and should be nested within a larger, more comprehensive process of institutional assessment that, in turn, should include a systematic process for the evaluation of current leaders. Taken together, these activities can inform whether a change in leadership approach is needed, while also identifying the leadership competencies desired as regular terms expire and new leaders are recruited. As depicted in Figure 19.1, a key outcome of this first step is an organizational decision as to whether the future should be more heavily weighted in terms of organizational continuity or discontinuity.

Developing a strong bench of potential leaders is the second major component needed for effective succession planning, as illustrated in Figure 19.2. In parallel with systematic efforts to identify desired or needed leadership competencies, an institution can intentionally develop the leadership skills of those who work at the college or university by affording opportunities to participate in in-house leadership programs or by relying on programs external to the organization.

Leadership development programs should be carefully monitored and assessed, as they can be the fundamental component to succession. Numerous benefits are derived from sponsoring programs that occur over weeks, months, or even longer that specifically focus on developing both knowledge and skills, and more generally, a culture that values and supports leadership development. Ideally, such programming extends beyond a classroom setting, provides a number of ongoing engagement opportunities for future leaders, and includes an opportunity to plan and implement unit or institutional improvement projects or activities as a component of the

Figure 19.1. Starting point for leadership succession planning in higher education.

process (Ruben et al., 2018). These components are depicted in Figure 19.3. Systematic leadership development efforts for internal employees require a substantial investment of time and other resources. However, these efforts may well be more cost effective than those required to recruit external candidates who then go through an intensive process of meeting individuals and learning about the new organization, engaging in "listening tours," and learning about the culture and climate of the institution.

Assuming that current employees have participated in well-designed leadership development programs, the final component of succession planning is an institutional commitment or willingness to give serious consideration to internal candidates when leadership openings occur (see Figure 19.4). This step may be the most difficult to implement for a variety of reasons, as described in the next section. However, taken together, the steps depicted

Figure 19.2. Developing a strong bench for leadership succession

Figure 19.3. Two critical components of leadership development programs.

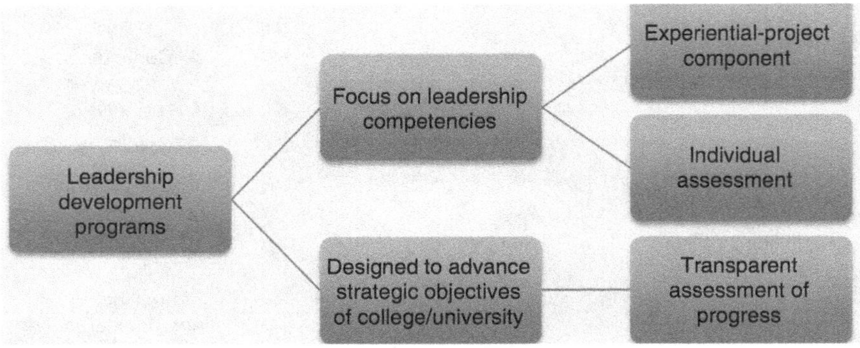

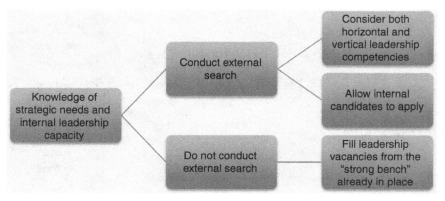

in Figures 19.1–19.4 represent a general model of leadership succession planning that can be implemented in higher education institutions.

Implementation Considerations

Given the diversity of institutions, a one-size-fits-all approach to succession planning is not realistic. There are several reasons why colleges and universities have limited succession plans that fall short of the talent management approaches used in the corporate sector. Historically, higher education has systematically underinvested in leadership development, instead relying on external searches to fill senior leadership posts carrying forth what is widely understood to be a long-standing cultural tradition (Mrig & Fusch, 2014).

Apart from cultural norms and traditions, many institutions are simply too small in size to have the capacity to develop a talent pool for internal

Figure 19.4. The final step in leadership succession planning: To search or not to search?

leadership succession. Succession planning requires an investment of human and financial resources. Colleges and universities may not have sufficient resources to conduct systematic competency identification and leadership training and development. Identification of future leaders and placement into leadership development programs can create internal friction and jealousy between those selected and those not selected. These circumstances can be challenging, especially within small departments; where they exist, more modest adaptations of the concepts of succession planning can be an option.

Finally, the academic culture and policies and procedures governing faculty promotions also render aspects of leadership succession planning for faculty members problematic. Faculty members might not want to invest their time and energy in leadership development, especially if advancement to a leadership position is not guaranteed, or if contributions in leadership roles are not appropriately valued, recognized, or rewarded. Such an investment during one's midcareer period, for example, might interfere with advancement to higher faculty ranks, particularly if training and one's contributions as an academic leader are not considered in promotion evaluation systems.

Many institutions offer academic leadership training programs for new chairs and even for new deans. In contrast, very few institutions offer leadership training programs for prospective chairs and prospective deans, with the exception of multicampus leadership development programs sponsored by the Big Ten Academic Alliance and other similar initiatives, discussed in chapter 18.

Factors Contributing to Effective Succession Planning

While there are many reasons for the pervasive lack of leadership succession planning in higher education, it is useful to consider the consequences of this general state of affairs and to reflect on what might be done to improve transitions to leadership in higher education. Best-practice approaches from other sectors can prove helpful as a guide for getting started. In the public sector, for example, succession planning has the best chance of being successful when

- senior leaders are involved and hold themselves accountable for developing new leaders,
- succession is linked to strategic planning and organizational assessment,
- needed leadership competencies are identified,

- a pool of talent is identified and developed with an eye toward future needs of the organization, and
- factors such as diversity, recruitment, and retention of leaders are considered (U.S. Office of Personnel Management, 2005).

There is every reason to expect that these same elements hold for leadership succession planning in higher education.

A Step-by-Step Approach to Leadership Succession Planning in Higher Education

Despite the diversity in types of institutions of higher education—especially in overall size and resource availability—we close this chapter by highlighting two steps that all institutions should take to move in the direction of leadership succession planning. We then present additional steps that, if adopted in full, provide the basis for a talent management approach to succession planning in higher education.

Leadership transitions need to be placed in the larger context of overall institutional assessment and accountability (Figure 19.1). Careful monitoring of progress toward institutional goals is part and parcel of the evaluation of current leaders. Such monitoring and ongoing assessment by supervisors of current leaders (including presidents and chancellors) should provide the foundation to determine the types of competencies that future leaders need. *Assessment of institutional progress is a critical and necessary component of leadership evaluation and leadership succession.* For example, if an institution judges that it is making good progress toward stated goals and is satisfied with its current trajectory, then a leadership transition might seek to maximize continuity and avoid disruption. On the other hand, if an institution judges that progress is severely lacking, then a leadership transition might seek to introduce discontinuity to disrupt and revise the current trajectory.

Whether leadership transitions are expected or unexpected, and whether external candidates or internal candidates are appointed, organizations have a greater chance of achieving successful outcomes when an ongoing process of institutional assessment, such as the excellence in higher education framework, discussed in chapter 13, is in place. Assessment can and should inform decisions about the need for radical changes or discontinuities in leadership versus relative stability or continuity in leadership. Either desired outcome—discontinuity or continuity—might result in an external or internal candidate assuming leadership of the unit, department, or institution. *The key is to connect institutional needs with leadership competencies.*

As described in chapter 9, leadership competencies have a vertical and a horizontal dimension. The vertical dimension—education and accomplishment in one's field—might be heavily weighted in the search and leadership transition process. If a school's top goal is increasing donations from individuals and foundations, prior success in development should be heavily weighted in screening candidates. Similarly, if a school wants to increase success with faculty applications for external research funding, then it makes sense to seek an accomplished researcher with a large grant portfolio. Note, however, that when needs for certain vertical competencies in the next leader have been identified, a possible next step is determining whether these capabilities might exist—or might be developed—in existing faculty and staff in anticipation of a vacancy.

To summarize, institutions need to preface searches by

- systematically assessing institutional needs and current leaders' performance and
- identifying future organizational directions and the leadership competencies needed to move forward.

The following list provides additional guidelines that will be important to success:

- Add leadership succession planning to the portfolio requirements of top leaders in the institution. A culture in which current leaders take responsibility for leadership succession, even their own replacements, ensures consideration of and conversations about leaders' roles in attainment of strategic organizational goals (Figure 19.2).
- Encourage and enable faculty and staff employees to enroll in leadership development programs to create a pool of internal candidates for future leadership positions. Building a strong bench is critical for leadership successions at an institution (Figure 19.3).
- Develop transition plans for key leadership positions that cover expected as well as unexpected vacancies. This step can include mandatory participation in either in-house or external leadership development programs for those who are newly appointed to leadership positions.
- Garner support and assistance from the necessary academic and institutional human resources departments to help manage the

process in which existing employees are identified as next in line for promotion (Figure 19.4).

- Establish a process to assess the outcomes derived from leadership succession planning.
- Modify plans within a continuous improvement framework.

Conclusion

Leadership succession planning entails a simultaneous and coordinated focus on developing human capital and organizational excellence, and as such, this form of planning can be a key tool for institutions striving for improvement and excellence. This result is more likely to occur when leadership succession planning is coordinated with vision setting, strategic planning, organizational assessment, and leadership development programming. Although leadership succession planning can be resource-intensive, over time the benefits to the organization should outweigh the costs needed for a successful program.

Adoption of the elements depicted in Figures 19.1–19.4 will move an institution of higher education in the direction of comprehensive, systematic, and intentional leadership succession planning. By adopting these leadership succession planning components, an institution is not obligated to promote a current employee who had completed training. The option to do so would be available, however, as would the option of searching externally. By taking a step-by-step approach, institutions of higher education can slowly expand into full-scale talent management approaches to leadership succession planning that reflect their particular needs, cultures, and traditions.

For Further Consideration

1. Approaches to leadership transitions
   Describe your department's or school's approach to leadership transitions.
   - Is the approach best described as ad hoc, one-to-one replacement, or talent management as described in this chapter?
   - Is your home unit's approach typical of the entire college or university?
   - Do your unit, college or university's policies documents designate a successor for the dean, president, or chancellor in cases of sudden death or disability? Do any other leadership positions have a successor designated by policy?

2. Leadership development programs

Consider the larger organization in which you operate.

- Does your institution offer leadership development programs, and if so, for whom: prospective leaders, newly appointed leaders, or both?
- Are these professional development programs linked to identified organizational needs, and do they focus on specific leadership competencies?
  Construct a 2 x 2 grid in which organizational needs and goals are columns and specific leadership competencies are rows. How many cells are filled, and how many are empty?

3. Leadership succession plan

Based on the previous set of questions, outline a leadership succession plan for your home institution, assuming one is not already in place. If a plan is in place, propose ways that it might be improved. Make sure your plan is realistic and takes into account your institution's culture.

Note

1. Richards adapted this framework from the Leadership Advantage Forum published by Personnel Decisions International.

20

INTO UNCHARTED WATERS

In This Chapter

- In what ways have the crises of recent years, including COVID-19 and racial unrest in the United States, added complexity to the work of leaders in higher education?
- How can an adaptation of the Excellence in Higher Education framework be used as a guide for renewal and reinvention?
- What role can visionary leaders and leadership play in transforming challenges into opportunities within their institutions?

The COVID-19 pandemic has ushered in a period of unprecedented disruption for higher education in the United States and internationally. Given the personal, economic, and health-system impacts of COVID-19, the consequences of the pandemic have been pervasive and game-changing, and may be permanently transformative for higher education. During this same period, we are confronted with painful reminders that racial, social, and economic cleavages pose their own persistent, intensified, and daunting challenges for the United States and many other countries throughout the world. These pervasive influences intersect and amplify one another in many ways, and they provide an immensely difficult backdrop for leaders across higher education.

It has been a time of uncertainty for leaders of departments, schools, and institutions of all types and sizes—a time when fundamental questions related to mission, values, plans, strategies, program and service offerings, and faculty and staff roles and responsibilities must all be considered (Buller, 2021; Cantwell & Taylor, 2020; Kelchen, 2020; Whitford, 2020). Will the missions of many of our institutions need to be reshaped? Will there be changes in the relationship among teaching, research, and service responsibilities? Will the programs and services typically associated with the residential campus need to be reinvented or perhaps even eliminated to accommodate new realities? Which administrative and support processes will be downsized, and

390

which will be ramped up? How will faculty and staff positions and responsibilities be affected, and how will these groups be engaged and supported in planning for short- and long-term change? How will budgets, resources, and the mechanisms for their allocation be adjusted to accommodate the changed environment?

How will racial, gender, and other issues related to representation, inclusion, and belonging be addressed within the ranks of faculty, staff, students, and leaders? And how will leaders be identified and developed who are equipped to foster transformative changes where they are needed?

More broadly, how will leaders guide the institution through a process of systematic review, reflection, and reinvention while fostering resilience and maintaining core values and a sense of community, and in what ways will the requisite decisions be made and communicated? And perhaps most important, how will our leaders and our institutions be better prepared for future challenges based on our responses in this extraordinary period in history?

These are among the questions we face as we complete our work on this second edition of the book, and these are the questions higher education faces as we all step into uncharted waters. Each of the previous chapters explore linkages to the current historical moment, and the concepts provided throughout the text can prove useful for leaders in navigating the many contemporary challenges facing higher education.

As we contemplate the current challenges facing colleges and university leaders, we have come to view the EHE framework (Ruben, 2016),[1] discussed extensively in chapter 13, as a particularly useful tool for leaders at this moment in time. The EHE framework, illustrated in Figure 20.1, was developed initially to guide assessment, planning, and continuous improvement in academic, professional, administrative, student life, or service units in "normal" times. With some revision, this model becomes extremely relevant for colleges and universities and constituent departments as they wrestle with key issues and formulate departmental and institutional plans to directly address the challenges ahead.

This concluding chapter presents a special adaptation of EHE—named *Excellence in Higher Education-Renewal* (EHE-R). EHE-R focuses specifically on issues that institutions and their constituent units confront as they engage in the necessary processes of review, reinvention, and renewal in addressing current challenges (Ruben, 2020a, 2020b, 2020c, 2021).

In the following pages, we summarize the elements of EHE-R which provide a helpful framework for collecting and cataloguing critical questions related to mission and vision, changing priorities, modifications in programs and services, adjustments in faculty and staff responsibilities, and processes for assessing and analyzing organizational functioning in the face

Figure 20.1. EHE: The framework and categories.

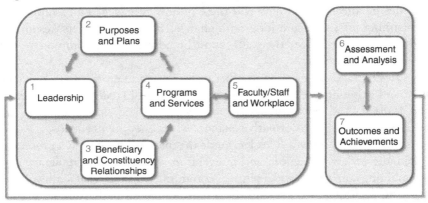

Source: Ruben (2016).

of a dramatically transformed environment. Perhaps most fundamentally, EHE-R helps to determine how leaders will guide and support the community through the process of review and reinvention. Also described are processes for using the framework at the institutional level, or within academic, professional, administrative, student life, support, and other units.

The EHE-R model, like the EHE framework from which it is adapted, is built on a foundation that recognizes the importance of each of the seven components of organizational effectiveness, adapted to focus on issues of relevance to organizational renewal:

- *leadership*—communicating core values and a forward-looking vision that underscores the importance of core purposes, aspirations, emerging strategic priorities, and the sense of community
- *purposes and plans*—creating a time-sensitive process for clarifying directions, aspirations, plans, strategies, goals, and action steps in a manner that engages faculty and staff in the planning efforts
- *beneficiary and constituency relationships*—listening to, understanding, and responding to the immediate and forward-looking needs of current and prospective students, parents, and other key constituencies and collaborators to sustain and ideally strengthen relationships going forward
- *programs and services*—reviewing mission-critical and support programs and services, considering whether particular functions should be expanded, contracted, restructured, or discontinued, and determining the criteria to be used in these determinations

- *faculty/staff and workplace*—recognizing and addressing faculty, staff, and community support needs, while also considering changes in roles, responsibilities, workplace practices, and workforce policies
- *assessment and analysis*—implementing processes and systems for assessment, analysis, and the effective and efficient sharing of information regarding current environmental conditions, progress and outcomes of organizational renewal efforts, and other issues of concern facing the institution
- *outcomes and achievements*—documenting and using information on outcomes and environmental, trend, and peer comparison insights to guide institutional renewal efforts, organizational alignment, forward planning, and day-to-day decision-making by leaders at all levels in all functional areas

This adaptation of the framework is meant to serve as a guide for organizational review, planning, and strategy formulation in situations where the needs may range from incremental and continuous improvement to extensive and transformative restructuring and reinvention.

EHE-R Categories

Following is a summary of each of the EHE-R categories and specific considerations for leading renewal and reinvention efforts in an academic context.

Category 1: Leadership

Category 1 examines the effectiveness of leadership approaches and governance systems in advancing the mission of an institution, department, or program; how leaders establish and communicate aspirations; how leaders set goals and promote innovation; how leaders allocate resources to accomplish common goals; and how leaders and leadership practices and performance are reviewed and evaluated. Even in the best of times, these are challenging issues, and they take on an even greater degree of importance in response to a broadly disruptive crisis.

As an institution moves into the early stages of renewal, it is incumbent on organizations and their leaders to address the critical relationships between leaders, faculty and staff, and other stakeholders, and to focus particular attention on issues of communication related to change and to consider the ways in which breakdowns in these areas can have extremely negative and lasting consequences that have the potential to undermine renewal efforts.

Category 2: Plans and Purposes

Clarifying and building consensus on an organization's purpose, aspirations, and goals, and developing and implementing plans based on the organization's mission, are central themes of category 2. This category also focuses on the importance of environmental scanning, benchmarking with other organizations, and aligning and coordinating plans and action steps throughout the organization. Also important in this category are considerations of how faculty and staff and other relevant stakeholders are engaged in defining aspirations and goals and in creating and implementing plans within the organization.

Adapting these general themes to a postcrisis environment is difficult but also very important. The biggest substantive issues here involve time and timing. Each unit/school/institution will need to determine the right time to undertake the planning process for the period ahead, how to prioritize the issues involved, and how to balance needs for expeditious forward movement with meaningful engagement. The guiding questions provided later in the chapter should be helpful in this regard.

Category 3: Beneficiary and Constituency Relationships

The focus of category 3 centers on stakeholders who benefit from, influence, or are influenced by the organization. Among the stakeholder groups considered—depending on the unit or school being considered—are faculty (full-time and contingent), current and prospective students, patients, future employers, alumni, members of relevant disciplinary or professional communities, governmental agencies, public and societal beneficiaries, internal institutional service units, and collaborators or suppliers in other academic or administrative units. The diverse array of relationships, all of which have particular expectations that are likely to have been disrupted in multiple ways during times of turbulence, makes this a complex and multifaceted topic during and following crises.

Category 4: Programs and Services

Establishing and maintaining mission-critical academic and administrative programs and services is the primary theme of category 4. The nature of the mission, programs, and services will vary substantially depending on whether the work of the unit involves academics, administration and support services, student services, facilities, athletics, or other functions. The category focuses on how an organization identifies, documents, evaluates, and regularly improves each mission-critical program and service, as well as how particular programs and services become priorities for refinement, restructuring, or discontinuation.

Higher education is much more accustomed to adding new programs and services than it is to downsizing, reimagining, reshaping, restructuring, or elimination, all of which may be options that merit consideration in post-crisis planning. In reviewing and prioritizing programs and services—and in decisions relative to changes—effectiveness, efficiency, expenses, and revenue generation are likely to be among the most critical criteria.

Category 5: Faculty/Staff and Workplace

The quality of the faculty and staff, and the nature of the organizational culture, climate, and workplace, are the topics of category 5. The category considers how the program, department, or institution recruits, supports, and retains faculty and staff; creates and maintains a positive workplace culture and climate; and recognizes and rewards accomplishments and superior performance. We know that traditional approaches to achieving these goals have often been less than perfect, particularly as they relate to colleagues of color, creating a situation where new and innovative approaches to diversity, equity, inclusion, belonging, and community enhancement are essential.

In a time of disruption, the usual focus on recruitment, orientation, recognition, and professional development of faculty and staff is likely to be accompanied, and perhaps replaced by, needs for technical, emotional, and financial support and issues related to possible reassignment, expanded or shifting roles and responsibilities, retraining and cross-training, and perhaps even temporary or more permanent layoffs. None of these options are easy or comfortable for anyone in the institution. What can be helpful in confronting this situation, in addition to effective faculty and staff communication and support mechanisms, is a systematic approach to thinking through questions of value and purpose, along with institutional, school, or unit priorities, and then implementing personnel changes with sensitivity, compassion, and appropriate transitional support.

Category 6: Assessment and Analysis

Category 6 focuses on the criteria, processes, systems, and internal communication channels through which assessment and analysis take place. The category emphasizes the methods and mechanisms through which an organization assesses, integrates, analyzes, and shares information regarding current environmental conditions, progress and outcomes regarding organizational continuity and renewal efforts, and other issues of concern. Also considered are the processes through which information on trends and information on peer and leading organizations is assembled, organized, and made accessible to leaders.

Information on progress and outcomes, environmental challenges and opportunities, and comparisons with peers is always central to strategy development and improvement activities; this resource becomes particularly critical in a period where expeditious and highly consequential decision-making is required of leaders. Data collection and access should be made as simple and automatic as possible, appropriately supported by technology, and to the extent possible, embedded in the normal workflow so that these activities do not require a major expenditure of additional time. If these processes work well, they provide accurate and timely sources of information and eliminate the need for the creation and use of shadow systems to complete scenario planning, assess progress on selected plans and goals, and contemplate decisions to postpone, expand, downsize, redesign, restructure, or discontinue specific programs or services.

Category 7: Outcomes and Achievements

The final category focuses on outcomes, with an emphasis on documenting and using outcomes information provided by the metrics, processes, and systems identified in category 6. The category calls for the use of information and evidence on environmental issues and trends and internal outcomes to highlight, communicate, and celebrate progress and achievements and to focus attention on areas where change is needed. Documented outcomes information is particularly essential for internal monitoring and external reporting and accountability, which are critical to continuing organizational improvement.

In times of reimagination and renewal, these functions take on added significance, providing the evidence needed for tracking, communicating, and recognizing accomplishments, and identifying gaps relative to internal mission(s), aspirations, continuity and renewal efforts, and other important functions throughout the organization. Of ultimate importance in this context is a focus on how evidence related to progress and outcomes is used for evaluating progress and establishing and guiding forward-directed plans and goals.

EHE-R: Applying EHE to Crisis Response, Reimagination, and Renewal

Many important questions may be posed in each of the seven categories of EHE-R (Ruben, 2021a; 2021b; 2021c). In the sections that follow, these questions are organized by category. The framework is designed to be applicable to any unit within a college or university or to an institution as a whole.

Each unit, school, or the leadership of the institution may prioritize and sequence these questions in a manner that makes sense for the challenges and timing at hand. The questions are intended for use by various constituency groups (e.g., college or school led by a dean; administrative unit such as student affairs led by a vice president; president's cabinet, etc.), as described in chapter 13.

1. Leadership
   - What is the future that leaders envision for the unit/school/institution in this new environment, and what are the guiding principles and values necessary to achieve this vision?
   - What preexisting leadership roles or structures need to be reimagined and refined? How will emergent leadership roles and decision-making protocols be coordinated with existing organizational structures, and how will communication infrastructures support both?
   - How will communication within the leadership team and throughout the unit/school/institution be effectively coordinated?
   - What are the most critical leadership goals now and going forward?
   - How will the values of diversity, equity, inclusion, and belonging be preserved and nurtured?
   - How can leaders sustain and strengthen the sense of community within the unit/school/institution? What messages are most essential at this moment in time, and how should they be disseminated?
   - What settings can be created to allow ideas and policies to be candidly discussed and evaluated by leaders at various administrative levels?
   - How can leaders make the best use of available information and interaction- and decision-support systems to strengthen strategic planning and implementation throughout the institution and its constituent units?
   - How can leaders ensure that decision-making protocols and processes instituted to increase expediency and predictability in such areas as health, finance, and personnel will not inadvertently undermine effective organizational functioning and employee morale and performance?
   - What leadership development needs and priorities exist, and how can these be addressed?
2. Purposes and plans
   - What will be the timing and process through which a vision for the future, shared priorities, plans, and goals for the unit/school/institution are formulated?

- How will organizational structures, personnel, and processes be involved in guiding the planning process?
- What current strengths, weaknesses, opportunities, and threats are important considerations in the planning processes, and what information is available to provide clarity in each area?
- How will consultation and creative problem-solving be enhanced to inform the new vision?
- How will faculty, staff, students, and other groups' perspectives be represented in planning? How will meetings be structured to benefit from the collective intelligence of the community?
- How will plans across the unit/school/institution be communicated, coordinated, and aligned, and how will common and cross-cutting priorities be determined?
- How will the institution or department consider contingencies related to resources, timing, and other uncertainties?
- What procedures, structures, and processes may hinder the planning process and plans, and how can these impediments be addressed?
- How can lessons learned from the present situation be captured for use in future planning?
- What chronic problems have plagued the unit/school/institution, and is there now an urgency and opportunity to address and resolve these ongoing issues?
- What opportunities for innovation and improvement have been created? What new or expanded program or service needs or opportunities have the crisis made apparent?
- How will difficult decisions about downsizing or eliminating certain programs and activities be made? How will the news of these decisions be shared?

3. Beneficiary and constituency relationships
   - How will students be served postcrisis? For example, consider how units/schools/the institution will address issues related to finances and health, campus residence, dining services, campus life, campus transportation, direct interaction with faculty, research engagement, advising, psychological and career counseling, sense of community, and others.
   - What other groups and organizations are traditionally served by the unit/school/institution? What specific benefits are being provided for each, and how will these needs be taken into account going forward?

- What programs, offices, and services should be available to provide academic, emotional, financial, and social support for students and other constituency groups? How will these programs and services be coordinated, and how will their availability be communicated?
- What groups are critical collaborators, partners, and suppliers for the unit/school/institution, and how will their expectations and future-oriented needs be assessed and addressed?
- What communication approaches will be needed to sustain relationships with each beneficiary and constituency group?
- What are the essential approaches for gathering, organizing, and disseminating information regarding the needs, concerns, and forward-looking expectations of faculty, staff, students, and other constituencies to guide planning and day-to-day decision-making?
- What important unit/school/institutional functions are realized through engagements with various constituency groups (e.g., collaborative research and community engagement), and how can these mutual benefits be preserved?
- Are there new constituencies that should become a focus of attention due to the impact of the crisis?
- How can units/schools/the institution serve as a critical partner in society-wide renewal efforts?

4. Programs and services
   - How will mission-critical, administrative, and support programs and services be systematically reviewed, inventoried, and prioritized, and what changes will be needed in these offerings going forward?
   - What criteria—and weightings of these criteria—should be used in reviewing and considering program/service prioritization and possible changes? For example, consider criteria such as mission centrality, alignment with aspirations, importance to stakeholders, distinctiveness, safety, resources required, revenue generation possibilities, redundancy, importance to faculty and staff, and reputational contribution.
   - What programs, services, or centers are candidates for initiation, improvement, expansion, downsizing, restructuring, or discontinuation?
   - How can virtual and other technologies be used to support and enhance various mission-critical functions and important administrative and support functions going forward?
   - What innovations are possible in mission-critical, administrative, and support processes? If these innovations are supporting a new vision

400 APPLIED TOOLS FOR LEADERSHIP

for the unit/school/institution, how can the new vision advance programs, services, and systems that are efficient, free of waste, and do not duplicate other functions? For example, consider adding more online teaching/learning technology and support systems, streamlining processes, expanding collaborations, eliminating duplication, sharing services, utilizing space and structures more efficiently, minimizing travel, enhancing safety, and expanding telecommuting and telemedicine options.

- What programs, services, and functions overlap with others, and what opportunities exist for closer coordination or integration?
- What opportunities exist for optimizing the relationship between centralization and decentralization in administrative areas based on current and anticipated circumstances? For example, consider finance, human resources, information technology, research support, facilities, transportation, sponsored research, external communication, safety measures, legal considerations, and changes that might become options due to current and anticipated circumstances.
- What opportunities for innovations in instruction, research, and community engagement are now made possible by the disruption of larger lectures and in-person proctored exams and current research and community outreach practices?

5. Faculty, staff, and workplace
   - How will faculty and staff uncertainties and morale issues related to health, safety, security of employment, transportation, and possible personnel changes be addressed?
   - What values and principles should be the focus of communication and engagement efforts with faculty and staff in the present situation and going forward?
   - How will enduring issues related to challenges in representation, equity, inclusion, and sense of community be effectively addressed?
   - What is the distribution of faculty and staff work roles and responsibilities, and what opportunities/necessities exist for recalibration, reallocation, temporary or longer term reassignment, cross-training, and professional development to address needed changes in workload and workplace priorities? How will right-sizing or downsizing be handled? How will institutional commitments to diversity, equity, and inclusion be taken into account in decisions relative to temporary or permanent workforce reductions?
   - What services will be needed to support faculty and staff in times of transition, reinvention, and renewal?

- What innovations in faculty and staff work practices might be considered? For example, consider technological innovations to facilitate virtual work, flex time and cross-training options, shift work, administration–union collaboration, and new approaches to allow for the balance of personal, family, and professional responsibilities.
- How can issues regarding faculty and staff morale related to the crisis in general and within the program/school/institution be best addressed?
- What communication approaches will be needed for two-way communication with faculty and staff, and how will these communication efforts be planned and coordinated?

6. Assessment and analysis
   - What information will be needed to monitor current environmental conditions, progress and outcomes of organizational renewal efforts, and other environmental issues of concern facing the institution?
   - Is there consensus on priority areas to be monitored?
   - Are metrics and methods for assessment and analysis agreed on and widely understood?
   - What processes and systems are available to assess, integrate, analyze, and share current information with decision-makers throughout the organization?
   - What information should be shared, when, how often, and with what audiences?
   - What relevant information is currently available, and what additional information and technological support are needed from internal and external sources to assist with assessment, analysis, dissemination of progress and outcomes information now and going forward? For example, will dashboard displays be created for easy access to data? Will improvement opportunities identified through assessment be documented and shared? Will a unit/school/institution case study narrative be developed?
   - How will information on strategies, innovations, and accomplishments of peer or leading institutions be gathered, analyzed, and shared?
   - How will information relative to progress, process improvement projects, and broader goals be communicated and used within the units, schools, and institution? What individuals, teams, or offices will coordinate these activities?
   - How can reimagination and renewal processes and activities become a focus for organizational research and the collection and sharing of best-practices information?

7. Outcomes and accomplishments
   - How is progress and outcome information being used for internal and external reporting and accountability?
   - How is information on environmental conditions, challenges, and opportunities being used?
   - How has progress and outcomes information been used to enhance leaders' forward planning, organizational alignment, and day-to-day decision-making?
   - What significant organizational achievements, innovations, and improvements have been realized?
   - What priorities for change have been identified based on reviews of information progress and outcomes to date?
   - How is information from peers and leaders being used?
   - What opportunities can be identified for institutional and scholarly research and cross-institutional sharing of outcomes assessment information and best practices?

Conclusion

For any organizational assessment, planning, or improvement program, an important question is whether the initiative has the intended value and impact, especially during disruptive periods when time and other resources are stretched thin. Experience and evidence suggest that the EHE-R 3.0 framework is useful in assessment, planning, and improvement within an institution, school, or unit of any type or size, drawing on accepted principles of organizational and performance excellence (Ruben et. al., in press). The modified EHE framework presented in this chapter adapts the basic EHE framework (2016a) to provide a guide for review, planning, and renewal in the postcrisis environment in which higher education now finds itself. The goal is for the EHE-R model to help leaders, faculty, and staff work together to create a viable and empowering road map to address the challenges of a very uncertain future.

We view the convergence of crises facing higher education not only as a historic challenge, but also a historic opportunity—an opportunity for ethical, effective, and values-based transformative leadership. Realizing opportunities is not a natural or automatic outcome. It requires visionary leadership and a strategic framework for review, strategy formulation, planning, innovation, and change.

The core values of higher education remain critical, and as leaders navigate these challenging circumstances, it is our hope that the EHE-R framework and the questions raised in this chapter and throughout this book will prove useful as we step deeper into uncharted waters. Faced with the uncertainty, ambiguity, and anxiety present in this moment, we are convinced that leadership matters now more than ever.

For Further Consideration

1. As you consider the impact of recent challenges on your unit, department, or institution, which of the categories discussed in this chapter requires the most urgent attention? In what ways might you use the questions provided in this chapter as a guide for addressing contemporary challenges and opportunities?
2. How might you draw on the EHE-R framework as you pursue renewal and reinvention efforts at the unit, department, or institutional level?
3. What challenges do you expect to encounter when leading renewal and reinvention, and how might the concepts and strategies discussed throughout this book be helpful in responding with intentionality and purpose?

Note

1. The EHE-R 3.0 (Ruben, 2021) framework and guide questions presented here represent an updated version from earlier publications (Ruben, 2020a, 2020b, 2020c). The author is particularly grateful for the insights and contributions of many individuals to the evolution of this model, including Joe Barone, Maury Cotter, Richard De Lisi, Phil Furmanski, Ralph Gigliotti, Rob Heffernan, Susan Lawrence, Laura Lawson, Barbara Lee, Gwen Mahon, Karen Novick, Bishr Omary, Jonathan Potter, Dave Raney, Lori Bush Shepard, Brian Strom, Al Tallia, and John Voloudakis.

A Snapshot View of the American Higher Education Sector

Institution, Students, and Distance Education (2016–2018)

This appendix provides a descriptive overview of the contemporary realities of the American higher education landscape, focusing on institutions, student demographics, acceptance, retention, and graduation rates, and enrollment in distance education courses and programs, drawing on recent statistics available from the U.S. Department of Education's National Center for Educational Statistics (McFarland et al., 2018). It is worth noting that this agency defines a higher education degree-granting institution as one that grants associate or higher degrees and that participates in Title IV federal financial aid programs.

Students and Enrollment Patterns

More than 19 million students were enrolled in higher education in fall 2016. At the undergraduate level, approximately 62% of students were enrolled on a full-time basis. At the graduate level, 57% of students were enrolled full-time. The vast majority of students are taught via traditional methods, but approximately one third of all students had taken at least one distance education course, and, at the graduate level, more than 25% of students were

TABLE A.1
Student Enrollment in Higher Education, Including Distance Education, Fall 2016

	Undergraduate	Postbaccalaureate
Full-time students	10.4 million	1.7 million
Part-time students	6.4 million	1.3 million
Percentage enrolled in any distance education course	31%	37%
Percentage enrolled exclusively in distance education	13%	28%

Note: Student data are for all types of IHEs combined.

TABLE A.2
Racial-Ethnicity Makeup of Higher Education Students, Fall 2016

	Undergraduate (%)	*Graduate (%)*
• White	54	53
• Black	13	12
• Hispanic	19	9
• Asian	7	7
• Two or more races	4	2
• Nonresident aliens	3	14
• Pacific Islander	< 1	< 1
• American Indian/Alaska Native	< 1	< 1

participating in fully online programs (see Table A.1). These numbers precede the rapid shift to remote instruction made necessary by the coronavirus pandemic, during which nearly all enrolled students were exposed to some degree of remote learning.

Racial-ethnicity compositions for undergraduate and graduate students are reported in Table A.2. White students represent slightly more than half of the overall enrollments at both the undergraduate and graduate levels.

Student Enrollment Patterns
In 2016, approximately 70% of high school graduates enrolled in higher education by the fall term following their graduation. This represents an enrollment of approximately 2.2 million undergraduate students, with female student enrollment rates about 5% higher than for male students. Approximately 46% of high school graduates enrolled in a 4-year institution; about 24% enrolled in a 2-year institution. These immediate enrollment rates did not vary appreciably from those in 2010. Although *higher education has a robust foundation of traditionally aged students at point of entry, this base shrinks over successive semesters/terms for the sector as a whole* because of retention and graduation rates. In fall 2016, degree-granting 4-year institutions had a total enrollment of 13,751,000 students; 2-year institutions enrolled 6,100,000. Public institutions enrolled 73% of all students; private schools enrolled 27% of all students.

Types of Institutions of Higher Education

From the standpoint of institutional makeup, higher education in the United States is a highly differentiated sector that has evolved within the public and private spheres to meet the diverse academic and economic needs of undergraduate and graduate students. Public community colleges provide access to postsecondary education for those who cannot afford to attend a 4-year institution due to the financial and/or time commitments required, or due to below-average high school academic performance. Access and opportunity are core aspects of missions for public community colleges. Community colleges offer degrees that render graduates eligible for employment or for enrollment in 4-year institutions. Four-year institutions are differentiated in that some focus exclusively on undergraduate education while others provide graduate and graduate-professional programs, and these institutions also vary as to how research intensive they are. Four-year institutions vary in terms of their admissions selectivity.

Overall, IHEs vary by types of degrees/certificates offered, the number of years required for completion of degree/certificate requirements, type of control (public, private nonprofit, and private for-profit), and most recently, by whether instruction is exclusively via distance education using modern technologies. Tables A.3 and A.4 provide snapshots that capture various aspects of institutional diversity. It is important to note that according to the U.S. Department of Education, the numbers of degree-granting IHEs decreased 7.8%, from 4,726 in 2012–2013 to 4,360 in 2016–2017. *This reverses a trend apparent in the 2 preceding decades, and it will be important for leaders to monitor how many and which IHEs close and/or merge in the coming decade as the sector experiences and fully absorbs the aftermath of the COVID-19 pandemic.*

In 2016–2017, about 61% of degree-granting IHEs with 1st-year undergraduates were 4-year institutions. About 41% of IHEs were public, 36% were private nonprofit, and about 24% were private for-profit institutions. Private for-profit PK–12 and postsecondary education are each expected to grow worldwide in the coming years (Duncan, 2019).

TABLE A.3
**Number of Degree-Granting Institutions With
1st-Year Undergraduates, 2016–2017**

	Type of Institution			
	Public	*Private Nonprofit*	*Private for-profit*	*(Total)*
Four-year	698	1295	402	(2395)
Two-year	885	97	518	(1500)
(Total)	(1583)	(1392)	(920)	(3895)

TABLE A.4
Numbers of Various Types of 4-Year Institutions, Fall 2016

	Type of Institution		
	Public	*Private Nonprofit*	*Private For-Profit*
Research university—very high	81	34	0
Research university—high	74	30	0
Doctoral/research	38	54	17
Master's college or university	271	412	58
Baccalaureate	223	460	172
Special focus	50	590	267
(Total)	(737)	(1580)	(514)

Differentiation within 4-year institutions is reported in Table A.4. The majority of 4-year institutions focus on baccalaureate and/or master's students and do not offer doctoral programs. Only 26% of public schools and 7% of private nonprofit schools offer doctoral degree programs. Private for-profit institutions are most heavily focused on undergraduate or special-focus (programs in one field only) students. Private for-profit institutions were not represented among research-intensive universities in fall 2016, but 75 such institutions offered one or more advanced degrees at the master or doctoral level.

This overview of differentiation of institutions in the higher education sector would be incomplete without mentioning the ways in which colleges and universities cater to particular types of students. According to the available U.S. Department of Education statistics, in 2016, the United States had 51 public and 51 private nonprofit historically Black colleges and universities (HBCUs) whose mission is to educate Black Americans. In 2016, there were 415 colleges/universities classified as Hispanic-serving institutions (25% or more Hispanic student enrollment). Finally, in this same year there were 38 women's colleges and 35 tribal colleges designed for Native American students.

Admissions Policies

IHEs also differ in terms of their admissions policies or acceptance rates for 1st-year (undergraduate) students. For 2-year institutions, the vast majority have an open admissions policy: 98% of public institutions, 70% of private nonprofit institutions, and 85% of private for-profit institutions accept all applicants with high school diplomas (or equivalent). Table A.5 provides an overview of admissions policies for 4-year institutions. Almost three quarters of all private for-profit institutions have an open admissions policy, in contrast to 22% of public and 15% of private nonprofit schools. At the opposite end of the admissions/acceptance rate spectrum, only 11% of public, 20% of private nonprofit, and 3% of private for-profit institutions accept less than 50% of all applicants.

Looking at the admission policies of various types of IHEs, it seems clear that the opportunity for Americans to attend a postsecondary institution is robust for those who have attained a high school diploma or its equivalent. *Virtually all 2-year and the majority of 4-year schools stand ready to accept the majority of applicants. This is an important fact for leaders to keep in mind, but it must be put in the context of student learning outcomes, such as retention and graduation rates.*

Retention and Graduation Rates
Retention rates of 1st-year undergraduates into their 2nd year of study average around 81% for 4-year public and private nonprofit institutions; 56% at private for-profits; and 62% for all types of 2-year institutions. Within 4-year institutions, retention rates vary by acceptance rates. Across all types of 4-year institutions with an open-admissions policy, retention rates average 59%. This is similar to the 1st-year retention rates at 2-year institutions, the vast majority of which have open admissions policies. The relationship between selectivity and retention is made apparent by examining the higher end of selectivity within 4-year institutions. At a high level of selectivity— admission of 25% or less of all applicants—1-year retention rates average 95%. Institutional leaders can track retention rates of 1st-year students relative to admissions standards to determine the relative success of their school against the larger sector.

It has become standard in higher education to define graduation rates relative to 150% of years of study required for the degree (i.e., 6 years for 4-year programs and 3 years for 2-year programs). Across all types of institutions, graduation rates are higher at 4-year than 2-year schools, but this difference is due, for the most part, to rates at public institutions (see Table A.6).

Public community colleges have open admissions policies and graduate 24% of the students they accept. Within 4-year institutions, public and private nonprofit institutions graduate 59–66% of their accepted students; private for-profit schools graduate less than 30% of their accepted students. This difference is due, in part, to differences in selectivity at the time of admission, as 74% of private for-profit IHEs have open admissions policies,

TABLE A.5
Admissions Policies/Acceptance Rates for 4-Year Institutions
With 1st-Year Undergraduates, 2016–2017 (% of total)

	Type of Institution		
	Public	*Private Nonprofit*	*Private For-Profit*
Open Admissions	22	15	74
75% or more accepted	33	27	18
50–75% accepted	34	38	6
Less than 50% accepted	11	20	3

while 22% or fewer of nonprofit, 4-year schools have open admissions policies. Within 4-year institutions, graduation rates approximate a linear relationship with acceptance rates: For institutions with open admissions, 32% graduate; for those who admit 50–75% of applicants, 61% graduate; and for the most selective institutions who accept less than 25% of applicants, 88% graduate. In general, as admission selectivity increases, so do year-to-year retention rates as well as graduation rates.

Distance Education
Modern technology has allowed new forms of curricula to be fashioned by individual professors, national professional organizations, or private companies. E-textbooks, real-world data and materials available from the internet, and other educational tools, including comprehensive learning management systems that allow online discussions and track individual student/group participation rates, are now ubiquitous in modern higher education. Tables A.7 and A.8 report on enrollment in distance education for undergraduate and graduate students, respectively.

TABLE A.6
Graduation Rates for 2010 Cohort (4-year IHEs) and for
2013 Cohort (2-year IHEs) by Type of IHE, Fall 2016

	Type of Institution			
	All IHEs	*Public*	*Private Nonprofit*	*Private For-Profit*
Four-year schools	60%	59%	66%	28%
Two-year schools	30%	24%	60%	60%

Note: Table reports 6-year and 3-year graduation rates for 4-year and 2-year IHEs, respectively.

TABLE A.7

Percentages of Undergraduate Students at Degree-Granting Institutions Who Enrolled Exclusively in Distance Education Courses, Fall 2016

	Type of Institution		
	Public	*Private Nonprofit*	*Private For-Profit*
Two-year schools	12%	35%	5%
Four-year schools	7%	15%	65%

In general, public colleges/universities have undergraduate enrollments in fully online programs at lower rates than do private colleges/universities. Overall, however, participation rates are modest—ranging from 5 to 35% of students—with the exception of private for-profit, 4-year schools. Here, 65% of students are enrolled exclusively in distance education courses. Nonprofit 4-year schools had a small percentage (7–15%) of students enrolled in fully online programs. This difference between enrollment rates in nonprofit and for-profit schools holds when graduate students are considered, although the percentages of students enrolled in distance programs are more robust at the graduate level for all types of institutions (see Table A.8).

A total of 20–24% of postbaccalaureate students were enrolled exclusively in distance courses at nonprofit (public and private) institutions. These percentages stand in marked contrast to the 84% of graduate students enrolled exclusively in distance education at for-profit institutions. More than 67% of graduate students enrolled in nonprofit institutions did not take any courses in a fully online format in fall 2016.

It will be interesting and important to track the percentages of undergraduate and graduate students enrolled in distance education courses in the next decade. It has been predicted for some time now that IHEs will

TABLE A.8

Percentages of Postbaccalaureate Students Enrolled in Distance Education Courses, Fall 2016

	Type of Institution		
	Public	*Private Nonprofit*	*Private For-Profit*
No distance courses	69%	67%	12%
Any distance courses	31%	33%	88%
Exclusively distance courses	20%	24%	84%

shift the mode of instructional delivery from face-to-face to distance as a way to maintain or increase enrollments, and perhaps to lower costs as well. To date, the use of distance education exclusively has been largely confined to private for-profit institutions offering 4-year programs and postbaccalaureate programs of study. There remains considerable room for growth in distance education programs at public and private nonprofit colleges and universities at both the undergraduate and graduate levels—a trend that will likely accelerate in response to the social distancing measures put in place because of the outbreak of the novel coronavirus and greater familiarity with the tools of online learning forced by the sudden shift to remote education in March 2020. The data reported in Tables A.7 and A.8 indicate that many colleges and universities were ill-prepared to offer fully online coursework and programs as the pandemic led to shutdowns in March 2020.

REFERENCES

Agnew, B. D. (2019). A study of critical incidents in higher education. In R. A. Gigliotti (Ed.), *Competencies for effective leadership: A framework for assessment, education, and research* (pp. 89–111). Emerald.

Aiken, C., & Keller, S. (2009, April). The irrational side of change management. *McKinsey Quarterly, 2.* https://www.mckinsey.com/business-functions/organization/our-insights/the-irrational-side-of-change-management#

Alger, J. R. (2015, November 2). Public or private good? The role of public higher education in modern society [Paper presentation]. Rutgers University, New Brunswick, NJ.

Allison, M., & Kaye, J., (2005). *Strategic planning for nonprofit organizations: A practical guide for dynamic times.* Wiley.

American College of Healthcare Executives. (2015, Fall). The Baldrige journey: In pursuit of excellence. *Frontiers of Health Service Management, 32*(1). https://www.nist.gov/system/files/documents/baldrige/enter/ACHE-FrontiersThe-Baldrige-Journey.pdf

Arnett, R. C., McManus, & McKendree, A (2018). *Conflict between persons: The origins of leadership.* Kendall Hunt.

Associated Press. (2015, February 4). Walker backs off removing "Wisconsin idea" from UW mission. *The San Diego Union-Tribune.* https://www.sandiegouniontribune.com/sdut-walker-budget-would-remove-wisconsin-idea-from-uw-2015feb04-story.html

Association for Talent Development. (2018). *2018 state of the industry report.* https://www.td.org/press-release/new-atd-research-investment-in-talent-development-on-the-rise

Association of American Colleges and Universities. (2004). *Taking responsibility for the quality of the baccalaureate degree.* Author. https://www.worldcat.org/title/taking-responsibility-for-the-quality-of-the-baccalaureate-degree/oclc/55126366

Association of American Medical Colleges & Kirwan Institute. (2017). *Proceedings of the Diversity and Inclusion Innovation Forum: Unconscious bias in academic medicine.* https://kirwaninstitute.osu.edu/research/proceedings-diversity-and-inclusion-innovation-forum-unconscious-bias-academic-medicine

Ayyad, C., & Andersen, T. (2000). Long-term efficacy of dietary treatment of obesity: A systematic review of studies published between 1931 and 1999. *Obesity Reviews, 1*(2), 113–119.

Baldrige National Quality Program. (2015a). *Home page.* National Institute of Standards and Technology. www.nist.gov/baldrige/

Baldrige National Quality Program. (2015b). *The 2015 criteria for performance excellence in education*. National Institute of Standards and Technology. http:// www.nist.gov/baldrige/enter/education.cfm

Association of American Medical Colleges & Kirwan Institute. (2017). *Proceedings of the Diversity and Inclusion Innovation Forum: Unconscious bias in academic medicine*. https://kirwaninstitute.osu.edu/research/proceedings-diversity-and-inclusion-innovation-forum-unconscious-bias-academic-medicine

Baldrige National Quality Program. (2015c, February 11). *More evidence that Baldrige criteria help organizations perform better*. National Institute of Standards and Technology. www.nist.gov/baldrige/2015_evidence_criteria.cfm

Baldrige National Quality Program. (2015d). *Why Baldrige?* National Institute of Standards and Technology. www.nist.gov/baldrige/enter/index.cfm

Baldrige National Quality Program. (2021). *Baldrige excellence framework: Education*. Baldrige Performance Excellence Program.

Barge, J. K., & Fairhurst, G. (2008). Living leadership: A systemic constructionist approach. *Leadership Quarterly, 4*(3), 227–251. https://doi.org/10.1177/1742715008092360

Bass, B., & Avolio, B. J. (1994). *Improving organizational effectiveness through transformational leadership*. SAGE.

Baylor University. (n.d.). *About Baylor*. https://www.baylor.edu/about/

Becker, C., Bianchetto, M., & Goldstein, L. (2012). Budget models and process: Challenges facing institutions today [Paper presentation]. Annual meeting of the National Association of College and University Business Officers, Washington, DC.

Bender, B. (2002). Benchmarking as an administrative tool for institutional leaders. In B. Bender & J. Schuh (Eds.), *Using benchmarking to inform practice in higher education* (pp. 113–120). Jossey-Bass.

Benne, K. D., & Sheats, P. (1948). Functional roles of group members. *Journal of Social Issues, 4*(2), 41–49.

Bennett, N. (2015, July 22). Our leader left. Who is left to lead? *The Chronicle of Higher Education*. https://www.chronicle.com/article/Our-Leader-Left-Who-s-Left/231159/?cid=at&utm_source=at&utm_medium=en

Bennis, W. (2007). The challenges of leadership in the modern world: Introduction to the special issue. American Psychologist. 62(1), 2–5. https://doi.org/10.1037/0003-066X.62.1.2

Bennis, W., & Nanus, B. (1985). *Leaders: The strategies for taking charge*. Harper & Row.

Benoit, W. L. (1995). *Accounts, excuses, and apologies: A theory of image restoration*. State University of New York Press.

Benoit, W. L. (1997). Image repair discourse and crisis communication. *Public Relations Review, 23*(2), 177–186. https://doi.org/10.1016/S0363-8111(97)90023-0

Benoit, W. L., & Pang, A. (2008). Crisis communication and image repair discourse. In T. L. Hansen-Horn & B. D. Neff (Eds.), *Public relations: From theory to practice* (pp. 244–261). Pearson.

Benson, J. A. (1988). Crisis revisited: An analysis of strategies used by Tylenol in the second tampering episode. *Central States Speech Journal, 39*(1), 49–66.

Berdahl, R. (2006). *Comments on the second draft of the Report of the Commission on the Future of Higher Education.* American Association of Higher Education.

Bertalanffy, L. V. (1968). *General system theory: Foundations, development, applications.* George Braziller.

Biemiller, L. (2017, September 6). After all but closing, Sweet Briar will shift curriculum and pricing. *The Chronicle of Higher Education.* https://www.chronicle.com/article/after-all-but-closing-sweet-briar-will-shift-curriculum-and-pricing/

Big Ten Academic Alliance. (n.d.). *Home page.* https://www.btaa.org/

Birnbaum, R. (1988). *How colleges work: The cybernetics of academic organization and leadership.* Jossey-Bass.

Blake, R. R., & McCanse, A. A. (1991). *Leadership dilemmas: Grid solutions.* Gulf Publishing.

Blumenstyk, G. (2015, March 9). Culture of change. *The Chronicle of Higher Education.* https://www.chronicle.com/article/Culture-of-change-Successful/228169/?key=QD91dgVjYXNKZX41NT1AbztcPSFsMB8mZX4cOihxblFREA==

Bok, D. (2013). *Higher education in America.* Princeton University Press.

Bolea, A., & Atwater, L. (2015). *Applied leadership development: Nine elements of leadership mastery.* Routledge.

Bolman, L. G., & Gallos, J. V. (2011). *Reframing academic leadership.* Jossey-Bass.

Booker, L., Jr. (2014). Crisis management: Changing times for colleges. *Journal of College Admission, 222,* 16–23.

Bowen, W. G., & Tobin, E. M. (2015). *Locus of authority: The evolution of faculty roles in the governance of higher education.* Princeton University Press.

Brancato, C. K. (1995). *New corporate performance measures.* Conference Board.

Bratton, W. J. (1998). *Turnaround: How America's top cop reversed the crime epidemic.* Random House.

Bratton, W. J. (1999). Great expectations: How higher expectations for police departments can lead to a decrease in crime. In Robert H. Langworthy (Ed.), *Measuring what matters: Proceedings from the Policing Research Institute meetings* (pp. 11–26). National Institute of Justice.

Brescia, S. A., & Cuite, C. L. (2019). Understanding coping mechanisms: An investigation into the strategies students use to avoid, manage, or alleviate food insecurity. *Journal of College and Character, 20*(4), 310–326.

Brown, D. (2011, February 28). Inside the busy, stressful world of air traffic control. *The Atlantic.* www.theatlantic.com/technology/archive/2011/02/inside-the-busy-stressful-world-of-air-traffic-control/71776/

Brown, D. J. (2014). *The boys in the boat: Nine Americans and their epic quest for gold at the 1936 Berlin Olympics.* Penguin.

Bruni, F. (2013, April 20). Questioning the mission of college. *The New York Times,* p. SR3.

Bryson, J. M. (2011). *Strategic planning for public and nonprofit organizations* (4th ed.). Jossey-Bass.

Buller, J. L. (2012). *The essential department chair. A comprehensive desk reference* (2nd ed.). Jossey-Bass.

Buller, J. L. (2014). *Change leadership in higher education: A practical guide to academic transformation.* Jossey-Bass.

Buller, J. L. (2021). *Academic leadership in the new normal.* Atlas Leadership.

Burkhart, P. J., & Reuss, S. (1993). *Successful strategic planning: A guide for nonprofit agencies and organizations.* SAGE.

Calareso, J. P. (2013). Succession planning: The key to ensuring leadership. *Planning for Higher Education, 41*(3), 27–33. https://doi.org/10.1177/0892020619881044

Camera, L. (2019, September 12). *Where the 2020 candidates stand on free college and student debt.* U.S. News & World Report. https://www.usnews.com/elections/student-debt-free-college-2020

Cantwell, B., & Taylor, B. J. (2020, April 16). It's time for radical reorganization. Crises spur intense competition among colleges. There's a better way. *The Chronicle of Higher Education.* https://www.chronicle.com/article/It-s-Time-for-Radical/248530

Cascio, W. F. (2011). Leadership succession: How to avoid a crisis. *Ivey Business Journal, 75*(3), 6–8.

Center for Talent Innovation. (2013). *Innovation, diversity, and market growth.* https://coqual.org/wp-content/uploads/2020/09/31_innovationdiversityand-marketgrowth_keyfindings-1.pdf

Centers for Disease Control and Prevention. (2014). Current cigarette smoking among adults—United States, 2005–2013. *Morbidity and Mortality Weekly Report, 63*(47), 1108–1112. https://www.cdc.gov/tobacco/data_statistics/fact_sheets/adult_data/cig_smoking/index.htm

Chatterjee, A., & Hambrick, D. C. (2007). It's all about me: Narcissistic chief executive officers and their effects on company strategy and performance. *Administrative Science Quarterly, 52*(3), 351–386. https://doi.org/10.2189/asqu.52.3.351

Chemerinsky, E., & Gillman, H. (2017). *Free speech on campus.* Yale University Press.

Cherniss, C. (2010). Emotional intelligence: Toward clarification of a concept. *Industrial and Organizational Psychology, 3*(3), 110–126. https://doi.org/10.1111/j.1754-9434.2010.01231.x

Cherniss, C., & Roche, C. W. (2020). *Leading with feeling: Nine strategies of emotionally intelligent leadership.* Oxford University Press.

Chronicle of Higher Education. (2020). *Here's a list of colleges' plans for reopening in the fall.* https://www.chronicle.com/article/heres-a-list-of-colleges-plans-for-reopening-in-the-fall/

Cole, D., Orsuwan, M., & Ah Sam, A. (2007). Violence and hate crimes on campus against international students and students of color: Uncovering the mystique. In M. C. Terrell & J. Jackson (Eds.), *Creating and maintaining safe college campuses: A sourcebook for enhancing and evaluating safety programs* (pp. 34–57). Stylus.

Collins, J. (2001). *Good to great. Why some companies make the leap . . . and others don't.* Harper Business.

Collinson, D., Jones, O. S., & Grint, K. (2017). "No more heroes": Critical perspectives on leadership romanticism. *Organization Studie*s, *39*(11), 1625–1647. https://doi.org/10.1177/0170840617727784

Connaughton, S. L., Lawrence, F. L., & Ruben, B. D. (2003). Leadership development as a systematic and multidisciplinary enterprise. *Journal of Education for Business, 79*(1) 46–51. https://doi.org/10.1080/08832320309599087

Connaughton, S. L., & Ruben, B. D. (2005). Millennium Leadership Inc: A case study of computer and internet-based communication in a simulated organization. In P. Zemliansky & K. St. Amant (Eds.), *Internet-based workplace communications: Industry and academic perspectives* (pp. 40–67). Idea Group.

Coombs, W. T. (1995). Choosing the right words: The development of guidelines for the selection of the appropriate crisis response strategies. *Management Communication Quarterly, 8*, 447–476. https://doi.org/10.1177/0893318995008004003

Coombs, W. T. (2006). *Code red in the boardroom: Crisis management as organizational DNA*. Praeger.

Coombs, W. T. (2015). *Ongoing crisis communication: Planning, managing, and responding* (4th ed.). SAGE.

Costa, G. (1993). Evaluation of workload in air traffic controllers. *Ergonomics, 36*(9), 1111–1120. https://doi.org/10.1080/00140139308967982

Cottrill, K., Lopez, D. P., & Hoffman, C. (2014). How authentic leadership and inclusion benefit organizations. *Equality, Diversity, and Inclusion, 33*(3), 275–292. https://doi.org/10.1108/EDI-05-2012-0041

Covey, S. R. (2013). *The 7 habits of highly effective people: Powerful lessons in personal change*. Simon & Schuster.

Cowan, S. (2014). *The inevitable city: The resurgence of New Orleans and the future of urban America*. Palgrave Macmillan.

Curry, J. R., Laws, A. L., & Strauss, J. C. (2013). *Responsibility center management: A guide to balancing academic entrepreneurship with fiscal responsibility*. National Association of College and University Business Officers.

Dawson, J. (2016). Benefitting the lab with Baldrige. *Medical Lab Management, 5*(3). https://www.medlabmag.com/article/1276/April_2016/Benefiting_the_Lab_with_Baldrige/

Day, D. V. (2001). Leadership development: A review in context. *Leadership Quarterly, 11*(4), 581–613. https://doi.org/10.1016/S1048-9843(00)00061-8

Day, D. V., Zaccaro, S. J., & Halpin, S. M. (Eds.). (2004). *Leader development for transforming organizations: Growing leaders for tomorrow*. Erlbaum.

DePree, M. (1999). My mentors' leadership lessons. In F. Hasselbein & P. M. Cohen (Eds.), *Leader to leader* (pp. 15–24). Jossey-Bass.

Dewey, J. (1933). *How we think*. D. C. Heath.

Dodd, A. H. (2004). Accreditation as a catalyst for institutional effectiveness. In M. J. Dooris, J. M. Kelley, & J. F. Trainer (Eds.), *Successful strategic planning* (New Directions for Institutional Planning, no. 123, pp. 13–25). Jossey-Bass. https://files.eric.ed.gov/fulltext/ED500983.pdf

Donathen, E. A., & Hines, C. A. (1998). Growing our own future leaders: A case study in Texas leadership training. *A Leadership Journal: Women in Leadership—Sharing the Vision, 2*(2), 93–106. https://doi.org/10.1177/107179190200900207

Dooris, M. J., Kelley, J. M., & Trainer, J. F. (2004). Strategic planning in higher education. In M. J. Dooris, J. M. Kelley, & J. F. Trainer (Eds.), *Successful strategic planning* (New Directions for Institutional Planning, no. 123, pp. 5–11). Jossey-Bass. https://doi.org/10.1002/ir.115

Dowling, D. W. (2009, March 11). Seven tips for difficult conversations. *Harvard Business Review.* https://hbr.org/2009/03/7-tips-for-difficult-conversat

DuBrin, A. J. (2013). Conclusions about crisis leadership in organizations. In A. J. DuBrin (Ed.), *Handbook of research on crisis leadership in organizations* (pp. 333–340). Edward Elgar.

DuBrin, A. W. (2004). *Leadership.* Houghton Mifflin.

Duncan, E. (2019, April 13–19). A class apart [Special report]. *The Economist, 431*(9138), 3–4.

Duneiere, M. (2000). *Sidewalk.* Farrar, Straus and Giroux.

Dwyer, M. (2019). A study of president-board communication competencies. In R. A. Gigliotti, (Ed.), *Competencies for effective leadership: A framework for assessment, education, and research* (pp. 113–133). Emerald.

Eddy, P. L., & Kirby, E. (2020). *Leading for tomorrow: A primer for succeeding in higher education leadership.* Rutgers University Press.

Edmondson, A. C. (1999). Psychological safety and learning behavior in work teams. *Administrative Science Quarterly, 44*(2), 350–383. https://doi.org/10.2307/2666999

Edmondson, A. C. (2019). *The fearless organization.* Wiley.

Edmunds, E. F., & Boyer, R. K. (2015, July 19). How great colleges distinguish themselves. *The Chronicle of Higher Education.* www.chronicle.com/article/How-Great-Colleges-Distinguish/231623/?cid=at&utm_source=at&utm_medium=en

Eisenberg, E. M. (1984). Ambiguity as strategy in organizational communication. *Communication Monographs, 51*(3), 227–242.

Ellerby, J. M. (2009, July 21). Views from both sides now. *Inside Higher Education.* www.insidehighered.com/views/2009/07/21/ellerby

Epstein, D. (2019). *Range: Why generalists triumph in a specialized world.* Riverhead Books.

Fairhurst, G. T., & Putnam, L. (2004). Organizations as discursive constructions. *Communication Theory, 14*(1), 5–26.

Fairhurst, G. T., & Sarr, R. (1996). *The art of framing: Managing the language of leadership.* Jossey-Bass.

Farris, D. A. (2020). *Understanding university committees: How to manage and participate constructively in institutional governance.* Stylus.

Fearn-Banks, K. (2011). *Crisis communications* (4th ed.). Routledge.

Feiner, M. (2004). *The Feiner points of leadership. The 50 basic laws that will make people want to perform better for you.* Warner Business Books.

Fiedler, F. E. (1967). *A theory of leadership effectiveness.* McGraw-Hill.

Flynn, W. J., & Vredevoogd, J. (2010). The future of learning: 12 views on emerging trends in higher education. *Planning for Higher Education, 38*(2), 5–10.

Fordham University. (n.d.). *Fellowship in higher education leadership.* https://www .fordham.edu/info/21272/gsas_funding/7058/fellowship_in_higher_education_ leadership

Freeh Report. (2012). *Freeh report of the actions of Penn State University.* www.scribd .com/doc/99901850/Freeh-Report-of-the-Actions-of-Penn-State-University

Freeman, R. E. (1984). *Strategic management: A stakeholder approach.* Pitman.

Furst-Bowe J., & Bower, R. A. (2007) Application of the Baldrige model in higher education. *New directions for higher education, 137*(5), 5–14. https://doi .org/10.1002/he.242

Gallup. (2021). *CliftonStrengths.* https://www.gallup.com/cliftonstrengths/en/ 252137/home.aspx

Geertz, C. (1973). *The interpretation of cultures.* Basic Books.

Genshaft, J. (2014). It's not the crime, it's the cover-up (and the follow-up). In G. M. Bataille & D. I. Cordova (Eds.), *Managing the unthinkable: Crisis preparation and response for campus leaders* (pp. 7–17). Stylus.

George, B. (2003). *Authentic leadership: Rediscovering the secrets to creating lasting value.* Jossey-Bass.

Georgetown University School of Medicine. (n.d.). *Home page.* som.georgetown.edu

Gigliotti, R. A. (2016). Leader as performer; Leader as human: A post-crisis discursive construction of leadership. *Atlantic Journal of Communication, 24*(3), 185–200.

Gigliotti, R. A. (2017). An exploratory study of academic leadership education within the Association of American Universities. *Journal of Applied Research in Higher Education, 9*(2), 196–210.

Gigliotti, R. A. (2019). *Crisis leadership in higher education: Theory and practice.* Rutgers University Press.

Gigliotti, R. A. (2020a). Sudden shifts to fully online: Perceptions of campus preparedness and implications for leading through disruption. *Journal of Literacy and Technology, 21*(2), 18–36.

Gigliotti, R. A. (2020b). The perception of crisis, the existence of crisis: Navigating the social construction of crisis. *Journal of Applied Communication Research, 48*(5), 558–576.

Gigliotti, R. A. (2021). The impact of COVID-19 on academic department chairs: Heightened complexity, accentuated liminality, and competing perceptions of reinvention. *Innovative Higher Education, 46,* 429–444. https://doi.org/10.1007/ s10755-021-09545-x

Gigliotti, R. A., Agnew, B. D., Goldthwaite, C., Sahay, S., Dwyer, M., & Ruben, B. D. (2016). Scholar-in-training; leader-in-training: The Rutgers University PreDoctoral Leadership Development Institute. In P. Blessinger & D. Stockley (Eds.), *Emerging directions in doctoral education: Innovations in higher education teaching and learning* (pp. 39–59). Emerald.

Gigliotti, R. A., & Dwyer, B. (2016). Cultivating dialogue: A central imperative for servant leadership. *Journal of Servant Leadership: Theory and Practice, 3*(1), 69–88.

Gigliotti, R. A., Dwyer, M., Brescia, S. A., Gergus, M., & Stefanelli, J. (2020). Learning leadership in higher education: Implications for graduate education. *Atlantic Journal of Communication, 28*(4), 209–223.

Gigliotti, R. A., & Goldthwaite, C. (2021). *Leadership in academic health centers: Core concepts and critical cases.* Kendall Hunt.

Gigliotti, R. A., & Qadri, M. J. (2017, September 12). Doctoral students as academic leaders. *Inside Higher Ed.* https://www.insidehighered.com/advice/2017/09/12/value-seeking-academic-leadership-skills-and-opportunities-graduate-student-essay?utm_source=Inside+Higher+Ed&utm_campaign=1961f45e62-DNU20170912&utm_medium=email&utm_term=0_1fcbc04421-1961f45e62-198628389&mc_cid=1961f45e62&mc_eid=3b9314975c

Gigliotti, R. A., & Ruben, B. D. (2015a). *Snapshots of academic and senior administrator leadership programs at Big Ten Institutions (BTAA)* (2nd ed.). Center for Organizational Development and Leadership/ Ten Academic Alliance.

Gigliotti, R. A., & Ruben, B. D. (2015b). *Academic leadership development matrix.* Center for Organizational Leadership, Rutgers University.

Gigliotti, R. A., & Ruben, B. D. (2017). Preparing higher education leaders: A conceptual, strategic, and operational approach. *Journal of Leadership Education, 16*(1), 96–114. https://doi.org/10.12806/V16/I1/T1

Gigliotti, R. A., & Ruben, B. D. (2018). *Snapshots of academic and senior leadership programs at Big Ten Academic Alliance (BTAA) universities* (4th ed.). Center for Organizational Leadership, Rutgers University. https://ol.rutgers.edu/wp-content/uploads/2020/06/snapshot-of-btaa-university-leadership-programs-2018-4th-ed-final.pdf

Gigliotti, R. A., & Ruben, B. D. (2019). A two-dimensional approach to preparing leaders. In R. A. Gigliotti (Ed.), *Competencies for effective leadership: A framework for assessment, education, and research* (pp. 29–38). Emerald.

Gigliotti, R. A., Ruben, B. D., Goldthwaite, C., & Strom, B. L. (2020). The collaborative design of a leadership education and development program for an academic health center: Implications for leadership education practice. *International Journal of Leadership in Education.* https://doi.org/10.1080/13603124.2020.1823487

Gigliotti, R. A., Ruben, B. D., & Wade, J. (2017). *Snapshots of academic and senior administrator leadership programs at big ten institutions (BTAA)* (3rd ed.). Center for Organizational Leadership/Big Ten Academic Alliance.

Gignac, G. (2010). On a nomenclature for emotional intelligence research. *Industrial and Organizational Psychology, 3*(2), 131–135. https://doi.org/10.1111/j.1754-9434.2010.01212.x

Gill, R. (2012). *Theory and practice of leadership* (2nd ed.). SAGE.

Gilley, J., Fulmer, K., & Reithlingshoefer, S. (1986). *Searching for academic excellence: Twenty colleges and universities on the move and their leaders.* Macmillan.

Gmelch, W. H., & Buller, J. L. (2015). *Building academic leadership capacity: A guide to best practices.* Jossey-Bass.

Gmelch, W. H., Hopkins, D., & Damico, S. (2011). *Seasons of a dean's life: Understanding the role and building leadership capacity.* Stylus.

Gmelch, W. H., & Miskin, V. D. (2004). *Chairing an academic department* (2nd ed.). Atwood.

Goffman, A. (2014). *On the run: Fugitive life in an American city*. University of Chicago Press.

Goleman, D. (1998). *Working with emotional intelligence*. Bantam.

Goleman, D. (2000). Leadership that gets results. *Harvard Business Review, 78*(2), 78–90.

Goleman, D. (2004, January). What makes a leader. *Harvard Business Review*. www .hbr.org/2004/01/what-makes-a-leader/ar/1

Gores, C. J. (2014). Courage, compassion, communication. In G. M. Bataille & D. I. Cordova (Eds.), *Managing the unthinkable: Crisis preparation and response for campus leaders* (pp. 147–156). Stylus.

Government Dashboards. (2015). *Home page.* https://www.idashboards.com/

Graen, G. B., & Uhl-Bien, M. (1995). Relationship-based approach to leadership: Development of leader-member exchange (LMX) theory of leadership over 25 years: Applying a multi-level multi-domain perspective. *The Leadership Quarterly, 6*(2), 219–247. https://digitalcommons.unl.edu/cgi/viewcontent.cgi?article=1059&context=managementfacpub

Grant, A. (2013). *Give and take: Why helping others drives our success*. Penguin.

Greenberg, M. (2014, September 5). You don't need a search firm to hire a president. *The Chronicle of Higher Education*. https://www.chronicle.com/article/you-dont-need-a-search-firm-to-hire-a-president/

Greenleaf, R. (1977). *Servant leadership*. Paulist Press.

Grint, K. (2001). *The arts of leadership*. Oxford University Press.

Guillén, L., & Ibarra, H. (2009). Seasons of a leader's development: Beyond a one-size fits all approach to designing interventions. *Academy of Management Proceedings, 1*, 1–6. https://doi.org/10.5465/ambpp.2009.44257934

Haberaecker, H. J. (2004). Strategic planning and budgeting to achieve core missions. In M. J. Dooris, J. M. Kelley, & J. F. Trainer (Eds.), *Successful strategic planning* (New Directions for Institutional Planning, no. 123, pp. 71–87). Jossey-Bass.

Healthcare Dashboards. (2015). *Home page.* https://www.idashboards.com/

Heaphy, M. S., & Gruska, G. F. (1995). *The Malcolm Baldrige National Quality Award: A yardstick for quality growth*. Addison-Wesley.

Heath, R. L., & O'Hair, H. D. (Eds.). (2009). *Handbook of risk and crisis communication*. Routledge.

Hecht, I. W. D., Higgerson, M. L., Gmelch, W. H., & Tucker, A. (1999). *The department chair as academic leader*. ACE Oryx Press.

Hernandez, M., Eberly, M. B., Avolio, B. J., & Johnson, M. D. (2011). The loci and mechanisms of leadership: Exploring a more comprehensive view of leadership theory. *Leadership Quarterly, 22*, 1165–1185. https://doi.org/10.1016/j.leaqua.2011.09.009

Hersey, P. (1984). *The situational leader*. Center for Leadership Studies.

Hersey, P., & Blanchard, K. H. (1969). Life-cycle theory of leadership. *Training and Development Journal, 23*, 26–34.

Ibarra, H. (2015). *The authenticity paradox: Why feeling like a fake can be a sign of growth.* Harvard Business Review Press.

Immordino, K. M., Gigliotti, R. A., Ruben, B. D., & Tromp, S. (2016). Evaluating the impact of strategic planning in higher education. *Educational Planning, 23*(1), 35–47. http://isep.info/wp-content/uploads/2016/04/23-1_4evaluatingimpact.pdf

Irvine, R. B., & Millar, D. P. (1998). *Crisis communication and management: How to gain and maintain control.* International Association of Business Communicators.

Jacob, R. (2004). An empirical assessment of the financial performance of Malcolm Baldrige award winners. *International Journal of Quality and Reliability Management, 21*(8), 897. https://doi.org/10.1108/02656710410551764

Jacob, R., Madu, C. N., & Tang, C. (2012). Financial performance of Baldrige award winners: A review and synthesis. *International Journal of Quality and Reliability Management, 29*(2), 233–240.

Jacobs, J. (1961). *The death and life of great American cities.* Random House.

Jaschik, S. (2015, January 20). Well-prepared in their own eyes. *Inside Higher Education.* www.insidehighered.com/news/2015/01/20/study-finds-big-gaps-between-student-and-employer-perceptions

Jasinski, J. (2004, December 9). Strategic planning via Baldrige: Lessons learned. In M. J. Dooris, J. M. Kelley, & J. F. Trainer (Eds.), *Successful strategic planning* (New Directions for Institutional Planning, no. 123, pp. 27–31). Jossey-Bass.

Jehn, K. A. (1997). A qualitative analysis of conflict types and dimensions in organizational groups. *Administrative Science Quarterly, 42*(3), 530–557.

Johnson, C. E., & Hackman, M. Z. (2018). *Leadership: A communication perspective* (7th ed.). Waveland.

Johnson & Johnson. (n.d.). *Our Credo values.* www.jnj.com/about-jnj/jnj-credo

June, A. W. (2010, December 10). Rutgers program helps Ph.D. students learn the ropes of academic leadership. *The Chronicle of Higher Education.* https://www.chronicle.com/article/rutgers-program-helps-ph-d-students-learn-the-ropes-of-academic-leadership/

Kalamazoo College. (n.d.). *Introduction and mission.* www.kzoo.edu/college

Kanter, R. M. (1983). *The change masters: Innovation and entrepreneurship in the American corporation.* Simon & Schuster.

Kaplan, R. S., & Norton, D. P. (1996). *The balanced scorecard.* Harvard Business School Press.

Kaplan, R. S., & Norton, D. P. (2001). *The strategy-focused organization.* Harvard Business School Press.

Kaplan, R. S., & Norton, D. P. (2004). *Strategy maps: Converting intangible assets into tangible outcomes.* Harvard Business School Press.

Kaplan, R. S., & Norton, D. P. (2006). *Alignment: Using the balanced scorecard to create corporate synergies.* Harvard Business School Press.

Katz, E., & Lazarsfeld, P. (1955). *Personal influence: The part played by people in the flow of mass communications.* The Free Press.

Katz, R. L. (1955). Skills of an effective administrator. *Harvard Business Review, 33*(1), 33–42.

Kegan, R. (1982). *The evolving self: Problem and process in human development.* Harvard University Press.

Kelchen, R. (2020, April 10). How will the pandemic change higher education? Professors, administrators, staff on what the coronavirus will leave in its wake. *The Chronicle of Higher Education.* https://www.chronicle.com/article/How-Will-the-Pandemic-Change/248474.

Kelderman, E. (2018, June 15). Sweet Briar College is placed on "warning" by accreditor. *The Chronicle of Higher Education.* https://www.chronicle.com/article/sweet-briar-college-is-placed-on-warning-by-accreditor/

Keller, G. (1983). *Academic strategy: The management revolution in American higher education.* Johns Hopkins University Press.

Kennedy, D. (1997). *Academic duty.* Harvard University Press.

Kerr, C. (2001). *The uses of the university.* Harvard University Press.

Keyton, J. (2011). *Communication and organizational culture: A key to understanding work experiences* (2nd ed.). SAGE.

Klann, G. (2003). *Crisis leadership: Using military lessons, organizational experiences, and the power of influence to lessen the impact of chaos on the people you lead.* CCL Press.

Kolowich, S. (2015, March 28). How Sweet Briar's board decided to close the college. *The Chronicle of Higher Education.* https://chronicle.com/article/How-Sweet--Board/228927

Kotter, J. P. (1996a). *Kotter's 8-step change model.* www.kotterinternational.com/the-8-step-process-for-leading-change/

Kotter, J. P. (1996b). *Leading change.* Harvard Business Press.

Kotter, J. P. (2012). Accelerate! *Harvard Business Review, 90*(11), 45–58. https://hbr.org/2012/11/accelerate

Krahenbuhl, G. S. (2004). *Building the academic deanship. Strategies for success.* American Council on Education.

Labaree, D. F. (1997). Public goods, private goods: The American struggle over educational goals. *American Educational Research Journal, 34*(1), 39–81. https://web.stanford.edu/~dlabaree/publications/Public_Goods_Private_Goods.pdf

Lawson, C. (2014). The power of leadership at a time of tragedy. In G. M. Bataille & D. I. Cordova (Eds.), *Managing the unthinkable: Crisis preparation and response for campus leaders* (pp. 37–46). Stylus.

Lederman, D. (2006, June 15). A stinging first draft. *Inside Higher Ed.* insidehighered.com/news/2006/06/27/commission

Lederman, D. (2007, March 21). Assessing the Spellings Commission. *Inside Higher Ed.* www.insidehighered.com/news/2007/03/21/commission

Lederman, D. (2019, March 8). The mood brightens: A survey of presidents. *Inside Higher Ed.* https://www.insidehighered.com/news/survey/2019-survey-college-and-university-presidents

Leist, J. C., Gilman, S. C., Cullen, R. J., & Sklar, J. (2004). Using Baldrige criteria to meet or exceed Accreditation Council for Continuing Medical Education standards. *The Journal of Continuing Education in the Health Professions, 24*, 57–63. http://doi.org/10.1002/chp.1340240109

Lerbinger, O. (1997). *The crisis manager: Facing risk and responsibility.* Erlbaum.

Lewin, K. (1952). Group decision and social change. In G. W. Swanson, T. M. Newcomb, & E. L. Hartley (Eds.), *Readings in social psychology* (pp. 459–473). Henry Heath & Co.

Lewin, K., Lippitt, R., & White, R. K. (1939). Patterns of aggressive behavior in experimentally created "social climates." *Journal of Social Psychology, 10,* 271–299. https://doi.org/10.1080/00224545.1939.9713366

Lewis, L. (2011). Organizational change: *Creating change through strategic communication.* Wiley.

Lewis, L. K. (2010). *Implementing change in organizations: A stakeholder communication perspective.* Wiley.

Li, T., & Yorke, J. A. (1975). Period three implies chaos. *American Mathematical Monthly, 82*(10), 985–992.

Liden, R. C., Wayne, S. J., Zhao, H., & Henderson, D. (2008). Servant leadership: Development of a multidimensional measure and multi-level assessment. *Leadership Quarterly, 19*(2), 161–177.

Lindell, M. K., Prater, C., & Perry, R. W. (2007). *Introduction to emergency management.* Wiley.

Lorenz, E. N. (1963). Deterministic nonperiodic flow. *Journal of Atmospheric Sciences, 20,* 130–148.

Loyola University. (n.d.). *About finance & administration.* http://finance.loyno.edu/about-finance-administration

Lucas, R., Goldman, E. F., Scott, A. R. & Dandar, V. (2018, February). Leadership development at academic health centers: Results of a national survey. *Academic Medicine, 93*(2), 229–236. https://doi.org/10.1097/ACM.0000000000001813

Luke, J. S. (1998). *Catalytic leadership.* Jossey-Bass.

Lukianoff, G., & Haidt, J. (2018). *The coddling of the American mind: How good intentions and bad ideas are setting up a generation for failure.* Penguin.

Luria, G., & Berson, Y. (2013). How do leadership motives affect informal and formal leadership emergence? *Journal of Organizational Behavior, 34*(7), 995–1015. https://doi.org/10.1002/job.1836

Luthans, F., & Avolio, B. J. (2003). Authentic leadership: A positive developmental approach. In K. S. Cameron, J. E. Dutton, & R. E. Quinn (Eds.), *Positive organizational scholarship* (pp. 241–261). Barrett-Koehler.

Machiavelli, N. (1532). *The prince.* www.constitution.org/mac/prince06.htm

Mamprin, A. (2002). *Five steps for successful succession planning.* https://leadersedge360.com/articles/Next%20in%20Line-5%20Steps%20for%20Successful%20Succession%20Planning.pdf.pdf

Mandelbaum, J. (2007). Managing the transition between chairs. *Effective Practices for Academic Leaders, 2*(8), 1–15.

Marcus, J. (2020, April 24). Transforming higher ed? *The New York Times.* https://www.nytimes.com/2020/04/23/education/learning/coronavirus-online-education-college.html

Marrelli, A., Tondora, J., & Hoge, M. (2005). Strategies for developing competency models. *Administration and Policy in Mental Health, 32*(5/6), 533–561.

Martin, J. (1992). *Cultures in organizations: Three perspectives.* Oxford University Press.

Maxwell, J. C. (1993). *Developing the leader within you.* Thomas Nelson.

Maxwell, J. C. (1995). *Developing the leaders around you.* Thomas Nelson.

Maxwell, J. C. (1999). *The 21 indispensable qualities of a leader.* Thomas Nelson.

Mayer, J. D., Salovey, P., & Caruso, D. R. (2000). Models of emotional intelligence. In R. J. Sternberg (Ed.), *Handbook of intelligence* (pp. 396–420). Cambridge University Press.

McCauley, C. D., Kanaga, K., & Lafferty, K. (2010). Leader development systems. In E. Van Velsor, C. D. McCauley, & M. N. Ruderman (Eds.), *Center for Creative Leadership handbook of leadership development* (pp. 29–61). Jossey-Bass.

McCauley, C. D., van Velsor, E., & Ruderman, M. N. (2010). Introduction: Our view of leadership development. In E. Van Velsor, C. D. McCauley, & M. N. Ruderman (Eds.), *Center for Creative Leadership handbook of leadership development* (pp. 1–26). Jossey-Bass.

McCombs, M. E., & Shaw, D. L. (1972). The agenda-setting function of mass media. *Public Opinion Quarterly, 36*(2), 176–187.

McCombs, M. E., Shaw, D. L., & Weaver, D. H. (2014). New directions in agenda-setting theory and research. *Mass Communication & Society, 17*(6), 781–802. https://doi.org/10.1080/15205436.2014.964871

McFarland, J., Hussar, B., Wang, X., Zhang, J., Wang, K., Rathbun, A., Barmer, A., Forrest Cataldi, E., & Bullock Mann, F. (2018). *The condition of education 2018* (NCES 2018144). https://nces.ed.gov/pubsearch/pubsinfo.asp?pubid=2018144

McGee, J. (2016). *Breakpoint: The changing marketplace for higher education.* Johns Hopkins University Press.

McGrath, J. E. (1962). *Leadership behavior: Some requirements for leadership training.* U.S. Civil Service Commission, Office of Career Development.

McIntire, M. E. (2015, October 20). Many colleges' new emergency plan: Try to account for every possibility. *The Chronicle of Higher Education.* www.chronicle.com/article/Many-Colleges-New-Emergency/233841/?key=UvQFoZhHCM9_6bonWiw3nxXlSiml_OgEstaSzwVmLiJSWmltSkI1cEN5NHBhUV80bFJoTy-1DRDJDNllzZk5yZXh1R2NpRzIyOS0w

McKenzie, L. (2020, June 8). Words matter for college presidents, but so will actions. *Inside Higher Ed.* https://www.insidehighered.com/news/2020/06/08/searching-meaningful-response-college-leaders-killing-george-floyd

McPherson, P. (2006, August 10). *NASULGC President Peter McPherson responds to the Commission on the Future of Higher Education Report.* National Association of State Universities and Land-Grant Colleges. https://www.historians.org/publications-and-directories/perspectives-on-history/october-2006/the-higher-education-commission-report-should-history-departments-be-concerned

Meyers, G. C., & Holusha, J. (1986). *Managing crisis: A positive approach*. Routledge.

Meza, A., Altman, E., Martinez, S., & Leung, C. (2019). "It's a feeling that one is not worth food": A qualitative study exploring the psychosocial experience and academic consequences of food insecurity among college students. *Journal of the Academy of Nutrition and Dietetics, 119*(10), 1713–1721. https://doi.org/10.1016/j.jand.2018.09.006

Michigan State University. (n.d.). *Office of Faculty & Organizational Development*. www.fod.msu.edu/

Middle States Commission on Higher Education. (2014). *Standards for accreditation and requirements of affiliation* (13th ed.). Author.

Middlebrooks, A., Allen, S. J., McNutt, M. S., & Morrison, J. L. (2020). *Discovering leadership: Designing your success*. SAGE.

Milikh, A. (2020, January 20). Preventing suicide by higher education. *CE Think Tank*. https://www.heritage.org/education/commentary/preventing-suicide-higher-education

Miller, C. (2006). *Issue paper 2: Accountability/consumer information*. Secretary of Education's Commission on the Future of Higher Education. www.ed.gov/about/bdscomm/list/hiedfuture/reports/miller.pdf

Mitroff, I. I. (1994). Crisis management and environmentalism: A natural fit. *California Management Review, 36*(2), 101–113. https://doi.org/10.2307/41165747

Mitroff, I. I. (2004). *Crisis leadership: Planning for the unthinkable*. Wiley.

Mitroff, I. I., Diamond, M. A., & Alpaslan, C. M. (2006). *How prepared are America's colleges and universities for major crises? Assessing the state of crisis management*. Society for College and University Planning. https://www.tandfonline.com/doi/abs/10.3200/CHNG.38.1.61-67

Mrig, A., & Fusch, D. (2014, February). *Innovative practices in higher-ed leadership development*. Academic Impressions. https://www.academicimpressions.com/PDF/LeadershipDevelopmentMD.pdf

Muffet-Willett, S. L. (2010). *Waiting for a crisis: Case studies of crisis leaders in higher education* [Unpublished doctoral dissertation. University of Akron].

Muffet-Willett, S. L., & Kruse, S. D. (2008). Crisis leadership: Past research and future directions. *Journal of Business Continuity & Emergency Planning, 3*(3), 248–258.

National Association of College and University Business Officers. (2011). *Challenge to change: A report of the NACUBO Baldrige Challenge 2010 Initiative*. https://www.researchgate.net/publication/267094810_Challenge_to_Change_A_Report_on_the_NACUBO_Baldrige_Challenge_2010_Initiative

National Association of College and University Business Officers. (2019, February 27). *Perceptions and priorities. Higher education dividends are strong but complex challenges lie ahead*. https://medium.com/nacubo/2019-perceptions-and-priorities-6d37a043af26

National Center for Education Statistics. (2018). *Postsecondary institutions and cost of attendance in 2017–18; degrees and other awards conferred, 2016–17; and 12-month enrollment, 2016–17*. https://nces.ed.gov/pubs2018/2018060rev.pdf

National Institutes of Standards and Technology. (2016, April 18). *Benefits of the Baldrige framework in U.S. health care: A summary of recent news.* https://www.nist.gov/news-events/news/2016/04/benefits-baldrige-framework-us-health-care-summary-recent-news

Nelson, M. D. (2014). Preparation, response, and recovery: The everydayness of crisis leadership. In G. M. Bataille & D. I. Cordova (Eds.), *Managing the unthinkable: Crisis preparation and response for campus leaders* (pp. 74–81). Stylus.

Neubert, M. J., & Taggar, S. (2004). Pathways to informal leadership: The moderating role of gender on the relationship of individual differences and team member network centrality to informal leadership emergence. *Leadership Quarterly, 15,* 175–194. https://doi.org/10.1016/j.leaqua.2004.02.006

Neustadt, R. (1960). *Presidential power and the modern presidents.* Wiley.

Nevin, J. (2020, April). *Student diversity measures.* Rutgers Center for Organizational Leadership.

North Central Association of Colleges and Universities, Higher Learning Commission. (2015). *The criteria for accreditation and core components.* www.ncahlc.org/Criteria-Eligibility-and-Candidacy/criteria-and-core-components.html

Northern Arizona University. (n.d.). *Mission & goals.* nau.edu/sbs/ssw/degrees-programs/mission-statement

Northouse, P. G. (2019). *Leadership: Theory and practice* (8th ed.). SAGE.

The Ohio State University. (2019). *Office of Human Resources, Difficult conversations: How to discuss what matters most. A high-level summary of the book by Stone, Patton and Heen.* https://gatewaytolearning.osu.edu/leadership-development/manage-your-employees/difficult-conversations/

Overton, A. R., & Lowry, A. C. (2013). Conflict management: Difficult conversations with difficult people. *Clinics in Colon and Rectal Surgery, 26*(4), 259–264. https://doi.org/10.1055/s-0033-1356728

Paris, K. (2004). Moving the strategic plan off the shelf and into action at the University of Wisconsin-Madison. In M. J. Dooris, J. M. Kelley, & J. F. Trainer (Eds.), *Successful strategic planning* (New Directions for Institutional Planning, no. 123, pp. 121–127). Jossey-Bass. https://eric.ed.gov/?id=EJ760566

Parker, E. T. (2015, December 3). *Hire a chief diversity officer, check!* Diverse Education. www.diverseeducation.com/article/79300/

Parks, S. D. (2005). *Leadership can be taught: A bold approach for a complex world.* Harvard Business Review Press.

Parrot, T. V. (2014). Working effectively with the media: Advice from the front line. In G. M. Bataille & D. I. Cordova (Eds.), *Managing the unthinkable: Crisis preparation and response for campus leaders* (pp. 170–180). Stylus.

Patterson, K., Grenny, J., McMillian, R., & Switzler, A. (2012). *Crucial conversations: Tools for talking when stakes are high.* McGraw-Hill.

Pauchant, T. C., & Mitroff, I. I. (1992). *Transforming the crisis-prone organization: Preventing individual, organizational, and environmental tragedies.* Jossey-Bass.

Payne-Sturges, D., Tjaden, A., Caldeira, K., Vincent, K., & Arria, A. (2017). Student hunger on campus: Food insecurity among college students and implications for academic institutions. *American Journal of Health Promotion, 32*(2), 349–354. https://doi.org/10.1177/0890117117719620

Perez, L. (2015, November 5–7). *Ethicak considerations in leadership.* [Paper presentation]. Committee for Institutional Cooperation Academic Leadership Program, University of Wisconsin–Madison, Madison, WI.

Peters, L., & O'Connor, E. (2001). Informal leadership support: An often overlooked competitive advantage. *Physician Executive, 27*(3), 35–39.

Pfeffer, J., & Sutton, R. I. (2000). *The knowledge-doing gap: How smart companies turn knowledge into action.* Harvard Business School Press.

Pfeiffer, J. W., Goodstein, L. D., & Nolan, T. M. (1986). *Applied strategic planning: A how to do it guide.* University Associates.

Pierce, S. R. (2011). *On being presidential. A guide for college and university leaders.* Jossey-Bass.

Platow, M. J., Haslam, S. A., Reicher, S. D., & Steffens, N. K. (2015). There is no leadership if no-one follows: Why leadership is necessarily a group process. *International Coaching Psychology Review, 10*(1), 20–37.

Porath, C. (2015, June 21). No time to be nice at work. *The New York Times.* https://www.nytimes.com/2015/06/21/opinion/sunday/is-your-boss-mean.html

Prince, H. (2001). Teaching leadership: A journey into the unknown. *Concepts and Connections: A Newsletter for Leadership Educators, 9*(3), 1–5.

Professionals in Higher Education Annual Report. (2020). College and University Professional Association for Human Resources. https://www.cupahr.org/surveys/professionals-in-higher-education/

Przasnyski, Z., & Tai, L. S. (2002). Stock performance of Malcolm Baldrige National Quality Award winning companies. *Total Quality Management, 13*(4), 475–488.

Quintana, C. (2018, July 24). Colleges are creating "a generation of sanctimonious, sensitive, supercilious snowflakes," Sessions says. *The Chronicle of Higher Education.* https://www.chronicle.com/article/colleges-are-creating-a-generation-of-sanctimonious-sensitive-supercilious-snowflakes-sessions-says/

Race Forward. (n.d.). *Race equity impact assessment toolkit.* https://www.raceforward.org/practice/tools/racial-equity-impact-assessment-toolkit

Regan, E. (2020). Food insecurity among college students. *Sociology Compass, 14*(6). https://doi.org/10.1111/soc4.12790

Richards, C. L. (2009). *A new paradigm: Strategies for succession planning in higher education.* [Unpublished doctoral dissertation, Capella University].

Ringer, J. (2019). *We have to talk: A step-by-step checklist for difficult conversations.* https://www.judyringer.com/resources/articles/we-have-to-talk-a-stepbystep-checklist-for-difficult-conversations.php

Roberts, S., & Rowley, J. (2004). *Managing information services.* Facet.

Rodas, D. (2020, April 4). *Leadership development: A view from executive search* [Paper presentation]. Rutgers Leadership Academy Presentation. New Brunswick, NJ.

Rost, J. C. (1993). *Leadership for the twenty-first century.* Praeger.

Rothman, S., Kelly-Woessner, A., & Woessner, M. (2010). *The still divided academy: How competing visions of power, politics, and diversity complicate the mission of higher education.* Rowman & Littlefield.

Rowley, D. J., & Sherman, H. (2001). Implementing the strategic plan. *Planning for Higher Education, 30*(4), 1–14.

Ruben, B. D. (1975). General systems theory: An approach to human communication. In R. W. Budd & B. D. Ruben (Eds.), *Approaches to human communication* (pp. 120–144). Hayden.

Ruben, B. D. (1976). Assessing communication competence for intercultural communication adaptation. *Group and Organization Studies, 1*(3), 1976, 334–354.

Ruben, B. D. (1977). Guidelines for cross-cultural communication effectiveness. *Group and Organization Studies, 2*(4), 470–479.

Ruben, B. D. (1978). Communication and conflict: A system-theoretic perspective. *Quarterly Journal of Speech, 64*, 202–210.

Ruben, B. D. (1989). Cross-cultural communication competence: Traditions and issues for the future. *International Journal of Intercultural Relations, 13*(3), 229–240.

Ruben, B. D. (1994). *Tradition of excellence: Higher education quality self-assessment guide.* Kendall Hunt.

Ruben, B. D. (1995). *Quality in higher education.* Transaction.

Ruben, B. D. (2001). We need excellence beyond the classroom. *The Chronicle of Higher Education, 47*(44), B15–16.

Ruben, B. D. (2004). *Pursuing excellence in higher education: Eight fundamental challenges.* Jossey-Bass.

Ruben, B. D. (2005). Linking communication scholarship and professional practice in colleges and universities. *Journal of Applied Communication Research, 33*(4), 294–304. https://doi.org/10.1080/00909880500278020

Ruben, B. D. (2006). *What leaders need to know and do: A leadership competencies scorecard.* National Association of College and University Business Officers.

Ruben, B. D. (2015). Intercultural communication competence in retrospect: Who would have guessed? *International Journal of Intercultural Relations, 48*, 22–23.

Ruben, B. D. (2016a). *Excellence in higher education: Workbook and scoring instructions* (8th ed.). Stylus.

Ruben, B. D. (2016b). *Excellence in higher education: A framework for the design, assessment, and continued improvement of institutions, departments, and programs* (8th ed.). Stylus.

Ruben, B. D. (2018a, September). *Leadership: Principles and pragmatics.* Academic Leadership Program-Big Ten Academic Alliance. https://www.btaa.org/leadership/alp/introduction

Ruben, B. D. (2018b, May 1). *The bumpy road to the promised land.* The Baldrige Foundation Outstanding National Leadership award in Education University lecture. Rutgers University. https://ol.rutgers.edu/wp-content/uploads/2020/06/baldrige-talk-text-official-reprint-final-05-17-18.pdf

Ruben, B. D. (2019). An overview of the leadership competency framework. In R. Gigliotti (Ed.), *Competencies for effective leadership: A framework for assessment, education and research* (pp. 19–28). Emerald.

Ruben, B. D. (2020a). *Guidance for college and university planning for a post COVID-19 world: Applying the Excellence in Higher Education Framework.* Stylus.

Ruben, B. D. (2020b). *Navigating through turbulent times: In search of a navigational system for this critical moment in the history of U.S. higher education.* Nuventive.

Ruben, B. D. (2020c). Contemporary challenges confronting colleges and universities: The Baldrige and Excellence in Higher Education approach to institutional renewal. *Chronicle of Leadership and Management, 1*(1), 13–35.

Ruben, B. D. (2021a) *Leadership competencies scorecard.* Rutgers Center for OL Leadership. https://ol.rutgers.edu/leadership-competencies-scorecard/

Ruben, B. D. (2021b) *Communication Style Inventory.* Rutgers Center for Organizational Leadership. https://ol.rutgers.edu/communication-style-inventory/ Rutgers Center for Organizational. https://ol.rutgers.edu/change-workbook/

Ruben, B. D. (2021c). *The excellence in higher education framework* (EHE-renewal, version 3.0). Rutgers Center for Organizational Leadership.

Ruben, B. D., Connaughton, S. L., Immordino, K., & Lopez, J. M. (2004). *What impact does the Baldrige/excellence in higher education self-assessment process have on institutional effectiveness?* [Paper presentation]. Annual Conference of the National Consortium for Continuous Improvement in Higher Education.

Ruben, B. D., De Lisi, R., & Gigliotti, R. A. (2017). *A guide for leaders in higher education: Core concepts, competencies, and tools.* Stylus.

Ruben, B. D., De Lisi, R., & Gigliotti, R. A. (2018). Academic leadership development programs: Conceptual foundations, structural and pedagogical components, and operational considerations. *The Journal of Leadership Education, 17*(3), 241–254. https://www.researchgate.net/publication/326709341_ Academic_Leadership_Development_Programs_Conceptual_Foundations_ Structural_and_Pedagogical_Components_and_Operational_Considerations

Ruben, B. D., & Fernandez, V. (2013). Growing your own: A proactive approach to leadership development. *The Higher Education Workplace* (pp. 37–40). https:// www.cupahr.org/issues/

Ruben, B. D., & Gigliotti, R. A. (2014). *Snapshots of academic and senior administrator leadership programs at Big Ten Institutions.* Center for Organizational Development and Leadership/Champaign: IL.

Ruben, B. D., & Gigliotti, R. A. (2016). Leadership as social influence: An expanded view of leadership communication theory and practice. *Journal of Leadership and Organizational Studies, 23*(4), 467–479. https://doi .org/10.1177/1548051816641876

Ruben, B. D., & Gigliotti, R. A. (2017). Are higher education institutions and their leadership needs unique? Vertical and horizontal perspectives. *Higher Education Review, 49*(3), 27–52.

Ruben, B. D., & Gigliotti, R. A. (2019a). The excellence in higher education model: A Baldrige-based tool for organizational assessment and improvement for colleges and universities. *Global Business and Organizational Excellence, 38*(4), 26–37.

Ruben, B. D., & Gigliotti, R. A. (2019b). *Leadership, communication, and social influence.* Emerald.

Ruben, B. D. & Goldthwaite, C. (2020). *Diagnosing your organization's culture.* Center for Organizational Leadership, Rutgers University. https://ol.rutgers.edu/research/guides-and-inventories/

Ruben, B. D., Goldthwaite, C., & Gigliotti R. (2021). Leadership and communication connections in academic health. In R. A. Gigliotti & C. Goldthwaite, *Leadership in academic health centers: Core concepts and critical cases* (pp. 59–76). Kendall Hunt.

Ruben, B. D., Goldthwaite, C., & Gigliotti, R. A. (2020). *Diagnosing your organization's culture.* Center for Organizational Leadership, Rutgers University.

Ruben, B. D., & Kealey, D. J. (1979). Behavioral assessment of communication competency and the prediction of cross-cultural adaptation. *International Journal of Intercultural Relations, 3*(1), 15–47.

Ruben, B. D., Lewis, L. K., Sandmeyer, L., Russ, T., Smulowitz, S., & Immordino, K. (2008). *Assessing the impact of the Spellings Commission: The message, the messenger, and the dynamics of change in higher education.* National Association of College and University Business Officers.

Ruben, B. D., Russ, T., Smulowitz, S. M., & Connaughton, S. L. (2007). Evaluating the impact of organizational self-assessment in higher education: The Malcolm Baldrige/Excellence in Higher Education Framework. *Leadership and Organizational Development Journal, 28*(3), 230–249.

Ruben, B. D., & Stewart, L. (2020). *Communication and human behavior* (7th ed.). Kendall Hunt.

Ruiz, R. R. (2011, October 13). Florida governor wants funds to go to practical degrees. *The New York Times.* thechoice.blogs.nytimes.com/2011/10/13/rick-scott/

Rutgers University. (n.d.). *Rutgers Center for Organizational Leadership.* https://ol.rutgers.edu/programs/plda/

Ruud, G. (2000). The symphony: Organizational discourse and the symbolic tensions between artistic and business ideologies. *Journal of Applied Communication Research, 28*(2), 117–143. https://doi.org/10.1080/00909880009365559

Sacharow, F. (2010, October). Preparing the next generation of academic leaders: New Rutgers institute trains pre-docs for transition from faculty to administration. *Rutgers Today.* https://ol.rutgers.edu/wp-content/uploads/2020/06/preparing-the-next-generation-of-academic-leaders.pdf

Salovey, P., & Mayer, J. D. (1990). Emotional intelligence. *Imagination, Cognition, and Personality, 9,* 185–211. https://ol.rutgers.edu/wp-content/uploads/2020/06/preparing-the-next-generation-of-academic-leaders.pdf

Sandmeyer, L. E., Dooris, M. J., & Barlock, R. W. (2004). Integrated planning for enrollment, facilities, budget, and staffing: Penn State University. In M. J. Dooris, J. M. Kelley, & J. F. Trainer (Eds.), *Successful strategic planning* (New Directions for Institutional Planning, no. 123, pp. 89–96). Jossey-Bass.

Scarborough, S. (2009). The case for decentralized financial management. *NACUBO Business Officer, 42*(10), 23–27.

Schein, E. H. (1999). *The corporate culture survival guide.* Jossey-Bass.

Schein, E. H. (2015). The concept of organizational culture: Why bother? In G. R. Hickman (Ed.), *Leading organizations: Perspectives for a new era* (3rd ed., pp. 280–291). SAGE.

Schneider, B. (Ed.). (1990). *Organizational climate and culture*. Jossey-Bass.

Schön, D. A. (1984). *The reflective practitioner: How professionals think in action.* Basic Books.

Schray, V. (2006). *Issue paper 14: Assuring quality in higher education.* Secretary of Education's Commission on the Future of Higher Education. https://www .ed.gov/about/bdscomm/list/hiedfuture/reports/schray2.pdf

Selingo, J. J. (2013). *College (un)bound: The future of higher education and what it means for students.* Houghton Mifflin.

Selingo, J. J. (2016). The decade ahead. The seismic shifts transforming the future of higher education. *The Chronicle of Higher Education.* https://store.chronicle.com/ products/2026-the-decade-ahead

Sendjaya, S., & Sarros, J. C. (2002). Servant leadership: Its origin, development, and application in organizations. *Journal of Leadership and Organization Studies, 9*(2), 47–64. https://doi.org/10.1177/107179190200900205

Sevier, R. A. (2000). *Strategic planning in higher education: Theory and practice.* Council for Advancement and Support of Higher Education.

Seymour, M., & Moore, S. (2000). *Effective crisis management: Worldwide principles and practice.* Cassel.

Shook, J., & Chenoweth, J. (2012). 100 top hospitals CEO insights: Adoption rates of select Baldrige Award practices and processes. *Truven Health Analytics.* https:// www.nist.gov/system/files/documents/baldrige/100-Top-Hosp-CEO-Insights-RB-final.pdf

Shrivastava, P. (1993). Crisis theory/practice: Towards a sustainable future. *Industrial & Environmental Crisis Quarterly, 7,* 23–42. https://doi .org/10.1177/108602669300700103

Silver, H. (2008). Does a university have a culture? *Studies in Higher Education, 28*(2), 157–169. https://doi.org/10.1080/0307507032000058118

Simons, H. W. (1974). The carrot and stick as handmaidens of persuasion in conflictful situations. In G. R. Miller & H. W. Simons (Eds.), *Perspectives on communication in social conflict* (pp. 177–178). Prentice-Hall.

Smircich, L., & Morgan, G. (1982). Leadership: The management of meaning. *The Journal of Applied Behavioral Science, 18,* 257–273. http://dx.doi.org/10.1177/002188638201800303

Smith, A. A. (2018, September 26). Free-college realities. *Inside Higher Ed.* https:// www.insidehighered.com/news/2018/09/26/free-college-proposals-shift-fit-state-needs-and-emulate-successful-examples

Smith, M. E. (2002). Success rates for different types of organizational change. *International Society for Performance Improvement, 41*(1), 26–33.

Smith, Z. (2007). *Creating and testing the higher education leadership competencies (HELC) model: A study of athletics directors, senior student affairs officers, and chief academic officers* [Unpublished doctoral dissertation, University of Nevada].

Snow, C. P. (2012). *The two cultures.* Cambridge University Press.

Sorensen, C. W., Furst-Bowe, J., & Moen, D. M. (2005). *Quality and performance excellence in higher education: Baldrige on campus.* Anker.

Southern Association of Colleges and Schools Commission on Colleges. (n.d.). *Home page.* https://sacscoc.org/

Spellings Commission. (2006). *A test of leadership: Charting the future of U.S. higher education.* Commission on the Future of Higher Education. https://www2.ed.gov/about/bdscomm/list/hiedfuture/reports/pre-pub-report.pdf

Spelman College. (n.d.). *About Spelman College.* https://www.spelman.edu/about-us

Spradley, J. P. (1979). *The ethnographic interview.* Wadsworth.

Sternick, E. D. (2011). Using Baldrige Performance Excellence Program approaches in the pursuit of radiation oncology quality care, patient satisfaction, and workforce commitment. *Frontiers of Oncology, 1,* 9.

Stincelli, E., & Baghurst, T. (2014). A grounded theory exploration of informal leadership qualities as perceived by employees and managers in small organizations. *International Journal of Business Management & Economic Research, 5*(1), 1–8.

Stolberg, S. G. (2015, June 20). Sweet Briar reaches deal to stay open. *The New York Times.* www.nytimes.com/2015/06/21/us/sweet-briar-reaches-deal-to-stay-open.html

Stone, D., Patton, B., & Heen, S. (1991). *Difficult conversations: How to discuss what matters most.* Viking.

Strauss, J. C., & Curry, J. R. (2002). *Responsibility-centered management: Lessons from 25 years of decentralized management.* National Association of College and University Business Officers.

Sue, D. W. (2010). *Microaggressions in everyday life: Race, gender, and sexual orientation.* Wiley.

Sue, D. W., Capodilupo, C. M., & Holder, A. M. B. (2008). Racial microaggressions in the life experience of Black Americans. *Professional Psychology: Research and Practice, 39*(3), 329–336. https://doi.org/10.1037/0735-7028.39.3.329

Sykes, C. J. (2016). *Fail U. The false promises of higher education.* St. Martin's.

Tagg, J. (2012). Why does the faculty resist change? *Change: The Magazine of Higher Learning, 44*(1), 6–15.

Tagiuri, R., & Litwin, G. L. (Eds.). (1968). *Organizational climate: Explorations of a concept.* Harvard University Press.

Teniente-Matson, C. (2019). A leadership competency study of chief business officers. In R. A. Gigliotti (Ed.), *Competencies for effective leadership: A framework for assessment, education, and research* (pp. 135–160). Emerald.

Thayer, L. (1968). *Communication and communication systems.* Richard D. Irwin.

Thayer, L. (2003). Communication: *Sine qua non* of the behavioral sciences. In R. W. Budd & B. D. Ruben (Eds.), *Approaches to human communication* (2nd ed., pp. 7–31). Spartan-Hayden.

Thelin, J. R. (2019). *A history of American higher education* (3rd ed.). Johns Hopkins University Press.

Tierney, W. G. (1988). Organizational culture in higher education. *The Journal of Higher Education, 59*(1), 2–29. https://doi.org/10.2307/1981868

The condition of education 2018. (2018). National Center for Education Statistics.

Tincelli, E., & Baghurst, E. (2014). A grounded theory exploration of informal leadership qualities as perceived by employees and managers in small organizations. *International Journal of Business Management and Economic Research, 5*(1), 2014, 1–8.

Tromp, S. A., & Ruben, B. D. (2010). *Strategic planning in higher education: A guide for leaders* (2nd ed.). NACUBO.

Tuckman, B. W. (1965). Developmental sequence in small groups. *Psychological Bulletin, 63*(6), 384–399.

Tuckman, B. W., & Jensen, M. A. C. (1977). Stages of small-group development revisited. *Group and Organization Management, 2*(4), 419–427.

Ulmer, R. R., Sellnow, T. L., & Seeger, M. W. (2018). *Effective crisis communication: Moving from crisis to opportunity.* SAGE.

University of Michigan. (n.d.). *Mission and integrity.* https://president.umich.edu/about/mission/

University of North Carolina. (n.d.). *University leadership education and development (ULEAD).* https://hr.unc.edu/training/ulead/

U.S. Department of Education. (2006, April 6–7). *Commission on the future of higher education.* https://www.connectlive.com/events/highered0406/

U.S. Department of Education. (2018). *Home page.* National Center for Educational Statistics. https://nces.ed.gov/

U.S. Office of Personnel Management (2005). *Succession planning process.* https://www.opm.gov/policy-data-oversight/human-capital-framework/reference-materials/leadership-knowledge-management/successionplanning.pdf

Useem, M. (1998). *The leadership moment.* Random House.

Vasquez, M. (2019, December 7). UNC's Silent Sam settlement was reached quickly. The blowback might last longer. *The Chronicle of Higher Education.* https://www.chronicle.com/article/UNCs-Silent-Sam-Settlement/247681

Velsor, E. V., McCauley, C. D., & Ruderman, M. N. (2010). *The Center for Creative Leadership handbook of leadership development.* Jossey-Bass.

Ward, D., & American Council on Education. (2006). *President to President, 7*(30). www.acenet.edu/Content/NavigationMenu/GovernmentRelationsPublicPolicy/PresidenttoPresident/Default877.htm

Watzlawick, P., Beavin, J., & Jackson, D. (1967). *Pragmatics of human communication: A study of interactional patterns, pathologies, and paradoxes.* Norton.

Weeks, W. B., Hamby, L., Stein, A., & Batalden, P. B. (2000). Using the Baldrige management system framework in health care: The Veterans Health Administration experience. *Joint Commission on Accreditation of Healthcare Organizations, 26*(7), 379–387. https://doi.org/10.1016/S1070-3241(00)26031-8

Weick, K. E. (1976). Educational organizations as loosely coupled systems. *Administrative Science Quarterly, 21*(1), 1–19.

Weick, K. E. (1988). Enacted sense-making in crisis situations. *Journal of Management Studies*, *25*, 305–317. https://doi.org/10.1111/j.1467-6486.1988.tb00039.x

Weick, K. E. (1995). *Sensemaking in organizations*. SAGE.

Weisburd, D., Mastrofski, S. D., Greenspan, R., & Willis, J. J. (2004, April). *The growth of Comstat in American policing*. Police Foundation Reports. www.assets.lapdonline.org/assets/pdf/growthofcompstat.pdf

Westchester Community College. (n.d.). *Mission and goals of the college*. https://www.sunywcc.edu/about/strategic-plan/mission/#:~:text=Westchester%20Community%20College%20provides%20accessible,economic%20development%20and%20lifelong%20learning

Western Association of Schools and Colleges. (2013). *Handbook of accreditation*. hilo.hawaii.edu/uhh/congress/documents/12WASCDraft2013HandbookofAccreditation.pdf

Wheatley, M. (2006). *Leadership and the new science: Discovering order in a chaotic world* (3rd ed.). Berrett-Koehler.

Whitford, E. (2020, June 24). Pandemic worsened public higher ed's biggest challenges. *Inside Higher Ed*. https://www.insidehighered.com/news/2020/06/24/coronavirus-pandemic-worsened-higher-eds-biggest-challenges-new-survey-shows

Wisniewski, M. A. (1999). Leadership competencies in continuing higher education: Implications for leadership education. *Continuing Higher Education*, *47*(1), 14–23. https://doi.org/10.1080/07377366.1999.10400361

Witherspoon, P. D. (1997). *Communicating leadership: An organizational perspective*. Allyn & Bacon.

Witt/Kieffer. (2013). *Leadership traits and success in higher education*. https://www.aascu.org/corporatepartnership/WittKieffer/Leadership.pdf

Woodhouse, K. (2015, April 28). Money talk. *Inside Higher Education*. www.insidehighered.com/news/2015/04/28/communication-issue-college-administrators-and-faculty-during-era-financial-change

Yukl, G. (2012). *Leadership in organizations* (8th ed.). Prentice Hall.

Zaleznik, A. (1992, March/April). Managers and leaders: Are they different? *Harvard Business Review*, 126–135.

Zeier, H. (1994). Workload and psychophysiological stress reactions in air traffic controllers. *Ergonomics*, *37*(3), 525–539.

Zemsky, R., Shaman, S., & Baldridge, S. C. (2020). *The college stress test. Tracking institutional futures across a crowded market*. Johns Hopkins University Press.

Zhang, Z., Waldman, D. A., & Wang, Z. (2012). A multilevel investigation of leader-member exchange, informal leader emergence, and individual and team performance. *Personnel Psychology*, *65*(1), 49–78. https://doi.org/10.1111/j.1744-6570.2011.01238.x

AUTHOR BIOGRAPHIES

Brent D. Ruben is a distinguished professor in communication at Rutgers University, where he also serves as senior university fellow and as advisor for strategy and planning in the Office of the Executive Vice President for Academic Affairs; he also was the founder of the Rutgers Center for Organizational Leadership. He is a member of the faculties of the Rutgers doctoral program in higher education and the Robert Wood Johnson School of Medicine. Ruben is author or coauthor of numerous publications in communication, leadership, and organizational assessment, strategy, and change, including *Visionary Leadership in Higher Education: Principles and Pragmatics of Organizational Excellence* (forthcoming); *Communication and Human Behavior* (Kendall Hunt, 2020), *Excellence in Higher Education Guide* (Stylus, 2016), and *What Leaders Need to Know and Do* (National Association of College and University Business Officers, 2006). Ruben was a founder of the Rutgers Department of Communication and first PhD program director of the School of Communication and Information. He was a founder and first president of the Network for Change and Continuous Innovation in Higher Education (NCCI), served as Rutgers' inaugural liaison, is a frequent contributor to the Big Ten Academic Alliance leadership programs, and serves as an adviser to colleges and universities nationally and internationally.

Richard De Lisi is an emeritus university professor of developmental psychology at Rutgers University and a senior fellow at the Rutgers Center for Organizational Leadership. De Lisi was a faculty member at Rutgers University in New Brunswick for 43 years and had more than 25 years of experience as a formal leader at the Rutgers Graduate School of Education, including chair of the Department of Educational Psychology, graduate program director for the doctorate in education program, graduate program director for the doctorate in higher education program, and dean of the Graduate School of Education from 2003 to 2014. Under De Lisi's leadership, the Graduate School of Education increased its online course offerings, developed its first online master's degree programs, developed teacher education and school counseling programs that received national accreditation, substantially expanded its doctorate in education program, developed a new doctorate in higher education program, and revised its doctorate in education program as an initial cohort member of the Carnegie Project on the education doctorate.

Ralph A. Gigliotti is assistant vice president for the Office of University Strategy and director of the Center for Organizational Leadership at Rutgers University where he provides executive leadership for a portfolio of academic leadership programs, strategic consultation services, and research initiatives. He also has part-time faculty appointments in the Department of Communication, PhD program in Higher Education, and Department of Family Medicine and Community Health at Robert Wood Johnson Medical School. He is author and coauthor of numerous books and articles exploring the intersection of communication, leadership, and crisis in higher education, including *Leadership in Academic Health Centers: Core Concepts and Critical Cases* (Kendall Hunt, 2021), *Crisis Leadership in Higher Education: Theory and Practice* (Rutgers University Press, 2019), and *A Guide for Leaders in Higher Education: Core Concepts, Competencies, and Tools* (Stylus, 2016). Gigliotti is a national examiner for the Malcolm Baldrige Performance Excellence program (National Institute of Standards and Technology, U.S. Department of Commerce). He is also actively involved in numerous boards and leadership teams, including the leadership team of the Training and Development Division for the National Communication Association and the Board of Directors for the Network for Change and Continuous Innovation (NCCI).

CONTRIBUTOR BIOGRAPHIES

Barbara E. Bender, EdD is senior associate dean of the School of Graduate Studies at Rutgers University and director of the Teaching Assistant Project as well as the Rutgers Academy for the Scholarship of Teaching and Learning. An expert on higher education governance, accreditation, and the graduate student experience, she is a member of the faculty of the Rutgers Pre-Doctoral Leadership Academy.

John A. Fortunato, PhD, is a professor at Fordham University in the Gabelli School of Business, in the area of communication and media management. His research interests include crisis management, sports media, and sponsorship marketing. He is the author of five books and more than 50 journal articles and book chapters. Dr. Fortunato received his doctorate degree from Rutgers University in the School of Communication and Information.

Christine Goldthwaite, PhD, is a communication scholar and the assistant director of the Rutgers Center for Organizational Leadership. In this role she oversees the coordination of the Rutgers Leadership Academy for midcareer faculty and staff from across the university and facilitates and consults in the areas of strategic planning, organizational assessment, workplace culture/climate, and communication design.

Sangeeta Lamba, MD, is professor of emergency medicine at Rutgers New Jersey Medical School. She serves as the vice chancellor for diversity and inclusion at Rutgers Biomedical and Health Sciences (RBHS). Her primary responsibility is to champion, lead, and implement a fully integrated strategy for diversity, and inclusion across RBHS, with a special emphasis on faculty support and advancement. Her research interests are medical education, communication skills training, and palliative care in the emergency department.

Susan E. Lawrence, PhD, is vice dean for undergraduate education in the School of Arts & Sciences; a fellow in the Center for Organizational Leadership; and an associate professor of political science at Rutgers–New Brunswick. She oversees undergraduate liberal arts and sciences education, curriculum development, strategic planning, assessment, advising, honors, and first-generation support programs. Representing the largest school at Rutgers–New Brunswick, she is recognized as providing critical informal cross-campus leadership for over 15 years.

cultural richness, 94
cultural sensitivity, 113
cultural traditions, 102, 105
culture, 21, 95, 96. *See also*
    organizational culture
culture of change initiative, 274
culture of leadership, 7
CUPA-HR. *See* College and University
    Professional Association for
    Human Resources
curriculum development, 86
curriculum vitae (CV), 5
Curry, J. R., 26
CV. *See* curriculum vitae
cyberthreats, 353

dashboards, 293, 308
data access, 395
data analysis, 301
data collection, 301, 395
day-to-day actions, 250, 252
day-to-day operations, 104
deans, 68–69, 72, 169, 173, 174, 369,
    374
debriefing, 180, 183, 185, 188
decentralized funding approaches, 27
decentralized solutions, 12
decision-making, 11, 101, 133, 175,
    177, 179, 250
  administrative, 328
  about appropriate locus of control,
    16
  collaborative, 160
  collegial, 106, 109, 169
  day-to-day, 302, 310
  developing road map for, 121
  economic issues and, 24
  foundation and context for, 247
  governance and, 65
  guiding, 252
  influences on, 25
  institutional mission and, 50
  operational, 25
  senior-level, 329

shifts in, 66
strategic, 21
structures of, 19, 84
decreased public confidence, xi, 35
degree completion, 290
degree-granting institutions, 405, 406,
    407
degree requirements, 71
delegation, 67
demographics, 112
DEO. *See* department executive officers
department chairs, 69, 72, 74, 169,
    175, 380
  requirements for, 87
  supportive, 88
  transition planning and, 374
department executive officers (DEO),
    354, 355, 356
department heads, 69, 72, 74
Department of Education, 106, 107,
    405, 407
determination, 136
developmental assignments, 216
developmental relationships, 216
dichotomies of leadership, 133–135,
    141
difficult conversations, 203
  close of, 199
  culture and climate for success in,
    201
  defining audience and, 194
  effective channels for, 196
  externalizing style and, 201
  goals of, 195
  plans of action for, 195–196
  points of possible difficulty in, 198
  reflecting on outcomes of, 196
  strategic communication and, 193,
    197
difficult messages, 193
dimensions of leadership, 9
Dimensions of Organizational Cultures
    Inventory, 104
direct language, 188

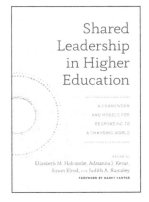

Shared Leadership in Higher Education

A Framework and Models for Responding to a Changing World

Edited by Elizabeth M. Holcombe, Adrianna J. Kezar, Judith Ramaley and Susan Elrod

"Today's higher education challenges necessitate new forms of leadership. A volatile financial environment and the need for new business models and partnerships to address the impact of new technologies, changing demographics, and emerging societal needs, demand more effective and innovative forms of leadership. This book focusses on a leadership approach that has emerged as particularly effective for organizations facing complex challenges: shared leadership.

Rather than concentrating power and authority in an individual leader at the top of an organization, shared leadership involves multiple people influencing one another across varying levels and at different times. It is a flexible, collective, and non-hierarchical approach to leadership. Organizations that have implemented shared leadership have been better able to learn, innovate, perform, and adapt to the types of external challenges that campuses now face and that will continue to shape higher education in the future."

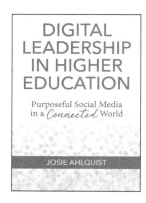

Digital Leadership in Higher Education

Purposeful Social Media in a Connected World

Josie Ahlquist

"If you want to learn both the why and the how behind online leadership in higher education, read this timely book, from cover to cover—from guidance, through development, to putting principles into action, it will be your north star."—*Scott Cline, Vice President of Enrollment Management and Auxiliary Services, California College of the Arts*

"I recommend this book for every higher education leader whether you have 100 or 100,000 followers. Reading it not only inspired me to review my own strategies and tactics, it also gave me purposeful questions as a chief marketing officer to put forward to our institution's social media managers."
—*Melissa Farmer Richards, Vice President for Communications and Marketing, Hamilton College*

"Josie Ahlquist breaks new ground with *Digital Leadership in Higher Education*. The book has a wide range of ideas that meets the reader wherever they are in their digital leadership journey."—*Walter M. Kimbrough, President, Dillard University*

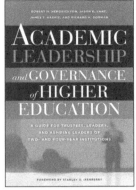

Academic Leadership and Governance of Higher Education

A Guide for Trustees, Leaders, and Aspiring Leaders of Two- and Four-Year Institutions

Robert M. Hendrickson, Jason E. Lane, James T. Harris, and Richard H. Dorman

Foreword by Stan Ikenberry

"This encyclopedic compendium of the history and challenges of virtually all aspects of higher education will serve as a handy reference for academic leaders and scholars. It should find a place in all college and university libraries as well as in the personal libraries of presidents. The book's perspective is that, to be successful, academic leaders must be focused on vision, mission, and core values; be able to adapt to a rapidly changing environment; and include key constituents in decision-making. The book is an important contribution to the higher education literature."
—*Rita Bornstein, President Emerita and Cornell Professor of Philanthropy and Leadership Development, Rollins College*

Practical Wisdom

Thinking Differently About College and University Governance

Peter D. Eckel and Cathy A. Trower

Foreword by Richard Chait

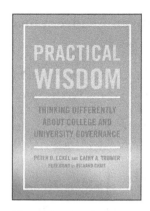

"As colleges and universities face increased scrutiny and mounting pressures, effective board governance has moved from a luxury to a necessity; if our institutions are to succeed in this environment, they need effective leadership from their Boards. Few are equipped to provide it. What a gift to have the wisdom of two distinguished leaders at our disposal during this critical time for higher education. Their extensive experience working with presidents and boards is displayed on every page of this book. Observations and suggestions are organized into clear and accessible essays that will prove equally valuable for public and private boards, presidents, and leaders. During a time of tumult and change, the wise counsel of *Practical Wisdom* serves as an essential guide to effective governance."—*Mary B. Marcy, President, Dominican University of California*

From the Foreword:

"*Practical Wisdom* astutely focuses on the means—tools, techniques, and templates—that enable trustees and, by extension, executives to determine, pursue, and achieve a core strategy aligned with core values. There's no more valuable contribution a book on governance can make."—*Richard Chait, Professor Emeritus of Higher Education, Harvard Graduate School of Education*